Fast Track C#

K. Scott Allen
Neil Avent
Syed Fahad Gilani
Jon D. Reid
Julian Templeman

Wrox Press Ltd. ®

Fast Track C#

Published by Wrox Press Ltd,
Arden House, 1102 Warwick Road, Acocks Green,
Birmingham, B27 6BH, UK
Printed in USA
ISBN 1-861007-11-6

Trademark Acknowledgments

Credits

Authors
K. Scott Allen
Neil Avent
Syed Fahad Gilani
Jon D. Reid
Julian Templeman

Technical Reviewers
Christian Darie
Mitch Denny
Michael Erickson
Slavomir Furman
Brian Hickey
Ben Hickman
Mark Horner
Brad Maiani
Kirk Montgomery
Simon Robinson
Gavin Smyth
Helmut Watson
Don Xie
Radomir Zaric

Managing Editor
Louay Fatoohi

Commisioning Editor
Julian Skinner

Technical Editors
Douglas Paterson
Helen Callaghan
David Barnes
Allan Jones

Project Manager
Claire Robinson

Author Agent
Cilmara Lion

Production Coordinator
Abbie Forletta

Production Assistant
Neil Lote

Indexing
Martin Brooks

Proof Reader
Dev Lunsford

Illustrations
Sarah Hall

Cover
Chris Morris

About the Authors

K. Scott Allen

Scott Allen has over ten years of software development experience across a wide range of technologies, from 8-bit embedded software to enterprise-scale web applications. Scott is currently a senior software developer for Butterfly.NET, a production studio, online publisher, and infrastructure provider for multiplayer games connecting players on PCs, consoles, and mobile devices. Scott graduated with an M.S. degree in computer science from Shippensburg University, and holds an MCSD certification. Scott lives in Hagerstown, Maryland with his wife Vicky, and sons Alex and Christopher. You can reach the author at bitmask@yahoo.com.

I'd like to thank Wrox press for giving me the opportunity to work on this project, and a special thanks to Julian Skinner, Claire Robinson, and Douglas Paterson for helping me along the way.

> My work here is dedicated to my parents: to my mom for her love and guidance, and my father for his love and wisdom.

Neil Avent

Neil Avent is a Freelance Consultant with a heavy interest in the .NET Framework and related technologies. He is currently a MCSD and just spent the last year working for a leading web hosting company in the UK. His main area of expertise lies in web enabling desktop applications. When not programming or writing he enjoys spending time with his wonderful daughter, Lauren. He can be contacted at neil@system-integration.co.uk.

Syed Fahad Gilani

A 21 year old bachelor, I am just about to begin a Masters Program in Computer Engineering at the Australian National University. I currently live in Lahore, Pakistan, and have been programming for the last thirteen years, managing to sell my first program at the age of ten. After completing my secondary education, I started teaching computer sciences and training computer professionals. I've been working as a Software Engineer for a variety of software houses over the last few years, working with a large range of languages and technologies. Over the years, I have worked on numerous private projects in various roles, which have been a great source of income. My interests include anything that's possible and anything that would manage to keep me awake through the night! Currently, I'm running Visual Sparks, a small software development company, teaching, training, and writing. If not working, you'd find me playing my guitar, jogging, eating, or back-flipping. I can be contacted at the following e-mail address: fahad_gilani@yahoo.com.

> This has been one of the finest experiences I've ever had. I would like to thank the Wrox team for helping me get into writing, for being supportive and for being so positive in their feedback
>
> During the course of writing, I've had tremendous support and encouragement from my family and friends. I'd like to thank my Dad for his smiles, my grandmother for her prayers and peanut biscuits, my sister for her patience, Adil Shafique for his doughnuts and other special friends for their continuing faith in me. I wish I could prove to be better.
>
> Finally, to all of you readers out there, I hope you have a great time learning C#! There's nothing like it.

Jon D. Reid

Jon is the Chief Technology Officer for Micro Data Base Systems, Inc. (http://www.mdbs.com), maker of the TITANIUM™ Database Engine and GURU® Expert System tool. His current area of interest is database development tools for the Microsoft .NET environment. He is a former editor for the C++ and Object Query Language (OQL) components of the Object Data Management Group (ODMG) standard, and has co-authored other Wrox titles including Beginning C#, ADO.NET Programmer's Reference, and Professional SQL Server 2000 XML. When not working, writing, or bicycling, he enjoys spending time with his wife and two young sons. Jon would like to thank his family, his employer, and Julian Skinner and the rest of the team at Wrox for their support and encouragement.

Julian Templeman

Julian has been a programmer for just over thirty years, and still enjoys it. He started as a real programmer, and so is pleased to see that Fortran may have a place in the .NET world. He spends most of his time running a training and consultancy company in London, mainly on Java, C++, COM, and .NET, and writes articles and books on programming topics.

Take the

Fast Track

to **C#**

Table of Contents

Table of Contents

Table of Contents

Table of Contents

Table of Contents

Introduction

C# is Microsoft's new language, designed specifically for its new platform, the .NET Framework.

The basic premise of .NET is quite simple: all .NET programs are compiled to an intermediate language (IL, or MSIL) rather than to native code that can be understood by the computer's processor. This IL code is then compiled to native code either when the application is installed, or when the application is run. Code run on the .NET Framework is managed by a run-time environment called the Common Language Runtime (CLR). This runtime provides memory-management features such as automatic garbage collection and type-safety checking, and is similar in some ways to Java's Virtual Machine.

The .NET Framework also provides a large number of base classes, whose functionality is available to all languages that use the CLR, and which allow the developer to achieve many common programming tasks. In the long term (if the .NET Framework is migrated to non-Windows platforms), these classes may provide a degree of platform-independence by avoiding the necessity of calling OS-specific APIs.

For the last few years, developers working chiefly on Microsoft platforms have had two principal languages to work with: they could choose the power of Visual C++, or the ease of use of Visual Basic. Although Visual Basic did allow a lot of power to those who were prepared to stretch it to its limits, and Visual C++ had a host of AppWizards designed to simplify life for the C++ developer, as a general rule applications built in Visual C++ took longer to develop, but had much better performance than those developed in Visual Basic.

The release of the .NET Framework changes all that in two ways. Firstly, Visual Basic .NET is much more powerful than its predecessor. All .NET languages compile to Intermediate Language, and can take advantage of the features supplied by the Common Language Runtime. Added to this are a number of more powerful features in Visual Basic.NET, such as true object-oriented features and exception handling with `Try...Catch`. However, probably the more important development is the creation of an entirely new language – C#, the subject of this book.

C# is a new language derived from C++, but designed to support Rapid Application Development in a similar way to Visual Basic. C# allows us to design both Windows and web applications quickly and easily using form designers; Visual Studio .NET takes care of much of the code, such as instantiating the controls and writing the definitions for event handlers. This of course comes on top of the features provided by the Common Language Runtime, such as automatic garbage collection. However, C# also gives us most of the power of C++, even allowing the use of direct access to memory addresses through pointers in blocks of "unsafe" code (code that bypasses C#'s type safety features). Add to this the fact that C# is the only language designed from the ground up for the .NET Framework, and it's clear why C# looks set to become the language of choice for .NET programming.

Who Is This Book For?

This book is for anybody who wants to learn about C# and the .NET platform. This book is not a beginner's book – we've assumed that you've got some programming experience, perhaps in Windows programming with Visual C++. Alternatively, you may be coming from a Java background and want to see what all the fuss is about. Some of the later chapters assume some basic knowledge of Microsoft technologies such as ADO, and COM.

What You Need to Use This Book

This book and the code it contains have been checked against the release version of Microsoft Visual Studio .NET. Its minimum requirements are therefore the same as those for that product: a PII-450 CPU, Microsoft Windows 2000 Professional or higher, at least 128 MB of RAM, and around 3GB of free space on your hard drive.

What Does This Book Cover?

This book is designed to provide an introduction to programming in C# on the .NET platform. As we have already implied, these two topics are closely connected. Because all code written for the .NET Framework will make extensive use of the .NET base classes, for example for input/output, data manipulation, and file handling, we cover these extensively, as well as the syntax of the C# language itself.

We start off by taking quick overviews of the .NET Framework, and C#, before moving on to look at the C# language in detail. Next we cover the basics of .NET programming – the .NET class libraries, building Windows applications, data access with ADO.NET, and the unit of .NET deployment – the assembly. Finally, we look at a few more advanced topics: integrating C# programs with COM and with Component Services, building ASP.NET web applications, and Web Services in C#.

Let's take a brief look at what we cover in each of the individual chapters of this book:

Chapter 1: Overview of .NET and the CLR

In this chapter we look at the .NET Framework, we look at some of the problems that the .NET Framework addresses, and we see how it does this. The Common Language Runtime (CLR) is discussed, along with Intermediate Language (IL) and the Common Type System (CTS).

Chapter 2: Introduction to C#

This chapter looks at the C# language – it starts with a discussion of why we need another programming language. C# is also compared to other programming languages currently in use. The chapter then looks at the types of application that can be built using C# in the .NET environment. Finally, we look at the C# compiler.

Chapter 3: C# Basics

This chapter is the start of the detailed look at C#. Throughout the chapter, any similarities and differences between C# and C++ and Java are noted. We look at the features of a C# program, including the data types, operators, and statements used in the language. Program control and loops are examined, and also the calling of methods and method overloading. Errors and how to handle them are also discussed.

Chapter 4: Object-Oriented Features of C#

This chapter looks at the functionality built into C# for working with objects. We begin with a discussion of enumerations, before going on to look at structs and classes. The members of classes – fields, properties, methods, and events – are all discussed. We also look at OO concepts such as inheritance, and see how they are implemented in C#. Other topics covered include interfaces and abstract classes, operator overloading, and indexers.

Chapter 5: Advanced C#

Now we go on to look at some of the more advanced features of C#. We start by looking at some advanced techniques involved with working with classes, such as variable argument lists. Next we look at C#'s preprocessor directives, which we can use to modify how our code is compiled, using pointers and unsafe code in C#, delegates, and events, before finally looking at XML documentation.

Chapter 6: .NET Programming with C#

Having finished our look at the C# language itself, this chapter starts dealing with how the language is used in the .NET environment. We look at reflection, which allows us to inspect types and objects at run time and find out what they are and what they can do. Then we look at .NET attributes, markers that we can apply to our code to provide additional run time information. Next, we look at collections and arrays, and finish off the chapter with a look at how .NET supports writing multithreaded applications in C#.

Chapter 7: Working with the .NET Base Class Library

This chapter takes us on a tour of some of the most commonly used base classes. We write example programs that show the base classes in action, and demonstrate how to perform common programming tasks in C# such as string manipulation, file handling, reading and writing to files, reading and writing XML, and XML serialization.

Chapter 8: Building Windows Applications

This chapter uses Windows forms to aid Rapid Application Development (RAD). After a quick look at creating applications without Visual Studio, the Visual Studio .NET IDE is used to add controls onto Windows forms. A sample Windows application is used to demonstrate creating menus, handling events, and other aspects of building Windows applications such as the standard dialogs. We then look at how to deploy applications from within Visual Studio .NET.

Chapter 9: Assemblies and ILDASM

In this chapter, we look at the concepts of assemblies and manifests. Assemblies are .NET components that include both the code itself and all the metadata needed to describe the component – its manifest. We explore the ILDASM tool which, allows us to view the contents of an assembly. The .NET Framework uses shared names to locate assemblies regardless of their physical location in the file system, so we see how we can create shared names for our assemblies. This allows assemblies to be shared by multiple applications. We also take a look at code access security.

Chapter 10: Data Access with ADO.NET

In this chapter, we look at data access on the .NET platform using ADO.NET, the latest of Microsoft's data access technologies. After a quick look at the data consumer, and provider classes, we look at the forward-only, read-only data reader, and using stored procedures and transactions in ADO.NET. Next, we see how to use the `DataSet` to access and update a database, and how to bind a `DataSet` to a `DataGrid`, and introduce some of Visual Studio .NET's built-in features for data access. Finally, we examine some of ADO.NET's functionality for working with XML.

Chapter 11: COM and COM+ Interoperability

Next, we look at integrating C# applications and components with existing code. First, we see how to call existing COM components from C# applications, using both early and late binding. Next, we discuss calling C# components as if they were COM components, by creating a wrapper COM object and exporting a type library.

After an overview of Component Services, we see how to use these features with .NET components. We look at creating transactional components under .NET and registering them with COM+ Services, and we see how to take advantage of some of the other main features of COM+ from our C# component, such as message queuing.

Finally, we look at calling unmanaged functions using PInvoke (Platform Invocation Services).

Chapter 12: ASP.NET

In our penultimate chapter, we see how to create web applications using ASP.NET, the latest incarnation of ASP. After an overview of the new features on offer, we show an example of creating a simple ASP.NET web application. We demonstrate the use of server-side controls in maintaining state and in validating user input. Finally, we look at configuring web applications, and some of the monitoring tools offered by ASP.NET.

Chapter 13: Web Services

Finally, we look at another, new kind of web application – the web service. Web services are a way of exposing the application logic on a server over the Internet. This allows the client to use the data on the server, without being tied to particular pre-constructed static or dynamic web pages. After a look at what web services are, and the protocols they use, we demonstrate how to build a Web service, and a client that will consume this service, and how to use asynchronous methods to handle possible interruptions to our service caused by network turmoil.

Conventions

We have used a number of different styles of text and layout in the book to help differentiate between the different kinds of information. Here are examples of the styles we use and an explanation of what they mean:

Bullets appear indented, with each new bullet marked as follows:

❑ **Important Words** are in a bold type font

❑ Words that appear on the screen in menus like the File or Window are in a similar font to the one that you see on screen

❑ Keys that you press on the keyboard, like *Ctrl* and *Enter*, are in italics

Code has several styles. If it's a word that we're talking about in the text, for example, when discussing the if...else loop, it's in this font. If it's a block of code that you can type in as a program and run, then it's also in a gray box:

```
public static void Main()
{
    AFunc(1,2,"abc");
}
```

Sometimes you'll see code in a mixture of styles, like this:

```
    // If we haven't reached the end, return true, otherwise
    // set the position to invalid, and return false.
    pos++;
    if (pos < 4)
        return true;
    else {
```

```
                    pos = -1;
                    return false;
             }
```

The code with a white background is code we've already looked at and that we don't wish to examine further.

Advice, hints, and background information come in an italicized, indented font like this.

> **Important pieces of information come in boxes like this.**

We demonstrate the syntactical usage of methods, properties (and so on) using the following format:

```
Regsvcs BookDistributor.dll [COM+AppName] [TypeLibrary.tbl]
```

Here, italicized parts indicate object references, variables, or parameter values to be inserted; the square braces indicate optional parameters.

Technical Support

If you wish to directly query a problem in the book with an expert who knows it in detail then e-mail support@wrox.com with the title of the book and the last four numbers of the ISBN in the subject field. A typical e-mail should include the following things:

❑ The **name**, **last four digits of the ISBN**, and **page number** of the problem in the Subject field.

❑ Your **name**, **contact information**, and the **problem** in the body of the message.

We *won't* send you junk mail. We need the details to save your time and ours. When you send an e-mail message, it will go through the following chain of support:

❑ **Customer Support** – Your message is delivered to one of our customer support staff, who are the first people to read it. They have files on most frequently asked questions and will answer anything general about the book or the web site immediately.

❑ **Editorial** – Deeper queries are forwarded to the technical editor responsible for that book. They have experience with the programming language or particular product, and are able to answer detailed technical questions on the subject. Once an issue has been resolved, the editor can post the errata to the web site.

❑ **The Authors** – Finally, in the unlikely event that the editor cannot answer your problem, they will forward the request to the author. We do try to protect the author from any distractions to their writing, however, we are quite happy to forward specific requests to them. All Wrox authors help with the support on their books. They will mail the customer and the editor with their response, and again all readers should benefit.

The Wrox support process can only offer support to issues that are directly pertinent to the content of our published title. Support for questions that fall outside the scope of normal book support is provided via the community lists of our http://p2p.wrox.com/ forum.

Source Code

All of the source code for this book is available at the wrox.com web site. When you arrive at http://www.wrox.com/, locate the title through our search facility or by using one of the title lists. Then, click on the Download Code link on the book's detail page, and you can obtain the code.

The files that are available for download from our site have been archived using WinZip. When you've saved them to your hard drive, you'll need to extract the files they contain using a decompression program such as WinZip or PKUnzip. When you extract the files, ensure that your software has the Use folder names (or some equivalent) option switched on.

Errata

We have made every effort to ensure that there are no errors in the text or the code. However, no one is perfect and mistakes do occur. If you find an error in this book, we'd be very grateful if you'd tell us about it. By sending in errata, you may save another reader hours of frustration, and you'll be helping us to provide information of even higher quality. Simply e-mail your discovery to support@wrox.com; your information will be checked and, if found correct, posted to the errata page or used in subsequent editions of the book.

To find errata on the web site, log on to http://www.wrox.com, and locate the title through the search facility. Then, on the book's detail page, click on the Book Errata link. On this page you'll be able to view any errata that have been already submitted and verified. You can also click the Submit Errata link to notify us of any errata that you may have found.

p2p.wrox.com

For author and peer discussion, join the **P2P mailing lists**. Our unique system provides **programmer to programmer™** contact on mailing lists, forums, and newsgroups, all *in addition* to our one-to-one e-mail support system. Be confident that your query is being examined by the many Wrox authors, and other industry experts, who are present on our mailing lists. At p2p.wrox.com you will find a number of different lists that will help you, not only while you read this book, but also as you develop your own applications.

To subscribe to a mailing list just follow these steps:

1. Go to http://p2p.wrox.com/.

2. Choose the appropriate category from the left menu bar.

3. Click on the mailing list you wish to join.

4. Follow the instructions to subscribe and fill in your e-mail address and password.

5. Reply to the confirmation e-mail you receive.

6. Use the subscription manager to join more lists and set your mail preferences.

Take the
Fast Track

to
C#

Overview of .NET and the CLR

Before we have an in-depth look at C#, we need to have a good understanding of the .NET Framework and the major part it plays in almost every aspect of C#. Of all the languages which are targeted to the .NET Framework, C# is the most tightly integrated with the Framework. The C# compiler produces code to run within the .NET Framework; in fact, you cannot run code generated from C# outside of the .NET Framework.

In this chapter we will have a close look at the following key ingredients of the .NET Framework:

❑   The Common Language Runtime (CLR)

❑   Microsoft Intermediate Language (MSIL or IL)

❑   The Common Type System (CTS)

❑   The Common Language Specification (CLS)

❑   Language Interoperability

❑   Assemblies

❑   The Garbage Collector

What is .NET?

In order to describe exactly what .NET is, we will begin by looking at the main components of .NET and how they work together.

There are quite a few new concepts (and acronyms) to get to grips with, so let's have a quick summary of the main items that work together to make .NET.

❑ **The Common Language Runtime (CLR)**
This handles running code within the .NET Framework and is responsible for managing the processes and threads that house the applications being executed. It is also known as the **.NET Runtime**.

❑ **Microsoft Intermediate Language (MSIL)**
The source code written in a .NET language such as C# is not compiled directly to native code, but to MSIL. During the process of Just-In-Time Compilation, the MSIL is compiled to native code. MSIL is often abbreviated to IL.

❑ **Common Type System (CTS)**
This is a collection of data types that all .NET languages must adhere to. This ensures that these languages can pass data between each other. This is a fundamental aspect of .NET's language interoperability.

❑ **Common Language Specification (CLS)**
This is a set of standards that defines boundaries on a language in order for it to be interoperable with other .NET languages. Together with the CTS, this allows other parties to develop compilers for .NET-enabled languages.

❑ **.NET Base Classes Library (BCL)**
This is a collection of classes which contain primitive data types and take care of all the functions previously covered by the Windows API, and more. This collection is a lot more intuitive than its API counterpart, and it is categorized into classes which expose functionality over many areas, including data access, file access and drawing operations.

❑ **Assemblies**
An assembly is the deployment unit of code that has been compiled into MSIL. An assembly contains a **manifest**, a section containing data pertaining to that code. This **metadata** describes various attributes about the code within the assembly. This is similar to the data that type libraries contain for COM components. Assemblies are either private to one application or shared so any application can access them.

❑ **Reflection**
This is the term given for programmatically exploring assemblies. There is a base class to handle this, and this can be used to programmatically find and use methods, classes and attributes.

❑ **Global Assembly Cache (GAC)**
This is where shared assemblies are stored; the contents can be viewed using Windows Explorer by navigating to `C:\WINNT\assembly`.

❑ **Managed Code**
Code designed to run within the .NET Framework is known as **managed code**. Code that does not run under the control of the .NET Framework is known as unmanaged code.

❑ **Just-in-Time (JIT) Compiler**
This is what the .NET compiler is generally known as, due to the fact that portions of code are compiled as needed while the application is running.

❑ **Application Domain**
An application domain is created and enforced by the CLR; allowing different applications to run within the same process without conflict. This can give great performance gains to applications that need to share data.

❑ **Garbage Collector**
The garbage collector is how the .NET Framework manages memory for the applications currently being executed. The garbage collector is controlled by the CLR and cleans up memory by deleting objects that are no longer needed. This minimizes the risk of memory leaks from applications run through the .NET Framework.

As you can judge from the above, the whole design inherent in how your application is run and managed within the .NET Framework is considerably different from what we have become accustomed to from developing applications that run on the Windows platform. Due to this design change, we will not have to contend with a few of the problems that have challenged us over the last few years. It is possible, however, that once .NET is more widely used in critical environments it will present its own quirks and challenges.

For the present, however, .NET is a totally new system that should be somewhat more friendly and productive than the previous system, which, due to the nature of progress, was really a mix of many technologies which didn't always fit together as seamlessly as one whole technology would have done.

.NET vs. Existing Problems with COM

Doubtless, if you have done any development on Windows and used DLLs, then you have come across a few problems. Perhaps you have installed an application that upon startup replaced a DLL with another with a higher version number. You may find an application that has been previously working has suddenly stopped working, and rolling back to a previous state to try and fix that application can be tricky; even then it may render your new application unusable. To add to your woes, an application could depend on several DLLs, each one of which depends on several further DLLs, which makes tracking down problems quite difficult. This problem has generally come to be known as DLL Hell or Versioning Problems.

Thankfully .NET appears to have the answer to these problems. The role of the DLL has been replaced by the assembly. An assembly does all that a DLL does, in that it holds code that can be used by one or many applications, but additionally it contains a manifest which holds metadata pertaining to that assembly. This removes the need to spend many hours trawling the Registry to find information about a DLL. There is a central store of shared assemblies known as the **global assembly cache (GAC)**, and upon installing .NET you will find the .NET base classes there. We will take a closer look at assemblies in Chapter 9; for now here are a few points worth noting:

❑ **Side by side versioning**
You can now have multiple versions of an assembly held on your machine. The version information is determined at run time and each application will use the version that it requires. This means that different applications can use separate versions of an assembly without affecting each other.

❑ **Shadow copying**
This allows an updated assembly to be placed onto your system without waiting for the old version to be unloaded from memory, which may require a reboot. This will come as a major relief for web developers who have struggled with IIS and DLLs.

❏   **Integrity checks**
   The manifest of an assembly contains a hash of the component that allows .NET to efficiently
   check the integrity of the assembly before loading it. This can help prevent code tampering;
   either by someone editing part of the file or by overwriting it.

COM and COM+

COM+ Services is not replaced by .NET, as it has some features such as Queuing and Distributed
Transactions that are not implemented in .NET. You can create .NET components that are able to use
COM+ Services. Your existing COM components will still work and you can use the COM
interoperability features in .NET, so that any new managed code will be able to call your COM
components. Because of the more advanced development and runtime environment in .NET, it is
probable that you would develop new .NET components rather than continuing to add to your existing
COM components. Chapter 11 looks at COM Interoperability and using COM+ Services.

Compiling and Executing a C# Application

Once you have finished writing code for an application, you compile the code first so it is in an
executable form. With .NET, compilation is a two-step process:

❏   Step 1 compiles your code into MSIL

❏   Step 2 occurs at run time when the MSIL is compiled into native machine code

This is shown in this diagram:

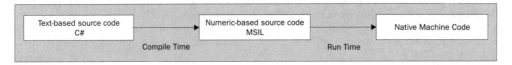

Compilation

The first stage in building and running an application, once the source code is in place, is to compile the
source code to MSIL. The source files are then in a state where they can be run within the .NET
runtime. Compiling code that is targeted within the .NET Framework gives a different result. The
executable and DLL files that you have after compilation no longer contain low-level assembly
commands which can be run through Windows; the files contain **Microsoft Intermediate Language
(MSIL)** which can be run through the **Common Language Runtime (CLR)**.

The compiled program, generated from your source code, will contain one or more assemblies. Each
assembly will contain the MSIL code that makes up your application as well as a manifest. The manifest
contains information detailing the code within that assembly.

Upon first glance MSIL bears more than a slight resemblance to Java byte code, but although they may share some of the same theoretical makeup, what actually goes on behind the scenes is vastly different. We will take a more in-depth look at MSIL in the next section. For now, it is worth noting that MSIL is its own language (as the name would suggest) rather than byte code, which is a stream of data that is fed into the Java VM, and, typically, interpreted. This gives MSIL much more power and flexibility; one benefit being that it can be compiled very quickly, either as a whole or in portions at a time.

Execution

When an application is run, it is under direct control of the Common Language Runtime. Before any code is compiled and run, several checks are performed by the CLR on the assembly or assemblies being loaded. The first thing done by the CLR is to load the initial assembly for your application. The integrity of this assembly is checked using the hash code in the manifest to ensure the assembly is in good condition.

Certain actions, such as file and network access, are restricted by the local Runtime Security Policy. This means that untrusted code, such as something downloaded from the Internet, cannot harm your system. The CLR will check the manifest for any permissions which the application may need to run. Applications can request permission to perform certain actions upon startup using attributes, or they may request permission during run time, when the action needs to be performed.

The CLR also performs one other very important check. It scans the code to ensure that it is memory type safe. This means that all memory access that the application will attempt is under the control of the CLR; if it is not, this check will fail and the code will only run if the Runtime Security Policy permits. For example, you can have blocks of unsafe code in C# that use pointers but this will force your code to fail this scan.

This check is performed because your application may need to run in the same process as other applications, providing a great performance gain for applications sharing information; nevertheless, if the CLR cannot verify how the application handles memory then there is a chance that the application could make the whole process unstable and force several applications to crash.

After all these checks have been passed, the CLR will actually run the code. It will either create a new process for the application or, at the application's request, add the main thread into an existing process which will then be shared with another application. The CLR will also create an application domain that allows the code to use its own area of memory without affecting anything else running within the same process. We will take a much closer look at this later in the chapter.

The CLR runs the code by passing the MSIL to the JIT compiler. The JIT compiler converts the MSIL into native instructions for the processor as needed. The JIT compiler will compile sections of code as and when the flow of execution requires them to be available. Once fully compiled, the code will be cached for subsequent use until the application is terminated. The resulting code may vary from one machine to the next, as the JIT compiler will optimize the code as it sees fit, depending on many factors, including your make and model of processor. This may seem like a slow process but the JIT compiler is very efficient, and in many cases code will execute with no real speed difference to native machine code.

While your code is being compiled and executed, the CLR will also be looking after other assemblies and processes in the same way. This allows applications to interact with other assemblies seamlessly, whatever language they were originally written in, as the JIT compiler only has to deal with MSIL. When necessary, the CLR will also call up the garbage collector to free up any unused memory; we will discuss the garbage collector in more detail later on in this chapter.

Microsoft Intermediate Language

We have mentioned Intermediate Language several times already in this chapter, as it is so integral to everything running within the .NET Framework. It is very easy to compare MSIL to Java byte code as they both provide a level of abstraction between your source code and the run-time instance of your code. MSIL is much more advanced than Java byte code, though; it is a language in its own right. With the .NET Framework there is a utility called `IlDasm.exe` that allows you to take apart an assembly in order to show the IL within that assembly. `IlDasm.exe` can be executed either through Windows or a command-line prompt.

Within the `FrameworkSDK` directory, which was created when you installed the .NET Framework, the `bin` subdirectory holds the tools and utilities that are shipped with the Framework. Depending on whether or not Visual Studio .NET is installed, you should find `IlDasm.exe` in one of the following directories:

```
C:\Program Files\Microsoft.NET\FrameworkSDK\bin
C:\Program Files\Microsoft Visual Studio .NET\FrameworkSDK\Bin
```

If you execute `IlDasm.exe` without any command line parameters the GUI will be displayed. You can load an assembly in here to view the manifest, namespaces and classes among other information. If you try to load an executable that contains native code rather than IL, then you will receive an error message. You can open some of the other tools such as `disco.exe` that are in the same directory as `Ildasm.exe` and view the contents of their assemblies. There is an option in the main menu for `Ildasm.exe` to dump the IL within the assembly to a text file. We will take a closer look at `Ildasm.exe` in Chapter 9.

What IL and Java byte code do share is that they utilize numeric rather than textual commands. This is a lot more efficient for a compiler and can be thought of as similar to assembler commands, where each command has a numeric substitute. In fact, due to the various optimizations the JIT compiler uses, the performance of IL is comparable to precompiled code. The JIT compiler, though advanced, is still in its infancy and should improve in future, at least according to Microsoft.

One of Java's main strengths is that the Java byte code can be interpreted on several different operating systems as the run-time instance has been ported to UNIX, Linux and Windows. This is not the case with MSIL at the moment, as the .NET Framework can only be installed on the Windows operating system. In the long term, there will almost certainly be a version of the Framework for other operating systems, and work is already underway on an open source version of the Framework for Linux.

MSIL is language-independent, as well as providing the potential to be platform-independent. The language-independent features of MSIL are immediately apparent with the Microsoft Languages Visual C++, C#, and Visual Basic .NET, as they all compile to MSIL and run within the .NET Framework. There are also other languages which are being .NET-enabled, including Eiffel and Perl. The ability of other vendors to target this medium will give .NET developers more choice in what language to use, and can only help make .NET more popular.

However, in order to provide language independence, MSIL needs to be a superset of the languages it supports, which is to say that a .NET language cannot perform an action which MSIL is not capable of executing. The following section will summarize what the MSIL language does support.

MSIL Programming Methodology

Fortunately for C++ and Java programmers, MSIL not only supports Object Oriented Programming (OOP) methodology, it actively encourages it. The implementation of OOP functionality in MSIL has brought in two items worth mentioning here; single inheritance and interfaces. All code must be within a class, therefore enforcing OOP design.

Single inheritance means a class can be directly derived from just one other class. However there is no limit to how many classes can be derived from a given class. All classes in MSIL are ultimately derived from a class called `Object`.

MSIL also supports **interfaces**. An interface is a set of properties and methods that a class derived from must implement. A class can derive from multiple interfaces, even though it is limited to deriving from just one class. Interfaces can be used in conjunction with attributes to communicate with a COM interface, discussed further in Chapter 11.

MSIL Data Handling

MSIL is very strict in the way it handles and controls variables. Each data type will fall into either a value or reference category. Value types hold data such as declaring a variable, whereas reference data types hold an address to some data in a similar fashion to a pointer in C++ or a Java reference type. Value and reference types are treated differently by MSIL; value data types are placed on the stack whereas reference types are stored on the heap (although if value types are declared as fields within reference types, they will be stored on the heap). This method of separating the two data types is very similar to that of the Java runtime environment.

One fundamental difference that will affect C++ developers directly is that the language is **type safe**. This means that each variable is marked as being a distinct type and is not allowed to exceed the boundaries of that data type. This prevents some casting methods, especially those using pointers although C# allows unsafe portions of code which avoids these restrictions. This means that apart from unsafe blocks of code, the .NET runtime does not lose control of what data type a variable is and therefore can always check it is not out of bounds.

This means a lot more care will need to be taken when writing code that deals with converting between data types, although within the base classes there is a class called `Convert` which has static members to perform many of the more common conversions for you. These type safe constraints and the data types used to enforce them is summarized by the Common Type System (CTS), which will be discussed further later in the chapter.

Summary of Intermediate Language

By supporting all the requirements in the CLS, MSIL forms a solid base for .NET applications. Programming for this environment imposes some constraints on the structure and content of your code, but this should result in cleaner code with fewer bugs. Here is a summary of the main aspects of MSIL:

- ❑ Object Oriented Design
- ❑ Single implementation inheritance of classes
- ❑ Interfaces

15

❏   Value and reference types

❏   Strong type system

Common Type System (CTS)

The CTS supports two categories of data types: **Value** and **Reference**. We have already mentioned that MSIL deals with the two categories in different ways. Reference data types hold a reference to an object and are placed on the heap. Value data types refer to variables and enumerations you declare within your code and are placed on the stack (unless the value type is declared as a field within a reference type, in which case it will be stored on the heap). The garbage collector will only evaluate and clear reference types when invoked to reclaim memory.

Within these two categories, there are a selection of data types that cover the base types found in C++ and Java. Additionally these types follow a hierarchical system, so it is clear how each of the data types relate to the others. This is shown in the diagram below:

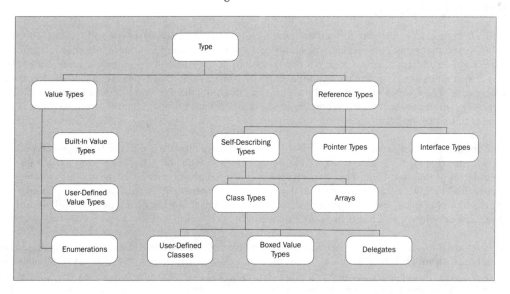

Here is a summary of the types in this diagram:

Type	Meaning
Value Type	Base class for any value types.
Built-in Value Types	Standard primitive types such as numbers and Boolean values, described in more detail below.
User-Defined Value Type	Types that have been defined in source code and stored as a value type. This type would hold a C# `struct`.

Type	Meaning
Enumerations	Set of enumerated values.
Reference Types	Base class for any data types accessed through a reference.
Self-Describing Types	Data types that provide information about themselves for the benefit of the garbage collector.
Pointer Types	Pointers, which are used in unsafe blocks of code.
Interface Types	Interfaces.
Class Types	Types that are self-describing but not arrays.
Arrays	A type containing an array of objects.
Delegates	Types that hold references to methods.
Boxed Value Types	A value type that is temporarily wrapped in a reference. We will discuss this in more detail further on in the chapter.
User-Defined Reference Type	Types that have been defined in source code and stored as a reference type. This type would hold a C# `class`.

The garbage collector will only evaluate and reclaim self-describing types. As you can see from the diagram, this includes class types, arrays and delegates. Interfaces don't actually occupy memory, so there is no need for the garbage collector to look at them, and pointers are only used in unsafe blocks of code, which are not evaluated by the garbage collector either.

Boxed value types are the odd one out among all these data types. You can convert a value type to an object, which allows variables to be treated as reference types as required. An example of this would be to pass a variable type as a type object to a method. This will be explored in Chapter 5 where we discuss custom casts.

The built-in value types contain the primitive types you expect to see with any language. There are too many to list here, so here is a selection:

Primitive Type	Description	Range
System.Boolean	Represents a Boolean value	true or false
System.Char	Represents a UNICODE character value	Any valid UNICODE character
System.DateTime	Represents a Date and Time value	IEEE 64-bit long integers that represent dates ranging from 1 January 0001 through to 31 December 9999 together with the time from 00:00:00 to 23:59:59

Primitive Type	Description	Range
System.Int32	Represents a 32-bit signed integer	-2,147,483,648 to 2,147,483,647
System.String	Represents a UNICODE string	Zero or more UNICODE characters

Each of these primitive types has a C# alias so they can be used within the language. From these primitive types, we can see that all string and char values accept UNICODE characters as standard. Additionally the string data type should come as a great relief to C++ programmers as it makes handling and manipulating strings so much easier than the methods used in C++. The names of the types are all prefixed with System as they all belong within that namespace.

System.Object

Every data type within the CLR is an object, and like all other objects within the .NET Framework, they are derived from System.Object. If you define your own custom types such as a class, structure, or enumeration, they will also derive from System.Object.

System.Object has four methods, available from all types as they are derived from this object. However, the Equals() and ToString() methods are overridden in most objects to provide better functionality and clearer output.

Method	Description
Equals()	Allows the object to be compared with another object.
GetHashCode()	Returns a hash code for the object. This is used by the Hashtable class to get a unique identity for an object.
GetType()	Returns a Type object that can be used to explore the methods, properties and events of a type. This is known as reflection.
ToString()	Returns a string representation of the type.

Common Language Specification (CLS)

The Common Language Specification is a set of language features that a language must support or adhere to if the language is to be CLS-compliant. However, the complete set of language features is quite considerable, so a language can support only a subset of the features of MSIL and CTS as long as it fully supports the CLS.

An example of a language not supporting all the features of MSIL is Visual Basic .NET. MSIL allows case-sensitive names but Visual Basic .NET does not. Visual Basic .NET does support all the features of the CLS, though, so it is still interoperable with your C# code which is case-sensitive, unless you have public or protected members whose names differ by case only, although this isn't advised.

The CLS is most important to those people who wish to create a compiler so that their language can target .NET. C# has only a few non-CLS-compliant features, so this shouldn't really affect your work to any great extent. If you do need to write non-CLS-compliant code it will run fine. Of course, the resulting code cannot be guaranteed to be completely accessible from other languages, however. Additionally you could put all of your non-CLS-compliant code in private implementations of your classes, as that would prevent other assemblies from accessing them.

There are a few things that could render your C# code non-CLS-compliant, such as using unsafe blocks of code. The C# data types `sbyte`, `ushort`, `uint` and `ulong` are not supported in the CLS, and using them as public or protected members will also make your code non-CLS-compliant.

Language Interoperability

Having looked at MSIL, CTS and CLS, we have gone though the basic components that allow .NET to give us language interoperability. Let's have a look at what is actually meant by language interoperability, and how .NET achieves this.

Until now, different programming languages have not been able to communicate with each other fluently. It was, however, possible for components to talk to each other using, for example, COM. This allowed components written in different languages to read each other's properties and invoke each other's methods. However, these calls were not done directly between the two components, data was marshaled across via COM. Additionally, the overhead of transferring the data between processes could be quite severe.

With the support built into .NET for language interoperability from the CLS and CTS, code can interact with other code regardless of what the initial language was, providing the code is CLS-compliant. This is one of the major benefits for developers targeting the .NET Framework. This means all of the following can be done:

❑ A type can inherit from another type written using another language

❑ An object can be passed to a method that belongs to another type written using another language

❑ An exception, once raised, can be passed through to code of a different language

❑ A debugger can step between methods in code and display the source code even if it means stepping between multiple languages

This is a big step forward for developers, especially those working in environments that see them exposed to more than one language, and are using COM to broker calls between DLLs. Visual Studio .NET provides an IDE that handles all the Microsoft .NET languages, in addition to Visual C++, and provides excellent debugging facilities. It is also possible for other languages to integrate into Visual Studio.NET.

The ability to pass across data types and their contents from one language to another is a benefit we can draw from the strong type safety enforced by MSIL. This ensures that when a data type is passed across, the JIT compiler can recognize the data type and deal with it appropriately.

The CLS ensures that once the data type has been successfully passed into the function, it is dealt with appropriately and safely so that the application does not crash and the data is not corrupted. This is done by strictly enforcing rules on the code being executed.

The .NET Base Class Library (BCL)

We have looked at most aspects of the .NET Framework but so far we have barely mentioned the Base Class Library. Again this is another element that can literally add so much functionality to your application.

The .NET Base Class Library is an extensive collection of various classes that replace, and in some cases improve the functionality provided by the Windows API. The classes are available for you to invoke and use yourself, several of which you can use to derive your own class.

These classes should be very easy for a Java developer to pick up and use, as they are intuitively named and are for the most part self-describing. C++ developers will find this a lot easier to use than the API equivalents, which can be cryptically named and sometimes lacking in documentation. The other major benefit of invoking methods rather than function calls is that the object can retain state; this can make many multiple-step operations easier to program, compared to the stateless function calls to the API.

Most tasks can be helped in some form with one or more of the base classes when using C#. Most of the chapters in this book will introduce you to at least one base class. We will begin our tour of the base classes in Chapter 7. Here is a list of some of the areas covered by the base classes:

- COM Interoperability
- Data Access (ADO.NET)
- Directory Access (replaces ADSI)
- File System Access
- Graphics (GDI+)
- .NET attributes and reflection
- Networking
- Accessing the Registry
- Windows-based services

Assemblies

We briefly touched on assemblies when we looked at some of the problems that exist within COM. Assemblies replace the role of the COM DLL, so let's take a look at what else they have to offer.

An assembly is a logical unit that contains compiled code targeted at .NET. Being a logical unit it can span one or many files, although the first file will contain all the metadata for the whole assembly. This is shown in the diagram below. Assemblies are discussed in more detail in Chapter 9.

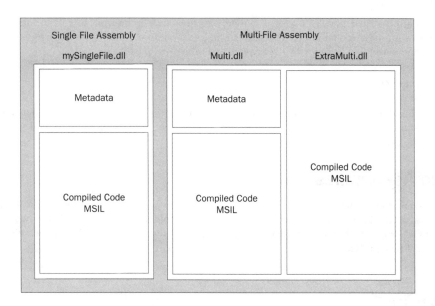

Metadata and Manifests

As we can see from the diagram above, every assembly has metadata that contains information pertaining to that assembly. The area that contains that metadata is called the manifest. This removes the need for any information about the assembly to be stored anywhere else. This is a big difference from COM, which stored information in Type Library files and in the Registry. The metadata will always contain the following information about an assembly:

❑ **Assembly file list**
Lists every file that contains data for this assembly

❑ **Referenced assemblies**
Lists all other assemblies, together with their version numbers, that this assembly needs to run its code

❑ **Type reference information**
This allows the classes and other resources to be found from within the assembly by the .NET runtime

❑ **Version information**
Each component has a version number, which is checked prior to each component being used

Shared Assemblies

Shared assemblies are accessible from any other .NET application. An example of this would be the .NET base classes. To make them visible to all applications, they are placed in the **global assembly cache (GAC),** which is managed by the .NET Framework.

There is a utility called `Gacutil.exe` provided with the .NET Framework to add and manage assemblies within the cache. `Gacutil.exe` can be found with the other framework tools and can used from the command line as follows to display all assemblies installed in the GAC:

```
>gacutil /l
```

By specifying the `/i` command-line option and the name of the DLL, we can install an assembly into the GAC; the `/u` command-line option uninstalls an assembly from the GAC. We shall see more of `Gacutil` in Chapter 9.

Private Assemblies

Private assemblies are used to store components designed to be run only with the application they are installed with. On installation they are copied to the same folder as the executable file rather than the GAC. It's as simple as that, no Registry entries to create or anything else. This has been given the name **zero-impact installation**.

Namespaces

Namespaces are used by .NET to place classes into logical groups. This allows you to have more descriptive names for your classes and lower the chances of different classes with the same name having a naming conflict. Say, for example, you defined a class called `Item` but there was already a class called by the same name in one of the other applications installed. This could cause a problem for the compiler, as it would not be clear which `Item` class you wanted to use. However, if your `Item` class was within the namespace `yournamespace` and the other `Item` class was within the namespace `thatnamespace` there would be no confusion over which class your code was referencing.

A namespace is used to keep a group of resources separate from everything else. The .NET base classes are within their own namespaces, such as `System` or `Sytem.Drawing`. This can be seen from the type and class names available to us, such as `System.Int32`.

You can also nest a namespace within another namespace. Microsoft guidelines recommend using your company name and the name of the project or package the code is relevant to. This could place our `Item` class into `Company.StockSystem.Item`, which would significantly decrease the chances of a name conflict.

Application Domains

Processes are used to run applications under Windows. Processes can utilize memory and other resources through Windows, and use threads to execute code that is within that process. Each process is isolated, meaning that no other process can directly affect it. This allows the programmer to have the confidence that the code will run on a machine and not be directly affected by something else that is running simultaneously. Additionally, if a process should crash, it will not affect all the other processes currently running.

This is all very good for the programmer, but processes incur a large overhead to create and run, and the system will suffer if too many are created. The overhead exists due to the conditions Windows imposes on each process to ensure that it is truly isolated. Each process has potentially 4 gigabytes of virtual memory, in which it can place its data and executable code. This 4 gigabytes of memory is then mapped to an area of physical memory that will not overlap between processes.

Each process can only read and write to memory by specifying an address from within its 4 gigabytes of virtual memory, and it has no access to the physical memory it is mapped to. Therefore, it cannot directly manipulate memory that belongs to another process. This can create another performance problem if two processes want to share data, as they cannot do that directly – unless of course all the code is running in the same process. However, if one crashes, all the others will also be closed down. Additionally, on Windows NT/2000/XP, each process has a security token that allows Windows to further control what it can and cannot do according to the security policy on the system.

Application domains are a way to keep classes isolated where necessary, yet allow them to run from the same process. This gives us considerable performance benefits in that data can be passed between components more freely, and there are fewer processes for the operating system to keep track of. This means that one process can hold several application domains, each of which will have its own thread to execute their code.

This diagram illustrates how application domains allow more than one application to run from a process, by sharing the memory within the process between the domains:

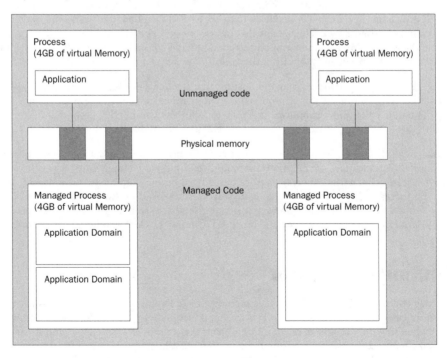

This cannot be done without the .NET Framework, as you would never have confidence that the process would retain its integrity once some other code has been placed in it. However, the .NET Framework ensures that all code within the process (for all the application domains) will be executed via the JIT Compiler. The rules imposed from the CLS, and the type safety restrictions from MSIL, ensure that each application domain will behave appropriately.

If code is not memory type safe, then it cannot share a process with other application domains. It will be placed in a process on its own with one application domain. Code is not memory type safe if the CLR cannot verify every attempt to access memory. As we mentioned earlier, unsafe blocks of code would fail the memory type safe checks.

JIT Compilation

The Just-In-Time Compiler is a core element of the .NET Framework. It is responsible for ensuring that MSIL is compiled to native machine code on demand, for every process running through the Framework.

This is no small task! You would think that if you had several applications running, the additional overhead of compilation on top of the resources needed to run would be significant enough to affect performance. Fortunately, the JIT Compiler has a few features designed to not only match the performance of applications using precompiled machine code, but to actually run your code even faster.

The JIT Compiler will not compile the entire application as it is loaded, which would create a slow start-up time. It only compiles portions of code as they are actually needed, and stores the native code until the application is closed down. This means that unless every function within an application is used every time the application is loaded, not all the code may be compiled, and looped code will only be compiled once and subsequently run from the compiler's cache of compiled code.

This method of compiling code on demand ensures that the compiler is not wasting time doing work that is not necessary to run the application. Where the compiler makes performance gains, though, is through the native code that it produces. It is able to tailor the compiled code to that of the processor it is to be run through, taking advantage of any optimizations available as it does so.

Previously the optimizations you applied to your code (if any) would apply to the processor that was used to build the application, or the processor supported by the development package. It was not general practice to check what processors were being used on the target machine and add code accordingly. Increasingly, processors have many methods to speed up execution that need to be explicitly prescribed in the machine code that is being sent to it, such as pairing up certain instructions. These optimizations can now be harnessed via the JIT Compiler, which should give a performance benefit.

The Garbage Collector

The garbage collector is how .NET manages memory for the applications currently being executed. It is a new feature to Windows programming. Previously, if using C++, you would have to explicitly delete an object when it was no longer needed. COM objects that had been instantiated and loaded kept a count of how many clients were accessing the component. When a process had finished using the component it needed to call the Release() method of the component so that the count would be lowered. If the count hit zero, which meant no-one wanted to use that component any more, it would then be deleted.

For the most part this worked fine; however it was easy for a programmer using C++ to forget to delete all his objects and create a memory leak. A memory leak is where an application does not release all the memory it used back to the operating system. One small leak is not a major problem for an operating system, but many leaks or a leak which is growing due to looping code can quickly drain the available resources, rendering the system practically unusable.

Memory leaks had the potential to cause more problems in conjunction with COM. When a process was terminated, Windows automatically reclaimed everything within that process, including the memory that had leaked while the process was running. With COM, though, there were processes designed to run all the time and never be closed down, such as custom DLLs for IIS. Therefore, if they leaked memory it would never be reclaimed, and additionally they might also be loaded several times, which multiplied any resulting memory leaks. Another side effect of COM was that if the count of an object never hit zero because a calling application never called the Release() method, it would be held in memory indefinitely.

The garbage collector is .NET's answer to this problem. This runs in a similar way to that of the garbage collector which is part of the Java runtime environment, and dynamically clears memory as needed from applications running within the .NET Framework. When the garbage collector is called by the CLR as memory needs to be cleared, the garbage collector checks all objects to see whether they are still accessible; if not, they will be deleted.

Your application, though, does not know when the CLR will call the garbage collector and you are not notified when it has been called. Code in the object destructor will be run when the garbage collector is called, but you cannot guarantee when this will be, so it is advisable not to put any time-critical code, such as closing a handle on a file, within the destructor.

You can specifically call the garbage collector at a specific point in your code if you so wish, although there are not many situations where this would be the best policy. If you have code to facilitate clearing up your object prior to deletion, it should be placed in a method called Dispose() which can be used to inform the garbage collector not to clear up this object. This is discussed further in Chapter 4.

Exceptions

.NET deals with exceptions using the try, catch and finally method which is similar to that used by C++ and Java. Due to the strong type system employed by MSIL, the performance hit for handling exceptions is not as great as it was with C++.

Exceptions are raised when an error occurs and take the form of an object derived from System.Exception in the .NET base classes. Going back to language interoperability, this gives the benefit that exceptions can be passed up to the calling object and understood, regardless of the language being used.

Security

There are two types of security for code running within the .NET Framework. You still get the role-based security you would be used to under NT/2000/XP, where the identity of the user account the code is running determines the level of trust. This could be used to prevent access to resources such as the Registry or file system.

Role-based security is fully supported under .NET, but it can now be complemented with code-based security. Code-based security allows you to specify the level of trust on an application that can work together with the appropriate role-based security. This means that as an administrator you can restrict code you are about to run if you feel it will be unsafe, and protect access to resources where needed. There is more discussion of this in Chapter 9.

Attributes

Attributes can be declared within your source code used to give the compiler extra information when compiling your code, or provide additional metadata within the assembly holding your code. An example of this would be to signify the threading model your application should start in, mark a method as obsolete, or to conditionally compile the method based on an earlier `#define` statement.

Under .NET you can define your own attributes in your source code, which can help with documenting your code and can be used with reflection to perform tasks based on your attributes.

Attributes will be covered in more detail in Chapter 6.

Summary

In this chapter, we have taken a quick look at all the main points of the core .NET technologies. We have seen how language interoperability has been created by a combination of .NET technologies and implemented through MSIL.

After reading this chapter, you should have a good understanding of the following concepts regarding the .NET Framework:

- ❑ Common Language Runtime (CLR)
- ❑ Common Language Specification (CLS)
- ❑ Common Type System (CTS)
- ❑ Microsoft Intermediate language (MSIL)
- ❑ JIT Compilation
- ❑ Assemblies (both private and shared)
- ❑ Application Domains
- ❑ Base Class Library (BCL)

Now we understand the basic concepts of .NET, we can move on and look at the C# Language.

Take the
Fast Track

to
C#

2

Introduction to C#

This chapter will give you an insight into the C# language. The C# language is a very modern language, especially when compared against languages such as C and C++ which have been in use for about twenty years. We will examine what strengths of other languages have been used to create C#, as well as what flaws have been left out. We will find out what benefits, if any, we can gain from using C# rather than our current language of choice, in terms of more reliable applications with shorter development times. Finally, we will look at what type of projects the C# compiler can produce and note what C#'s most important features are.

Why Do We Need C#?

In a world where new products are being released on a regular basis, it is natural to have some skepticism about the new product. New languages, though, are few and far between. It can take a considerable amount of time for a developer to retrain to become productive using the new language. Therefore, unless a new language can offer some benefits over existing languages, developers may stick to whatever language they know best. We'll take a brief look at some of the problems of the most popular current languages that are used for modern application development, and see how C# claims to have improved on these.

Before the release of the .NET Framework and .NET-enabled languages, the most popular choices for development on the Windows platform were C++ or Visual Basic. There are many other languages available, including Delphi and Perl, to mention just a few. However, they never really matched the popularity of C++ or VB. C++ came in many flavors; you could use Visual C++ or Borland C++ which gave you an IDE allowing a graphical approach to building forms, and there were many other compilers that could be run from the command line. Visual Basic could only be compiled if the IDE was installed, but was quite advanced and promoted quick development of Windows Forms and COM components.

This presented a dilemma for developers when trying to decide what language to learn or develop their applications in. Many of the less popular languages could present a problem if you needed to work in a team environment with other developers using a different language. Trying to decide between C++ and VB was not the easiest decision either. C++ has all the power and speed you expect, but it is reasonably difficult to learn and couldn't really be described as a rapid development tool even when being used by seasoned C++ developers. However, Visual Basic is practically at the other end of the scale, as it does not perform nearly as well as C++ and some of the more advanced features of C++ were not easy to implement, if they existed at all. In its favor, however, Visual Basic is very easy to learn in comparison to C++, and allows much quicker development times.

Java is in use on the Windows platform but is not terribly popular for application development. It is available in two flavors, the Java SDK from Sun and J++, which is part of Visual Studio. In many respects Java could be seen as a step ahead of C++ for development, due to the managed environment, but unfortunately it doesn't have the speed of compiled C++ code. J++ was also the cause of a legal battle between Microsoft and Sun, which probably did not encourage developers to take up the language.

This meant that there was not really a language that could be seen as a halfway house between C++ and VB. The gap between the languages was so large that experienced or professional VB developers found great difficulty in picking up C++. Additionally, in the programming environment we are facing today, the development time involved in building and maintaining applications with C++ is becoming increasingly hard to bear.

Problems with Existing Languages

Let's review the strengths and weaknesses of the main languages in use today in a little more depth, so we can better evaluate C# against our needs.

C and C++

C++ is a reasonably old language now. Its roots lie in the 1970s, when Bjarne Stroustrup added the facility to add classes to the language C, thus creating C++. C++ has many attractive features:

❑ It can be used on almost every platform, although code will only run on the platform it was compiled on

❑ It gives the developer a high level of control over the system, more so than most other languages

❑ It provides compiled code that executes quicker than other languages

C++ is also a flexible language in that you can develop an application using a procedural or object-oriented design. Despite its age, it has kept its popularity, mainly due to the high level of control it gives to the developer, although this has slipped as of late due to the increasing need for quicker turnaround of working applications from initial specification.

The main problem with C and C++ is that they are complex languages, which means that it takes longer to build applications with them. It is also very easy to make mistakes that can be hard to track down. Some of the more common bugs are listed here:

❑ C++ supports multiple inheritance of objects which can lead to a number of problems, one being ambiguity problems between base classes.

❑ You can easily mistake the assignment operator = for the comparison operator ==. In doing so your conditional statement will return the result True and overwrite the left hand side value in the process. No explicit error will be flagged to alert you to the problem.

❑ It is possible to read from a variable before it has been initialized, or is outside the bounds of an array. In doing so, you will receive bad data, and additionally writing to memory that has not been allocated to your code can cause instability for your application, or in some cases the whole system.

❑ With C and C++, you can directly allocate memory for the resources your application needs. It is also up to you to free the memory when you have finished using it. Failure to do so leads to memory leaks which, if severe, can force a system to be inoperable.

If your application requires fine control over the system, or as much speed as you can get out of your system, then your only choice may be C or C++. However, the complexity of these languages can lead to problems that are hard to debug and increase development time. Due to the continual increase in processing power and storage space, the extra power and efficiency that can be achieved from using C or C++ is no longer quite so important for most scenarios, and a slightly easier language to work with, that does not sacrifice too much control or speed, may be more attractive for many developers.

Visual Basic

Visual Basic has only been regarded as a more serious tool since the later versions (Visual Basic 5 and 6) were released. These allowed the creation of class modules, which allow an object-oriented methodology to be used. However, several important capabilities, such as inheritance and polymorphism are not available. Additional keywords, such as addressof, allow you to use more of the API, while at the same time enjoying the Rapid Application Development (RAD) system of Visual Basic. This allows you to drop controls onto a form and only provide code for events generated by that control.

The syntax of Visual Basic is also clear and easy to understand; variables are initialized upon creation and contents can be swapped between types easily. There is also a Variant data type that allows the user to use data without specifying whether it was numerical or string-based, as the compiler would attempt to work it out from looking at the data. The Variant data type is used for all variables in VBScript, which is essentially a cut-down version of Visual Basic to provide scripts for web applications, or to replace DOS scripts.

Visual Basic also came in one more flavor, Visual Basic for Applications. This was embedded into several applications such as Microsoft Office and Visio. This allows you to enhance your documents with portions of Visual Basic code that could respond to events raised from actions within those documents.

With all of this flexibility it is easy to see how Visual Basic has become as popular as it has. Unfortunately it comes with its own Achilles heel – the VB runtime DLL. For Visual Basic code to run, the runtime DLL needs to be installed on the machine, and this prevents standalone applications from running without it being installed first. As VB applications run all of their commands through the external DLL, it makes them perform a lot slower than their C or C++ counterparts. Additionally, developers find it increasingly difficult, if not impossible, to code more complex tasks using Visual Basic.

Java

Java was developed by Sun Microsystems, and was an attempt by Sun Microsystems to provide a language which was like C++ in design, but more suited for a distributed environment. This was released as an answer to the demands being placed on developers due to the emerging Internet and its related technologies, which involved creating applications that could talk to each other and exchange data between various locations, and possibly different platforms.

This philosophy leads to what many people see as Java's main strength – platform independence. It gives Java coders the power to run their code under Windows, UNIX or Linux, providing the Java runtime environment is installed. This is achieved by compiling Java source code into Java byte code, which can then be interpreted on the destination computer into the desired native code by the local Java Virtual Machine (JVM). Some later versions of the JVM are able to compile Java byte code rather than interpret it, which gives a performance benefit to running code.

Java offered other improvements over C++:

❑ Multiple inheritance is not allowed, although implementation is provided as an alternative

❑ Java is a strongly-typed language, which prevents some common errors

❑ Procedural design is not allowed, as all code has to be included within a class

These changes are present in C# and we will discuss the benefits they bring fully later in the chapter.

Another main benefit of Java byte code is that security can be enforced via the runtime environment, giving the user confidence to run code downloaded from the Internet. The runtime environment prevents actions such as writing directly to the file system or accessing the Registry. This allows the creation and use of Java applets that will typically run from within web pages, regardless of whether you are browsing the page from Windows, Macintosh or a UNIX machine as long as the appropriate JVM is installed.

Due to these benefits, Java has become a feasible choice for developers who wish to develop applications that can utilize more than one platform for all the various components. However, producing an application such as a web browser that could run on all operating systems was not an easy effort. Due to the different graphical methods between operating systems, it was almost impossible to produce one graphical interface that would fit all. However, for server-side applications that do not rely on a GUI, Java has become a popular choice.

Thanks to the more modern design of Java it is not as complex as C++, although good Java coders are just as scarce as their C++ equivalents, if not more so. Many Visual Basic developers found the transition to C++ or Java quite hard due to the way Visual Basic hid so much from the developer. This probably had as big an influence as any other on why Java development is not more widespread on the Windows platform.

Interestingly enough, quite a few ideas that are implemented in the design of Java and the Java runtime environment can be found in a similar guise in C# and the .NET framework. Here are a few of them:

- ❏   A central framework that managed the code and enforced security
- ❏   A garbage collector that helped memory management
- ❏   Procedural design not allowed; all code must be within a class
- ❏   A collection of base classes for basic functionality

Enter C#!

Now we have seen the main choices of languages for our development needs and some of the main disadvantages or problems we could face, let's take a look at C# and see whether it is going to make life easier for us as developers.

Some of the benefits we list here are inherited from the .NET Framework. Code generated using C# will always run under the Framework. The strengths of the .NET Framework and runtime environment are discussed in more detail in Chapter 1, although we will briefly review what aspects are utilized as part of C#. This means that some of these benefits may apply to other languages targeted at .NET, so we will look at how different C# is from managed C++, J# and Visual Basic .NET.

Strengths of C#

C# is a language that has built on the experience of developers, using languages such as C++, Java and Visual Basic to create a more modern, productive environment for producing applications for the .NET platform. C# boasts a syntax which is similar to that of C++ and Java. There is also full support for object-oriented programming and creation of components.

C# is also more tightly integrated with the .NET Framework than any other .NET-aware language, allowing you full access to all the benefits of writing for the .NET platform. This includes easy conversion of components into XML Web Services that can be accessed over the Internet, regardless of the platform or language of the other system.

In the next few sections of this chapter, we will review the main strengths of C#, both as a language and its gains from utilizing the .NET Framework.

Simplicity

Despite having a syntax which is remarkably similar to that of C++, there are many differences which make the language easier to read and maintain. Most of these are fairly subtle, such as referring to an object using the . operator in C#, instead of either the :: or -> operators with C++.

Your code is held in a single file, making it easier to maintain, rather than using header files or Interface Definition Language (IDL) files. Additionally, the source code to create forms and controls is part of your main code, and not hidden from view or held in a separate file.

Variables and Type Safety

C# is a type safe language; this means that the data types you are working with need to be defined, so that the compiler can ensure that no commands are run that will violate the rules of that data type. Additionally, data types cannot be inadvertently changed; if you wish to convert one data type to another you must perform an explicit conversion by using a cast operation to do so.

Every access of a data type is checked by the compiler. Variables need to be initialized before they can be used, or the compiler will flag up a warning. When you access an array, the compiler automatically checks whether you are in-bounds. Checks like these prevent you from reading bad data from memory space that has not been properly allocated to hold your data.

Consider this piece of C++ code:

```
int i;
if (i)
{
    ...
}
```

The C# compiler will not compile the code shown above and will generate an error instead. To amend this code so it will compile, we need to initialize our variable so that we know what data will be held in it, and we have to use a conditional operator (!=) so that there will be a Boolean value returned to the if statement.

Conditional statements such as an if statement always require a Boolean value to determine whether the condition imposed was true or false. This will leave us with the following code, which will compile successfully:

```
int i = 0;
if (i != 0)
{
    ...
}
```

Initially this may appear more restrictive, in that you have less freedom to do what you want with your variables, but the trade-off is more readable code that is less likely to contain errors. C# provides an extremely rich collection of built-in data types, such as decimal and string, which are very flexible and remove the need for more cryptic C-style data types. The built in char and string data types support Unicode values and make dealing with characters and strings so much easier and quicker than C++.

A type safe environment like this can bring other benefits as well. As the runtime environment has close control of your variables and objects, it can employ a garbage collector to clear out items that are no longer in scope. This is another powerful feature, as it automatically clears up objects for your code, preventing the most common cause of memory leaks in the process.

Flow Control Statements

The flow control statements in C# are for the most part identical to that of C++ and Java. C# also includes the VB keyword foreach to loop through the items within an array or collection.

Switch statements operate slightly differently with C# than they do in C++. Each case statement will break if true, unless you explicitly note that it should not. This stops the switch statement falling through to multiple case statements, which was a useful but error prone feature of C++.

Mature Object-Oriented Functionality

C# is a fully object-oriented language, allowing all the functionality that you would expect, such as encapsulation, polymorphism and inheritance. Because C# is a more modern language than C++ and Java, the opportunity has come up to remove or alter several aspects of object-oriented functionality to simplify the design and implementation of your classes.

C# allows only single inheritance, which means that each class can only be derived from one other class. There is no limit to the number of classes that your derived class can be used to create, though. The prevention of multiple inheritance stops the creation of classes that are hard to work with and amend because they are based on several inherited classes. Deriving from multiple interfaces is allowed, though. Additionally, the methods within your classes are non-virtual by default, which makes it much more unlikely that they will be mistakenly over ridden.

Namespaces are used to group your classes and other objects. You can nest one namespace within another, doing so with information such as your company name, and the current project will ensure that the possibility of naming conflicts with other code is very remote.

C# prohibits the use of global methods or variables in the same manner as Java. This ensures your application uses an OO style rather than falling back into a procedural style, which was easy to do with C++. You can create static members within your classes, though, which can be used to give similar functionality to global variables and functions.

Another benefit of C# being a fully object-oriented language is that you can treat everything as an object. This includes variables, structures and enumerations. For example you could call the `ToString()` method of an integer to get a string representation of its contents.

Unsafe Code

C# allows you to define blocks of code as **unsafe**. Code executed within these blocks is not restricted by all the safety rules that the rest of your code obeys. This allows you to use features such as pointers to directly access memory and gives you more freedom in what data types you can pass to DLLs outside the .NET Framework, such as the Windows API.

Since code in these blocks is not subject to the type safety and management rules of the runtime environment, it will fail the checks that the runtime environment puts each section of code through. This means that in some environments the code will not have sufficient permission to run, as it will not have the same level of trust as code which is not marked as unsafe.

XML Documentation

Another feature of C# is that you can embed XML documentation in with your code. Lines can be marked in a similar fashion to standard comments, but information can be held within XML tags. The compiler will recognize these tags and can produce documentation from them. We will look at this in more detail in Chapter 6.

Common Language Runtime

As we discussed in detail in Chapter 1, C# code is compiled into MSIL and then run within the .NET runtime environment. Due to the very close relationship between C# and the .NET Framework many of the possible benefits that could be gained from using the CLS are seen with C#.

The .NET Base Classes

The .NET Framework contains an extensive collection of base classes. These are a collection of classes that can be utilized via your code to perform a whole host of basic functions that replicate the bulk of the functionality that can be found from the Windows API, as well as some new features. The base classes are a lot easier to navigate than the API though, due to the intuitive class-based structure. Methods within the classes have descriptive names, so it is easy to decide what methods to use, many of which are richly overloaded giving you flexibility in what format you pass data across to them. We begin our tour of the .NET base classes in Chapter 7.

Data Access

The obvious choice for accessing data with C# is ADO.NET. ADO was a great model for accessing data from a variety of sources, although it was more suited to Visual Basic than C++. ADO.NET improves greatly on ADO, offering much greater support for working with disconnected sets of data, which is much more appropriate for distributed environments. There is also a separate class designed purely for accessing SQL Server. This allows your code to work much faster with SQL Server than using the standard OLE DB classes. We look at ADO.NET in Chapter 10.

XML

The standard format for data storage within the .NET Framework is XML. The `System.Xml` namespace has all the functionality you need to read, write and validate XML documents. ADO.NET also has native support for XML, so much so that it uses XML to send data to external sources such as a Web Form or your application. Such tight integration between ADO.NET and XML allows you to deal with XML data in a remarkably intuitive fashion. We will see XML in Chapters 7 and 10.

C# Compared to Java

Java coders will not only find the process of how C# compiles to an intermediate language and runs within a managed environment familiar, but also notice many similarities in the syntax used by Java and C#.

One benefit Java has over C# is platform independence, due to the different versions of the Java runtime for the various operating systems. At the moment .NET Framework can only be installed on the Windows platform, but it is almost certain that in the future it will exist in some form on other operating systems.

C# does have several advantages over Java, mostly due to the .NET runtime being more powerful than the Java runtime. The runtime gives C# a much more powerful set of base classes than Java, together with language interoperability. Additionally the ability to include blocks of unsafe code, which can run without some of the runtime restrictions, is not allowed in Java.

C# Compared to Other .NET Languages

We have seen that C# is an excellent language in its own right, and reviewed many of the useful features that it brings to us as developers. Now we need to compare it to the other languages that are available to produce applications aimed at the .NET runtime.

Managed C++

It is possible to run your existing C++ code within the .NET Framework, utilizing benefits such as garbage collection and code-based security. This can be done with header files provided with Visual Studio .NET, and some minor alterations to your class definitions.

Managed C++ does not give you any comparable speed difference for the most part over C#. Together with the improvements C# has over C++ which we noted above, this makes C# much more attractive for developing new components and applications.

Visual Basic .NET

Visual Basic .NET should not be confused with VB5/6, which we discussed at the beginning of the chapter. Visual Basic has had a major overhaul to bring it up to .NET standard, and in many respects should be treated as a different language.

Due to the nature of integration with the .NET Framework, Visual Basic .NET is practically on a par with C# for functionality. However, unlike C#, it is not case sensitive. One feature Visual Basic .NET does lack, though, is the ability to utilize blocks of unsafe code, which essentially is not a major problem.

However, Visual Basic .NET is still widely different from C# in its syntax, which for the most part resembles VB. Despite this, Visual Basic .NET will not be that much easier for VB developers to pick up and become productive with, due to the number of differences between VB and Visual Basic .NET.

J#

J# is currently in Beta 1 stage at the time of writing this book. It is a full .NET language in that the compiler produces MSIL for use in the .NET runtime, and does not offer any support or compatibility for the Java runtime produced by Sun. This also means that you cannot create Java applets for use in web pages using J#.

The language is very similar to Java and VJ++, and there are tools for converting VJ++ source code into J#. There are additional base classes installed as part of J# which are designed to replicate some of the class libraries within the JDK.

Due to J# and C# both running within the same runtime, there will probably not be much difference between the functionality of the languages once J# is fully released. There will be minor syntax differences between the two languages, but probably little else.

JScript.NET

JScript was Microsoft's interpretation of ECMAScript, which was better known as JavaScript. JScript was used primarily for scripting the client-side portion of web sites, although it could also be used for server-side scripting within an Active Server Page (ASP).

JScript has been ported to .NET, but it retains a major difference from C# in that, by default, it is a loosely-typed language, which is in complete opposition to the strong type system that C# relies on. In doing so JScript.NET retains full backwards compatibility with existing JScript code.

C# Applications

With C# we can create practically any type of application for the .NET Framework. In a distributed environment allowing access to the Internet, it is more important than ever for a language to support a lot more than the basic client-side form-based application. Thanks to the wealth of features within the .NET Framework, we have the capability to create several different types of applications and components, allowing us to write code that will be relevant to a wide variety of scenarios. Here we will go through some of the various projects you can create either wholly or partially with C#.

ASP.NET

Like all the other technologies within the .NET Framework, ASP.NET is a completely new system for web development rather than a mere upgrade of ASP, the technology it is designed to replace.

Active Server Pages are used to generate web pages dynamically via processing on the web server. This is done by inserting blocks of code (either VBScript or JScript) within an HTML file to create dynamic content where it is needed. This could be used, for example, to populate an HTML table with records from a database.

There were a few problems with this – ASP code was interpreted rather than compiled, which made it run relatively slow. Additionally, having the HTML and ASP code in the same file made maintenance quite difficult. Some HTML editors did not work well with embedded ASP, and quite often designers and developers would be working on the same file, leading to problems of overwriting each other's work or keeping the whole file up to date.

ASP could use COM objects, so that compiled code could also be used once it had been installed on the web server. This enabled ASP to access data through ADO and allowed functionality that couldn't be replicated via VBScript or JScript.

To create a fully functioning web site, this system of work often meant using several different technologies together to build the final product. This was compounded further in an *n*-tier scenario that could utilize technologies such as MTS and COM+.

ASP.NET is a solution to these problems that have plagued ASP web developers, and it also contains some great new features. ASP.NET is not a direct replacement for ASP, so you can still run existing code alongside ASP.NET, even within the same web site.

The main benefits ASP.NET has over ASP could be summarized as follows:

- ❑ ASP.NET promotes structured code using classes, as opposed to blocks of code among HTML
- ❑ Your code is contained in a separate file from your HTML
- ❑ ASP.NET can use any .NET-aware language, such as C#
- ❑ ASP.NET substantially increases performance over ASP – partially due to a more advanced system of caching pages
- ❑ Must better support for tracing and debugging
- ❑ Support for Web Server Farms

Web Forms

This is the main programming model for ASP.NET. Using Visual Studio .NET, you can build a Web Form in an almost identical fashion to a Windows form. A Web Form takes the place of the traditional web page. You no longer need to insert blocks of ASP code within the page unless you wish to do so, you just place controls onto the Web Form. This can make it easier for designers and developers to work on the same page.

Mobile ASP.NET

Although not part of the standard .NET installation, there is a Mobile Internet Toolkit available from Microsoft to help develop your ASP.NET applications for use on mobile phones and other mobile devices. This enables ASP.NET to generate WML and cHTML as needed to provide the appropriate display on mobile devices.

Web Controls

These are the controls you can use to populate your web forms. ASP.NET renders the controls depending on what browser is being used; this feature can be used to display the control properly whether using Internet Explorer, Netscape Navigator or even a portable device. One benefit of these is that controls can raise events from the web page for your code to handle.

All the code exists within a class that is located in a separate file from the web form. This means that a designer can work on the web form while the developer works on the code independently. This event-driven model is vastly different from ASP, and allows you to have better structured code and keep more of your code server-side, preventing the need to use DHTML for all of your data validation. This is vastly different from ASP where any items on a form were only capable of sending information back when the page was submitted back to the browser.

Web Services

The Internet has proved to be a very successful medium for transferring data from user to user via e-mail and from machine to user in the form of HTML. However, if your application wants to transfer data to another remote application, you quickly run into problems.

There have been technologies developed for this purpose, such as DCOM and CORBA, but although they work fine on a LAN, there are problems using them across the Internet. The traffic can be a little inefficient and large in size, which slows the process more than it would across a LAN. Additionally, there is the problem of firewalls and possible bad networking conditions to overcome.

Web services could well be the solution to this problem. Web services use technologies such as HTTP, XML and SOAP that are standard throughout the industry, rather than just Microsoft-specific.

It is possible that in the near future we may be in the position where web services (in a looser sense than the .NET implementation) will be able to talk to other web services regardless of what operating system, and even what applications are on the target machine. This may sound like just wishful thinking, but the same thing could have been said a few years ago about tight interoperability between languages, such as we are seeing now in the .NET Framework.

It is very simple to mark your code as part of a web service when using C#; you simply have to add a [WebMethod] attribute to the relevant methods within your classes. Visual Studio .NET maintains a discovery file within your ASP.NET application which allows your methods to be found and accessed. Data between web services is transported as XML using SOAP as the protocol.

Windows Applications

With C# you get the excellent support for the classic client-side application that uses Windows forms to display the user interface that you have come to expect from Microsoft development languages. The Visual Studio .NET IDE makes the creation of forms and their contents very quick and simple. The process is similar to creating a form using Visual Basic 6, and is a lot easier than C++.

Windows Controls

The items you add onto a Windows form are known as Windows Controls, and they replace Active X Controls (or OCXs as they were also known). Windows Controls are capable of displaying onto the containing form within the area given to it, and receive events from user interaction with the control. They do not have to display anything on the form that holds them, however, and an impressive suite of controls is available for use, offering functionality in many different areas.

Windows Services

Windows Services usually run in the background without requiring any direct user interaction. There is excellent support for services within the base classes. This gives you basic functionality for services allowing you to create a service without writing code to register your application as a service and handle talking to the Service Control Manager. This relieves a lot of basic work that would normally be needed to make your application behave like a normal service and respond to actions from the Service Control Manager.

Class Libraries

In many ways a class library is similar to a COM DLL, as denoted by the name, although the library contains classes, whereas a DLL could just have easily held functions. This is enforced, as all code must be within a class when using C#.

A class Library is held within an assembly and therefore has several major benefits over the older COM DLL. Possibly the most beneficial of these is that you do not have to register the assembly as you would a DLL. An assembly can either be copied to the same directory as the executable file, which will access it if it needs to be kept private, or installed into the global assembly cache if it is going to be made public to all .NET applications.

Assemblies also support side-by-side versioning, so that if you use a common class library for some functionality in your application, you can be confident that the component will not get updated – which could have an adverse effect on your application.

It is still possible for an application running within the .NET Framework to access a COM component, rather than being restricted to assemblies. COM Interoperability is possible, although not as efficient as working with code within the actual framework. This enables legacy code to be utilized with new code built for the .NET Framework. There are utilities distributed with the .NET Framework to assist those working with COM components.

Console Applications

You can create console applications with C#, although it is not especially useful for a full application in a Windows environment. The console is a great method for reporting data if your code does not have access to a GUI. Instances where this is useful would include debugging or testing components.

The C# Compiler

In a break from tradition with most professional languages produced by Microsoft, the C# compiler is currently given away freely with the .NET Framework. This is great in the sense that anyone can download the .NET Framework from Microsoft, write some C# code using Notepad, and compile from the DOS prompt.

It is obviously going to be more productive to use an IDE than Notepad and a DOS prompt, and Visual Studio .NET not only provides all the functionality you could ask for to develop your C# applications, but for the most part it makes it as quick and painless as possible. The built-in help is clear and concise, IntelliSense auto-completes where possible, and it allows you to build Windows forms and Web Forms with an intuitive IDE.

Due to the fact that the compiler can be used freely without Visual Studio .NET, there are now many other C# development environments available, such as the Antechinus C# Programming Editor and SharpDevelop.

Using the Compiler

The C# compiler is very simple to use – it is just a case of executing it from a command prompt with switches to control the output. If you intend to use the compiler from the command prompt frequently, it may be worth setting the PATH environment variable so that the compiler can always be found. There are two locations which you may wish to add, one within your framework where the C# compiler can be found, and another within your installation of Visual Studio .NET where other command line tools like ildasm.exe can be found. The locations vary depending on your OS and installation choices, but typically you will want to set your PATH environment variable to include the following (with the second location depending on whether you have Visual Studio .NET installed):

```
C:\Program Files\Microsoft.NET\FrameworkSDK\bin
C:\Program Files\Microsoft Visual Studio .NET\FrameworkSDK\Bin
```

To specify your source file and output file you would write something like:

```
>csc /out:Executable.exe Source.cs
```

We saw earlier that C# can be used for a variety of project types; you specify which type with the /target or /t switch. So, to create an application using Windows forms, we could execute the following:

```
>csc /out:Executable.exe Source.cs /t:winexe
```

Response Files

In addition to adding all your options to the command line each time you wish to compile some code, you can also specify a response file that holds the options for you.

To replicate the build above with a response file, the response file contents would be as below:

```
# My comments go here
/t:winexe
/out:Executable.exe
Source.cs
```

We would execute the following line without our switch options, as any items in the file would override the items on the command line:

```
>csc @responsefile1.txt
```

RSP File

Located with the C# compiler is a file named csc.rsp which contains options which will always be processed, unless you specify the /noconfig option. By default the RSP file contains references to the common framework libraries, but you may want to add common options or a reference to an assembly that you always use.

Here are some of the more commonly used compiler options:

Option	Description
/out:<file>	Output file name
/target:exe	Build a console executable
/target:winexe	Build a Windows executable
/target:library	Build a library
/target:module	Build a module that can be added to another assembly
/recurse:<wildcard>	Include all files in the current directory and subdirectories according to the wildcard specifications
/unsafe[+|-]	Allow unsafe code to compile
/resource:<resinfo>	Embeds the specified resource
/reference:<assembly> /r:<assembly>	Imports metadata from an assembly file. You can specify the full path to the assembly, or anywhere specified by the PATH environment variable, or a relative path starting at the current project. If more than one file is specified, they are separated by semicolons.

Summary

In this chapter we have had a good look at many aspects of the C# language. This is a language that benefits from a modern, well thought out design. Learning from the problems developers have been experiencing from their languages has enabled the C# designers to incorporate features to avoid those pitfalls. The benefits that are gained from the .NET Framework to manage code while running C# enables developers to quickly and efficiently produce code that should be more robust and bug-free than ever before.

❑   C# has also proved to be a very flexible language which is able to provide functionality in many key areas which will become increasingly important over time

❑   The native support for XML is very strong and that will become more relevant for your programming needs in the near future

❑   With all the additional features of ASP.NET, a browser-based solution is now looking increasingly attractive over a more static form-based solution for many scenarios

Despite the rich functionality and powerful benefits C# has over many other languages, the compiler is freely available. You can pick up a free or cheap C# editor over the Internet, so the language can be picked up and used by anyone who wishes to do so. However, the Visual Studio .NET IDE is by far the most advanced offering, and is essential for more complex projects, especially those utilizing more than one language.

Take the **Fast Track** to *C#*

3

C# Basics

This is the first of four chapters on the core of the C# language, in which were going to cover the basic syntax elements. The second chapter is going to look at the specific object-oriented features of C#, the third chapter will concentrate on more advanced topics, and the final one will deal with some .NET specific features – such as threading and reflection – and how they're implemented in C#.

Since C# has so many similarities to both Java and C++, I'll use some special paragraphs in the text to point out special features of interest to C++ and Java programmers. Feel free to ignore the ones that don't apply to you!

In this chapter, we're going to cover the following topics:

- ❑ How to build and run C# programs
- ❑ How C# programs are structured
- ❑ Basic C# syntax
- ❑ How to call methods
- ❑ How to handle errors using exceptions
- ❑ How to send output to the console

Starting Out

Every programmer knows that the first program you write in a new language is one that prints "Hello world!" to the console. I've no desire to break with tradition, so here is the simplest C# version:

```
using System;

// Here's a Hello World program in C#
namespace Wrox.FTrackCSharp.Basics.Hello
{
    class Hello
    {
        public static int Main()
        {
            Console.WriteLine("Hello world!");
            return 0;
        }
    }
}
```

You can type this code into Notepad, and save it into a file with a .cs extension (hello.cs), which is the default extension for C# code. Save this in the C:\FTrack\Basics directory. Note that, like all C-derived languages, C# is case-sensitive, so you have to type everything with the correct case. Note especially that the name of the main method is Main() with a capital M!

Assuming you've got the .NET Framework SDK installed, you can compile the program by invoking the C# compiler from the command line:

C:\FTrack\Basics>csc hello.cs

When you examine the directory, you'll see that this has produced an executable called hello.exe, which you can run from the command-line just like any other executable.

Executables in C#

The executable produced by the C# compiler is a standard Windows PE (Portable Executable) format file. Such a PE file contains the compiled IL code, plus code for loading the runtime, which will run the program on any machine that has the .NET runtime installed.

The small size of the executable is due to the fact that .NET code dynamically links to the .NET Framework class libraries, so the executable only has to contain the IL for the code that you actually write.

Using Visual Studio .NET

You can easily create the same Hello World program using Visual Studio .NET. Start up the IDE, and use the File | New | Project... menu item to bring up the New Project dialog. Make sure that Visual C# Projects is selected in the Project Types pane, and Console Application in the right-hand Templates pane. Pick a suitable location for the project, and give it the name Hello.

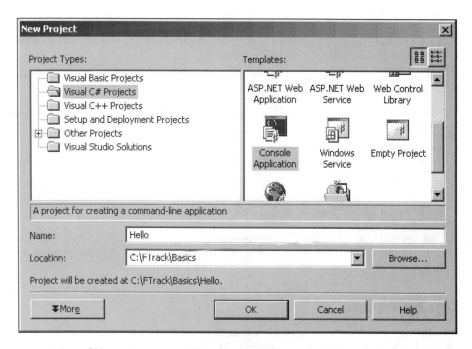

When you click on **OK**, a new project will be created for you, and the IDE will display the skeleton code in the editor. Replace the TODO comment lines with the same Console.WriteLine() statement from the Notepad version, and you'll end up with code that looks like this:

```
using System;

namespace Wrox.FTrackCSharp.Basics.Hello
{
    /// <summary>
    /// Summary description for Class1
    /// </summary>
    class Class1
    {
        /// <summary>
        /// The main entry point for the application
        /// </summary>
        [STAThread]
        static void Main(string[] args)
        {
            Console.WriteLine("Hello world!");
        }
    }
}
```

You'll notice a few differences from the hand-coded version. I'll list them briefly here, and most of them will be covered in more detail in later chapters.

47

❑ The class is enclosed in a namespace. Namespaces provide a higher level of scoping than the class, and they are used to group related types. Namespaces are discussed in more detail in the next chapter.

❑ The namespace takes its name from the project, and the one class it contains is called Class1 by default. You are quite at liberty to change either or both of these names.

❑ The '///' comments are C# XML documentation comments, and are explained in more detail in Chapter 5.

❑ [STAThread] is an example of an attribute attached to a method. This attribute is specifying the threading model for the Main() method. Attributes are discussed in Chapter 6.

❑ The Main() method in this version takes an argument and has a void return type, whereas in the Notepad version it had no arguments and returned an int. Main() is special, and it can either return an int or void, and can optionally take command-line arguments.

You can compile this code by selecting Build Solution from the Build menu, or by pressing *Ctrl+Shift+B*. You can then run the program by pressing *Ctrl+F5*, or by selecting Start Without Debugging from the Debug menu.

Program Structure

Before moving on to look at the basic syntax elements in detail, let's look briefly at the structure of the Hello World program, as this shows (in just about the simplest program possible) the overall structure of C# programs.

The first important point to note is that C# is a *pure OO language*, which means that everything has to be part of a class. This idea will be familiar to Java programmers, but will be new to those who are coming from C++. In C#, all functions and data items have to be class members, and only certain keywords – such as using – can occur outside a class definition.

Java Note
A C# source file can contain as many classes as you like, and there's no link between the name of the file and the name of a public class within the file. You can also have more than one public class per file.

In C++, main() would be a global function, but in C# it has to be part of a class. So in this application the Hello class exists simply in order to hold the Main() method. Main() is a static member of the class; the idea of static members in C# is the same as in C++ or Java, denoting a member that belongs to the class rather than to any instance.

The Console.WriteLine() method is used to output a line of text ending with a new line. We'll cover basic I/O in more detail later in this chapter.

The using directive at the top of the program is the only line of code that occurs outside a class definition. Its purpose is effectively to tell the compiler how to resolve names, by telling it what namespaces it can use as type prefixes. Namespaces and the using keyword are described in more detail in Chapter 6.

> **Java Note**
>
> C#'s using directive is very similar in operation to Java's import keyword, in that it saves the programmer having to use fully qualified names in code.

> **C++ Note**
>
> The using directive may look similar to the C++ #include directive, but the task it performs is completely different. #include includes source code at compile time, whereas using merely tells the compiler which namespaces to look in for any types which aren't referred to by their fully qualified names, or aren't in the default or global namespace.

Basic Syntax

This section will examine the basics of C# syntax, comparing and contrasting with C++ and Java as appropriate.

Comments

C# has three commenting conventions, two of which will be immediately familiar to Java and C++ programmers. A double slash // starts a comment that continues to the end of the current line, while /* and */ are used to delimit comment text which may be within a single line, or be spread over multiple lines.

```
// Comment to the end of the line

/* A comment
   over more than
   one line */

x = /* A comment within a line */ 5;
```

The third style of comment is the documentation comment, which starts with three slashes /// and continues to the end of the line. This comment type is used to generate XML documentation from C# code, and it is explained more fully in Chapter 5.

> **Java Note**
>
> The XML documentation feature in C# is very similar to JavaDocs. Apart from the different commenting syntax used in C#, a major difference is that the output is in XML rather than Java's default HTML.

Types

This section introduces the types that are available in the C# language.

Value and Reference Types

OO languages have a fundamental problem: how to represent the most basic of data types, such as integers, characters, and simple user-defined types such as a `Point` structure that contains only X and Y coordinates.

From the design point of view it would be nice if everything were a class, because this makes it possible to have a unified type system. The problem is that there are considerable overheads to using classes. Object allocation and destruction takes time, and using method calls for simple operations (such as adding or copying two integers) will impact efficiency considerably.

It is much more efficient to make the basic types bit patterns, which can easily be manipulated, and which can be created on the program stack. The problem is that now the language has a two-tier type system, with objects and 'other types' that aren't objects. This doesn't allow for a unified type system, and it is awkward when you need to use a basic type in a context that requires an object, such as using a collection class.

.NET gets around this problem by dividing types into **value types** and **reference types**.

Java Note
Java uses a two-tier type system. The basic types (such as `int` and `double`) are represented as bit patterns, just as they are in C++. Wrapper classes (such as `Integer` and `Double`) are provided in `java.lang` to wrap the basic types so that they can be used as objects.

Reference Types

Reference types include classes, interfaces, and arrays. For the minute, let's restrict the discussion to classes, and introduce the others in the sections (and chapters) that follow. Reference types are created on the managed heap, usually using the new operator.

```
// Creating a reference type
Foo f = new Foo();
```

C++ Note
Reference types are always created on the heap, regardless of how they are instantiated (strings are reference types in C#, but aren't usually created using the new operator). In fact, new can also be used to initialize structs, which are value types.

What you get back when you create a Foo object is a reference to a Foo, which works the same as a reference in Java, or similarly to a pointer in C++. Here are some of the characteristics of reference types:

❏ They can contain all the things you'd expect in a class, such as methods, properties, constructors - and so on

❏ They're always created on the managed heap

❏ They're always accessed using references

❏ Copying, assignment and parameter passing is always by "reference"

❏ They are automatically garbage-collected

Why do we have "reference" in quotation marks above? In C#, everything is actually passed by value by default, but in the case of reference types, the value is just a reference to the location on the heap where the actual object is stored. The distinction between this form of passing parameters and genuine passing by reference may seem pedantic, but it does affect how parameters behave.

Consider this code, which converts the first letter of a string to upper case, and the remainder of the string to lower case:

```
using System;

class Class1
{
    static void Main(string[] args)
    {
        string s = "heLLO";
        InitialCaps(s);
        Console.WriteLine(s);
    }

    public static void InitialCaps(string s)
    {
        switch (s.Length)
        {
            case 0:
                break;
            case 1:
                s = s.ToUpper();
                break;
            default:
                s = s[0].ToString().ToUpper() +
                    s.Substring(1, s.Length - 1).ToLower();
                break;
        }
    }
}
```

Although strings are reference types, the output from this code will be unchanged from the original value: heLLO, rather than the intended Hello. This is because strings are immutable – when a string is modified, instead of altering the existing object, a new string object is actually created on the heap. This means that the original object is unaffected when we modify the string within the InitialCaps() method, and the changes aren't propagated back to the calling method. In order for the method to work as intended, we need to explicitly pass the parameter by reference using the ref keyword:

```
using System;

class Class1
{
    static void Main(string[] args)
    {
        string s = "heLLO";
        InitialCaps(ref s);
        Console.WriteLine(s);
    }
```

```
public static void InitialCaps(ref string s)
{
    switch (s.Length)
    {
        case 0:
            break;
        case 1:
            s = s.ToUpper();
            break;
        default:
            s = s[0].ToString().ToUpper() +
                s.Substring(1, s.Length - 1).ToLower();
            break;
    }
}
}
```

This code outputs our desired Hello string. We'll look at the `ref` keyword and method parameters later in this chapter.

Garbage Collection

Reference types in C# – and, in fact, all .NET languages – are automatically destroyed as required. Managing memory by hand is difficult in all but the simplest applications, and failure to deallocate memory correctly can result in memory leaks (at best) or program crashes.

The runtime engine keeps track of references to objects, and periodically the garbage collector is run in order to clear up objects that can no longer be reached. This may happen when there is not enough memory to allocate new objects, or a collection can be requested from code. The .NET garbage collector is generational, in that it doesn't try to collect all unused objects every time, but divides them into generations. If collecting the newest, most recently released objects provides enough memory, it doesn't bother with older generations. The garbage collector normally runs concurrently on a separate thread, although it is possible to run the collector on the same thread as the application.

C# classes can contain a destructor (also known as a finalizer), which is a method that is called when an object is reclaimed by the garbage collector. Finalizers are discussed in more detail in Chapter 4.

> *To read more about the .NET garbage collection mechanism, see the two articles by Jeffrey Richter in the November and December 2000 issues of MSDN Magazine, and also Jeffrey Richter's book "Applied Microsoft .NET Framework Programming" (Microsoft Press, ISBN 0-735614-22-9). If you have the MSDN Library installed, either as part of Visual Studio .NET or independently, you'll find these two articles in electronic form. You can also find them on the MSDN web site at http://msdn.microsoft.com/msdnmag/issues/1100/GCI/GCI.asp for the November 2000 article, and http://msdn.microsoft.com/msdnmag/issues/1200/GCI2/GCI2.asp for the December article.*

Value Types

A **value type** is a sequence of bits normally stored on the program stack, and so they behave in the same way as the basic built-in types in Java or C++. The C# built-in types are almost all value types, and you can create your own value types by using the `struct` and `enum` keywords. How you do this is covered in the following chapter.

Value types do not need to be created using new, but instead can use standard local variable declaration. In the following code fragment, Point is a value type:

```
// Creating a value type
Point p;
```

When a value type is instantiated, its data members will be initialized to default values (for example, zero for a numeric field). However, we can also use the new operator to instantiate a struct using a constructor that initializes the members to specific values.

Here are some of the characteristics of value types:

❑   They are very similar to reference types, but there are one or two limitations, such as the fact that they can't inherit from reference types, and cannot be used as superclasses.

❑   They are created on the stack, so creation and destruction is efficient because it doesn't involve allocating and freeing a separate chunk of memory. (Value-type members of reference types are actually stored on the heap, but since this memory has already been allocated when the object was instantiated, this still holds true.)

❑   They are accessed directly, so access is efficient.

❑   By default, they are copied and passed by value, not by reference.

❑   They are not subject to garbage collection.

Microsoft recommends that you use value types for types that meet one or more of the following criteria:

❑   Act like primitive types

❑   Are smaller than 16 bytes or so in size

❑   Are immutable

❑   Should possess value semantics

Boxing

All types in C# ultimately inherit from the Object class, which we met briefly in Chapter 1. The Object class lives at the base of the inheritance tree; because of this, you can define generic container classes to hold references of type object, and they will then be able to hold any type. How can you store a value type in such a container? In Java, you have to wrap the basic type in a class wrapper, so that an int is wrapped in an Integer object, which can then be stored. The problem is that this has to be done manually, both to store the basic type and to retrieve the value later. C#, on the other hand, provides a way to convert to and from objects as required, and this means that value types have the efficiency of basic bit-patterns, along with the usability of objects. This conversion usually occurs automatically, although you may occasionally have to use a cast, as described below.

When a value type is **boxed**, it is implicitly converted to an object: an object instance is allocated, and the value of the value type is copied into the box. The following picture shows the boxing process in action.

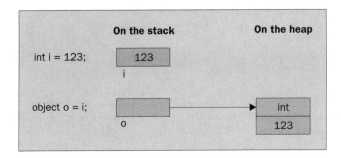

An integer is created on the stack, and then assigned to an object. An object is created on the managed heap that contains the type, and a copy of the value. Note that boxed objects always contain a copy of the value, so alterations made to the boxed copy never affect the original value type.

It is also possible, although rarely necessary, to box values explicitly in code using a cast:

```
// Explicitly boxing a value
int i = 123;
object o = (object)i;
```

Note how the cast syntax is similar to both C++ and Java.

Unboxing converts the boxed object back into a value type again, and is performed manually using a cast.

```
// Box a value
int i = 123;
object o = i;

// Unbox it
int j = (int)o;
```

The cast is effectively saying "check whether the type in the boxed object is an int, and if so, extract the value and copy it into j". If the boxed type isn't an int, an InvalidCastException will be thrown.

Note that you can, of course, only unbox a boxed object. Trying to unbox an arbitrary reference is going to cause a run-time error.

The Common Type System (CTS) and the Common Language Specification (CLS)

As we mentioned in Chapter 1, there are two important concepts often used when discussing .NET languages – the **Common Type System (CTS)** and the **Common Language Specification (CLS)**.

The Common Type System defines how types are declared, used and managed in the runtime. It is the definition of the way in which the runtime implements the features of .NET languages, such as reference and value types, arrays, delegates, interfaces and pointers.

Not everything in the CTS will be implemented by every .NET language, so the Common Language Specification defines a subset of features that must be supported by every language. If you write code that is CLS-compliant, you will be able to interoperate with any other CLS-compliant .NET language.

You don't normally have to worry about CLS compliance in your code except in one area. Some of the basic .NET value types are not CLS-compliant, so there is no requirement for all .NET languages to support them. The table in the next section marks those types that aren't CLS-compliant, and you'll see that the set of non-compliant types includes unsigned integers. This means that you shouldn't use unsigned integers in any code that is designed for interoperability with other .NET languages, because they may not be able to work with your C# code. This is especially true of Visual Basic .NET, which doesn't support unsigned integer types.

C#'s Built-in Types

The following table lists C#'s built-in types. All are value types except the last two – `string` and `object` – which are reference types. Types marked with an asterisk are not CLS-compliant.

Name	Corresponding .NET Framework Type	Description
sbyte*	System.SByte	8-bit signed integer
short	System.Int16	16-bit signed integer
int	System.Int32	32-bit signed integer
long	System.Int64	64-bit signed integer
byte	System.Byte	8-bit unsigned integer
ushort*	System.UInt16	16-bit unsigned integer
uint*	System.UInt32	32-bit unsigned integer
ulong*	System.UInt64	64-bit unsigned integer
float	System.Single	Single-precision floating point
double	System.Double	Double-precision floating point
bool	System.Boolean	Boolean value
char	System.Char	Unicode character
decimal	System.Decimal	Precise decimal with 28 significant digits
object	System.Object	Generic object reference
string	System.String	Unicode string
void	System.Void	The void type

The `void` type doesn't really fit with the others: it represents the 'return type' of a method that doesn't return anything, and isn't used as a parameter type.

The C# names are simply synonyms for the corresponding .NET Framework type. You can use the Framework types in your code, but it is more usual to use the C# types instead.

```
// The next two lines are equivalent
int n = 3;
System.Int32 n  = 3;
```

Numeric literals are declared as you'd expect from a C-type language. Floating point values are double by default, and you can use F to denote single precision (for instance, 12.7F). U can be used to denote unsigned literals, and L longs. The precise decimal type is denoted by an M suffix, as in 12.77M.

```
int n = 3;
double d = 12345.67;
float f = 12.7F;
decimal dc = 100000.0M;
```

C++ Note
All these types have fixed sizes, and will be the same size on any system. This removes some of the problems traditionally associated with porting C and C++ code between architectures, and is pretty vital for writing distributed applications.

Java Note
You can choose between signed and unsigned integer types. If you choose unsigned, you obviously get extra magnitude because the sign bit can be used.

A Word about Characters

C# has the basic char value type and the string reference type, both of which use 16-bit Unicode characters. The Unicode wide-character encoding has become the standard for languages that are used for web programming, because the Unicode character encoding is large enough to hold a wide variety of national character sets.

A char is an unsigned 16-bit integer, and as such can hold the 65536 values that form the Unicode character space. Character literals can be written in several forms:

❑   As a character enclosed in single quotes, 'A'

❑   As a quoted hexadecimal value, such as '\x002D' or '\x3A'

❑   As an integer with a cast, (char)32

❑   As a Unicode value, \u002D

String literals can be written in two forms, quoted and @-quoted (called verbatim strings). Quoted string literals are simply enclosed in double quotes, and support the normal range of C-style escape sequences, such as \n for a newline character and \t for tab. If you put an '@' symbol in front, it turns into a verbatim string where escape sequences are not processed, making it rather more convenient for expressing path names. Verbatim strings can also contain line breaks.

```
"quoted string"
@"c:\temp\newfile"      // escape sequences not expanded
"c:\\temp\\newfile"     // use '\\' to get a literal backslash
```

Constants

A variable can be made unmodifiable by using the `const` keyword. If a variable is declared as `const`, it must be initialized since, by definition, a constant can't have its value changed later.

```
const int i;            // error! You must provide a value
const int i = 3;        // OK
```

A `const` variable can be initialized using an expression, but this expression must be one that can be evaluated by the compiler.

```
const int m = 10;
const int n = m * 4;    // OK - compiler knows value of m
int p = 3;              // non-const value
const int q = p + 4;    // error
```

Operators

The table below lists all the operators supported by C#:

Category	Operators
Arithmetic	+ - * / %
Logical	& | ! ^ ~ && || true false
String concatenation	+
Increment and decrement	++ --
Bit shifting	<< >>
Comparison	== != < > <= >=
Assignment	= += -= *= /= %= &= |= ^= <<= >>=
Member access	.
Indexing	[]
Cast	()
Conditional	?:
Delegate operations	+ - += -=
Object creation	new
Type information	is sizeof typeof

57

Category	Operators
Overflow exception control	`checked unchecked`
Indirection and address	`* -> [] &`
Conversion	`as`
Memory allocation	`stackalloc`

Most of these operators will be familiar to C++ and Java programmers. Here are a few brief notes on those that are new:

❑ is checks the run-time type of an object, while as converts an object to a compatible type.

❑ typeof obtains a System.Type object that describes a type. Type is described in Chapter 6.

❑ stackalloc is used to allocate a block of memory on the runtime stack. It is covered in Chapter 5.

❑ checked and unchecked are unusual in that they can be used both as operators and keywords. They are used to control the overflow-checking context for integer arithmetic operations and conversions, and are discussed later in this chapter.

Precedence follows a logical pattern, as shown in the following table. The operators with highest precedence are at the top of the table:

Group	Operators
	`() . [] x++ x-- new typeof sizeof checked unchecked`
Unary	`+ - ! ~ ++x --x` casts
Multiplication	`* / %`
Addition	`+ -`
Shifting	`<< >>`
Relational	`< > >= <= is`
Equality	`== !=`
Logical AND	`&`
Logical XOR	`^`
Logical OR	`|`
Boolean AND	`&&`
Boolean OR	`||`
Conditional	`?:`
Assignment	`= *= etc`

These operators have been provided to work with the predefined types, and it is possible to make them work with user-defined types by defining your own versions of some of these operators, a process known as **operator overloading**, which is covered in Chapter 5.

Creating and Initializing Variables

Reference and value types are declared and initialized differently. Value types can be directly declared and initialized, as shown in the examples below:

```
int n;               // uninitialized int
long l = 327;        // initialized long
float f = 3.13F;     // float initialized from
                     // single-precision literal
```

Just as in C++ and Java, local value-type variables (declared on the stack) aren't initialized to anything, although the compiler will warn you if you try to use an uninitialized variable.

Reference types, on the other hand, are created in two parts: the reference variable, and then the object itself. The code below supposes that we have a reference type called `Person`, and shows how to create a `Person` object:

```
// Create a Person
Person p1 = new Person();
```

The new operator creates a new `Person` object on the managed heap and returns a reference to it, which is assigned to `p1`. The variable `p1` is a reference variable that can point to a `Person` object – think of a pointer in C++ or an object reference in Java.

C++ Note

If you think of reference variables as similar to pointers, you won't be too far wrong. You have to create the pointer variable, and make it refer to something, but you don't have to de-reference it when you use it.

It is also possible to declare a reference that doesn't refer to anything:

```
// Create an uninitialized Person reference
Person p;
```

An uninitialized reference has a value of `null`, and it is possible to assign `null` to a reference in order to "unlink" it from an object. As with pointers in C++ and references in Java, you need to make the reference refer to an object before it can be used. Trying to use an uninitialized reference will usually give you a compiler warning, and in any event will certainly result in your code being terminated by an exception at run-time.

C++ Note

You can only instantiate reference types on the heap in C#. There's no way to create stack-based objects, as all class instances are accessed by reference.

Assignment of references copies the reference, and not the object referred to:

```
// Create a new string and store the reference
string s = "abc";
string s2;
s2 = s;    // s2 and s refer to the same object
```

Variable Comparisons

Because of this behavior, you also have to be careful when comparing references, since by default the == and != operators compare the reference, not the content of the objects. You can compare content by overloading the == and != operators, as described in Chapter 4.

Suppose we have a Name class that stores employee names. We can create two instances that contain the same value, but a comparison will fail because the two references point to different objects – they aren't "equal".

```csharp
using System;

// TestNames.cs

namespace Wrox.FTrackCSharp.Basics.TestNames
{
    class TestNames
    {
        public static void Main()
        {
            // Create a new string and store the reference

            Name n1 = new Name("fred smith");
            Name n2 = new Name("fred smith");

            if (n1 == n2)
                Console.WriteLine("This shouldn't happen!");
            else
                Console.WriteLine("Objects aren't equal...");
        }
    }
    // Simple Name class
    public class Name
    {
        private string n;

        public Name(string s)
        {
            n = s;
        }
    }
}
```

If you want to compare object content, you use the Equals() method which all classes inherit from the Object superclass, and which will be explained in the next chapter.

In the `string` type the `==` and `!=` operators have been overloaded to provide content comparison.

```
using System;

// StringCompare.cs

namespace Wrox.FTrackCSharp.Basics.StringCompare
{
   class Class1
   {
      public static void Main()
      {
         // Create a new string and store the reference
         string s = "abc";
         string s2 = "abc";

         if (s == s2)
            Console.WriteLine("Strings are equal");
         else
            Console.WriteLine("This shouldn't happen!");

      }
   }
}
```

On compiling and executing this code, you will find that the output is Strings are equal.

This makes programming string comparisons much more intuitive for most programmers.

String Construction

Note that there's a special construction syntax for building strings from a string literal. Instead of using new, you simply use the string literal on the right-hand side of the assignment:

```
// This will give a compiler error
string s1 = new string("abc");

// The correct way
string s1 = "abc";
```

The documentation says that the constructor that constructs a string from a literal has been omitted for "performance reasons".

Arrays

C# supports three types of array: one-dimensional, rectangular, and jagged. I'll introduce them briefly here, and cover them in more detail in Chapter 6.

One-dimensional arrays are declared as follows:

```
// A 10 element array of ints
int[] array1 = new int[10];
```

Note how the left hand of the assignment declares an `int[]` variable – a reference to a one-dimensional array. The right hand of the assignment creates the ten `int`s, and assigns the reference to the array variable. Note that the size of the array is not defined by the array variable; `array1` is "a reference to an array of integers", and it is the declaration on the right-hand side that specifies how many elements make up this array.

C++ Note

The square brackets have to be placed after the type, and not after the array variable name.

Java Note

Java allows you to place the square brackets after the type, or after the array variable name. In C#, you have to place the brackets after the type, and placing them after the name isn't supported.

Arrays are used the same way as in Java and C++, using zero-based indexing. The valid range of indexes for the array in the code above is zero to nine, because there are ten elements:

```
// Set some elements
array1[0] = 1;
array1[9] = 6;
```

C++ Note

Arrays are objects in their own right, and not a shorthand for pointer arithmetic. They know their bounds, and an exception will be thrown if you try to access an invalid element.

Arrays of Reference and Value Types

Arrays of reference and value types are created rather differently. When you create an array of value types, the value types are created on the stack, and you can assign to them directly.

```
// ints are value types
int[] array1 = new int[10];

// Assign to elements directly
for(int i = 0; i < 10; i++)
    array1[i] = i * i;
```

The elements in an array of reference types are object references, and they are initialized to `null` when the array is created. This means that you have to assign objects to the elements – creating them if necessary – before you can use them.

```
// Person is a reference type
Person[] array2 = new Person[3];

// Create objects and assign them to array elements
array2[0] = new Person("Fred");
array2[1] = new Person("Bill");
array2[2] = new Person("Scott");
```

Initializing Arrays

C# arrays support aggregate initialization, using either of the following syntax forms:

```
// Declare and initialize an array of ints
int[] array1 = { 1,2,3,4,5 };

// Alternative syntax
int[] array1 = new int[] { 1,2,3,4,5 };
```

The second form is more cumbersome, and only has to be used in one circumstance; if you create an array object and then want to initialize it later, you have to use the new syntax:

```
// This gives a compiler error
int[] array1;
array1 = { 1,2,3,4,5 };

// This is correct
int[] array1;
array1 = new int[] { 1,2,3,4,5 };
```

Multi-Dimensional Arrays

There are two types of multi-dimensional arrays: rectangular and jagged (also sometimes known as "arrays of arrays"). In rectangular arrays each row is the same length, whereas in jagged arrays each row can be a different length if required. Here's how to declare and use a rectangular array:

```
// A 3-by-3 element array of ints
int[,] array2 = new int[3, 3];

// Fill in the elements
for(int i = 0; i < 3; i++)
    for(int j = 0; j < 3; j++)
        array2[i, j] = i + j;
```

Note how the declaration of the array variable uses a comma to denote the rank of the array. The number of commas within the square brackets on the right and left hand sides of the declaration must obviously balance.

The aggregate initialization of rectangular arrays is a simple extension of the one-dimensional case:

```
// A 3-by-3 element array of ints
int[,] array2 = { {1, 2}, {3, 4}, {5, 6} };
```

Jagged arrays can have row of differing lengths, and are declared in a way that will be familiar to C++ and Java programmers. Here's an example showing how to create and use a jagged array:

```
using System;

// JaggedArrayExample.cs

namespace Wrox.FTrackCSharp.Basics.JaggedArrayExample
```

```
{
   class Test
   {
      public static void Main()
      {
         // A 3 row jagged array of ints
         int[][] array3 = new int[3][];

         // Create the rows
         array3[0] = new int[2];
         array3[1] = new int[3];
         array3[2] = new int[4];

         // Fill in the elements and output the elements
         for(int i = 0; i < 3; i++)
         {
            for(int j = 0; j < i+2 ; j++)
            {
               array3[i][j] = i + j;
               Console.Write(array3[i][j]);
            }
            Console.WriteLine();
         }
      }
   }
}
```

Aggregate initialization is also supported, as shown here:

```
// A 2 row jagged array of ints. The first row has two elements,
// and the second has three.
int[][] array3 = new int[][] { new int[] { 1, 2 };
                               new int[] { 1, 2, 3 }; }
```

Statements

In this section we're going to look at the selection and looping statements supported by C#.

Note before we start that C# uses the same block structuring as C++ and Java, with curly brackets delimiting blocks of code.

The goto Statement

Let's get this one out of the way right at the start; there is a fully working goto in C#. It works the same way that it does in C/C++, taking a reference to a label elsewhere in the code:

```
goto label1;
   // intervening code
label1:
   // more code here
```

Although you are never going to use a goto in a fully structured OO language, it turns out that there's one place where you may well need to use it, and that's to jump between cases in a switch statement.

The C# compiler will also check for some cases of goto abuse, such as trying to jump into a block, but it still isn't recommended for general use.

C++ Note

C# is less strict than C++ in that it will let you declare variables between the goto statement and the label. It will, however, still flag an error if you try to use a variable whose initialization has been skipped by a goto.

The if Statement

The C# if statement is identical to the one found in Java, and very similar to the one in C++. A statement or block of statements is executed if the expression in round brackets evaluates to true. The if can optionally be followed by one or more else ifs, and/or an optional else.

```
if (x == 0)
    Console.WriteLine("X is zero");
else if (x < 0)
{
    Console.WriteLine("X is negative");
    x = 0;
}
else
    Console.WriteLine("X is positive");
```

C++ Note

The expression in an if statement must resolve to a bool value. The link with C has finally been broken, and you can no longer use integers.

The for Statement

The for statement is the first of four iteration statements that C# supports.

C++ and Java Note

There are four iteration constructs in C# rather than three. We've got the familiar for, do and while loops, plus a new one that has come from Visual Basic, foreach.

The C# for statement is the same as the equivalent constructs in C++ and Java, and it works in exactly the same way. The loop is driven by three expressions in parentheses – an initializer expression, a condition expression, and an iterator expression:

```
for (initializer; condition; iterator)
    statement;
```

The initializer expression lets you declare a variable local to the loop and set its value, which can be used to count the number of times the loop is executed. The condition expression is commonly used to test that expression, and the iterator expression provides a place where you can increment the value of the loop control variable. An example will show how it works:

```
for (int i = 0; i < 10; i++)
    Console.WriteLine(...);
```

The initializer expression declares an int and sets its value to zero; note that the variable i is local to the loop. Each time around the loop, the int is incremented, and the loop continues while its value is less than 10. The increment expression is executed at the end of each iteration, and the condition is checked at the beginning.

As in C++ and Java, missing out all three expressions is one way of obtaining an infinite loop:

```
for(;;)
{
    // endless loop
}
```

The break and continue Keywords

The break and continue statements can be used to control iteration. The break statement will exit from the immediately enclosing for, do, while, foreach, or switch statement. As the code below shows, break provides a good way to exit from an infinite loop:

```
for (;;)
{
    // Get a number from the console
    Console.Write("Enter a number: ");
    string s = Console.ReadLine();
    // Convert the string to an integer
    int n = Convert.ToInt32(s);

    // If it is negative, break, otherwise print the value
    if (n < 0)
        break;
    Console.WriteLine("Number is {0}", n);
}
```

The code asks for a number, and reads the user's response with Console.ReadLine(). This method returns a string, so it is necessary to convert it to an integer using one of the methods provided by the Convert class.

The continue statement works with iteration statements, and will terminate the current iteration, causing a jump to the end of the block forming the body of the loop:

```
for (int i = 1; i < 20; i++)
{
    // Only write out even numbers
    if (i % 2 == 1)
        continue;
```

```
    Console.WriteLine("i is {0}", i);
}
```

The do and while Statements

The do and while statements are very similar to one another, both looping until a Boolean expression evaluates to false. As the code example shows, the only difference between them is that the body of a do loop will always execute at least once, whereas a while loop may execute zero times.

```
int total = 0;
int n = 0;
// while loop may execute zero times
while (n < 10)
{
    total += n;
    n++;   // increment the counter
}

int m = 10;
// do loop always executes the body once
do
{
    total -= m;
    m--;
}
while (m > 0);
```

The foreach Statement

The foreach statement lets you iterate over the elements in arrays and collections, and is very similar to Visual Basic's For Each construct. Here's a simple example to show how it is used:

```
int[] arr1 = new int[] {1, 2, 3, 4, 5};
foreach (int i in arr1)
{
    Console.WriteLine("Value is {0}", i);
}
```

When applied to an array, the content of the foreach loop is repeated for each element in the array, and the same mechanism applies to collections. This means that foreach is simple to use with the collections provided in the System.Collections namespace, such as List and HashTable – or, in fact, with any object that implements IEnumerable.

The switch Statement

The switch statement is similar to the one found in other C-type languages. It selects between alternatives based upon the value of a switch expression.

C++ and Java Note

Although the C# switch is similar to those in Java and C++, there are a few differences hiding here to catch the unwary, the major one being that you no longer fall through from case to case if you omit the break *and* there's code in the case.

The switch expression must be a constant, and can be an integer type (including char) or a string. This means that we can write code like this:

```
switch (name)
{
    case "Jim":
        Console.WriteLine("It's Jim!");
        break;
    case "Jon":
        Console.WriteLine("It's Jon!");
        break;
    default:
        Console.WriteLine("Must be someone else...");
        break;
}
```

If you want to "fall through" from one case to the next, it isn't enough to simply omit the break; you have to use a goto to signal your intention to the compiler, as shown in the next example. This is done so that you won't introduce an error by inadvertently omitting a break. Note that you don't have to do this if the cases don't contain any code.

```
using System;

namespace Wrox.FTrackCSharp.Basics.SwitchExample
{
    public class Test2
    {
        public static void Main()
        {
            string s = "abAcdEefgjIk";

            // Loop over each character in the string
            for (int i = 0; i < s.Length; i++)
            {
            switch (s[i]) {
                case 'a':
                    Console.WriteLine("Lower-case ");
                    break;
                case 'A':
                    Console.WriteLine("A found");
                    break;
                case 'e':
                    Console.Write("Lower-case ");
                    goto case 'E';
                case 'E':
                    Console.WriteLine("E found");
```

```
            break;
        }
    }
}
}
}
```

Defining and Calling Methods

Defining and calling methods in C# closely follows the Java model. This means that every method has to have a declaration that follows the pattern below, where the items in square brackets are optional:

```
[modifiers] return-type method-name([parameter-list])
```

Every method has to have a return type; if the method doesn't return a value, its return type is void. The return value is specified in the method body using a return statement, which works just like return in C++ and Java – every possible execution path must contain a return statement, unless an exception is thrown. If it's possible for the method to execute normally without returning a value of the appropriate type, a compiler error will be thrown.

A method need not take any parameters, in which case the method name is followed by empty parentheses. As in C++ and Java, you're free to ignore the return value if you don't need it.

The method return type may be preceded by one or more modifiers; if there's more than one, they are separated by white space. Method modifiers will be covered in the next chapter, when we talk about classes. How parameters are passed through to a method depends on whether they are value types or reference types. If a parameter to a method is a value type, it is passed (as you might expect) by value, which means that a copy of the parameter is passed to the method. Any changes made to the local copy inside the method will not affect the value of the original parameter. When a reference type is passed to a method, what gets passed is a reference to the object, and this means that any changes you make in the method will affect the object itself – there's no copying involved.

What if you want to pass a value type into a method and modify it? C# provides two ways of doing this using the ref and out keywords.

Marking a parameter with the ref keyword means that any modifications you make to its value will persist, just as if it was a reference type.

```
void refMethod(ref int n)
{
    n += 3;
}
...
int p = 3;
refMethod(ref p);      // value of p will be changed
```

Note the use of ref int as the parameter type, and the use of the ref keyword in the method call to tell the compiler to pass by reference rather than by value.

If you don't assign a value to p before making the call, the compiler will give you an error because you're using an uninitialized variable.

C++ Note

Because C# checks for uninitialized variables and gives an error at compile time if they are used, it is much less likely that you'll forget to initialize variables and get completely unpredictable output and bugs as the result.

As we saw earlier, ref can also be used with reference-type parameters. In this case, the variable in the calling scope will still be affected, even if a new object is assigned to the parameter within the method body.

If it is intended that the method is going to assign a value to the parameter, as opposed to modifying its existing value, then an out parameter should be used. Like ref, out means that the parameter reference in the method refers to the original variable in the calling code. The difference between them is that a ref parameter must be initialized before the method is called, whereas an out parameter doesn't have to be.

```
void outMethod(out int n)
{
    n = 3;
}
...
int p;              // uninitialized
outMethod(out p);   // value of p will be set
```

Note that even if an out parameter does have an initial value, that initial value is not passed across to the method.

C++ Note

C# doesn't support either default or anonymous parameters, but it does have the params keyword, which lets you define methods with variable parameter lists.

Method Overloading

Like Java and C++, C# allows you to declare more than one method with the same name. This practice is called **overloading**, and we'll see numerous examples when we cover classes in the next chapter.

Overloaded methods must differ in the number and/or type of parameters they take, and this enables the compiler to tell which one should be called by the context of the call. Note that the method return type is not significant, as it is always possible to ignore a return value; this means that you can't have two overloaded methods that only differ in their return type. Here are two overloaded methods:

```
long square(int n)
{
    return n*n;
}
```

```
double square(float x)
{
   return x*x;
}
```

Both are called square(), but one takes an int as a parameter, while the second takes a float. This means that the compiler can tell which version to call, depending on whether an int or a float has been passed as an parameter:

```
long l = square(3);           // int version
double d = square(3.0F);      // float version
```

C++ Note

In C++ you could implement the two square() methods using a template. C# doesn't support templates, although some form of template-like functionality may be added in future versions.

Error Handling

C# supports exceptions in very much the same way as Java and C++, and the following section assumes that you know something about how exceptions work in one or both of those languages.

What isn't immediately apparent is that the exception handling mechanism is implemented at the level of the runtime engine, and isn't specifically a C# feature. This means that exceptions are common to all .NET languages, so that it is possible to throw an exception from C# and catch it in some Visual Basic .NET or Managed C++ code, or vice versa. This makes mixed-language programming in the Windows environment much easier than it has ever been. It also means that exceptions are used more commonly in .NET than in C++, where their use is optional.

To signal an error, you throw an exception using a throw statement:

```
void PrintString(string s)
{
   // check for a null argument
   if (s == null)
   {
      throw new System.Exception("null argument");
      // execution never gets here
   }
}
```

An exception is tagged with an object reference, identifying the type of error that has occurred. In C#, what you throw has to be a System.Exception object, or derived from System.Exception. As with Java and C++, once a throw statement has been executed normal execution stops and the runtime goes off looking for an exception handler, so any code after the throw will not get executed.

C++ Note

Unlike in C++, you can't throw an instance of just any type in C#. The thrown value has to be a reference to a `System.Exception` object (or an object of a derived class).

Exceptions are handled by using `try`, `catch` and `finally` blocks. Code that may give rise to an exception is enclosed in a `try` block, which is followed by one or more `catch` blocks:

```
public void DoDivide(int a, int b)
{
    int result = 0;

    try
    {
        // This will fail if b is zero
        result = a / b;
    }
    catch(DivideByZeroException e)
    {
        Console.WriteLine("Exception occurred: " + e);
    }

    // We'll get here after the handler has been executed
    Console.WriteLine("Result was {0}", result);
}
```

Note how the `catch` block has a `DivideByZeroException` as an argument, which is passed by reference. If b is zero when the code executes, the divide-by-zero exception will be triggered and the handler code will get executed, resulting in output like this:

```
Exception occurred: System.DivideByZeroException: Attempted to divide by zero
    at xyz.Class1.Test(Int32 n) in C:\FTrackCSharp\Chapter03\class1.cs at line 32
Result was 0
```

If you know – or suspect – that more than one kind of exception may occur during execution of a `try` block, you can chain `catch` blocks together and they'll be checked in order to see which one (if any) is going to handle the exception.

C++ and Java Note

You have to order your `catch` blocks correctly in C#. If you code a `catch` (derived from `System.Exception`) block after a `catch` (`System.Exception`) block you'll get a compiler error, because the second `catch` will never be reached.

A `catch` block that will catch any exception is called a **general catch clause**. These blocks don't specify an exception variable, and can be written like this:

```
try
{
    // code which may fail
```

```
   }
catch
{
    // handle error
}
```

This is rather a last-resort kind of error handler and shouldn't be used very often, because you lose the information that came with the exception, so you don't know what is wrong.

C++ Note
General catch clauses are equivalent to `catch{...}`

And finally...

The use of `try` blocks means that control can leave a piece of code in several ways:

❏ If there's no error, execution will resume after the `try` block

❏ If there is an error and a suitable catch handler follows the `try` block, the handler will be executed. This handler could contain a `return` statement to pass control out of the method

❏ If no suitable handler exists, the exception handling mechanism will move up the call stack, looking for a handler

The fact that execution can go in one of several directions after execution of a `try` block means that it can be hard releasing resources – such as files or database connections – that have been used within a method. The optional `finally` block provides a way to release resources tidily.

If a `finally` block is attached to a `try`, it will be executed before the `try` is left, and after any possible exceptions are caught in the `catch` clauses. This will happen no matter how control leaves the `try`, whether it is due to normal termination, to an exception occurring, a `break` or `continue` (or `goto`) statement, or a `return`.

The following code shows how this might work in practice. The method reads a file whose name is passed in as a parameter, and lists it to the console. The mechanics of reading a file will be covered in a later chapter; for now, concentrate on the error handling:

```
static void ReadFile(string name)
{
    StreamReader sr = null;

    try
    {
        sr = File.OpenText(name);
        string line = sr.ReadLine();
        while(line != null)
        {
            Console.WriteLine(line);
            line = sr.ReadLine();
        }
    }
```

```
    catch(Exception e)
    {
        Console.WriteLine(e.Message);
    }
    finally
    {
        if (sr != null)
            sr.Close();
    }
}
```

Note how the file is closed in the `finally` block; this code will be executed whether an exception occurs or not.

A `finally` block can occur with or without `catch` blocks. Note that it is an error to transfer control out of a `finally` block using `break`, `continue`, `return` or `goto`. If an exception occurs during execution of a `finally` block, it is passed to the enclosing `try`; if another exception was being processed at this point, it will be lost.

Exception Classes

There are a number of exception classes provided in C#, all of which inherit from the `System.Exception` class. You can find a full list in the C# online help.

When catching these, remember that some of them inherit from others (for example, an `OutOfMemoryException` is derived from `SystemException`, which is in turn derived from `Exception`), and if you're going to catch at different levels in the hierarchy, you need to get them in the right order:

```
try
{
    // code which may fail
}
catch (OutOfMemoryException e)
{
    // this one must come first
}
catch (SystemException se)
{
    // this one must come second, as it can't hide the first one
}
```

You can make up your own exception classes by deriving from one of these, typically `System.Exception`.

checked and unchecked

Two keywords, `checked` and `unchecked`, can be used to control overflow checking for arithmetic operations and conversion of integer types.

Note that `checked` and `unchecked` are slightly unusual, in that these keywords can act as both operators and statements.

If an operation is checked, an exception will be thrown if overflow occurs; if it is unchecked, the overflowing bits will be silently discarded.

```
public void CheckIt(int a, int b)
{
    int result = 0;
    try
    {
        result = checked(a * b);
    }
    catch(OverflowException e)
    {
        Console.WriteLine(e);
    }

    Console.WriteLine("Result is {0}", result);
}
```

Depending on the values passed in, the result may overflow an int. If this is the case, the checked expression will result in an exception being thrown. If checked was replaced by unchecked, the unchecked expression will simply lose bits.

If you don't use either, the result you get will tend to depend on other factors, such as compiler options. As well as using the two operators to check expressions, the checked and unchecked keywords can be applied to whole blocks of code:

```
// all operations in the block are checked
checked
{
    aNumber = largeNumber * largeNumber;
    number1 = number2 + number3;
}
```

Console I/O

We've already seen simple use of the Console.WriteLine() method to produce text output. In this section we'll look in a little more detail at console I/O, and look at other .NET I/O mechanisms in Chapter 7.

Console I/O is provided by the System.Console class, which gives you access to the standard input stream (Console.In), standard output stream (Console.Out), and standard error stream (Console.Error).

The standard input stream gets character input, by default from the keyboard although this can be redirected to obtain input from other sources, such as files. The standard output stream writes to the screen by default, but can also be redirected to output to other destinations, such as files. The standard error stream is like the standard output stream, in that it usually displays output to the screen. The reason for having two output streams is that it lets you write normal output to Console.Out and error messages to Console.Error, so that if you got an error when standard output is being redirected to a file, you'll still see it on the screen.

Although it is possible to use the standard streams for I/O, calling methods such as
`Console.In.ReadLine()` and `Console.Out.WriteLine()`, it is more usual to use the static
methods provided by the `Console` class, as described in the following sections.

Console Input

`Console.Read()` returns a single character as an `int`, or –1 if no more characters are available.
`Console.ReadLine()` returns a string containing the next line of input, or `null` if no more lines
are available.

Note that just hitting the *Enter* key will not result in `null` being returned. Instead you'll get a zero-length
string returned, which you can test using the `Length` property of the string type:

```
Console.Write("Please enter your name: ");
string name = Console.ReadLine();
while (name.Length == 0)
{
    Console.Write("Please enter your name: ");
    name = Console.ReadLine();
}

Console.WriteLine("Your name is {0}", name);
```

The code checks the length of the input string, and keeps asking for input as long as nothing is entered.

Console Output

`Console.Write()` outputs one or more values without a newline character, while
`Console.WriteLine()` does the same but appends a newline.

`Write()` and `WriteLine()` have numerous overloads, so that you can easily output many different
types of data. There is one for each of the basic types (such as `short` and `long`) and `string`, plus
several for producing formatted output.

If you want to produce formatted output, you use a version of `WriteLine()` which takes a string
containing a format and a variable number of objects:

```
Console.WriteLine(format, object1, ...)
```

C++ Note
C# doesn't support variable argument lists in the way C and C++ do.

Format strings contain static text, plus markers that show where items from the argument list are to be
substituted, and how they are to be formatted. In its simplest form a marker is a number in curly
brackets, the number showing which argument is to be substituted:

```
"The value is {0}"      // use the first argument
"{0} plus {1} = {2}"    // use the first three arguments
```

The more general form of a format looks like this:

```
{N[,M][:FormatString]}
```

As we've already seen, 'N' is the zero-based number of the argument to be substituted, and it can optionally be followed by an integer specifying a field width. If the field width value is negative the value will be left-justified within the field; if positive, right-justified.

```
{1}              // output the second argument
{0,-8}           // output the first argument,
                 // left justified, in a field
                 // eight characters wide
```

These can optionally be followed by a formatting specification, which consists of a character and optionally a precision specifier.

```
{1:D7}           // output the second argument as an
                 // integer, field width of 7, padded
                 // with zeros
{0:E4}           // output in exponent notation with four
                 // decimal places
```

Here's an example showing how to print an invoice number in a fixed field width:

```
void PrintInvoiceNumber(int invoice)
{
    Console.WriteLine("Invoice: {0:D6}", invoice);
}
```

Given an invoice number of 1000, the method will print

```
Invoice: 001000
```

The table below shows the list of format characters. Note that although I've given them in uppercase, they can be specified in either upper or lowercase.

Format Character	Description	Notes
C	Locale-specific currency formatting	
D	Integer, with optional zero padding	If a precision specifier is given, for instance {0:D5}, the output will be padded with leading zeros

Format Character	Description	Notes
E	Scientific	The precision specifier sets the number of decimal places, which is 6 by default. There is always one figure before the decimal point.
F	Fixed-point	The precision specifier controls the number of decimal places. Zero is acceptable.
G	General	Uses E or F formatting, depending on which is the most compact
N	Number	Produces a value with embedded commas, for example 32,767.44
X	Hexadecimal	The precision specifier can be used to pad with leading zeros

As well as these formatting characters, you can also use placeholder characters to map out formats. Here's an example:

```
Console.WriteLine("{0:00000}", 123);
```

The output from this will be 00123, because the format outputs a digit wherever one is available, and outputs a zero where there isn't one. The # placeholder is similar, but this outputs a space instead of a zero.

Summary

This chapter has examined the basic syntax of C#, and we've seen that it is very similar in many ways to both C++ and Java, but has tried to overcome some of the shortcomings of both languages.

The main features we've covered are:

❑   C# is a case-sensitive language

❑   All C# programs must have a Main() method

❑   C# types are based on the underlying language-independent .NET types

❑   16-bit Unicode encoding is used for characters

❑   C# supports structured error handling

❑   The Console class is used for console I/O

Object-Oriented Features of C#

This chapter is going to introduce some of the more advanced features of the C# language, starting with enumerations, and moving onto object-oriented features such as structs, classes, interfaces and inheritance.

C++ and Java programmers will find that there are considerable similarities between C# and their languages, but they'll also find some new– and some changed – features in addition.

Enumerations

An enumeration is a data type consisting of a set of named integer constants:

```
enum Weekday {Mon, Tue, Wed, Thu, Fri, Sat, Sun};
```

Each of the named constants has a value, which by default starts at zero and increases by one for each succeeding member. So, in the example above, Mon has the value 0, Tue is 1, and so on. You can give explicit values to any or all of the constants; any that you don't specify get a value one more than the preceding constant:

```
enum Error {FileNotFound=100, AccessDenied=200, UnknownError=500};
```

You can also use expressions to initialize enum values, provided that the expressions consist of values that have already been defined. For example:

```
enum Error {FileNotFound=100, AccessDenied=FileNotFound+100,
            UnknownError=FileNotFound+400};
```

The default type of the enum is int; but if you wish to, you can declare enumerations that use other integral types:

```
enum Weekday : short {Mon, Tue, Wed, Thu, Fri, Sat, Sun };
```

You can use the byte, sbyte, short, ushort, int, uint, long and ulong types as the base types for enumerations.

You can declare variables of enum type in your code. Note the need to qualify the enum member name:

```
// Declare an enum
enum Weekday {Mon, Tue, Wed, Thu, Fri, Sat, Sun};

Weekday w = Weekday.Mon;

if (w == Weekday.Mon)
    Console.WriteLine("It's Monday");
```

It is possible to convert between an enum and its base type using a cast:

```
Weekday w = Weekday.Mon;

int nDay = (int)w;
```

All enums inherit from the System.Enum class, and so you can use any of the members of this class on your enum types. The following table lists some of the more useful members of this class; note that they are all static methods.

Member	Description
Format()	Converts a value in an enumerated type to its string equivalent
GetName()	Gets the name of the value in an enumerated type that has the specified value
GetNames()	Gets an array of strings containing the names of all the values in an enumerated type
GetUnderlyingType()	Returns the underlying integer type for an enumeration
GetValues()	Retrieves an array containing the values of the constants in an enumeration
IsDefined()	Returns true if a constant with the specified value exists in an enumeration
Parse()	Converts a string containing the name or numeric value of a constant to an enumeration object
ToObject()	Returns an instance of the specified enumeration type set to the specified value

For example, the `Enum.Parse()` static method can be used with our `Weekday` enum as follows:

```
Weekday day = (Weekday)Enum.Parse(typeof(Weekday),"fri",true);
Console.WriteLine(day);
```

`Enum.Parse()` converts a string into a value of the enumeration. The version here takes three parameters, the first parameter is the `Type` of the enumeration, obtained with the `typeof` keyword, the second is our string to convert and the value of `true` indicates that we will ignore the case when performing the conversion. `Enum.Parse()` actually returns an object reference; in the code above, Fri is displayed, to obtain the value of the enumeration corresponding to Fri we would have to cast to an `int` with `(int)day`. We shall see more about casting later in the chapter.

Structs

A struct in C# is essentially a scaled-down class, designed for situations where you may simply want to group some data together. A C# struct is defined using the `struct` keyword:

```
// A struct called ComplexNumber

struct ComplexNumber
{
    public double Re;
    public double Im;
}
```

Unlike classes, which are reference types (as we shall see in the next section) structs are value types. This means they will be stored on the stack, and aren't garbage collected. Structs in C# have other features of classes, such as implementing constructors and methods, although they do not support inheritance (except that they derive from `System.Object`), nor can they be used to derive from.

The members of a struct are accessed using dot notation:

```
using System;

namespace Wrox.FTrackCSharp.OOCSharp.ComplexNumberStruct
{
    // A struct called ComplexNumber

    struct ComplexNumber
    {
        public double Re;
        public double Im;
    }

    public class Test
    {
        public static void Main(string[] args)
        {
            ComplexNumber z1;        // Declare a Complex Number
```

```
        z1.Re = 1;       // Set the Real part of z1
        z1.Im = 2;       // Set the Imaginary part of z1

        Console.WriteLine("z1 = {0}+{1}i", z1.Re, z1.Im);
    }
  }
}
```

It is quite possible to nest structs, and you can use the dot notation to access all levels within the nested structure:

```
using System;

namespace Wrox.FTrackCSharp.OOCSharp.ComplexCircleStruct
{
    // A struct called ComplexNumber

    struct ComplexNumber
    {
        public double Re;
        public double Im;
    }

    // A ComplexCircle with a complex number origin and radius
    struct ComplexCircle
    {
        public ComplexNumber Origin;
        public double Radius;
    }

    public class Test
    {
        public static void Main(string[] args)
        {
            ComplexCircle c;       // Declare a ComplexCircle

            // Set the coordinates
            c.Origin.Re = 2;
            c.Origin.Im = 3;
            c.Radius = 4;

            Console.WriteLine(
                "Complex Circle: Centre {0} + {1}i Radius: {2}",
                c.Origin.Re,c.Origin.Im,c.Radius);
        }
    }
}
```

In this case, the members of ComplexNumber will be accessed in exactly the same way as in the previous example.

Defining Methods for Structs

Defining methods for structs is the same as defining them for classes, which we shall look at in more detail later. Here we add a method to the ComplexCircle struct that decides if another complex lies on the boundary of the circle.

```
using System;

namespace Wrox.FTrackCSharp.OOCSharp.OnBoundary
{

    // Use ComplexNumber struct from earlier

    struct ComplexCircle
    {
        public ComplexNumber Origin;
        public double Radius;

        public bool OnBoundary(ComplexNumber z)
        {
            double t1 = z.Re - Origin.Re;
            double t2 = z.Im - Origin.Im;

            return ((t1*t1 + t2*t2) == Radius*Radius);


        }
    }
    public class Test
    {
        public static void Main(string[] args)
        {
            ComplexCircle c;          // Declare a ComplexCircle

            // Set the coordinates
            c.Origin.Re = 2; c.Origin.Im = 3;
            c.Radius = 4;

            Console.WriteLine(
                    "Complex Circle: Centre {0} + {1}i Radius: {2}",
                    c.Origin.Re,c.Origin.Im,c.Radius);

            ComplexNumber z1,z2;
            z1.Re = 6; z1.Im = 3;
            z2.Re = 4; z2.Im = 4;
            Console.WriteLine("6 + 3i is on the boundary : {0}",
                                      c.OnBoundary(z1));
            Console.WriteLine("4 + 4i is on the boundary : {0}",
                                      c.OnBoundary(z2));

        }
    }
}
```

Struct Constructors

A struct can have one or more **constructors** that are used to initialize struct instances when they are created. Following normal C++ and Java practice, a constructor is a function that has the same name as the struct and no return type.

```
struct ComplexNumber
{
    public double Re;
    public double Im;

    // Constructor
    public ComplexNumber(double xval, double yval)
    {
        Re = xval;
        Im = yval;
    }
}
```

Note that structs cannot contain parameter-less constructors. If you create a struct instance without specifying any parameters, its members are automatically set to their default values (null for objects and zero for primitive types). Note also that unlike classes, structs cannot have *destructors*.

Order of Declaration

C++ programmers may be wondering about the order of declaration of the class and the struct in the previous code example. C#, like Java, doesn't require forward references to type definitions in the sourcecode. Before compiling any code that could possibly refer to the inner type, the compiler has parsed the entire sourcecode and discovered all the types.

This means that you can define types in any order you want, regardless of how they reference each other, and the compiler will sort out the references.

Not only is there no need for forward declarations, there is also no place for header files. Since all code has to be part of a class and has to be physically located within the curly brackets that define the class body, there is no place for any of the items that normally live in header files, such as function prototypes (there aren't any in C#), constant definitions (must be part of a class), preprocessor defines (there is no symbol substitution in the C# preprocessor) or struct/class definitions (they're all part of the source code).

Classes

The concept of the class is at the heart of OO programming.

This example shows a very simple implementation of a class that represents a bank account:

```
using System;

namespace Wrox.FTrackCSharp.OOCSharp.Account2
```

```
{

    public class Account
    {
        private double balance;        // a data member
        private double overDraftLimit;
        private string name;


        public void Deposit(double amt)
        {
            // Check parameter
            if (amt < 0.0)
                throw new ArgumentOutOfRangeException(
                                        "Deposit: invalid argument");

            // deposit cash
            balance += amt;
        }

        public void Withdraw(double amt)
        {
            // Check parameter
            if (amt < 0.0)
                throw new ArgumentOutOfRangeException(
                                        "Withdraw: invalid withdrawal");

            // withdraw cash
            if (balance - amt + overDraftLimit < 0.0)
                throw new ArgumentOutOfRangeException(
                                        "Withdraw: not enough funds");
            else
                balance -= amt;
        }

        public void Report()
        {
            Console.WriteLine("Account Name: {0}",name);
            Console.WriteLine("Balance : {0}",balance);
            Console.WriteLine("Overdraft Limit : {0}",overDraftLimit);
        }
    }

    public class AccountTest
    {
        static void Main(string[] args)
        {
            // Main method to test out the Account class

            // Create new account
            Account a1 = new Account();
            // Deposit and withdraw
            a1.Deposit(5000.0);
            a1.Withdraw(2000.0);
```

```
        a1.Report();

    }
  }
}
```

There are several important points to note about this definition. The first is the use of the `class` keyword, which defines the class as a reference type, rather than a value type. It also gives a hint to users that `Account` contains some functionality, and isn't simply a container for other data types.

C++ Note
Note that in C# you don't need a semicolon at the end of the class definition.

The `Account` class consists of declarations of data members – in this case just the balance, name of the account holder, and the overdraft limit – and definitions of methods. Note that all the declarations and definitions take place between the opening and closing curly brackets. Note here that our data members are all private – in the *Properties* section later, we will "expose" these fields as properties.

C++ Note
C# doesn't separate class definition from implementation. Classes are defined and implemented in the same place, so there's no place for header files, and it means that a class has to be implemented in one piece, in one file.

Class methods are invoked using exactly the same dot notation used for structs. You'll notice that in the `Main()` method in the code above, `new` is used to create an instance of `Account`, because a class is a reference type:

```
// Create an account
Account a1 = new Account();
```

You may be wondering what value the balance has immediately after the `Account` object has been created, but before `Deposit` has been called. The answer here is 'zero', because unlike in C++, data members in C# classes are set to sensible default values: zero for numeric types, `false` for Booleans, and `null` for references, and structs are zeroed out.

You'll notice that methods and data members are qualified by `public` or `private` access modifiers. These have the same meaning as in Java and C++, `private` meaning that a class member is not accessible to any code outside the class. In effect, it can't be accessed outside the opening and closing parentheses that bracket the class content. `public`, on the other hand, means that anyone can use the member. We can also see `public` applied to the class itself, which means that this class can be used from anywhere.

There are three other access modifiers – `protected`, `internal` and `protected internal` – which we'll discuss later on.

Constructors and Destructors

A constructor is a method called when an object of a class type is constructed, and is used for initializing the object. A constructor method has several characteristics:

- ❑ It has the same name as the class
- ❑ It has no return type
- ❑ It doesn't return any value

Constructors can be overloaded, and which one will get called depends on the arguments you give to new.

C++ and Java Note
If you don't specify any constructors for a class, C# does provide a default constructor that zeroes out everything. If you supply any constructors, no default one is supplied.

Constructors are usually `public`, but can also be `private` or `protected` (which relates to inheritance, and is discussed later in the chapter). Marking all the constructors `private` means the class can't be used as a base class for inheritance.

We will add some constructors to our `Account` class. With no constructors specified, a newly created `Account` object will have the default values for the fields. We will add a no argument constructor to provide each new account with an introductory gift of $1, a $500 dollar overdraft limit, and another constructor to fill in more details of the account:

```
// Constructors for Account class
public Account()
{
    balance = 1.0;
    overDraftLimit = 500.0;

}

public Account(double amt, string nm, double overDrftLmt)
{
    // set up the opening balance
    balance = amt;
    overDraftLimit=overDrftLmt;
    name=nm;
}
```

And we add these lines to the `Main()` method for testing purposes:

```
Account a2 = new Account(1000.0,"Count Dracula",500);

    // Deposit and withdraw

a2.Withdraw(1250.0);
```

```
        a2.Report();
        a2.Deposit(8000.0);
        a2.Report();
```

Destructors

A **destructor** (also known as a **finalizer**) is the logical opposite to a constructor, in that it is a method called when an object is reclaimed by the garbage collector.

C++ Note
Destructors in C# are *not* the same as in C++, and are used much less frequently. Read this section carefully!

Java Note
C# destructors are very similar to Java's finalize() method, and have all the same disadvantages.

The following example code shows the syntax used for a destructor:

```
public class Destructable
{
    ~Destructable()
    {
        // Bid farewell
    }
}
```

The name of a class destructor is the class name preceded by a tilde (~). They are always public (though not declared as such), and like constructors they have no return type. They also take no arguments, so there can only ever be one for a class.

Note that structs cannot have destructors.

I said above that a destructor is called when an object is destroyed, and it is worth taking a minute to explain just how this works. Like Java, C# manages dynamically allocated memory for you, and uses a **garbage collector**, running on a separate thread, to reclaim the memory for unused objects. An object becomes unused when the last reference to it disappears, so that it can no longer be accessed. Such objects are candidates for garbage collection, and the process of calling the destructor when an object is reclaimed is called **finalization**.

The problem is that you can't tell when an object is going to be reclaimed by the garbage collector, because the C# runtime schedules garbage collections when it feels they're necessary (for instance, when memory is getting short). As a final kicker, you also can't tell the order in which destructors will be called.

In C#, it is the responsibility of any client code to notify your object when it no longer needs it. To achieve this, if your class is resource-intensive, it should implement the IDisposable interface, which requires the IDisposable.Dispose() method to be implemented. Dispose() should be called explicitly by any client code when your object is no longer required. A destructor is effectively a backup for the case of client code that doesn't call Dispose().

The code for the cleanup of resources should go in the Dispose() method; having done this, there is no need for the destructor to be called so we can issue the GC.SuppressFinalize() call to request that the finalizer method should not be called. The typical code for this situation is as follows:

```csharp
public class ResourceConsumer : IDisposable
{
    public void Dispose()
    {
        Dispose(true);
        GC.SuppressFinalize(this);
    }

    protected virtual void Dispose(bool disposing)
    {
        if (disposing)
        {
            // Cleanup of managed resources here
        }
        // Cleanup of unmanaged resources
    }

    ~ResourceConsumer()
    {
        Dispose(false);
    }
}
```

Note that ResourceConsumer implements IDisposable with the : IDisposable syntax; we shall see more of this in the *Interfaces* section.

Dispose(bool) should not be called from anywhere else in your code – it is only invoked from within the destructor or Dispose(). When the client calls Dispose(), we pass onto Dispose(true) and all resources will be cleaned up, and we have no need to call the finalizer.

Alternatively, if the destructor has been invoked, we know that this must have been done by the garbage collector, so we know we have no need to clean up the managed resources – this is the role of the garbage collector. The destructor calls Dispose(false), and the value of false means that only the unmanaged resources will be attended to.

This all means that client code can call Dispose() and the resources will be cleaned up; if the client code fails to call Dispose(), then the destructor will be called at some point when the object is garbage-collected, and the resources will be cleaned up.

Note that it is possible to influence the behavior of the garbage collector using various methods from the `System.GC` class. We have already seen `SuppressFinalize()`, and there is `Collect()` to force a collection, and `RequestFinalizeOnShutdown()` to ask the garbage collector to execute all destructors on exit.

The actual behavior of the garbage collector is quite complex, especially so for classes that have destructors. If you're interested in the mechanism, it is well described in two articles by Jeffrey Richter in the November and December 2000 issues of MSDN Magazine. If you have MSDN installed on your machine, you'll find both these articles available in electronic form.

Constant and Read-Only Members

The `const` modifier can be used to declare constant members of classes:

```
public class Account
{
    private const string sortCode = "12-00-23";
    ...
}
```

One problem you may encounter is that the values of `const` members are calculated at compile time, so you can't use `const` to define a member whose value can't be set in this way. To get around this, C# provides the `readonly` modifier, which specifies that the member can have its value set once only in a constructor, and afterwards is read-only. In the example below, we're setting the sort code to the string value passed into the constructor.

```
public class Account
{
    private readonly string sortCode;

    public Account(string sc)
    {
        sortCode = sc;
    }

}
```

The this Reference

As in both Java and C++, the `this` keyword is used within a method to denote the object that called the method. It's quite common to use `this` to disambiguate local and class variables that have the same name, as shown here, where `this.SortCode` refers to the member of class `Account`, and `sortCode` without a prefix refers to the constructor argument:

```
public class Account
{
    private readonly string sortCode;

    public Account(string sortCode)
```

```
    {
        this.sortCode = sortCode;
    }

}
```

Properties

It is considered bad programming practice to give users of a class public access to data members, because of the implications for integrity. For this reason it is very common practice in OO languages to give access to data members via "get and set" (or **accessor**) methods, like this:

```
public class Account
{
    private string name;

    public void setName(string nm)
    {
        // do any checking you need, then...
        name = nm;
    }

    public int getName()
    {
        return name;
    }
}
```

This is a reasonable way to give access to members, but suffers from two drawbacks: firstly, you have to code the accessor methods up manually, and secondly, users have to remember (or figure out) that they have to use these accessor methods to work with data members.

The .NET languages have the idea of accessing data members through get and set code built into the language, in the form of **properties**. The difference between using get/set methods and properties is that to a user, using a property looks like they're getting direct access to the data, whereas in fact the compiler is mapping the call onto the get/set methods. This idea – mapping data access onto get/set methods – was pioneered in Visual Basic, and is one of the VB ideas that has been borrowed by C#. We shall add `Balance`, `Name`, and `OverDraftLimit` properties to our `Account` class.

Here's how the code above could be written to use a property:

```
public class Account
{
    private string name;

    // A property called Name
    public string Name
    {
        get
        {
            return name;
```

```
        }
        set
        {
            name = value;
        }
    }
}
```

The class now implements a single property called Name, of type string, which we can manipulate using the get and set clauses. Note how the set clause makes use of the special variable value, which represents the value passed in from the user. The type of value is determined by the type of the property.

You can use the property just as you would use a public data member:

```
Account a = new Account();

a.Name = "The Wolfman";
string myName = a.Name;
```

You can omit the set clause if you want to model a read-only property, and a method should be used instead of a write-only property. In fact, we set our Balance property to be read-only:

```
public double Balance
{
    get
    {
        return balance;
    }
}
```

You don't have to simply return the value of a variable in a get clause, you can use any code you like to calculate or obtain the value of the property. This means that properties don't have to be tied to a data member, but can represent dynamic data. Since properties can be inherited, and you can use the abstract and virtual modifiers with them, derived classes can be required to implement their own versions of the property methods.

The set accessor can also be used to perform data validation – here we add an OverDraftLimit property to our Account class that only allows positive values for the overdraft limit, and throws an ArgumentOutOfRangeException otherwise:

```
public class Account
{

    // A property called OverDraftLimit
    public double OverDraftLimit
    {
        get
        {
            return overDraftLimit;
        }
        set
```

```
    {
        if (value<0)
            throw new ArgumentOutOfRangeException(
                                    "Invalid overdraft limit");
        else
          overDraftLimit = value;
    }
  }
}
```

Note that in C#, the names of public properties, like all public members of a class, should be Pascal cased, so the first letter of each word in the name should be capitalized.

Static Members

C# supports the same notion of static members as C++ and Java: members that belong to the class as a whole rather than to any individual instance.

Static data members and static methods can be declared using the `static` keyword, as shown in this example. Here we set a `static Penalty` property for the `Account` class, which is to be applied ruthlessly to any account that makes use of its overdraft facility:

```
private static double penalty;

public static double Penalty
{
    set
    {
       penalty = value;
    }
    get
    {
       return penalty;
    }
}
```

Static members are accessed using the class name rather than an object reference:

```
Account.Penalty = 25;

double thePenalty = Account.Penalty;
```

C++ Note
In C#, static members must be accessed through a class name. You can't access them via an object, as you can in C++.

Constructors are used to set or calculate the initial values for object data members, and there is an equivalent mechanism that can be used for static members, called the **static constructor**. You can use the static constructor for any operation that needs to be performed once per class.

```
namespace Wrox.FTrackCSharp.OOCSharp.Account
{

    public class Account
    {
        private double balance;
        private static double penalty;        // a static data member

        // A static constructor
        static Account()
        {
            // calculate the penalty based on the phase of the moon
        }
    }
}
```

You can see from the example code that a static constructor is coded up like a constructor, with the addition of the static keyword. We know that this constructor will be called once before the first instance of the class is created, and before any static members of the class are used, but you don't know exactly when that will be. Note also that there's no access modifier on static constructors, and there's also no such thing as a static destructor.

Inheritance

The principle of inheritance is one of the fundamentals of OO, giving us the ability to *derive* new classes from ones that have already been written.

> *Note that reference types can be used to build inheritance hierarchies. Value types cannot be used in this way.*

Here's an example showing how we could derive a new class from Account:

```
public class SavingsAccount : Account
{
}
```

Note the : Account, which sets up the inheritance relationship. That's all you need to do to set up inheritance, and if we left it there, we'd effectively have two classes with different names but exactly the same behaviour, since SavingsAccount has inherited all the members of Account, and hasn't added any functionality of its own.

In this example, Account is the **base class** (or **superclass**) of SavingsAccount, and SavingsAccount is a **derived class** (or **subclass**) of Account.

Here's how we could use the derived class:

```
static void Main(string[] args)
{
    // Create a check account
```

```
    SavingsAccount s1 = new SavingsAccount();

    // Deposit and withdraw
    s1.Deposit(5000.0);
    s1.Withdraw(2000.0);
}
```

C++ Note

C# only allows single inheritance. Interfaces, discussed later in this chapter, can be used when you need to inherit from multiple base types, but there's no multiple code inheritance.

In addition, only public inheritance is supported in C#, hence there is no need for the `public` keyword before the base class name.

Using Base Class References

Derived classes can be accessed through base class references, as you'd expect:

```
// Create a check account
SavingsAccount s1 = new SavingsAccount();

// Refer to it through a base class reference
Account a1 = s1;
```

Remember that, since `Account` is a reference type, you now have two references to the same object.

Protected Access

A third level of access control, `protected`, limits access to a method to the defining class itself and to any classes derived from it. In the following example code, subclasses of `Account` can call `Withdraw()`, but classes unrelated to `Account` cannot:

```
public class Account
{
    private double balance;        // a data member
    . . .
    protected void Withdraw(double amt)
    {
        // Perform some checks
        balance -= amount;
    }
}
```

Calling Base Class Constructors

When a subclass object is created, its base class constructor is also called, and so on up the chain until there are no more base classes.

Base class constructors that take no arguments – known as **default constructors** – are called automatically. If the base class constructor takes arguments, you have to call it in your derived class constructors, as the following example shows:

```
public class SavingsAccount : Account
{
    public SavingsAccount(double amt) : base(amt)
    {
    }
    ...
}
```

Here, if a `SavingsAccount` is created with a `double` passed into the constructor, that `double` is passed on to the base class constructor. The compiler sees `base(amt)` as meaning "pass amt through to the base class constructor which takes one double as an argument". In this case, `Account` has a suitable constructor, so the compiler can find and use it.

The base class constructor is called before the derived class constructor code (if any) is executed. This means that constructor code actually gets executed from the top downwards, with the most-derived class code being executed last.

Virtual Methods

Virtual methods are supported in C#, as they are in C++ and Java, with a change in syntax in order to make it clearer to the programmer when methods are being overridden, in order to prevent some problems that can arise in C++ due to accidental overriding.

You declare a method as virtual by using the `virtual` modifier in the base class:

```
public class Account
{
    ...

    public virtual bool Withdraw(double amt)
    {
        ...
    }
}
```

When you override a virtual method in a derived class, you use the `override` keyword to signal that you are overriding a virtual method:

```
public class SavingsAccount : Account
{
    ...

    public override bool Withdraw(double amt)
    {
        ...
    }
}
```

C++ Note

You must use the `override` keyword in C# when you're overriding a virtual method. The `virtual` keyword is only valid in the class that defines the top of the virtual tree. Making this distinction between the original and overriding methods helps to prevent accidental overriding.

Hiding Base Class Methods

If you don't declare a method to be `virtual`, but still provide a new version of the method in a derived class, this new method is said to *hide* the base class version. To hide a method, its needs to be modified with the `new` keyword; the C# compiler will warn you if you omit the `new` modifier:

```
public class SavingsAccount : Account
{
    ...

    public new bool Withdraw(double amt)
    {
        ...
    }
}
```

The new method won't take part in the virtual function mechanism, so if I access a `SavingsAccount` object using an `Account` reference, I'll get the `Account` method called:

```
Account s1 = new SavingsAccount();

// These call Account's deposit and withdraw methods, even though
// we're referencing a SavingsAccount object
s1.Deposit(15000.0);
s1.Withdraw(2000.0);
```

Accessing Base Class Members

You may need to call a method in a base class from time to time. Since C# only supports single inheritance, you can do this using the `base` keyword without having to specify the actual name of the base class, since the compiler can work out which one it is.

For example, all our `Account` class requires is that there are sufficient funds in an account to make a withdrawal. However, the Savings Account has a minimum withdrawal of $50. The derived class `SavingsAccount` will decide if this withdrawal exceeds this minimum, and if so, call the base class method to actually make the withdrawal.

```
public class SavingsAccount : Account
{
    public new void Withdraw(double amt)
    {
```

```
            if (amt >= 50)
                base.Withdraw(amt);
            else
                throw new ArgumentOutOfRangeException(
                        "SavingsAccountWithdraw : Insufficient Withdrawal");
        }
    }
```

Note that you don't have to do this for all base class methods, but only ones where you want to modify the functionality in some way.

Java Note
base is in many ways the equivalent of Java's super keyword.

Abstract Classes and Methods

Abstract base classes are created by qualifying the class name with the abstract modifier:

```
    public abstract class Account
    {
        ...
    }
```

As you'd expect, you can't create instances of an abstract class, although you can still use references to Account to refer to derived objects.

```
    // Try to create an account
    Account s1 = new Account();              // Error!

    // Create a savings account
    Account s1 = new SavingAccount();        // OK
```

You can also create abstract methods by using the abstract modifier on a method definition. By marking a method as abstract, you ensure that derived classes have to implement it if they aren't also to be considered abstract.

```
    public abstract class Account
    {
        ...
        public abstract bool Withdraw(double amt);
        ...
    }
```

Abstract methods are implicitly virtual, since derived classes have to override them, and they don't contain any implementation, so there's no method body. Note that you can declare a class as abstract without it having to contain any abstract methods, but a class that contains abstract methods has to be declared as an abstract class.

> **Java Note**
>
> The presence of an abstract method in a class doesn't implicitly make the class abstract. You have to use the abstract modifier on the class as well.

Preventing Derivation

You may have reasons – arising from design or security factors – for not wanting anyone to use a class as a base class. If that's the case, you can mark the class as `sealed`.

```
public sealed class MySecureClass
{
    ...
}
```

Any attempt to derive from this class will result in a compiler error. It should be obvious that `sealed` and `abstract` are mutually exclusive modifiers for a class, since the one prevents inheritance while the other mandates it.

Casting

> **C++ Note**
>
> Casting in C# is much safer than in C++, and doesn't need to be discouraged as much because of run-time type checking.

Casting in C# uses the Java (and C) style cast syntax:

```
Account acc = new SavingsAccount();
...
SavingsAccount chk = (SavingsAccount)acc;       // OK
```

If the cast fails at run-time, you'll get a `System.InvalidCastException` thrown.

There are also a number of methods provided by the `System.Convert` class to help you convert to and from various types. For instance, the `Convert.ToDouble()` static method has numerous overloads, including one that tries to convert a string. For example:

```
double d = Convert.ToDouble ("123.45");
Console.WriteLine("{0}", d);
```

If the conversion works, the double value will be assigned to d. If it fails, a `System.FormatException` will be thrown. Classes may also support other conversion methods where appropriate, such as `ToBoolean()` and `ToChar()`. Note that `System.Convert()` will not throw an exception if the conversion will result in a loss of precision.

The predefined value types all support a static `Parse()` method which converts a string into the type, throwing an exception if unable to do so:

```
string s = "123.45";
double d = double.Parse(s);
Console.WriteLine(double*2);
```

We shall look at user-defined conversions in the next chapter.

The Object Class

C#'s `object` type is mapped onto the `System.Object` class. This class is important because all other .NET (and hence C#) data types inherit from it, even if they don't specifically say so. Unlike Java and C++, this even includes the simple, built-in value types such as `int` and `long`.

This means that there are certain methods that all types inherit, and which can provide useful functionality. The `Object` class has seven methods, which are summarized in the following table:

Method	Description
Equals()	Determines whether two objects are the same
Finalize()	Called when an object is garbage collected
GetHashCode()	Computes a hash code for an object
GetType()	Returns a `Type` object that represents the type of an object
MemberwiseClone()	Performs a shallow copy of a object
ReferenceEquals()	Returns `true` if two references are referring to the same object
ToString()	Returns a string that represents an object

The `ToString()` method returns a string which represents the object in some way. By default it simply returns the name of the class, but you'll frequently want to override it for your own classes. A primitive type will return a string that represents the value; for example `30.ToString()` returns `"30"`. For most value types, it is pretty obvious what this string will represent. In our example here, we will use the `Account` class's `ToString()` method to display the name of the account holder and the account balance, fulfilling the role of the `Account.Report()` method we already have:

```
using System;

namespace Wrox.FTrackCSharp.OOCSharp.Account
{
    public class Account
    {
        // Account class code
        public override string ToString()
        {
            return "Account Holder : "+name+"\nBalance : "+balance;
```

```
        }
    }
}
```

Note the use of the `override` method qualifier, because we want this to be treated as a virtual function. Note also the use of `"\n"` in the return string, to signify a new line.

`Equals()` is a very important method, and can be used to compare the content of objects. Because C# uses a system of object references, the `==` operator normally compares references:

```
if (r1 == r2) ...
```

The code above evaluates to `true` if `r1` and `r2` are referring to the same object.

C++ Note

Think of comparing pointers. If you use the `==` operator with a pair of pointers, the addresses in the pointers are compared.

In the previous chapter, we had two `Name` objects that both held the same string `"Fred"`, compared them with the `==` operator, and found the comparison to be false. This was simply because the two `Name` objects were different objects, although they had the same content.

C# provides the `Equals()` method to let you compare object content. The default implementation of `Equals()` is equivalent to `==`, but any class can override it to implement its own custom object comparison. In the example below, we override `Equals()` to compare the content of two `Name` objects:

```
using System;

namespace Wrox.FTrackCSharp.OOCSharp.TestEquals
{
    public class Name
    {
        private string nm;
        public Name(string s)
        {
            n = s;
        }

        public override bool Equals(object o)
        {
            return (nm.Equals(((Name)o).nm));
        }
    }
    class TestNames
    {
        public static void Main()
        {
            Name n1 = new Name("fred smith");
```

```
Name n2 = new Name("fred smith");
Name n3 = n2;        // n2 and n3 point to the same object

Console.WriteLine(n1==n2);         // False
Console.WriteLine(n2==n3);         // True
Console.WriteLine(n1.Equals(n2));  // True
Console.WriteLine(n2.Equals(n3));  // True
    }
  }
}
```

Note that because Equals() is inherited from the top-level Object class, its argument is the most general thing possible, an object. This means that we need to cast it to a Name before we can access any members of the Name class. If the cast fails, you'll get a System.InvalidCastException thrown, which you'll have to handle.

ReferenceEquals() is a static member that compares two references, and returns true if they're the same. In the example above, calling ReferenceEquals() has the same effect as using ==, with n2 and n3 being considered "equal".

The next method, GetHashCode(), returns a hash code which identifies an object, and has to be considered along with Equals(). A hash code is an integer key, calculated in a way that makes it unlikely that two objects will end up with the same code. These codes can be stored in a hash table, and it can make searching for particular objects very efficient.

GetHashCode() is related to Equals() in that objects which are "equal" according to Equals() must return the same hash code. This means that in most cases if you override Equals() you'll also need to provide your own version of GetHashCode() – the compiler will warn you of this accordingly. What would you return as a hash code? If there's a unique integer value associated with your objects (such as a bank account number) then use that. If there isn't a unique integer, you could make one up out of the hash codes for other members of the object. For our Name example, we'll simply use nm.GetHashCode():

```
public override int GetHashCode()
{
    return (nm.GetHashCode());
}
```

MemberwiseClone() performs a shallow copy on an object. Shallow copying means that only the 'top level' of an object is copied, so that if an object contains references, the references are copied rather than the objects they refer to. Not all classes want to support shallow copying, so MemberwiseClone() is made protected. Consider the Account class that we've been using in this chapter: you probably want each instance of Account to be unique, with one instance representing one account.

If a class wants to support shallow copying, it can provide a wrapper function that calls MemberwiseClone(). For example, in our Account class, we can add the following to the class definition:

```
public Account Copy()
{
    object o = MemberwiseClone();
```

```
        return (Account)o;
    }
```

In the `Main()` method of our `Account` example, adding the following shows us the result of the shallow copy:

```
Account a2 = new Account(3000.0,"Count Dracula",true);

// Deposit and withdraw
a2.Deposit(5000.0);
try
{
    a2.Withdraw(4000.0);
}
catch(Exception e) {Console.WriteLine(e);}

a2.Report();
Account a3 = new Account();
// Display the current status of this account
a3.Report();
// Now perform the shallow copy
a3 = a2.Copy();
// Now display the new status of this account
a3.Report();
```

In order to implement deep copying, a class has to implement the `ICloneable` interface, which has a single `Clone()` method. Implementing interfaces is covered later in the chapter.

C++ Note
In C++ shallow copying happens by default, and you implement a copy constructor to solve any problems that need a deeper copy.

Finally, there's `GetType()`, which lets you obtain type information about an object, returning you a `Type` object which you can query. We discuss this further in Chapter 6.

Operator Overloading

Like C++, C# supports the idea of operator overloading, meaning that operators can be defined to work with classes where it makes sense.

As an example, consider a `Currency` class. It would be useful (and intuitive) in code if we could simply add two `Currency` objects using the '+' operator, rather than having to use a custom `add()` method.

Operator overloading lets us define a new '+' operator that works with `Currency` objects; we're overloading the '+' symbol, in the same way that a function name can be overloaded.

The principle is the same as in C++, although the set of operators that can be overloaded is smaller in C#.

Operators	Overloading Behaviour
`+ - ! ~ ++ --` true false	Unary operators can be overloaded
`+ - * / % &	^ << >>`	Binary operators can be overloaded
`== != < > <= >=`	Comparison operators can be overloaded
`&& ||`	Can't be overloaded
`[] ()`	Can't be overloaded
`+= -=` etc.	Can't be overloaded
`= . ?: -> new is as sizeof typeof`	Can't be overloaded

Note the following points:

❑   `&&` and `||` can't be directly overloaded, but are evaluated using `&` and `|` which can be overloaded.

❑   `[]` can't be overloaded, and you're supposed to use indexers instead.

❑   `()` can't be overloaded. Instead, define new conversion operators.

❑   Compound assignment operators can't be overloaded. This is because they are always decomposed so that `+=` is evaluated as a `+` followed by an `=`.

❑   Logical operators must be overloaded in pairs, so `==` and `!=` must be done together.

C++ Note

In C# there is only one overload for the `++` and `--` operators, so you can't separately overload the prefix and postfix versions.

Here's an example of overloading some operators in our `Currency` class:

```
public class Currency
{
    double val;

    public Currency(double val)
    {
        this.val = val;
    }
    public static Currency operator+(Currency lhs, Currency rhs)
    {
        return (new Currency(lhs.val + rhs.val));
    }

    public static bool operator==(Currency lhs, Currency rhs)
    {
        return (lhs.val == rhs.val);
    }
```

```
    public static bool operator!=(Currency lhs, Currency rhs)
    {
        return (lhs.val != rhs.val0);
    }
}
```

Note that all the operator overload functions have the keyword `operator` plus the operator symbol, so we get `operator+`, `operator==` and so on. Note also how if we want `operator==` the compiler will force us to define `operator!=` as well.

Furthermore, all operator overloads are static methods of the class.

Interfaces

An interface in C# is a reference type, similar to a class, but which contains only abstract members. Interfaces are often used to model behavior that will be implemented differently by derived classes; if inheritance models an 'is a' relationship, interfaces model a 'can do' relationship that is independent of class inheritance.

Java Note
C# interfaces are very similar to Java interfaces, and work in very much the same way.

C++ Note
An interface in C# can be considered very similar to a C++ abstract base class which contains only pure virtual functions. There's never any implementation in a C# interface. C# interfaces are not COM interfaces!

A typical interface might look like this:

```
interface IPrintable
{
    void Print();
}
```

There are a couple of things to note about this definition. An interface looks like a class definition, but its only purpose is to define a set of methods, and not to implement them.

For this reason, the interface definition only includes the definitions of methods, and no implementation code. Interfaces can only contain methods, properties, and indexers (covered later in this chapter), plus events, which we'll explain in the next chapter. They can't contain constants, fields (or data members), constructors and destructors, or any type of static member. If you think back to our discussion on abstract classes, you may realise that an interface is very similar to an abstract class that contains only abstract methods.

Note that all the members of an interface are public by definition, and the compiler will give you an error if you try to specify any other modifiers on interface members.

In order to use an interface you inherit from it, just as you would from a class. The difference between inheriting from a class and inheriting from an interface is that you have to implement all the members defined in the interface. Here we shall define an interface IBankAccount, which our Account class will implement.

```
public interface IBankAccount
{
    void Deposit(double amt);
    void Withdraw(double amt);
    double Balance
    {
        get;
    }
}
```

Note that the interface name is prefixed with an 'I'; this is not required, and is a naming convention which has been inherited from Microsoft COM, but can be useful to help separate interfaces from classes.

For the IBankAccount interface, we amend its code declaration as follows:

```
public class Account : IBankAccount
```

Conveniently, our Account class already implements all the methods of the IBankAccount interface, plus some others. The compiler will enforce this, so you'll get a compilation error if you don't implement all the methods specified in the interface.

What advantages does using interfaces give you? There are two main ones. C# doesn't support multiple inheritance, but interfaces can be used to give some semblance of multiple inheritance because although you can only inherit from one class, you can inherit from (or "implement") as many interfaces as you like. In our example here, the Account class will implement the IBankAccount and the IPerson interface:

```
interface IBankAccount
{
    // Code from above
}

public interface IPerson
{
    string Name
    {
        get;
        set;
    }

    string Address
    {
        get;
        set;
    }
}
```

```
public class Account : IBankAccount, IPerson
{
    // Existing Account code - also need to implement
    // the Address property specified in IPerson

    private string address;

    public string Address
    {
        get
        {
            return address;
        }
        set
        {
            address=value;
        }
    }
}
```

In the Account class we need to implement both the Name and Address properties of the IPerson interface, but the Account class already has a Name property defined, so only the Address property code is shown here.

The second (and more important) use for interfaces is to describe behaviour. In the example above, class Account inherits from and implements the IBankAccount and IPerson interfaces. This means that by the usual rules of inheritance an Account object can be considered to be an instance of both IBankAccount and IPerson, and that means that we can pass an Account object where one of the interface types is specified:

```
public class TestingI
{
    public void DoSomething(IPerson p)
    {
        Console.WriteLine("I am not satisfied with "+p.Name+".");
    }
}
public class Account : IBankAccount, IPerson
{
// Account code
}
public class AccountTest
{
    static void Main(string[] args)
    {
        Account a = new Account(1000.0,"Count Dracula",500);
        TestingI t = new TestingI();
        t.DoSomething(a); // Pass the Account object to the method
    }
}
```

The `TestingI.DoSomething()` method doesn't care exactly what kind of object it is passed, as long as it implements the methods of the `IPerson` interface. Since the method is thinking of the object in terms of `IPerson`, it can only call methods defined in `IPerson`, and not any others defined as part of `Account`.

This idea of **interface-based programming** is powerful. It lets us design functionality by specifying the members of an interface. We have already seen that the `IDisposable` interface is at the heart of C#'s destruction mechanism – provider classes should implement this interface and define the `Dispose()` method, which is to be called by client code when it has finished with the object.

Interfaces and Inheritance

Interfaces provide a way to implement multiple inheritance of type. C# (and .NET languages in general) only allows inheritance from a single base class.

As an example, consider some birds:

❑ Hawks can fly but can't swim

❑ Ostriches can't fly or swim

❑ Penguins can swim but can't fly

❑ Cormorants can both fly and swim

One possible design, using interfaces, looks like this:

```
interface IFlying
{
    void Fly();
}

interface ISwimming
{
    void Swim();
}

// Hawk is a Bird that can fly
class Hawk : Bird, IFlying
{
    public void Fly() { ... }
}

// Cormorant is a Bird that can fly and swim
class Cormorant : Bird, IFlying, ISwimming
{
    public void Fly(){ ... }
    public void Swim(){ ... }
}
```

The functionality common to all of these birds is provided by the `Bird` base class, and the optional functionality is provided as a series of interfaces.

Note that interfaces can inherit from one another, which means that any class that implements the interface is going to have to implement the accumulated methods of all the interfaces:

```
interface ISwimming
{
    void Swim();
}

// Anyone implementing IDiving will have to provide Swim() as well
interface IDiving : ISwimming
{
    void Dive();
}
```

Indexers

Indexers are an elaboration of properties, and are used where you want to access some class property by index, in an array-like manner. They are useful in cases where a class is a container for other objects. Note that indexers can't be static members of a class.

C++ Note
Indexers are roughly equivalent to the overloaded [] operator.

The syntax used for writing indexers may look a little strange:

```
public double this[int index]
```

Indexers are declared using the this[] syntax. The return type determines what will be returned, in this case a double. The parameter in square brackets is used as the index; in this example we've used an int, but there's no need for it to be numeric.

Here we will add an indexer to our ComplexNumber struct, so that z.Re can be accessed with z[0], and z.Im can be accessed with z[1].

```
using System;

namespace Wrox.FTrackCSharp.OOCSharp.Indexers
{

    public class IndexTest
    {
        ComplexNumber z;

        public IndexTest(double a, double b)
        {
            z.Re = a;
```

```
        z.Im = b;
    }

    // Indexer definition
    public double this[int index]
    {
        get
        {
            // do some bounds checking
            if (index < 0 || index > 1)
                throw new IndexOutOfRangeException(
                                "Cannot get element "+ index);

            if (index==0)
                return z.Re;
            else
                return z.Im;
        }
        set
        {
            if (index<0 || index>1)
                throw new IndexOutOfRangeException(
                                "Cannot set element " + index);
            if (index==0)
                z.Re = value;
            else
                z.Im = value;

        }
    }
}

struct ComplexNumber
{
    public double Re;
    public double Im;
}

public class Test
{
    public static void Main()
    {
        IndexTest it = new IndexTest(3,4);

        Console.WriteLine("Index 0 is {0}", it[0]);
        Console.WriteLine("Index 1 is {0}", it[1]);
        try
        {
            Console.WriteLine("Index 2 is {0}", it[2]);
        }
        catch (IndexOutOfRangeException e) {Console.WriteLine(e);}
    }
}
}
```

You can overload indexers by giving them different parameter types, and it is possible to have indexers with more than one parameter, allowing you to create objects that act as multidimensional arrays.

Summary

This chapter has shown how C# implements OO features. Many of the basic elements are similar to their counterparts in C++ and Java, but there are significant differences, such as the support for properties.

Here are the main features we've looked at in this chapter:

- ❑ C# supports enums and structs
- ❑ Structs and enums are value types, which means they are stored on the stack and are not garbage collected, although a struct is essentially a scaled-down class
- ❑ Classes are reference types, which means they are created on the heap and garbage collected
- ❑ Properties let you define get and set methods for accessing data members
- ❑ C# supports inheritance, but only single inheritance is supported
- ❑ All classes are ultimately derived from the object class
- ❑ Virtual methods are used to implement polymorphism
- ❑ Interfaces are used to define functionality without implementation
- ❑ Interfaces can be used to provide some of the features of multiple inheritance
- ❑ Indexers are useful for classes that manage collections, and let you retrieve data using an array-like notation

5

Advanced C#

Chapters 3 and 4 have introduced you to the basics of C# language. This chapter will introduce several more advanced features, including:

- ❏ Using variable argument lists with methods
- ❏ User-defined conversions
- ❏ The preprocessor
- ❏ Using pointers and unsafe code
- ❏ Delegates and events
- ❏ XML documentation

More about Classes

Now, let's talk a little more about classes in C#.

Variable Parameter Lists

In C# you can define methods that can be called with variable numbers of parameters, whose types you may not know in advance. A good example is the `Console.WriteLine()` method that we've been using throughout the code, which can take a variable number of parameters after the format string. Variable parameter lists in C# are a feature that is common to all .NET languages. This means that you can write a function that takes a variable number of parameters in C# and use it in Visual Basic .NET code.

The key to handling variable parameter lists lies in the fact that all objects can be referred to through an `object` reference. Variable parameter lists are implemented using the `params` keyword together with a reference to an array object, or indeed any type of array:

```
using System;

namespace Wrox.FTrackCSharp.Advanced.Test
{
    public class Test
    {
        public static int Main()
        {
            AFunc(1,2,"abc");
            return 0;
        }

        // AFunc takes a variable number of parameters
        public static void AFunc(params object[] args)
        {
            int numArgs = args.Length;

            Console.WriteLine("Number of args is {0}", numArgs);
        }
    }
}
```

The method is passed an array of `object` references, and we can use the `Length` property to find out how many references the array contains. As an aside, using `Length` like this is how you can find out how many command-line parameters you've been passed in the `Main(string[] args)` method.

We can call the method like this:

```
AFunc(12, 2, "abc");
```

and it will be passed an array of three `object` references, each of which refers to one of the parameters.

How does it work? The first thing to note is that if the compiler can find an overload for the method whose parameter list matches those in the method call, then it will use that overload and no variable parameter list will get generated.

If the compiler can't find an overload of the method that matches the parameter list but it *does* find a version with the `params` keyword, it will use that one and automatically build an `object` array to hold the parameters, boxing value types as necessary. So the call above is equivalent to coding:

```
object[] o = new object[3];
o[0] = 12;
o[1] = 2;
o[2] = "abc";

AFunc(o);
```

Note that in this example we've used an array of object references, but you can use any type you like. If you do want to use object and don't know exactly what you're going to get passed, you'll probably want to use reflection – discussed in Chapter 6 – to find out details about what the array references.

Because the compiler does extra work in creating the array and populating the elements, it will be more efficient to provide overrides for versions of methods that you know you'll need, such as a specific (int, int, string) version if you're going to use that a lot.

User-Defined Conversions

User-defined conversions let you define operators for a class to convert objects to and from other types. This is often done for value types, and other classes that are wrappers around some single value. As an example, you may want to define an operator for a string class that can convert to and from arrays of chars.

Note that you can't redefine existing conversions – such as int to long – or provide a user-defined conversion between base and derived types.

C++ Note
These are very similar to C++ type conversion operators.

As a practical example we'll use the Currency class we built in the previous chapter. This class is basically a wrapper around a double value, with some extra information and functionality added in, and we'll add operators to convert Currency objects to and from doubles.

Here's how the class looks with the two new operators added:

```
using System;

namespace Wrox.FTrackCSharp.Advanced.Currency
{

    public class Currency
    {
        private double val;     // the amount

        public Currency(double amt)
        {
            val = amt;
        }

        public static explicit operator Currency(double val)
        {
            Currency c = new Currency(val);
            return c;
        }

        public static implicit operator double(Currency c)
        {
            return c.val;
        }
    }
}
```

The first thing to note about these conversion operators is that they are always implemented as static methods. The name of the operator is the type being converted *to*, and the single parameter is the type being converted *from*. So, in the above example, the first conversion is from double to Currency, and the second is from Currency to double.

You'll notice that these methods are qualified by the explicit and implicit modifiers, which determine in what context a conversion will be done. If an operator is qualified with explicit, it means that a cast has to be used to apply the conversion, as in

```
Currency c1 = (Currency)12.4;
```

However, the programmer does not have to explicitly supply the cast.

```
double d = c1;
```

Which should you choose? Since implicit conversions can take place without your knowledge, you should be careful that they couldn't go wrong and present the programmer with an unexpected surprise. This means that implicit conversions shouldn't throw exceptions, and shouldn't be able to lose any data. If you can't guarantee this, make your conversion explicit so that the programmer knows when they're using it.

Now that we've defined conversion operators, we can write code like this:

```
double d = c1 + 12.4;
```

The implicit conversion operator will convert the Currency into a double before invoking the '+' method.

The Preprocessor

The C# compiler supports C-style preprocessor directives in order to provide a conditional compilation mechanism.

C++ Note
Not all C++ preprocessor functionality is supported. In particular, the C# preprocessor has no #include facility, does no code substitution, and #define is simply used to define identifiers for use with #if. For example, the C# pre-processor does not support macros. Note also that in C# preprocessing is not a separate step before compilation. Preprocessor directives are processed as lexical elements while the compiler performs lexical analysis as the first part of the compilation process.

#define, #undef and #if

#define and #undef are used to define and undefine pre-processor identifiers in code.

```
#define someName
#undef someOtherName
```

Identifier naming conventions follow those for C# variables. It isn't an error to #undef a name more than once. Note that, similarly to C++, the # character must be the first non-whitespace character on a line, and that you can also have spaces between the # character and the rest of the directive.

C++ Note
Unlike in C++, you can't assign a value to an identifier, but simply define it.

The preprocessor #if mechanism can be used to conditionally include or omit blocks of code:

```
// Define a preprocessor symbol
#define debug

using System;

namespace Wrox.FTrackCSharp.Advanced.Define
{
    public class PreprocTest
    {
        public static void Main()
        {
            #if debug
                Console.WriteLine("This is debug output");
            #endif
        }
    }
}
```

Blocks of code are delimited by #if and #endif, and will be included if the appropriate identifier has been defined. Preprocessor identifiers must be defined before any 'real' code, which means putting them before the using declarations.

The #elif and #else keywords provide an if...elif...else mechanism:

```
// Define a preprocessor symbol
#define debug

using System;

namespace Wrox.FTrackCSharp.Advanced.Define
{
    public class PreprocTest2
    {
        public static void Main()
        {
            #if debug
                Console.WriteLine("This is debug output");
            #elif release
                Console.WriteLine("This is release output");
            #endif
        }
    }
}
```

You can nest #ifs inside one another:

```
#define debug

#if debug
    #if logToConsole
        Console.WriteLine("Logging to console");
    #endif
#endif
```

Since you can use logical operators with #if, the above code is equivalent to

```
#define debug

#if debug && logToConsole
    Console.WriteLine("Logging to console");
#endif
```

You can use !, ==, !=, && and || with #if. This means you can write code such as

```
#if debug == true
```

to test whether a symbol is defined, which is exactly the same thing as simply writing #if name.

As is the case with all C++ compilers, you can also define preprocessor identifiers on the command line if you're using the command-line C# compiler.

You can also conditionally include or exclude entire methods by using the conditional attribute. Attributes are discussed in more detail in Chapter 6.

#warning and #error

These two preprocessor control lines will cause a warning or an error to be emitted at compile time.

```
#undef debug

using System;

namespace Wrox.FTrackCSharp.Advanced.Define
{
    public class PreprocTest3
    {
        public static void Main()
        {
            #if debug
                Console.WriteLine("This is debug output");
            #elif release
                Console.WriteLine("This is release output");
            #else
            #error Must have either debug or release defined
            #endif
```

```
                    }
                }
            }
```

#line

The #line directive can be used to alter the file name and line number information which is output by the compiler in warnings and error messages. It isn't very likely to be used in application code, and is typically used for programs that emit C# code based on some input script.

#region and #endregion

Visual Studio .NET C# IDE has an extremely useful outlining feature that can be used to expand or hide blocks of text. The #region and #endregion directives are used to delimit blocks of text so that the editor will know how to expand and collapse them. In the following example, the region is entitled This is a region.

```
#region This is a region
    // code
#endregion
```

The title for the region is optional, but if you don't include it, you won't have any useful text displayed when the region is hidden. Note that regions can be nested, and that a #region block cannot overlap with an #if block.

Delegates

It is common in Windows programming to use callbacks, where client code provides a function that the Windows API calls back to at some point. These are used where an API function needs client code to provide some customized behavior. As an example, consider the EnumFonts API function, which enumerates all the fonts available on a specified device. The C prototype for the API function looks like this:

```
int EnumFonts(
    HDC hdc,                    // device context
    LPCTSTR lpFaceName,         // font typeface name
    FONTENUMPROC lpFontFunc,    // callback function
    LPARAM lParam               // extra data
);
```

Notice the third argument, which specifies the address of a callback function. The EnumFonts API enumerates all the fonts provided by the device specified by the device context, and calls the callback function for each font it finds. The client callback function can then take whatever action it wants, such as adding the name of the font to a listbox.

FONTENUMPROC is a type that defines what the callback function has to look like. It is a C function pointer, and so the address of any suitable function can be passed into the API, and will be called at run time. The problem is that there is no way to find out until run time whether the pointer being passed in really points to a suitable function (or even to a function at all!). If the pointer isn't valid, you can expect to get a run-time crash.

121

Similar functionality is provided in C# by delegates, which are like function pointers but are type-safe, secure, fully managed objects. The fact that they're managed objects means that the runtime guarantees that a delegate will always point to a valid function of declared type. Delegates are used in many places in C#, such as for callbacks and event handlers, so it is essential to appreciate how they work.

Delegates have some conceptual similarities to interfaces, in that both are used to link pieces of code that are otherwise unrelated. Interfaces, however, are related to classes, can contain methods, properties, indexers and events, and are defined at compile time. Delegates, on the other hand, can only refer to a single method and are defined at run time. The coupling between client and "server" is less in delegates than in interfaces, so that links can easily be made at run time. If there are a lot of callbacks implemented between the same pair of classes, it might be better to use an interface instead of a number of delegates.

It is easiest to explain delegates using a code example, so consider a class that wishes to let callers perform an arithmetic operation on two integers:

```
namespace Wrox.FTrackCSharp.Advanced.ArithTest
{

    public class ArithTest
    {
        int n, m;

        // Delegate definition
        public delegate int ArithOp(int a, int b);

        // Constructor to store values
        public ArithTest(int a, int b)
        {
           n = a;
           m = b;
        }

        // Method to manipulate the members using the delegate
        // object passed in
        public int DoOp(ArithOp ar)
        {
        return ar(n, m);
        }
    }
}
```

The class declares a delegate called ArithOp, which provides a 'template' for a method that takes two ints and returns an int.

The DoOp() method takes an ArithOp delegate as an argument, passes it the two int arguments, and returns the result. In effect, a delegate is a reference to a method rather than a data member, and it enables you to pass around method references and execute them.

Any other class can define a method with the appropriate signature – one that takes two ints and returns an int – and **bind** it to the ArithOp delegate. A reference to the delegate can then be passed to the DoOp() function, and the delegate will execute the appropriate function when it is invoked.

C++ Note

You may be thinking that delegates sound like function pointers, and you'd be correct. There are several differences between them: one is that C# delegates are much safer than function pointers, due to their type safety. A second is that a single delegate can bind to both static and non-static class members, whereas C++ requires two different types of function pointer.

How do we call the `DoOp()` method? First, we need to define the methods that are going to perform the actual operations:

```
namespace Wrox.FTrackCSharp.Advanced.ArithTest
{
   public class ArithTest
   {
      // Same code as example above
   }

   public class DoTest
   {
      // Method to add two integers
      public int AddOp(int a, int b)
      {
         return a + b;
      }

      // Static method to subtract two integers
      public static int SubOp(int a, int b)
      {
         return a - b;
      }
   }
}
```

These are simply functions whose signature (in other words, its return type, and the number and type of its arguments) matches that of the delegate. Methods that are bound to delegates can be static or non-static, and we've used one of each in the example code.

Next, we have to create the delegates themselves, so add the following lines to this class:

```
using System;

namespace Wrox.FTrackCSharp.Advanced.ArithTest
{
   public class ArithTest
   {
      // Same code as example above
   }

   public class DoTest
   {
      // Method to add two integers
      public int AddOp(int a, int b)
```

```
    {
        return a + b;
    }

    // Method to subtract two integers
    public static int SubOp(int a, int b)
    {
        return a - b;
    }
```

```
    public static void Main(String[] args)
    {
        // Create a DoTest object
        DoTest dt = new DoTest();

        // Create two delegates
        ArithTest.ArithOp add = new ArithTest.ArithOp(dt.AddOp);
        ArithTest.ArithOp sub = new ArithTest.ArithOp(DoTest.SubOp);
    }
}
```

Delegate objects are created by passing in the name of the method to be used by the delegate. The AddOp() method is not static, so the delegate needs to be bound to an instance of DoTest; the SubOp() method is static, so the corresponding delegate is bound to the class method.

The compiler will issue an error message if the function passed to the delegate constructor doesn't have the correct signature. You can now see where the name 'delegate' comes from, because the delegate object will simply delegate the actual processing to the method we pass it. Note how the manipulating functions – AddOp and SubOp – are defined by the calling class, and not by ArithOp.

Having created these two objects, we can now use them. Insert the following lines into your code:

```
    public static void Main(String[] args)
    {
        // Create a DoTest object
        DoTest dt = new DoTest();

        // Create two delegates
        ArithTest.ArithOp add = new ArithTest.ArithOp(dt.AddOp);
        ArithTest.ArithOp sub = new ArithTest.ArithOp(DoTest.SubOp);

        // Create an ArithTest object
        ArithTest at = new ArithTest(5, 3);

        // Do the operations using the delegates
        int resultOne = at.DoOp(add);
        int resultTwo = at.DoOp(sub);

        // Print out the results
        Console.WriteLine("The first result is " + resultOne);
        Console.WriteLine("The second result is " + resultTwo);
    }
```

We execute the DoOp() method, passing in a reference to the delegate objects we've created. Within DoIt() itself, the delegate gets called, and it simply hands the processing on to the AddOp() and SubOp() methods.

In the next section, we will look at creating multicast delegates which will accept more than one method.

Events

All GUI programming is based on the concept of events, where an object notifies interested parties that something significant has occurred. Examples of events include a button object notifying its parent form that it has been pressed, or a list box notifying other controls that its selection has changed. The notification involves the originating object invoking a specific function on the observing object.

.NET takes the idea of events and makes it more general, so that now any class can **publish** a set of events, to which other objects can **subscribe** at run time. Events are no longer restricted to GUI programming, and this means that you can, for example, code up a FileSystem class which will notify interested parties whenever files are added or deleted, or a database table class which can notify observers when its contents have been changed. Events implement the Publish/Subscribe (Observer) design pattern as described in the original design patterns book ("Design Patterns," by Gamma et al., Addison-Wesley, 0-201-63361-2). This pattern defines a one-to-many relationship between objects, so that when one object (called the **publisher**) raises an event (changes state), then all its dependents (called **subscribers**) are notified.

Events in C# are based on delegates, with the event source defining one or more callback functions using delegates. The publishing class defines a delegate and the subscribing classes provide methods that implement it, which can be assigned to the delegates, and then called when an event is raised. A callback function, as traditional Windows programmers will know, is a function which one piece of code defines and another implements; in other words, one piece of code says "if you implement a function which looks like this, I can call it." A class that wants to raise events defines callback functions as delegates, and the listening object then implements them. Once again, an example will be the easiest way to show how it works. Suppose that in a banking application we want various objects in the system to be able to obtain information on interest rate changes.

We can add a class called RateChanger which gets data on various interest rates from some external source, and a RateChanger object can notify other objects in the banking system when an interest rate changes. In this case we'll use a class called RateObserver so we can show simply how events are set up, but we could just as easily add the code to the Account class. We'll use the classes like this:

```csharp
using System;

namespace Wrox.FTrackCSharp.Advanced.Event
{
    public class TestEvent
    {
        public static int Main(string[] args)
        {

            RateWatcher rw = new RateWatcher();

            RateObserver obs = new RateObserver("One",rw);
```

```
        RateObserver obs2 = new RateObserver("Two",rw);

        rw.Notify("base", 5.7);

        return 0;
    }
}
```

The `RateWatcher` is created and starts monitoring the interest rates. We then create two `RateObservers`, passing them a reference to the `RateWatcher` object. The `RateObserver` tells the `RateWatcher` that it is interested in being notified, and so its callback method will get called whenever the `RateWatcher` detects that the interest rate has changed.

The delegate method that is used for the notification takes two arguments, and this signature is defined by the event system. The first is a reference to the object that has originated the notification, and the second contains any data that needs to be passed as part of the notification process. In our example, we'll want to pass over the name of the rate (such as "base" for the base rate) and the new value. This second argument is a reference to a class derived from the system class `EventArgs` (you can define the class yourself or use one that Microsoft have defined, but it should be derived from `System.EventArgs`):

```
class RateEventArgs : EventArgs
{
    public readonly string RateName;
    public readonly double NewRate;

    public RateEventArgs(string name, double rate)
    {
        RateName = name;
        NewRate = rate;
    }
}
```

A `RateEventArgs` object simply holds the name of a rate and the new value for the rate. Since these are only used once in the notification call, we can use read-only properties to fix the values.

We're now in a position to implement the `RateWatcher` class itself. The first task is to define the delegate that will be used for callbacks. As I mentioned above, event delegates take two arguments, one representing the sender object, and the second the data passed with the event:

```
// This class watches the rates, and uses Notify() to notify observers when
// the rate changes.
class RateWatcher
{
    public delegate void RateChangeHandler(object sender,
                                           RateEventArgs e);
```

We then add to our class a reference to an event object:

```
    // Declare an event called RateChanged, of type RateChangeHandler
    public event RateChangeHandler RateChanged;
```

This line defines an event object of type `RateChangeHandler`, called `RateChanged`. The `RateChangeHandler` contains the event (object) and clients add methods to this event. Clients will create delegate objects that refer to their own handlers and will then attach those delegates to the event.

The final part of `RateWatcher` is the method that identifies that the event has occurred and raises the event that calls back to the client:

```
    // Call this method to notify observers that something has occurred
    public void Notify(string name, double val)
    {
        RateEventArgs r = new RateEventArgs(name, val);
        if (RateChanged != null)
            RateChanged(this, r);
    }
}
```

If the event reference is `null`, then no-one has registered with us. If it isn't `null`, we create a `RateEventArgs` object to hold the event data, and then use the delegate to call back to the client.

Now we need to implement the client, in the form of the `RateObserver` class:

```
    /// This is the class that wants to be notified when a rate changes
    class RateObserver
    {
        RateWatcher watcher;
        string myName;

        //  The constructor takes a RateWatcher object, which is going to notify
        //   this RateObserver
        public RateObserver(string name, RateWatcher r)
        {
            myName = name;

            watcher = r;

            watcher.RateChanged +=
            new RateWatcher.RateChangeHandler(RateHasChanged);
        }

        // Define the notification method
        public void RateHasChanged(object sender, RateEventArgs e)
        {
            Console.WriteLine("{0}: Rate '{1}' has changed to {2}",
            myName, e.RateName, e.NewRate);
              Console.ReadLine();
        }
    }
```

First, we implement the constructor to store away the reference we're passed. We also implement the delegate in the form of the `RateHasChanged()` method, which takes the two arguments that were defined in `RateWatcher`. The final piece of the jigsaw is to link our callback method to the event reference in the watcher object:

```
...
watcher = r;

watcher.RateChanged +=
new RateWatcher.RateChangeHandler(RateHasChanged);
```

Using standard delegate syntax, we create a `RateWatcher.RateChanged()` delegate, passing it a reference to our callback method, and save it to the public member of the watcher. You may have spotted the += being used in this assignment – this is a very useful property of delegates that allows you to chain delegate references together. Thus, if two clients register themselves with the same `RateChanger`, their delegates will get concatenated, and when `OnRateChange` is called in the watcher, both callback methods will get called one after the other. This is called a **multicasting** delegate.

As well as using += to register event handlers, you can also use -= to deregister them, should the client want to stop receiving notifications. You can add a `Remove()` method to the `RateObserver` class that uses -= to deregister the observer object:

```
...
Console.WriteLine("{0}: Rate '{1}' has changed to {2}",
myName,e.RateName,  e.NewRate);
  Console.ReadLine();

}
public void StopNotifications()
{
    // Tell the watcher we no longer need notification
    watcher.RateChanged -=
    new RateWatcher.RateChangeHandler(RateHasChanged);
}
```

Compile and run this program, and you should receive the following output:

```
>csc TestEvent.cs
Microsoft (R) Visual C# .NET Compiler version 7.00.9447
for Microsoft (R) .NET Framework version 1.0.3617
Copyright (C) Microsoft Corporation 2001. All rights reserved.


>TestEvent
One: Rate 'base' has changed to 5.7
Two: Rate 'base' has changed to 5.7
```

Unsafe Code

C++ programmers may be thinking by this point that while they can see the advantages of garbage collection and accessing variables via references, they miss pointers and being able to directly manipulate memory.

C#, in attempting to marry the best features of both C++ and Java, provides a way to let programmers use pointers just as you would in C or C++, but to do so in a way that doesn't conflict with the operation of the GC. In effect, C# lets you write code which runs outside the control of the memory management mechanism. For example, it is possible to directly access memory, to perform conversions between pointers and integral types, to take the address of variables, and so on. This code is called **unsafe code**, because there's a possibility that you can introduce all the problems that pointers and direct memory access bring with them, and because there is no way for the .NET runtime to check or control what is going on in unsafe code. Since unsafe code could potentially cause unverifiable problems, it cannot be used in components that are going to be downloaded from external sources, such as the Internet.

Why would you want to do this, and step outside the safe memory management provided for you by the .NET runtime? There are several possible reasons. Firstly, there's efficiency – using references to access objects imparts an extra layer of indirection, and the GC mechanism itself must add its own overheads. For certain critical blocks of code, you may want to be as efficient as possible, and using pointers may give you that edge.

Secondly, you may want to import some C or C++ code into C# that uses pointers, and you don't want to have to convert the pointers to references. Thirdly, you may want to use a system call or COM interface method that requires a pointer as an argument.

Blocks of code where you want to work outside the control of the GC and use pointers have to be marked as 'unsafe', which tells both the runtime and anyone reading the code what you're doing. You can mark blocks of code or whole methods as `unsafe`:

```
public class Test
{
   ...
   public unsafe void DoSomething()
   {
      ...
   }

   public void DoSomethingElse()
   {
      unsafe
      {
         // do something unsafe in here
      }
   }
}
```

If you want to use unsafe blocks or functions in your code, you will have to set the /unsafe compiler option, or they will be treated as errors. This can be used on the command line if you are using `csc.exe`, or set in the project property pages when using Visual Studio .NET.

A Brief Introduction to Pointers

For anyone who may not have come across C-style pointers before, here's a brief explanation. We access objects in C# using references, and this means that whenever we use an object we're actually dealing with two entities – the reference, and the object to which it refers. Only the reference knows the actual address of the object and that address isn't accessible to users, so the GC can move the object around in memory, and provided it fixes up the reference, users will be none the wiser.

A pointer, on the other hand, is a variable that holds an address; this address is the value of the pointer variable, it is visible and may be modified by the user. So using pointers means that you're directly playing with memory addresses, and here's where the problems start. As far as the GC is concerned, pointers are bad news, because it can no longer move objects around as it wishes. Pointers are also inherently unsafe, because they rely on correct values being used for the addresses they hold; if a bad value gets assigned to a pointer, it can end up accessing incorrect memory locations, resulting in possible memory corruption or programs crashing. Indeed, it is estimated that a very large number of bugs in C and C++ code result from pointers, which is one of the reasons why Java doesn't support them, and why C# handles them specially. You should therefore only use pointers in C# code when you absolutely have to.

Pointer variables are declared using the * notation:

```
int* pi;        // pointer to an int
char* pch;      // pointer to a char
```

Pointer variables are typed, so that `int*` declares a 'pointer to `int`', and can only be used to hold the address of an `int`. If you try to make it hold the address of any other type, the compiler will complain. In fact, a pointer simply holds an address, and the type tells the compiler how the memory at that address should be regarded: If it is a `char` pointer, it references memory in two-byte chunks; if it is an `int`, four-byte chunks, and so on. This means that you can use a pointer to refer to one or more integers (or characters, or whatever) and there has to be some other way to tell the compiler *how many* elements are stored at the address. In C and C++ this is the cause of many 'buffer overrun' bugs.

Pointers can also be set to the special value `null`, which indicates that they are not pointing to anything. It is good practice to initialize pointers to `null`, because an uninitialized pointer will contain a random value, which could be treated as an address later in the code, and lead to all sorts of errors. If pointers are initialized to `null`, any attempt to use the pointer will generate a run-time error.

```
int* pi = null;        // pointer initialized to null
```

You need to use the & operator to take the address of the variable and assign it to a pointer. Once you have a pointer to a variable, you can use the -> operator to access its members. This operator is used to access members through a pointer, in the same way that . is used to access members through a reference. Needless to say, since the -> operator works with pointers, it can only be used within an unsafe context.

```
// This method can use unsafe code
public unsafe void UsePoint(Point2D p)
{
    Point2D* pp = &p;
    Console.WriteLine("p is ({0},{1})", pp->x, pp->y);
}
```

It is very common to use pointers to access arrays, making the pointer hold the address of each element in turn as we move through the array. You'll see how to do this in the example in the very next section.

The fixed Keyword

Before moving on, let me mention an important fact that should be fairly obvious: pointer variables can only be declared and used within unsafe blocks, because the garbage collector has to be warned about them.

We've already said that the use of object references means that the garbage collector can move the actual objects around in order to make efficient use of memory. If we want to use pointers, the objects we want to reference obviously mustn't be moved around by the garbage collector while we're using them, and C# provides the fixed keyword to tell the garbage collector not move an object while it is being referenced by a pointer. Using fixed to stop the garbage collector from moving an object is known as **pinning** the object. Pinning is something that you want to do as little as possible, because when used to excess, it can prevent the garbage collector from doing its job efficiently. It isn't possible in C# to declare a pointer to a reference type, but pinning is useful for those times when you want to declare a pointer that points to a value type that is a member of a reference type.

The following code example shows how to pin an object:

```
using System;

namespace Wrox.FTrackCSharp.Advanced.Unsafe
{
    class Test
    {
        static void Main(string[] args)
        {
            int[] arr = new int[5] { 10, 20, 30, 40, 50 };
            UseArray(arr);
        }

        static unsafe void UseArray(int[] ar)
        {
            fixed (int* pa = &ar[0])
            {
                for (int i = 0; i < arr.Length; i++)
                    Console.WriteLine("ar[{0}]={1}", i, *(pa + i));
            }
        }
    }
}
```

This method is passed a reference to a normal managed int array object. We use fixed to get an int* pointer to the start of the actual object in memory, so that the address of the object ar is stored in the pointer variable pa. We can then use pa within the fixed block to access the elements of the array. The * operator is used to **dereference** the pointer, returning the value stored at the address the pointer holds. Note the use of **pointer arithmetic** in this sample: the expression (pa+i) is defining an offset from address pa, the 'units' of the offset being the size of the type being pointed to. Since the pointer pa is an int*, the offset is going to increase by four bytes – one int worth – each time around the loop.

And of course, while we're using pa in this block, the garbage collector won't touch the object referred to through ar. When we exit from the fixed block, the pointer goes out of scope, and the garbage collector can then take control of the object once more.

Note that you don't need to use fixed for value types, because they're allocated on the stack, so the garbage collector isn't going to move those around. That means that we can do traditional C-style manipulation of value types via pointers, the only proviso being that the pointers must be declared in an unsafe block.

stackalloc Keyword

The stackalloc keyword allows C# programmers to allocate memory on the stack within an unsafe context, in the same way that alloca does in C and C++. As its name implies, the memory is allocated dynamically on the stack (not the heap), and so is automatically released when the function in which it is allocated returns. For this reason, stackalloc can only be used to initialize local variables within functions. Note that stack size is limited, so stackalloc should be used sparingly.

Here's an example showing how to allocate an array of integers using stackalloc.

```
// stackalloc can only be used in an unsafe context
public unsafe void UseInts()
{
   // Allocate the array
   int* pi = stackalloc int[10];

   // Populate the array
   int* p = pi;
   for (int i = 0; i < 10; i++)
      *p++ = i * 2;

   // See what we have
   p = pi;
   for (int i = 0; i < 10; i++)
      Console.WriteLine(*p++);
}
```

XML Documentation

Our final topic in this chapter covers C#'s documentation facilities. Java programmers will be familiar with javadoc; an application that processes special tags in Java source code, and produces HTML pages as its output. The idea, based on the *literate programming* system invented by Donald Knuth, is that you write the code documentation at the very best time – as you're writing the code. You can then automatically generate the documentation from the code, and it should be easy to keep code and documentation up to date.

C#'s version is different to javadoc in two main ways. Firstly, it is processed by the compiler and not by a separate tool, and secondly, it generates XML rather than HTML. The reason for generating XML is that it is relatively easy to apply a cascading or XSL stylesheet to XML in order to generate HTML, but because XML tags mark up content rather than presentation, you can also use the documentation for purposes other than just display.

Text that is to be processed into XML documentation is provided in special comments that use three slashes /// instead of the normal two.

The compiler also supports a set of documentation tags that you can use within XML comments. Some of these are simply standard tags to which you'll have to attach your own meaning when you process the XML, but a few of them are processed by the compiler. You can also make up and use your own XML tags in order to extend the set. The following table lists the standard tags, and you can see an example showing how they're used in code later in the chapter.

Tag	Description
`<c>`	Marks text within a line up as code, for instance: `Here is some <c>code</c>`
`<code>`	Marks multiple lines as code
`<example>`	Marks up a code example
`<exception>`	Documents which exceptions a class may throw
`<include>`	Includes documentation comments in another file
`<list>`	Inserts a list into documentation. Uses `<listheader>` and `<item>` tags.
`<para>`	Delimits paragraphs in comment text, and is commonly used within `<summary>` elements.
`<param>`	Marks up a method parameter
`<paramref>`	Indicates that a word is a method parameter
`<permission>`	Documents access to a member
`<remarks>`	Adds a description for a member
`<returns>`	Documents the return value for a method
`<see>`	Provides a cross-reference to another member
`<seealso>`	Provides a 'see also' section in a description
`<summary>`	Provides a short description of an object
`<value>`	Describes a property

The compiler will check several of these tags during compilation. `<param>` and `<paramref>` are checked to make sure that the parameters you're using do actually exist. The `<see>` and `<seealso>` tags are checked to make sure that the entities named in the cross-reference exist, and to expand them to their full names, including class and namespace. The `<exception>` tag is processed to make sure that the exception class referenced in the tag exists, and the compiler also ensure that files referenced in `<include>` tags can be found. Finally, `<permission>` tags are checked to ensure that the entities they refer to exist.

Producing Documentation

The documentation /// comments will be treated as normal comments by the compiler, unless you use the /doc:filename compiler option to tell it to generate the XML. The following command line will compile the myclass.cs file, and place the generated XML into myclass.xml:

```
>csc /doc:myclass.xml myclass.cs
```

Unfortunately, you're on your own after that, because nothing is provided to help you turn your XML into anything readable.

You are better off if you're using Visual Studio .NET, because a tool is provided that generates a set of HTML pages rather than a raw XML file. We will try this with the program we just built, by copying it into a newly created C# Project file. We will place the comments within the web comment tags and then select Build Comment Web Pages... from the Tools menu, and you'll see the following dialog displayed:

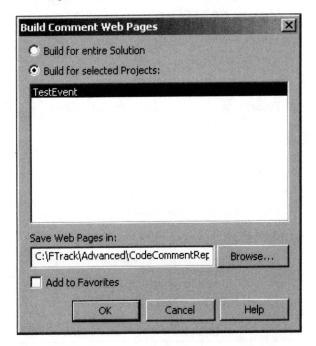

You can choose to generate documentation for the entire solution, or selected projects. When you press OK, a series of pages is generated in the directory specified in the dialog. The figure below shows one of the resulting pages:

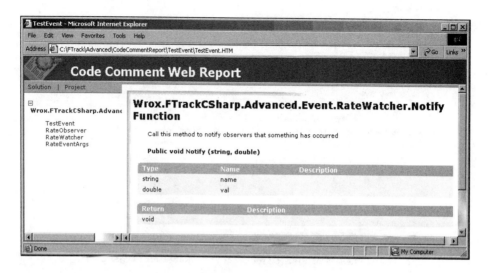

An XML Documentation Example

To show you how to format this code for translation into XML, here's the `TestEvent` program documented up using the XML documentation tags. If you're using the Visual Studio editor, typing the third slash on a comment will put in a skeleton summary block for you. If you're using some other editor (such as Notepad) you'll have to type all the XML in yourself.

```
using System;

namespace Wrox.FTrackCSharp.Advanced.Event
{
    /// <summary>
    /// Test Event class
    /// </summary>
    public class TestEvent
    {
        /// <summary>
        /// Create a RateWatcher...
        /// </summary>
        /// <param name="args"></param>
        /// <returns></returns>
        public static int Main(string[] args)
        {
            ...

        }
    }


    /// <summary>
    /// This is the class that wants to be notified when a rate changes
    /// </summary>
    class RateObserver
    {
        RateWatcher watcher;
```

```csharp
    string myName;

    /// <summary>
    /// The constructor takes a ratewatcher object, which is going to
    /// notify this RateObserver
    /// </summary>
    /// <param name="name"></param>
    /// <param name="r"></param>
    public RateObserver(string name, RateWatcher r)
    {
        ...
    }

    /// <summary>
    /// Define the notification method
    /// </summary>
    /// <param name="sender"></param>
    /// <param name="e"></param>
    public void RateHasChanged(object sender, RateEventArgs e)
    {
        ...
    }
    public void StopNotifications()
    {
        // Tell the watcher we no longer need notification
        ...
    }
}

/// <summary>
/// This class watches the rates, and uses Notify() to notify observers
when the rate changes.
/// </summary>
class RateWatcher
{
    /// <summary>
    /// Here's the delegate that defines the method observers must implement
    /// </summary>
    public delegate void RateChangeHandler(object sender,
                                           RateEventArgs e);

    /// <summary>
    /// Declare an event called RateChanged, of type RateChangeHandler
    /// </summary>
    public event RateChangeHandler RateChanged;

    /// <summary>
    /// Call this method to notify observers that something has occurred
    /// </summary>
    /// <param name="name"></param>
    /// <param name="val"></param>
    public void Notify(string name, double val)
    {
        ...
    }
```

```
        }

        /// <summary>
        /// This class holds the notification information
        /// </summary>
        class RateEventArgs : EventArgs
        {
            /// <summary>
            /// private name and rate members
            /// </summary>
            public readonly string RateName;
            public readonly double NewRate;

            /// <summary>
            /// construct the object
            /// </summary>
            /// <param name="name"></param>
            /// <param name="rate"></param>
            public RateEventArgs(string name, double rate)
            {
                ...
            }
        }
}
```

You can see that classes and methods are documented by placing the XML comments immediately before the class or method concerned. <summary> tags are used for the bulk of the documentation, with others inserted to add emphasis as necessary. Assuming that the sourcecode is held in TestEvent.cs, you can produce the XML with the following command line:

```
>csc /doc:TestEvent.xml TestEvent.cs
```

Here's an extract from the XML file that's produced:

```
<?xml version="1.0"?>
<doc>
    <assembly>
        <name>TestEvent</name>
    </assembly>
    <members>
        <member name="T:Wrox.FTrackCSharp.Advanced.Event.TestEvent">
            <summary>
            Test Event class
            </summary>
        </member>
        <member name="M:Wrox.FTrackCSharp
            .Advanced.Event.TestEvent.Main(System.String[])">
            <summary>
            Create a RateWatcher...
            </summary>
            <param name="args"></param>
            <returns></returns>
        </member>
```

```
<member name="T:Wrox.FTrackCSharp.Advanced.Event.RateObserver">
    <summary>
    This is the class that wants to be notified when a rate changes
    </summary>
</member>
. . .
```

This is a standard XML file built from nested tags. All the members of the assembly are denoted by <member> tags, and you can see how the compiler has added the full name of the member as a name attribute. The T, F and M prefixes denote types, fields, and members respectively.

Summary

In this chapter we've seen some of the more advanced features of C#. In particular:

❑   Variable method argument lists can be handled using the params keyword.

❑   User-defined conversions can be defined by using the implicit and explicit keywords.

❑   Delegates are similar to C++ function pointers, and provide a way for a class to specify behavior without implementing it.

❑   Events are based on delegates, and provide a way for classes to provide a notification service to interested parties.

❑   C# has a preprocessor that provides a subset of the functionality provided by the traditional C preprocessor. This is mainly used for conditional compilation, and macros aren't supported.

❑   Pointers and memory manipulation can be used with 'unsafe' code blocks. Variables can be referenced by address within these blocks, and pinning can be used to fix objects so that the garbage collector won't move them around.

❑   Special comments within the text can be used to produce XML documentation.

Take the
Fast Track

to
C#

6

.NET Programming with C#

The previous three chapters have focused on the C# language itself. This chapter starts dealing with how the language is used in the .NET environment, and will introduce you to:

- ❑ Namespaces and the `using` keyword
- ❑ Reflection and the `Type` class
- ❑ Attributes
- ❑ Collections and arrays
- ❑ Threading

Namespaces and the Using Keyword

This section introduces the concept of namespaces and shows how they are constructed and used. It also shows how the `using` keyword can make using namespaces easier.

Namespaces

C++ programmers will already be familiar with namespaces, and Java programmers have a similar construct in the Java package. For those that aren't familiar with the concept, here's an illustration.

Suppose that two developers are working on different parts of a large application. One is dealing with basic customer details, and develops a class called `Address`. The other is working with networking code, and also wants to have a class called `Address` to represent an IP address on the Internet. There will be a problem using both these classes together in one application because their names clash.

Namespaces are used to provide a higher level of scoping than type names. If the two `Address` classes belong to different namespaces, their names will be unique and can be used together without any name clash. Namespaces are thus very useful to anyone writing code that may be used by anyone else, because they enable you to minimize the chance of name clashes, while allowing you to choose the type names that make sense to you.

Formally, the `namespace` keyword is used to declare a scope:

```
namespace CustomerDetails
{
    public class Address
    {
        ...
    }
}

namespace Net
{
    public class Address
    {
        ...
    }
}
```

The two `Address` classes are defined in different namespaces, and so are unique. The full names of the two classes are `CustomerDetails.Address` and `Net.Address`, which shows how the dot notation is used for namespace member access as well as class member access.

A type name that includes the namespace information is called a fully qualified name. For example, `System.Collections.ArrayList` is a fully qualified name.

Java Note
C# namespaces look like Java packages, but there is no link between a namespace name and a directory structure. Classes defined in a namespace do not have to live in any particular directory.

Unlike a class declaration, a namespace can be defined in more than one source file. Note that namespace names can contain periods. This apparent structure is simply there to let you create hierarchical names; it has no compile- or run-time significance. The namespaces that form the .NET Framework all start with `System`, for instance `System.Xml`, `System.Collections` and `System.Data`. The idea is that a company can use this naming scheme to have all their namespace names starting with the same unique prefix.

Nested Namespaces

You can define one namespace inside another, as shown in the following code fragment. This can be useful when structuring code; for instance, a company could define a top-level namespace that holds all the company code, and within that a separate namespace for each product:

```
namespace AcmeCorp
{
    namespace DiskTrasher
    {
        class Cruncher
        {
            ...
        }
    }
}
```

As you'd expect, the full name of the class would be `AcmeCorp.DiskTrasher.Cruncher`. This ability to make hierarchical namespace names means that a namespace defined as:

```
namespace One.Two.Three
{
    public class X
    {
        ...
    }
}
```

is functionally equivalent to the following nested declaration:

```
namespace One
{
    namespace Two
    {
        namespace Three
        {
            public class X
            {
                ...
            }
        }
    }
}
```

Using Namespaces in Programs

This section is going to consider how to use code that lives in a namespace in your own applications.

Assemblies

In order to know how to use namespaces in programs, you have to know something about assemblies. This topic is covered in a lot more detail in Chapter 9, but I'll present just enough of an introduction to let you work with namespaces.

143

Compiled C# classes live in assemblies, which can be DLLs or EXEs, and which are the basic unit of packaging and distribution of .NET code. An assembly consists of one or more files, and can include code plus any other data needed by the assembly, such as bitmaps or sound files. The system assemblies that ship with the .NET Framework are all DLLs, and this is generally true of any assembly that is going to be used by other applications.

Referencing Assemblies

In order to use a class from another assembly, you have to give the compiler a reference to the assembly so that it can find the class. The reason for this is that, like Java, .NET uses compiled code to make compile-time and run-time checks, so it has to know about the assemblies for every type that you use in your programs.

How do you know what assembly a class lives in? For the .NET Framework classes, the requisite page in the online help will tell you in the Requirements section at the bottom of the page. Here's the Requirements section from the help page for the `System.Array` type:

```
Namespace: System
Platforms: Windows 98, Windows NT 4.0, ...
Assembly: Mscorlib (in Mscorlib.dll)
```

This tells you that the class is defined in the `mscorlib` assembly, which is physically located in `mscorlib.dll`.

Once you know which assembly the class is defined in, you can tell the compiler. If you're compiling from the command line, you use the `/reference` option to specify the name of the assembly:

```
>csc /reference:AssemblyA.dll;AssemblyB.dll /out:myprog.exe input.cs
```

This example will compile the file `input.cs` to produce the executable `myprog.exe`, and it will use the two assemblies `AssemblyA.dll` and `AssemblyB.dll`. Note how a semicolon is used to separate the names where multiple assemblies are specified. You don't need to do this for any classes that are defined in the `mscorlib` assembly, because that is the one assembly that the compiler automatically knows about.

If you're using Visual Studio .NET and you're working with a C# project, you add a reference to the assembly. Open the Solution Explorer, and expand the project tree to show the **References** folder; if you expand this folder, you'll see the list of references that are automatically added to every C# project in Visual Studio.

To add a new reference, right-click on **References** to pop up a context menu.

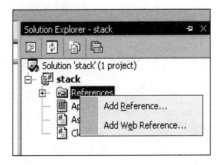

Selecting **Add Reference** will open the **Add Reference** dialog. Select the .NET tab, and then scroll down the list until you find the assembly you're interested in. Select it in the list box and press **Select** to add it to the list to references. You can add as many references as you like before pressing **OK**.

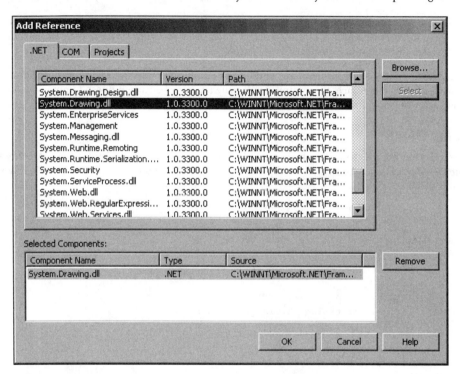

The using Directive

Once you've added a reference to an assembly, you can use any type in the assembly by using its fully qualified name. In the figure above I added a reference to `System.Drawing.dll`, which contains the `System.Drawing` namespace. One of the classes in `System.Drawing` is `Pen`, so once I've added the reference, I can create a `Pen`:

```
System.Drawing.Pen p =
        new System.Drawing.Pen(System.Drawing.Color.DarkGreen);
```

Using fully qualified names like this gets very tedious after a while, so you can use the `using` directive to provide a shortcut. Here's the equivalent code with a `using` directive:

```
// Add a using directive for System.Drawing
using System.Drawing;

...

// Create a Pen and use a Color
Pen p = new Pen(Color.DarkGreen);
```

The using directive appears at the top of the file, and lets you use the types in a namespace without having to fully qualify them. In effect, whenever it sees a type that it doesn't recognize, the compiler will use the namespaces in using directives to prefix the unknown type name, to see if one matches.

A using directive will not give you access to any nested namespaces. Each namespace needs its own using directive. In addition, a nested namespace can reside in a different file so that, for example, System.Data lives in a different file to System.

You can have multiple using directives at the top of a file. If you try to reference a type that is defined in more than one namespace, the compiler will issue an error because it doesn't know which one to use. In that case, you should use the fully qualified name for the type, in order to remove ambiguity.

The using Block

There's another use for the using keyword, which we'll cover here for completeness. A **using block** defines a scope at the end of which an object will be disposed, and the simple program below shows how it is used:

```
using System;

namespace Wrox.FTrackCSharp.DotNetProg.Using
{
    class MyClass : IDisposable
    {
        public void Print()
        {
            Console.WriteLine("MyClass.Print");
        }

        // Implement Dispose
        public void Dispose()
        {
            Console.WriteLine("MyClass.Dispose");
        }
    }

    class Class1
    {
        static void Main(string[] args)
        {
            Console.WriteLine("Before using block");
            using (MyClass md = new MyClass())
            {
                md.Print();
            }
            Console.WriteLine("After using block");
        }
    }
}
```

MyClass implements the IDisposable interface, which specifies a single Dispose() method. The using statement in the Main() method creates a MyClass object, which is used within the block. At the end of the block the reference md goes out of scope, and the Dispose() method on the MyClass object is automatically called.

Reflection and the Type Class

Reflection is a feature of the .NET Framework that lets you inspect types and objects at run-time and find out what they can do. You can take an object and find out what class it belongs to, what its superclass is, and what methods, properties and fields it has. You can even create an instance of a class where the class is determined at run-time instead of compile-time, and invoke methods on it. Reflection is mostly used by writers of tools and compilers, but it can be useful in application programs as well.

The `System.Reflection` namespace contains a large number of classes that implement the reflection functionality; in the rest of this section we will discuss some of the more interesting classes. Before we do, though, we need to talk about the `Type` class.

The Type Class

The key to using reflection is the `System.Type` class. A `Type` object represents a .NET type: a class, an interface, a value type, an array or an enumeration. Once you've obtained a `Type` object, you can use its methods and properties to find out about the type.

How do you obtain a `Type` object? There are a number of ways. Firstly, the `typeof` operator takes a type name and returns you a `Type` that represents it:

```
// Get a Type object representing the Foo class
Type t = typeof(Foo);
```

The second way is to use the `GetType()` method that every type inherits from `System.Object`:

```
// Get a Type object representing the Foo class
Foo f = new Foo();
Type t = f.GetType();
```

The third is to use the static `Type.GetType()` method:

```
// Get a Type object representing the Foo class
Type t = Type.GetType("Foo");
```

You may be wondering why there are three basic ways of getting a `Type` object. The `Object.GetType()` and `Type.GetType()` methods let you get a type based on a reference or a type name, and can be used from any .NET language. The point of `typeof` is that you use it if you know at compile-time what type you want to get a `Type` object for, and you don't want to instantiate an object of that type first. `Object.GetType()` is used where you have a reference to an object (and you don't need to know at compile-time what the type is – the actual object may be of a derived class). `Type.GetType()` is similar to the `typeof` keyword – you supply the name rather than an object, but since the name is in a string variable, you don't need to know it at compile-time.

All of these return you exactly the same `Type` object. Once you've got a `Type` object, you can find out about the type it represents, and the following table lists some of the members you can use to do this.

Member	Method/ Property	Description
Assembly	Property	Returns an `Assembly` object representing the type's assembly
Attributes	Property	Gets the standard attributes associated with the type as a `TypeAttributes` object
BaseType	Property	Returns a `Type` object representing the superclass of the current type, but returns a `null` reference if you use this on `System.Object`, as it has no superclass.
FullName	Property	Returns the full name of the type, including namespace
IsAbstract	Property	True if the type is abstract
IsArray	Property	True if the type is an array
IsClass	Property	True if the type is a class
IsCOMObject	Property	True if the type is a COM object
IsEnum	Property	True if the type is an enumeration
IsInterface	Property	True if the type is an interface
IsPointer	Property	True if the type is a pointer
IsPublic	Property	True if the type has public access
IsSealed	Property	True if the type is sealed
IsValueType	Property	True if the type is a value type
Module	Property	Returns a `Module` object representing the module in which the type is defined
Namespace	Property	Returns a string representing the namespace for this type
FindMembers()	Method	Returns a filtered array of `MemberInfo` objects
GetConstructor(), GetConstructors()	Method	Returns details of one or more constructors for this type
GetCustomAttributes()	Method	Returns details of any custom attributes defined for this type
GetEvent(), GetEvents()	Method	Returns details of one or more events for this type
GetField(), GetFields()	Method	Returns details of one or more public fields for this type

Member	Method/ Property	Description
GetInterface(), GetInterfaces()	Method	Returns details of one or more interfaces implemented by this type
GetMember(), GetMembers()	Method	Returns details of one or more members of this type.
GetMethod(), GetMethods()	Method	Returns details of one or more methods implemented by this type
GetProperty(), GetProperties()	Method	Returns details of one or more properties of this type
GetTypeArray()	Static method	Gets the type of objects in an array
InvokeMember()	Method	Invokes a method, or accesses a property or field of a type
IsInstanceOfType()	Method	Determines whether a specified object is an instance of a particular type
IsSubclassOf()	Method	Determines whether the current Type is a subclass of a specified Type

Here's an example to show how you can use the Type class.

```
using System;
using System.Reflection;

namespace Wrox.FTrackCSharp.DotNetProg.UseType
{
    // A test interface
    interface IOne
    {
        void Method1();
    }

    // A test class
    public class Test : IOne
    {
        // Fields
        public int fieldOne;
        private int fieldTwo;
        public string fieldThree;

        // Constructors
        public Test()
        {
        }
        public Test(int a)
        {
        }
```

```
        // A property
        public double propOne
        {
            get { return 3.0;}
            set {}
        }

    // Implement IOne
    public void Method1()
    {
    }

    // A method
    public void AMethod(int n)
    {
    }
}

class Class1
{
    // Test reflection
    [STAThread]
    static void Main(string[] args)
    {
        // Get type objects
        Type t1 = typeof(IOne);
        Reflect(t1);
        Type t2 = typeof(Test);
        Reflect(t2);
    }

    static void Reflect(Type t)
    {
        Console.WriteLine("Type name: {0}", t.FullName);

        // Basic info
        if (t.IsPublic)
            Console.Write(" public");
        else
            Console.Write(" non-public");

        if (t.IsAbstract)
            Console.Write(" abstract");

        if (t.IsClass)
            Console.Write(" class");
        else if (t.IsInterface)
            Console.Write(" interface");

        Console.WriteLine();

        // Fields
        FieldInfo[] fi = t.GetFields();
        foreach(FieldInfo f in fi)
            Console.WriteLine(" Field: {0}", f.Name);
```

```
    // Methods
    MethodInfo[] mi = t.GetMethods();
    foreach(MethodInfo m in mi)
      Console.WriteLine(" Method: {0}", m.Name);

    // Properties
    PropertyInfo[] pi = t.GetProperties();
    foreach(PropertyInfo p in pi)
       Console.WriteLine("  Property: {0}", p.Name);
    }
  }
}
```

The program first adds a `using` directive for the `System.Reflection` namespace, in order to be able to use the types from that namespace without having to use fully qualified names.

You'll see two types defined at the top of the code: a simple interface called `IOne`, and a class called `Test`. The main program creates a `Type` object for each of these types, and then calls the `Reflect()` function, which prepares a brief report on the type. The `"Is"` group of properties are used to print out basic information about the type, and then the `"Get"` methods are used to retrieve details of the fields, methods and properties. Notice how you work with fields, methods and properties in the same way. You can use the properties and methods of the `FieldInfo`, `MethodInfo` and `PropertyInfo` classes to find out more about class members, but space doesn't permit a full discussion here.

When you run the program, you should see output like this:

Loading an Assembly

The `System.Reflection.Assembly` class represents an assembly, and its static `Load()` method lets you load assemblies dynamically at run time. This can be used to obtain information about the types defined in a certain assembly. There are many times when this facility is useful. As an example, think of printer drivers. The user of a program can choose which printer to use at any time, and the code needs to load the requisite driver on the fly.

The following code fragment shows how you can load an assembly. It uses the simplest of the overloads of the `Load()` method, which takes the name of the assembly:

```
using System;
using System.Reflection;

...

Assembly asm;

try
{
    asm = Assembly.Load("MyAssembly");
}
catch(Exception e)
{
    Console.WriteLine(e.Message);
}
```

The assembly is going to be found using .NET's location rules for assemblies (discussed in Chapter 9), and Load() will throw an exception if the assembly can't be found. To use an assembly that is located anywhere on your file system, use the LoadFrom() method with the path name of the assembly. The current assembly that the code is running from can be returned with the GetExecutingAssembly() method. For example, GetExecutingAssembly().FullName will display the name and further information about the current assembly. We shall see more of Load() in Chapter 9.

Creating Objects Dynamically and Invoking Members

Once you've loaded an assembly, it is possible to create instances of the types contained in the assembly, and to invoke members of those instances dynamically. This idea – deciding what to create and what to do with it at run-time – is called **late binding**. If you've done any COM programming, you'll have come across COM's implementation of late binding, the IDispatch interface.

Dynamically creating objects is done by the System.Activator class, with the overloaded CreateInstance() method. This code fragment shows how to create an object using CreateInstance():

```
using System;
using System.Reflection;

...

Assembly asm;
Type t = null;
object o= null;

try
{
    asm = Assembly.Load("MyAssembly");
    // Get a Type object to represent the type
    t = asm.GetType("MyNamespace.MyType");

    // Create an instance
    o = Activator.CreateInstance(t);
}
catch(Exception e)
```

```
{
    // Handle the error
}
```

The `Assembly.GetType()` method returns a `Type` object, and will throw a `ReflectionTypeLoadException` if no such type exists in the assembly. If no exception is thrown, the `Type` object can be passed to `Activator.CreateInstance()` to create an instance. There are a lot of exceptions that can be thrown by this method, so it needs to be in the `try` block as well.

Now that you have an object, you can invoke methods and access properties using the classes in the reflection namespace. You met the `MethodInfo` class in the previous section, where it was used to report on the methods implemented by a type. It also has an `Invoke()` member, which will execute the method represented by the `MethodInfo`, taking any arguments you may need to pass in.

To finish the example, suppose that `MyType` has a `Square()` method that takes a `double`, squares it and returns the result:

```
using System;
// MyAssembly.cs
namespace Wrox.FTrackCSharp.DotNetProg.MyAssembly
{
    public class MyType
    {
        public double Square(double n)
        {
            return n*n;
        }
    }
}
```

We compile this into a class library with the following command-line syntax:

C:\FTrack\DotNetProg>csc /target:library MyAssembly.cs

Here's a piece of code that invokes the `Square()` method, and displays the result:

```
using System;
using System.Reflection;

namespace Wrox.FTracCSharp.DotNetProg.InvokeTest
{
    class Class1
    {

        static void Main()
        {
            Assembly asm;
            Type t = null;
            object o = null;
            try
            {
```

```
                    asm = Assembly.Load("MyAssembly");

                    // Get a Type object to represent the type
                    t = asm.GetType("Wrox.FTrackCSharp.DotNetProg.MyAssembly.MyType");

                    // Create an instance
                    o = Activator.CreateInstance(t);

                    // Find the method
                    MethodInfo mi = t.GetMethod("Square");

                    if (mi != null)
                    {
                        // Build the argument list
                        object[] argarray = { 3.0 };

                        // Invoke the method
                        double d = (double)mi.Invoke(o, argarray);
                        // Write the answer
                        Console.WriteLine(d.ToString());
                    }
                }
            }
            catch(Exception e)
            {
                Console.WriteLine(e);
            }
        }
    }
}
```

The `Type.GetMethod()` function is used to retrieve a `MethodInfo` by name, and it returns a `null` reference if no such method can be found. Arguments are passed to `MethodInfo.Invoke()` as an array of objects; in this case there is only one, but it still has to be passed as an array.

The `Invoke()` method is called, passing in the object and the parameter array. The result (if any) is returned as an object, so it has to be cast to the appropriate type before it can be used.

Attributes

In most programming languages, all information has to come from the code, and the forms of information that you can express are fixed, or at best extensible through limited mechanisms such as macros.

In all .NET languages, **attributes** are extra items of declarative information that can be attached to code elements, whether they be assemblies, classes, interfaces, methods, method parameters, data members or properties. Once you've associated an attribute with an entity in your code, it can be queried at run-time by anyone making use of your class, using **reflection**.

Attributes are implemented by attribute classes. A number of standard attributes are provided with C#, and we'll see shortly how it is possible to write your own.

The .NET Framework uses standard attributes for a variety of reasons. They are used to describe how to serialize data, to specify characteristics that are used to enforce security, and limit optimizations by the just-in-time (JIT) compiler so the code remains easy to debug. Attributes can also record the name of a file or the author of code, or control the visibility of controls and members during development of Windows Forms applications.

The following table lists some of the most commonly used standard attributes, and those who have had any experience with using IDL for COM programming will recognize several of them.

Attribute Name	Description
AttributeUsage	A "meta attribute" that is used to determine what elements another attribute can be applied to
Conditional	Conditionally includes a method in a class
Obsolete	Marks an entity as obsolete; the compiler will give a warning or error if it is used
Guid	Specifies a GUID for the class or interface
In	Indicates that a parameter is passed from caller to method
Out	Indicates that a parameter is passed from method back to caller
Serializable	Marks a class or struct as serializable
NonSerialized	Marks a data member or property as being transient, only needed in a [Serializable] class

Using Attributes

As an example, here's how you'd use one of the standard attributes that controls conditional inclusion of methods in a class:

```
#define Debug

using System;
using System.Diagnostics;

namespace Wrox.FTrackCSharp.DotNetProg.Conditional
{
    public class Test
    {
        [Conditional ("Debug")]
        public static void TraceOutput()
        {
            Console.WriteLine("Some conditional output...");
        }

        public static void Main(string[] args)
        {
            Console.WriteLine("Main method");
            ConditionalMethod();
```

```
        }
    }
}
```

You can see from the code that in C# attributes are specified in square brackets, and are placed immediately before the element they apply to. The conditional attribute is provided for the benefit of the compiler; it takes the name of a preprocessor symbol `Debug` as its argument; if that symbol is defined, the method `TraceOutput()` and all calls to it are included in the compilation. If the symbol isn't defined, then all traces of `TraceOutput()` are omitted from the compiled code.

Note that the name of the attribute class is `ConditionalAttribute`, but when you use it in code you don't have to use the `Attribute` suffix. You can refer to it either as `ConditionalAttribute` or just `Conditional`, because the compiler first looks for the plain class name (`Conditional`), and if that doesn't work, it appends `Attribute` and tries again. This short-cut is provided by the C# compiler so that you don't have to type `Attribute` so many times!

Since the preprocessor symbol is defined at the start of the file, both the definition and the call will be compiled. We'd expect to see output like this:

Main method
Some conditional output...

If we remove or comment out the definition of DBG, we'd see this output:

Main method

There are a few restrictions on methods that can be used with the `Conditional` attribute, the main one of which is that they can only have a `void` return type. This effectively prevents such methods being used in expressions, where it would be impossible to selectively discard calls.

Writing Custom Attributes

The first step to writing your own attributes is to create an attribute class, which inherits from `System.Attribute`:

```
using System;

[AttributeUsage(AttributeTargets.Class)]
public class IsDrawingPluginAttribute : System.Attribute
{
}
```

This attribute, `IsDrawingPluginAttribute`, is going to be used to mark classes that are plug-ins for a mythical drawing program. As a matter of convention, attribute class names usually end with `Attribute`.

The main thing to note about this example is that the attribute class itself has an attribute, `AttributeUsage`. This is really a meta-attribute, because it is an attribute that applies to attributes!

`AttributeUsage` is used to determine which elements in a program this attribute can be applied to, and in this case we can apply it to classes. The `AttributeTargets` enumeration contains methods that let you tie down what you want your attributes to be used on, and you can use `AttributeTargets.All` if you're not fussy.

The above definition isn't complete, because attribute classes must have at least one public constructor. Since our attribute has no data associated with it, the constructor is very simple indeed, and our completed simple attribute would therefore look like this:

```
using System;

[AttributeUsage(AttributeTargets.Class)]
public class IsDrawingPluginAttribute : System.Attribute
{
    public IsDrawingPluginAttribute ()
    {
    }
}
```

We'd compile this class up as part of an assembly, and have its assembly available when we want to use it. In client code, we'd use it on a class like this:

```
[IsDrawingPlugin]
public class Plugin
{
}
```

Note once again that you don't have to use the `Attribute` suffix when naming attributes.

AttributeUsage

The `AttributeUsageAttribute` class has two properties that may be useful when creating custom attributes.

`AttributeUsageAttribute.AllowMultiple` controls whether multiple occurrences of this attribute are allowed on a single program element. You might want to do this if the attribute can take parameters, as explained a little later on. The default is `false`, so the following code would generate a compiler error:

```
[IsDrawingPlugin]
[IsDrawingPlugin]
public class Plugin
{
}
```

If you want to allow multiple occurrences of the attribute, set this property to `true`:

```
[AttributeUsage(AttributeTargets.Class, AllowMultiple=true)]
public class IsDrawingPluginAttribute : System.Attribute
{
    public IsDrawingPluginAttribute ()
    {
    }
}
```

This example shows how to use parameters with attributes, and these are covered in more detail in the next section.

`AttributeUsageAttribute.Inherited` controls whether this attribute is inherited by classes that derive from the one on which the attribute is specified. It defaults to `true`, but can be set to `false` if you don't want the attribute to be inherited.

```
[AttributeUsage(AttributeTargets.Class, Inherited=false)]
public class IsDrawingPluginAttribute : System.Attribute
{
    public IsDrawingPluginAttribute ()
    {
    }
}
```

A More Complex Attribute Example

For a more complex example that uses arguments, consider an attribute that can be used to attach information about who writes a particular class:

```
using System;

[AttributeUsage(AttributeTargets.All)]
public class AuthorInfoAttribute : System.Attribute
{
    private string name;

    public AuthorInfoAttribute(string name)
    {
        this.name = name;
    }
}
```

Note how we're using `AttributeTargets.All` so that this attribute can be used on all program elements.

Positional and Named Parameters

Attributes take two kinds of parameters, known as **positional** and **named**. Positional parameters are used as arguments to attribute constructors, and must be specified every time the attribute is used, so you use them for data that is central to the operation of the attribute. The string `name` in the example above is a positional parameter.

Named parameters are represented by a non-static data member or property in the attribute class. They are optional, and if used, they are identified by their name. We can add optional `Date` and `Comment` named parameters to our class like so:

```
using System;

namespace Wrox.FTrackCSharp.DotNetProg.CustomAtts
{
    [AttributeUsage(AttributeTargets.All)]
    public class AuthorInfoAttribute : System.Attribute
```

```
    {
        private string name;
        private string date;
        private string comment;

        public AuthorInfoAttribute(string name)
        {
            this.name = name;
        }

        // Read-only property to return the name
        public string Name
        {
            get
            {
                return name;
            }
        }

        // Property to get and set a Date member
        public string Date
        {
            get
            {
                return date;
            }
            set
            {
                date = value;
            }
        }

        // Property to get and set a Comment member
        public string Comment
        {
            get
            {
                return comment;
            }
            set
            {
                comment = value;
            }
        }
    }
}
```

We've only added a get property for the name, because that's set via the constructor. The positional and named parameters could be used like this in code:

```
[AuthorInfo("julian")]
[AuthorInfo("julian", Date="27/03/02")]
[AuthorInfo("julian", Date="27/03/02", Comment="First revision")]
```

The first version just uses the one positional parameter, which has to be included in all uses of this attribute. The second and third use one and both of the named attributes respectively. Note that named parameters always have to occur after position parameters when constructing attributes.

To use the attribute, you simply include it at the top of a class definition. If you want to specify more than one attribute, you can use a comma-separated list or separate sets of square brackets:

```
[IsDrawingPlugin, AuthorInfo("julian",
                            Date="27/01/02", Comment="First revision")]
public class Plugin
{
   ...
}
```

Or:

```
[IsDrawingPlugin]
[AuthorInfo("julian", Date="27/01/02", Comment="First revision")]
public class Plugin
{
   ...
}
```

Note that only a subset of the .NET types can be used for attribute parameters, as shown in the following list:

❑ bool, byte, char, double, float, int, long, short and string

❑ object

❑ System.Type

❑ A public enum

❑ Arrays of the above

Using Attributes

You can use reflection on objects that you create to find out about the attributes they support, using the Type.GetCustomAttributes() method. This example uses the Plugin class that was introduced in the previous section:

```
using System;
using System.Reflection;

namespace Wrox.FTrackCSharp.DotNetProg.UseCustomAtts
{
   [IsDrawingPlugin]
   public class Plugin
   {
   }

   public class Test
```

```
    {
        public static void Main (string[] args)
        {
            // Get a Type object representing the Plugin class
            Type t = typeof(Plugin);

            // Get the array of custom attributes
            object[] attribs = t.GetCustomAttributes(false);

            // List them
            foreach (object o in attribs)
            {
                if (o.GetType().Equals(typeof(IsDrawingPluginAttribute)))
                    Console.WriteLine("Supports IsDrawingPlugin attribute");
                else
                    Console.WriteLine("Not a plugin");
            }
        }
    }
}
```

We start by getting a `Type` object that represents the class we want to examine, and then call its `GetCustomAttributes()` method to retrieve an array of objects, each of which represents an instance of an attribute class. The `false` argument tells the method not to search derived classes, mainly because – in this case – there aren't any!

We then walk through this collection using `foreach`, testing the type of each member to see whether it is an `IsDrawingPluginAttribute` object. If it is, then the class supports that attribute and we report the fact. Notice that we use `Equals()` when comparing types, because the code is dealing with references to `Type` objects.

Using an attribute class that has parameters is simply a matter of accessing the members of the attribute object. In the following code, note how we need to cast the `object` reference into an `AuthorInfoAttribute` in order to access its members:

```
using System;
using System.Reflection;

namespace Wrox.FTrackCSharp.DotNetProg.UseCustomAtts
{
    [IsDrawingPlugin]
    [AuthorInfoAttribute("Johnny", Date="2/2/2002")]
    public class Plugin {
    }

    public class Test
    {
        public static void Main(string[] args)
        {
            // Get a Type object representing the Plugin class
            Type t = typeof(Plugin);

            // Get the array of custom attributes
```

```
        object[] attribs = t.GetCustomAttributes(false);

        // List them
        foreach (object o in attribs)
        {
            if (o.GetType().Equals(typeof(IsDrawingPluginAttribute)))
                Console.WriteLine(Supports IsDrawingPlugin");
            else if (o.GetType().Equals(typeof(AuthorInfoAttribute)))
                Console.WriteLine(
                    "AuthorInfo: name={0}, date={1}",
                    ((AuthorInfoAttribute)o).Name,
                    ((AuthorInfoAttribute)o).Date);
        }
    }
  }
}
```

Collections and Arrays

The final section of this chapter looks at how collections of objects are handled in C#, starting with arrays, and moving on to the .NET Framework collection classes.

Arrays

C++ Note:
Arrays in C# work very differently from their C++ counterparts!

Arrays in C# are objects in their own right, and are accessed through a reference variable. The following code shows how to declare references to int arrays:

```
int[] arr;          // declare one int array reference
int[] arr2, arr3;   // declare two array references
```

Note that the type is int[] ('reference to int array'), and that the type applies to all variables in the statement. You don't put any value in the square brackets because you're not declaring the array itself here, just a reference to it.

Java Note
The square brackets have to appear immediately after the type in C#. The alternative C-style declaration allowed in Java won't work here.

Once you've declared the array reference, you can construct the array itself:

```
int[] arr;          // declare the array reference
arr = new int[25];  // create a 25 element int array
```

You use new the same as you would for any other object, and the size of the array you want is specified in square brackets after the type. Array sizes are fixed, and can't be changed after creation; if you need a dynamic array, consider using one of the collection classes defined in the System.Collections namespace, discussed in the following section.

Once you've created an array you can access its elements, using zero-based addressing. This means that the valid subscripts for a 25-element array run from [0] through to [24], and any attempt to access an element outside those bounds will result in an exception being thrown at run time.

```
using System;

namespace Wrox.FTrackCSharp.DotNetProg.SimpleArray
{
   class Test
   {
      public static void Main()
      {
         int[] arr = new int[25];      // declare 25 element int array
         arr[0] = 1;                   // first element
         arr[24] = 10;                 // last element
         arr[25] = 12;                 // error!
      }
   }
}
```

How do you give initial values to your array elements? Apart from the obvious – assigning them one by one, as in the code above – you can also provide a list of initial values in braces:

```
int[] arr = new int[] { 1,2,3,4 } ;
// which can be shortened to...
int[] arr = { 1,2,3,4 };
```

Note that if you do this, you don't have to provide a size for the array as the compiler can work it out for itself.

If you need to, you can create arrays that aren't zero-based by using the System.Array class. This isn't recommended, though, as .NET languages will expect arrays to be zero-based.

The System.Array Class

All arrays in .NET languages are derived from System.Array, which provides two advantages. Firstly, arrays are now the same in all .NET languages and can be freely passed around. Declaring an array in C# and passing it to a Visual Basic .NET function is now quite trivial.

The second advantage is that all arrays inherit the methods and properties of System.Array, which are summarized in the following table:

Member	Type	Description
IsReadOnly	Property	True if the array is read-only
IsSynchronized	Property	True if the array is thread-safe
Length	Property	Gets the total number of elements in all dimensions of the array
Rank	Property	Gets the number of dimensions of the array
BinarySearch()	Static method	Uses a binary search to locate an element
Clear()	Static method	Clears all or part of an array
Clone()	Method	Creates a shallow copy of the array
Copy()	Static method	Copies all or part of an array to another array
CopyTo()	Method	Copies all elements from a 1D array to another 1D array
GetEnumerator()	Method	Returns an enumerator (see the following topic for details of enumerators)
GetLength()	Method	Returns the number of elements in one dimension of the array
GetLowerBound()	Method	Returns the lower bound of a specified dimension
GetUpperBound()	Method	Returns the upper bound of a specified dimension
GetValue()	Method	Gets the value of a specified element
IndexOf()	Static method	Returns the index of the first occurrence of a value in all or part of a 1D array
Initialize()	Method	Calls the default constructor of the array to initialize all members
LastIndexOf()	Static method	Returns the index of the last occurrence of a value in all or part of a 1D array
Reverse()	Static method	Reverses the order of the elements in all or part of a 1D array
SetValue()	Method	Sets the value of a specified element
Sort()	Static method	Sorts the elements in a 1D array

Multidimensional Arrays

C# supports two types of multidimensional arrays – **rectangular** and **jagged**. In rectangular arrays, as their name implies, every row is the same length. A jagged array, on the other hand, is simply an array of one-dimensional arrays, each of which can be of a different length if desired.

The following example demonstrates how to declare and initialize rectangular arrays:

```
using System;

namespace Wrox.FTrackCSharp.DotNetProg.CubeDemo
{
    class Cube
    {
        static void Main()
        {
            char[] symbols = new char[] { ' ', '-', '|', '/' };

            int[, , ] cube;
            char[,] projected;

            cube = new int[10,10,10];
            projected = new char[20,20];

            // Setup the boundaries of the cube
            for (int i = 0;i<10;i++)
            {
                cube[i,0,0] = 1; cube[i,9,0] = 1;
                cube[i,9,9] = 1; cube[i,0,9] = 1;
                cube[0,i,9] = 3; cube[9,i,9] = 3;
                cube[0,i,0] = 3; cube[9,i,0] = 3;
                cube[0,0,i] = 2; cube[9,0,i] = 2;
                cube[0,9,i] = 2; cube[9,9,i] = 2;
            }
            // Now we "project" cube onto projected
            for (int y=9;y>=0;y--)
            {
                for (int x=0;x<10;x++)
                {
                    // Comment out the if line for hidden line removal
                    for (int z=0;z<10;z++)
                        if (cube[x,y,z]!=0)
                            projected[y+z,x+y] = symbols[cube[x,y,z]];
                }
            }
            // Now we display the cube
            for (int i=19;i>=0;i--)
            {
                for (int j=0;j<20;j++)
                    Console.Write(projected[i,j]);
                Console.WriteLine();
            }
        }
    }
}
```

The syntax for declaring jagged arrays is different. A jagged array is an array of 1D arrays (each of which can be of a different length), and this means that you have to declare the jagged array itself plus each of the 1D arrays which makes it up. An example should make it clear:

```
using System;

namespace Wrox.FTrackCSharp.DotNetProg.JaggedArray
{
    class Test
    {
        public static void Main()
        {
            int[][] jagged;                 // A 2D jagged array of ints
                                            //  called jagged.
            jagged = new int[5][];          // 5 rows in this array;

            for (int i=0; i <5; i++)
            {
                jagged[i] = new int[i+1];       // i+1 columns in the i-th row

                for (int j=0; j < i + 1;j++)
                {
                    jagged[i][j] = j;
                }
            }

            for (int i= 0; i<jagged.Length; i++)
            {
                Console.Write("Row {0} : ",i);
                for (int j=0; j<jagged[i].Length; j++)
                    Console.Write(jagged[i][j]);

                Console.WriteLine();
            }
        }
    }
}
```

Notice the difference in the way you access the two types of array. With rectangular arrays all indices are within one set of square brackets, while for jagged arrays each element is within its own square brackets.

Collections

The .NET Framework class library contains two namespaces that define collection classes: System.Collections and System.Collections.Specialized. All the collections in these two namespaces work with object references, so value types will be boxed before they are stored in a collection.

All the collection classes are based on a series of interfaces that are used to define the functionality required by various types of collection. It is quite possible to produce your own collections by implementing these interfaces in your own classes:

Interface	Description
ICollection	Defines size, enumerators and synchronization methods for all interfaces
IComparer	Exposes a method that compares two objects
IDictionary	Represents a collections of key/value pairs
IDictionaryEnumerator	Enumerates the elements in a dictionary
IEnumerable	Exposes an enumerator, which supports simple iteration over the elements in a collection
IEnumerator	Supports simple iteration over a collection
IList	Represents a collection whose elements can be accessed by index.

The major classes in System.Collections are summarized in the following table:

Class	Description	Interfaces Implemented
ArrayList	A dynamically resizable array	ICollection, IList, IEnumerable, ICloneable
BitArray	A compact array of bit values, used to represent flags	ICollection, IEnumerable, ICloneable
Hashtable	A collection of key/value pairs organized by the hash code of the key	ICollection, IDictionary, IEnumerable, ICloneable, ISerializable, IDeserializationCallback
Queue	A first-in, first-out collection	ICollection, IEnumerable, ICloneable
SortedList	Represents a collections of key/value pairs whose elements can also be accessed by index	ICollection, IDictionary, IEnumerable, ICloneable
Stack	A push-down (first in, last out) stack	ICollection, IEnumerable, ICloneable

And the next table summarizes the major classes in System.Collections.Specialized:

Class	Description	Interfaces Implemented
HybridDictionary	Implements IDictionary using a ListDictionary while the collection is small, and the switching to a Hashtable	ICollection, IDictionary, IEnumerable

167

Class	Description	Interfaces Implemented

`ListDictionary`	Implements small collections using a singly linked list	`ICollection,`
		`IDictionary,`
		`IEnumerable`

`NameValueCollection`	A collection of key/value pairs in which both keys and values are strings	`ICollection,` `IEnumerable`
`StringCollection`	A collection of strings	`ICollection, IList,` `IEnumerable`
`StringDictionary`	A hash table with the key strongly typed as a string	`IEnumerable`
`StringEnumerator`	Supports simple enumeration over a `StringCollection`	

One major benefit of these classes is that – unlike Java's collections or the C++ STL library – these are cross-language, and so can be used with any .NET language. It is easy to create a `Hashtable` in C# and pass it to a Visual Basic .NET or Managed C++ function. To give you a feel for how they work, I'll concentrate on two of the most commonly used of these classes: `ArrayList` and `Hashtable`.

The ArrayList Class

An `ArrayList` is a dynamically resizable array; if you look up the entry for `ArrayList` in the online help, you'll see that it implements four interfaces: `ICollection`, `IList`, `IEnumerable` and `ICloneable`. These interfaces provide the key to how the collection classes work, by specifying the common features provided by the various types of collection.

For instance, `IList` is implemented by collections whose elements can be accessed by index, so it will be implemented by array-like collections. It won't be implemented by hash tables or dictionaries, because these aren't accessed by element. `IList` defines methods such as `Add()`, `Clear()`, `Contains()`, `Insert()` and `Remove()` and `IndexOf()`. Classes that implement `IList` also have an `Item` property, which is used to get and set particular items in the collection. C# uses the `Item` property as an indexer, so you can use square brackets to access elements in an `IList`.

The `ICollection` interface is implemented by most collections, and defines three properties and one method:

❑ `Count` returns the number of elements in the collection

❑ `IsSynchronized`, if implemented by a class, returns `true` if access to the collection is thread-safe

❑ `SyncRoot`, if implemented by a class, returns an object that can be used to synchronize access to a collection

❑ The `CopyTo()` method copies the elements of an `ICollection` to an array

`IEnumerable` is implemented by classes that support the ability to enumerate over the collection of elements. Classes that implement `IEnumerable` have a `GetEnumerator()` method that returns a reference to an `IEnumerator` object.

The following program demonstrates how you can create and use an `ArrayList`:

```
using System;
// Needed for the collections
using System.Collections;

namespace Wrox.FTrackCSharp.DotNetProg.ArrayListProgram
{
    class Test
    {
        [STAThread]
        static void Main(string[] args)
        {
            // Create an ArrayList
            ArrayList al = new ArrayList();

            // Add some elements
            al.Add("An element");
            al.Add(3.7);
            al.Add(5);
            al.Add(false);

            // List them
            Console.WriteLine("Count={0}",al.Count);
            for(int i = 0; i < al.Count; i++)
                Console.WriteLine("al[{0}]={1}", i, al[i]);

            // Remove the element at index 1
            al.RemoveAt(1);

            // List them
            Console.WriteLine("Count={0}",al.Count);
            for(int i = 0; i < al.Count; i++)
                Console.WriteLine("al[{0}]={1}", i, al[i]);
        }
    }
}
```

The program starts by creating an empty `ArrayList`, and adding four items to it. The `Add()` method can take any object as an argument, so you can use it to build heterogeneous collections, if you wish. The `Count` property tells you how many items are in the collection, and the indexer lets you refer to the elements by index. All indexing is zero-based, to keep them the same as arrays, so the `RemoveAt(1)` method call removes the second element from the collection.

Note that the indexer, and any other 'get' methods, return a plain object reference. If you need to work with an item once you've retrieved it, you'll have to cast it to the appropriate type.

Enumerators

Iterating over the elements in the collection using a `for` loop and an indexer works very well, but it has the drawback that you have to remember how to iterate over a particular type of collection. `ArrayLists` use indexers, but what about `StringCollection` or `Hashtable`?

Enumerators provide a collection-independent way of iterating over a collection. If a collection implements `IEnumerable`, it will have a `GetEnumerator()` method which will return you an `IEnumerator` reference when called. `IEnumerator` only has three members:

❑ The `MoveNext()` method, which moves the enumerator to the next element, and returns `false` when there are no more

❑ The `Current` property, which returns a reference to the current element

❑ The `Reset()` method, which resets the enumerator back to the start of the collection

Here's how you would use an enumerator with an `ArrayList`:

```
IEnumerator ie = al.GetEnumerator();

while(ie.MoveNext())
    Console.WriteLine(ie.Current);
```

If you know that the collection implements `IEnumerable`, you don't have to remember how to iterate over its members. Note that this iteration only provides read-only access to the elements of the collection.

The Hashtable Class

`Hashtable` is an example of a keyed class, where items are stored and retrieved by key rather than by index. This means that it doesn't implement `IList`, but it does implement `IDictionary`.

As well as the normal `Add()`, `Clear()` and `Remove()` methods, `Hashtable` contains a number of methods that use keys and values, such as `ContainsKey()` (and `Contains()`, which also looks for a key), `ContainsValue()`, `Keys()` (to retrieve the collection of keys), and `Values()` (to retrieve the collection of values).

You can use any class you like for the key, but you may need to override a method in the class so it can be used efficiently as a key. Hash tables use a hash key (or hashcode) to determine where to store the values in its table. Every class inherits the `GetHashCode()` method from `System.Object`, but this generates a very general-purpose hash key. If you want high performance hash tables, you'll need to override `GetHashCode()` and generate your own hash keys. This can be quite a specialized task, and if you need to do it, you may want to consult a book on data structures and algorithms.

The following sample shows how you can create and use a `Hashtable`. Note how the indexer for `Hashtable` takes a key value:

```
using System;
// Needed for the collections
using System.Collections;

namespace HashT
{
    class Class1
    {
        [STAThread]
        static void Main(string[] args)
        {
```

```
        // Create a Hashtable
        Hashtable ht = new Hashtable();

        // Add some items with string keys
        ht.Add("Phone Bill", 250.0);
        ht.Add("Electricity Bill", 200.0);
        ht.Add("Heating Bill", 150.0);
        ht.Add("Internet Access", 50.0);

        // Look for an item by key, and retrieve it
        if (ht.Contains("Phone Bill"))
            Console.WriteLine("Phone bill = {0}", ht["Phone Bill"]);
        else
            Console.WriteLine("No phone bill!");
    }
  }
}
```

Threading

This section is going to examine the support that .NET gives C# programmers who want to write multithreaded code. Threading is a complex subject, and this brief section can only give an outline of what is available. This section assumes that you have a basic knowledge of what writing multithreaded code involves; there isn't space to introduce the basics here.

Application Domains

A traditional Win32 process consists of an address space containing one or more threads and associated resources, as shown in the figure below.

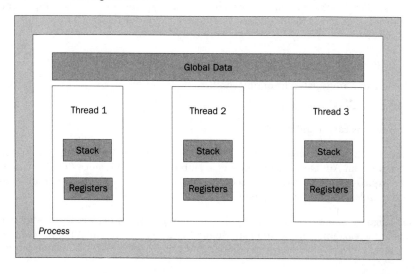

Every thread has its own set of register values and its own stack, which means that each thread's local variables are unique. Every thread has equal access to the process' global data.

.NET application domains, or AppDomains, are "processes within a process". One Win32 process can host any number of application domains, each of which is completely isolated from all others in the process. Communication between AppDomains uses the same remoting mechanisms as communication between processes.

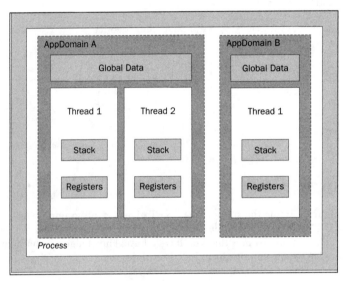

Since AppDomains cannot interact with one another except through remoting mechanisms, different threads within the same process can be completely isolated from one another by creating them in different AppDomains. Code in one AppDomain can communicate with data in another AppDomain, but strict marshaling rules apply. Most types are marshaled by value across boundaries between AppDomains, so that that if a reference is passed between AppDomains, the data representing the object is serialized, sent across the boundary, and deserialized to produce a copy of the object in the second AppDomain.

There are three properties of AppDomains that make them particularly useful:

❑ AppDomains are isolated from one another

❑ AppDomains can have their own security settings

❑ AppDomains can be unloaded

We've already seen how AppDomains within a process are completely isolated, and this isolation makes it possible to unload an AppDomain and all the assemblies it contains, since they have no external dependencies. AppDomains can also have security policies applied to them, so that different parts of a process can run under different security policies.

The common language runtime creates one AppDomain per process by default. If you want to create other AppDomains in the current process, you can use the CreateDomain() method in the System.AppDomain class. The details of creating and using AppDomains is outside the scope of this book.

The System.Threading Namespace

The System.Threading namespace contains classes that enable you to write multithreaded code in C#, and the main members are listed in the following table:

Class	Description
AutoResetEvent	Notifies one or more waiting threads that an event has occurred
Interlocked	Provides atomic operations for variables that are shared by multiple threads
ManualResetEvent	Notifies one or more waiting threads that an event has occurred
Monitor	Provides a mechanism to synchronize access to objects
Mutex	A synchronization primitive that can be used across processes
ReaderWriterLock	A lock that implements single writer/multiple reader semantics
Thread	Creates and controls a thread
ThreadPool	Manages a pool of threads that can be used to perform tasks such as asynchronous I/O or processing timers
ThreadStart	A delegate that represents the method that will handle the Start event of a thread
Timer	Provides a timer
WaitHandle	Encapsulates system-specific objects that wait for exclusive access to shared resources

The Thread Class

The most important class in the table above is Thread, the class that represents an operating system thread. The most significant members of the class are listed in the following table:

Member	Type	Description
IsAlive	Property	Returns true if the thread is still alive
IsBackground	Property	Returns true if the thread is a background thread
Name	Property	Gets or sets the name of the thread
Priority	Property	Gets or sets the current thread priority
ThreadState	Property	Gets or sets the current thread state
Abort()	Method	Terminates the thread
GetDomain()	Static method	Gets the AppDomain in which the current thread is executing

Table continued on following page

Member	Type	Description
Interrupt()	Method	Interrupts a thread that is in the WaitSleepJoin state
Join()	Method	Blocks the thread until another thread terminates
Resume()	Method	Resumes a thread that has been suspended
Sleep()	Static method	Causes a thread to sleep for a period
SpinWait()	Static method	Causes a thread to wait a specified number of times
Start()	Method	Causes the operating system to change the thread state to Running
Suspend()	Method	Suspends the thread if it isn't already suspended

The following example shows the Thread class in use:

```
using System;
using System.Threading;

namespace Wrox.FTrackCSharp.DotNetProg.Threads
{
    class ThreadTest
    {
        private char theChar;
        private int theInterval;

        public ThreadTest(char c, int i)
        {
            theChar = c;
            theInterval = i;
        }

        public void Show()
        {
            Console.Write(theChar);
            for(int i = 0; i < 5; i++)
            {
                Console.Write(theChar+":"+i+":");
                if (theInterval > 0) Thread.Sleep(theInterval);
            }
            Console.Write(theChar);
        }
    }

    class Class1
    {
        [STAThread]
        static void Main (string[] args)
        {
            // Create three ThreadClass objects
            ThreadTest tc1 = new ThreadTest('A', 20);
            ThreadTest tc2 = new ThreadTest('a', 10);
            ThreadTest tc3 = new ThreadTest('-', 50);
```

```
        // Create three threads
        Thread t1 = new Thread(new ThreadStart(tc1.Show));
        Thread t2 = new Thread(new ThreadStart(tc2.Show));
        Thread t3 = new Thread(new ThreadStart(tc3.Show));

        // Start them
        t1.Start();
        t2.Start();
        t3.Start();
    }
  }
}
```

A Thread object represents a single native operating system thread, and it starts running the code in one method on that native thread when it is started. When Thread objects are created, they are passed the method they are to execute using a delegate. Since in C# methods can only exist as part of a class, it is very common to find classes, like ThreadClass in the example, that contain one method that is going to be executed on a thread.

The ThreadTest class has a single method, Show(), which simply prints out our chosen character, theChar, displays the numbers 0 to 5 along with our character, waiting for a period (determined by theInterval) after each display, and then displaying the chosen character again. The function that is going to be executed by the thread cannot take any arguments and has to return void, so if you need to use any variables within this method, you have to pass them in via the constructor.

The Main() function creates three ThreadTest objects with different parameters, then creates three threads and starts them running. By varying the parameters, you can see how the threads are scheduled against one another. When you run the program the precise characters you'll get will depend on the interval you specify when creating the ThreadTest objects.

A Word about Suspend() and Resume()

The Suspend() and Resume() methods let you pause and restart a running Thread, but be very careful how you use these methods. Threads can be suspended and resumed from outside the thread's code by any code that has a reference to the thread object. If the thread is in the process of doing something critical, such as updating a database table, that operation will be suddenly stopped, and you could end up with a half-updated table. By the time the operation resumes, it is possible the table may have been corrupted. Also, a thread may have a lock on some resources, and cannot release the lock if it is suspended from outside; the resources will remain locked until the thread is resumed.

The Thread.Abort() method can be used to forcibly terminate a thread. Before .NET, aborting a thread was not recommended because, like suspending, it could leave resources locked or in a half-updated condition. The Abort() method raises a ThreadAbortException that can be caught by the thread code, so the thread has an opportunity to clear up, and therefore, aborting a thread in .NET is acceptable.

Locking Resources

If resources can be accessed by more than one thread running concurrently, there's a serious danger that the resource could be corrupted, or that the code running on one thread could access a value which is about to be updated, and no longer valid. This could lead to subtle and hard-to-trace bugs that could compromise your application.

In C#, we can prevent other threads accessing a block of code with the `lock` keyword. The `lock` syntax is similar to that for the `using` block:

```
lock (expression)
{
    // Code in critical section
}
```

The expression is the object for which we want to obtain the lock. This must be a reference-type object, and is usually either `this`, to lock a class instance, or the `Type` object of a static member that is to be locked.

Let's have a quick look at the `lock` statement in action. In this example, we use a static `ArrayList` field to store an arbitrary array of integers. We define a static method to add a simple checksum onto the end of this array by adding up the values in it, and finding the modulus of this sum and the number of elements in the array. The method then writes the value of this checksum to the console. Within our `Main()` method, we start off two threads that execute this method asynchronously, so that we can see how locking the `ArrayList` ensures that its data isn't corrupted:

```csharp
using System;
using System.Threading;
using System.Collections;

namespace Wrox.FTrackCSharp.DotNetProgs.Locking
{
    class LockDemo
    {
        // The static ArrayList member that the threads will access
        static ArrayList al;

        static void Main(string[] args)
        {
            // Instantiate the ArrayList and add some values
            al = new ArrayList();
            al.Add(1);
            al.Add(2);
            al.Add(4);
            al.Add(8);
            al.Add(16);

            // Set off two threads concurrently to run a method which
            // accesses our ArrayList
            ThreadStart addCheckSum = new ThreadStart(AddCheckSum);
            Thread t1 = new Thread(addCheckSum);
            Thread t2 = new Thread(addCheckSum);

            t1.Start();
            t2.Start();
        }

        // The AddCheckSum method adds a checksum integer
        // to the end of the ArrayList, based on its current values
        static void AddCheckSum()
```

```
        {
            int checksum = 0;

            // Lock the class so it can't be accessed
            // by both threads at the same time
            lock (typeof(LockDemo))
            {
                foreach(object element in al)
                    checksum += (int)element;

                Thread.Sleep(5);
                al.Add(checksum % al.Count);
            }

            // Display the value of the last element (i.e., the checksum)
            Console.WriteLine(al[al.Count - 1]);
        }
    }
}
```

Notice that we lock the `ArrayList` before we start calculating the checksum, and don't release the lock until after we have added the checksum to the end of the list. This ensures that the list can't be altered by another thread before the list is updated. The call to `Thread.Sleep()` is added simply to simulate further processing, and provide a delay between calculating the checksum and adding it to the array.

When we run the program above, we should see that the checksum is correctly calculated both times (the second time including the new checksum as part of the array):

```
1
2
```

However, if we comment out the line `lock (typeof(LockDemo))`, and then rebuild and rerun the application, we get a different result:

```
1
1
```

This time, the first thread doesn't have time to add the new checksum to the array before the second thread calculates the new checksum, so the second thread calculates exactly the same value as the first, and adds a corrupt value to our `ArrayList`.

Summary

In this chapter We've had an introduction to using .NET features in C#. In particular, we've seen:

❑   How code can be organized using namespaces and the `using` keyword

❑   The uses of reflection and the `Type` class to get run-time information about types and manipulate them

❑   What attributes are, and how they are defined and used

❑   How arrays work in C#, and how the .NET Framework provides useful collection classes and interfaces

❑   How the `System.Threading` namespace and the `Thread` class enables you to write multithreaded code

Working with the .NET Base Class Library

7

This chapter is all about the .NET base class library – the vast number of .NET classes supplied by Microsoft. Since the extent of the .NET base class library is vast, we will be concentrating on some of the most widely-used ones and will demonstrate their ease of use and how effective their implementation is.

The .NET base classes provide the kind of basic functionality that is needed by many applications to perform such things as system, Windows, and file handling tasks. C#, having almost no built-in libraries of its own, uses the .NET base class library instead. So does Visual Basic .NET for that matter, and indeed any .NET-aware language. To a large extent the .NET base classes can be seen as replacing the previous Win32 API and a large number of Microsoft-supplied COM components. The base classes are simpler to use, and you can easily derive from them to provide your own specialist classes. Not only are these libraries easy to use, they are quite simple to understand; a welcome relief for C++ developers!

In this chapter, we will be looking at the base classes for:

- ❑ String handling
- ❑ Handling files
- ❑ Reading and writing to files and streams
- ❑ Reading and writing XML
- ❑ XML Serialization

.NET Class Library Namespaces

Due to the fact that there are literally hundreds of base classes, they are all managed and contained in their respective namespaces. Here are some of the most useful namespaces, some of which we will come across in this chapter, and the chapters that follow:

Namespace	Description of its contents
System	Contains frequently used classes and primitive data types
System.Collections	Contains various types of collection objects; arrays, bit arrays, queues, lists, hash tables and dictionaries.
System.Diagnostics	Classes used in debugging applications
System.IO	File handling and streams
System.Xml	For manipulating and transforming XML
System.Net	Contains classes used for making remote requests, over the Internet or a network
System.Windows.Forms	Windows forms controls
System.Data	Contains classes that constitute most of the ADO.NET architecture
Microsoft.CSharp	Contains classes that support compilation and code generation using C#
Microsoft.Win32	Classes used for Registry access and handling events raised by the operating system

String Handling in C#

We all come across strings one way or the other, sometimes for storing user input or sometimes for manipulating or formatting text. C# offers you a variety of string-handling features, from simple text manipulation to multiple string encoding.

We shall now dip into further details of the design and use of C# strings, but before we carry on with our demonstrations, it should be noted that the C# string keyword is in fact an alias for the System.String class. The System.Text namespace offers us the StringBuilder class for string handling with better performance – we shall look at this class shortly.

The System.String Class

As remarked in Chapter 3, a string in C# is not constructed with the new keyword, you simply use the string literal on the right-hand side of the assignment to construct the string. Before we look at manipulating string objects in C#, we will first look at two important properties of a string in C#:

❑   A string is immutable

❑   A string is interned

A String is Immutable

To understand strings in C# better, let us first look at a simple example console application, which takes a string, casts it to an object, and compares this to another object cast from a modified version of the same string:

```
using System;

namespace Wrox.FTrack.BaseClasses
{
    class SimpleStringCompare
    {
      static void Main(string[] args)
      {
          string strOne = "Strings are immutable";
          object objA = (object)strOne;
          strOne = strOne.Insert(21, " in C#");    /* String Modified */
          object objB = (object)strOne;
          if(objA == objB)
             Console.WriteLine("The two objects are the same");
          else
             Console.WriteLine("The two objects differ from one another");
      }
    }
}
```

The code produces the following output:

The two objects differ from one another

To describe the string data type, we can safely claim that strings represented by the string data type in C# are immutable, which means they cannot be modified once created. Any attempt in modification will result in the creation of a new string. This, of course, is carried out transparently behind the scenes.

If you look at these lines from the above example:

```
object objA = (object)strOne;
strOne = strOne.Insert(21, " in C#");    /* String Modified */
object objB = (object)strOne;
```

181

you can see that logically the two objects we created refer to the same string and so they should, logically, refer to the same location. An attempt to modify the string's contents creates a new string altogether, and thus the condition in the next line from the code:

```
if(objA == objB)
```

is actually `false`, and the output of the program is "The two objects differ from one another".

Of course, if you comment out the line that modifies `strOne`, then "The two objects are the same" will be the output. Since the string wasn't modified, the two objects will point to the same location.

As a new string is created every time a string is modified, it should be noted that if you need to do a lot of string concatenation and manipulation, you should use the `StringBuilder` class, since using the ordinary `string` type for this purpose would result in a substantial performance overhead. We shall move onto the `StringBuilder` class later on.

A String is Interned

In addition to strings being immutable, they are also interned. This means that if two or more string constants hold duplicated data, they all point to just one location, which of course can lead to some unexpected results. Observe the following:

```
string strOne = "Immutable strings are interned";
string strTwo = "Immutable strings are interned";

Console.WriteLine(strOne == strTwo);    // True
Console.WriteLine(strOne.Equals(strTwo)); // True
Console.WriteLine(strOne.CompareTo(strTwo)); /* Prints 0 for True */
Console.WriteLine((object)strOne == (object)strTwo);
        /* True, both refer to the same location */
```

It is the following line that is of most interest:

```
Console.WriteLine((object)strOne == (object)strTwo);
```

We explicitly compare the two objects, and to our surprise, the result that we would have initially expected to be `False`, since the two objects supposedly point to different locations, is in fact `True`.

Manipulating Strings

Working with strings in C# isn't much of a hassle. Manipulating strings in the old days of traditional C/C++ programming used to take quite a bit of work as strings were nothing but an array of characters, and tasks such as copying strings or parsing strings would take up much of a developer's time. We will now look into some code examples to see how easy concatenation, indexing, formatting and encoding strings is in C#:

```
using System;
namespace Wrox.FTrackCSharp.BaseClasses.StringTinkering
{
```

```
class StringModifying
{
   static void Main()
   {
      string text = "I like working";
      text += " in C++";  // Concatenation using the overloaded operator
      text = text.Replace("++", "#");
      Console.WriteLine(text);
   }
}
```

As you can see, two strings were seamlessly concatenated using the overloaded += operator. Similarly, we used the Replace() method which takes two parameters, the first parameter being the string or character you want replaced and the second parameter is the string or character that you want to replace with. In our case, we replaced the "++" from the final string with "#".

In a C# string, characters are accessed with a zero-based index, consistent with all other indexing in the CLR, and we can loop the characters in a string with a foreach loop. The following example illustrates this, and uses the Length property of the string, which returns the total length of the string.

```
using System;
namespace Wrox.FTrackCSharp.BaseClasses.LoopThruString
{
   class LoopThruString
   {
      static void Main()
      {
         string text = "Take the Fast Track to C#";
         for(int i = text.Length - 1; i >= 0; i--)
            Console.Write(text[i]);

         Console.WriteLine("");

         foreach(char c in text)
            Console.Write(c);
      }
   }
}
```

When run from the command prompt, the output will be the following:

```
Command Prompt                                                    _ □ ×
C:\FTrack\BaseClasses>LoopThruString
#C ot kcarT tsaF eht ekaT
Take the Fast Track to C#

C:\FTrack\BaseClasses>_
```

Trimming Strings

The `System.String` class implements methods for trimming strings. This can be necessary when taking input from a user or while parsing a string and you're left with white spaces or blank spaces on either side of the string, or you want certain characters to be removed from the string. For example:

```
char [] cEat = {'s', 'o', 'o', 'n'};

string text = "  This string is going to be eaten sosoonon    ";
strString = text.Trim();         // Trims the white spaces
strString = text.TrimEnd(cEat); // eats characters given in array

Console.WriteLine(text);
```

The final output would be The String is going to be eaten .

Padding Strings

You can right-align your strings or left-align them with white spaces or a custom alignment character, as the code snippet below demonstrates:

```
string text = "Align me";

Console.WriteLine("The length of string before being aligned was {0} and is " +
                  "now {1}", text.Length, text.PadLeft(15, ' ').Length);
```

This would pad the string, with a space character, to the left with a total width of 15 characters – this is the total width of the string plus the padding. The output would be The length of string before being aligned was 8 and is now 15.

The StringBuilder Class: Mutable Strings

In contrast to a string represented by a `string` data type being immutable in C#, the `StringBuilder` class, from the `System.Text` namespace, represents a mutable string. Such a string, created with the new keyword unlike an ordinary string, starts with a predefined size of 16 characters and grows dynamically as more string data is added. This string can grow without bound or to a configurable maximum. The following example illustrates modifying two `StringBuilder` objects.

```
using System;
using System.Text;

namespace Wrox.FTrackCSharp.BaseClasses
{
    class SimpleStringBuilderCompare
    {
        static void Main(string[] args)
        {
            StringBuilder myString = new StringBuilder("This is a mutable string");
            object objA = (object)myString;
            myString.Insert(24, " in C#");  /* Modification */
            object objB = (object)myString;
```

```
        if(objA == objB)
            Console.WriteLine("The two objects are the same");
        else
            Console.WriteLine("The two objects differ from one another");
    }
  }
}
```

This code produces the following output since the `StringBuilder` class permits us to modify the string's contents without creating another instance of it; thus the `StringBuilder` string is mutable:

The two objects are the same

There are further methods within the `StringBuilder` class for dealing with these string-like objects. For example, the `Append()` method, with its variety of overloads, has far superior performance to using ordinary string concatenation, for reasons we have discussed earlier.

The File System with C#

The .NET Framework class library provides a number of classes that you can use for accessing the file system and perform tasks such as creating, copying, deleting, and moving files, and obtaining file information. All of these classes, and more, come from the `System.IO` namespace, which provides you with other useful classes such as the generic `Stream` class for reading and writing (we'll talk about this in a while). Before we go any further, let's look at what classes the `System.IO` namespace has to offer for file and folder management:

Class	Purpose
FileSystemInfo	An abstract class that represents any file system object, such as `FileInfo`, or `DirectoryInfo`.
FileInfo	Represents any file. Provides instance methods for file handling.
File	A class that cannot be instantiated. It provides static file handling methods such as copying or deleting files.
DirectoryInfo	Represents any folder. Provides instance methods for folders.
Directory	A class that cannot be instantiated. It provides static directory handling methods such as listing files or getting information about the directory.
Path	A class that provides static methods for processing directory strings in a cross-platform manner.

Files and Folders

This section will concentrate on using the `FileInfo` and the `DirectoryInfo` classes, but since we've mentioned the `FileSystemInfo`, `File`, and `Directory` classes it would be fair to give you a little insight as to how they go about performing similar tasks and how they differ.

To start with, here's a code snippet that shows `FileSystemInfo` at work, outputting the time at which a certain file and a certain directory were created:

```
FileSystemInfo fileSysInfo = new FileInfo(@"C:\FTrack\BaseClasses\Readme.txt");
Console.WriteLine(fileSysInfo.CreationTime.ToString());

FileSystemInfo dirSysInfo = new DirectoryInfo(@"C:\FTrack\BaseClasses\Temp");
Console.WriteLine(dirSysInfo.CreationTime.ToString());
```

> *It is at this point that we point out the importance of the @ that precedes the string. This symbol, if placed before a string, indicates a string literal in C# so that escape prefixes for the \ character are not needed; usually, the \ symbol in a string indicates the start of an escape sequence. The code could be also be written using \ \ instead of \, which would indicate a single \ in the pathname. Thus "C:\ \FTrack\ \BaseClasses\ \Temp" produces the same string as @"C:\FTrack\BaseClasses\Temp".*

`FileSystemInfo` is an abstract class for any type of file system object, and as such, supports generic operations. Since the `FileInfo` and the `DirectoryInfo` classes are specifically there to represent any file or folder on a file system, we will now turn our attention towards them.

To be able to perform functions on a file, you instantiate a `FileInfo` class by passing the path to the file as a string to its constructor. For example:

```
FileInfo fileOne = new FileInfo(@"C:\FTrack\BaseClasses\ReadMe.txt");
```

It should be noted that if, for instance, the `ReadMe.txt` file does not exist in the pathname mentioned, an exception would not be thrown when the object is created, but only when you try to call a method that would require the file's presence. For this purpose, the `FileInfo` and the `DirectoryInfo` classes implement the `Exists` property, which can be used to check whether the object exists, and if so, whether it is of the appropriate type. For example, a `FileInfo` object pointing to a directory or a `DirectoryInfo` object pointing to a `File` would give a `false` if checked with the `Exists` property.

Here's an example of using a `FileInfo` object, which will create a new `ReadMe.txt` file if one does not currently exist in the `C:\FTrack\BaseClasses` directory.

```
using System;
using System.IO;

namespace Wrox.FTrackCSharp.BaseClasses.FileCreate
{
    class FileCreate
    {
        static void Main(string[] args)
        {
```

```
        try
        {
            FileInfo fileOne = new FileInfo(@"C:\FTrack\BaseClasses\ReadMe.txt");

            if(!fileOne.Exists)
            {
                fileOne.Create();
            }
            else
                throw new Exception("Cannot create! File exists.");
            Console.WriteLine(fileOne.Exists.ToString());
        }
        catch(Exception ex)
        {
            Console.WriteLine("Error: {0}", ex.Message);
        }
    }
}
```

In the code above, we create a `FileInfo` object, pointing it to
`C:\FTrack\BaseClasses\ReadMe.txt`. The `Exists` property of the `FileInfo` object is used to
decide if the file exists. If the value of the property is `false`, we create a new file using the `Create()`
method, and if the property is `true`, we throw an exception complaining that the file already exists.

When run, everything seems to go fine; the code executes, the program quits without a warning or an
error, and better yet, the file `ReadMe.txt` now appears in `C:\FTrack\BaseClasses`. However, the
last line of code gives us `false` as an output. This is because when the object was first created, it
pointed to a file that never existed, but when the `Create()` method was called, a new file was created
but the object's state was not refreshed. In order to make the change take effect in your code, you have
to explicitly call another member function, inherited from the `FileSystemInfo` class, that refreshes
the object's state, namely, the `Refresh()` method. Let us now re write the code and see what happens
(make sure you delete the `ReadMe.txt` file from the directory before running the code again):

```
FileInfo fileOne = new FileInfo(@"C:\FTrack\BaseClasses\ReadMe.txt");
if(!fileOne.Exists)
{
    fileOne.Create();
    fileOne.Refresh();
}
else
    throw new Exception("Cannot create! File exists.");
Console.WriteLine(fileOne.Exists.ToString ());
```

For handling folders, the code isn't very different from what we just saw, apart from the fact that we use
`DirectoryInfo` rather than `FileInfo`. Here's an example:

```
try
{
    DirectoryInfo dirOne = new DirectoryInfo(@"C:\FTrack\BaseClasses\Testing");
```

```
      if(!dirOne.Exists)
      {
         dirOne.Create();
         dirOne.Refresh();
      }
      else
         throw new Exception("Folder already exists.");
      System.Console.WriteLine(dirOne.Exists.ToString());
      }
   catch(Exception ex)
   {
      Console.WriteLine("Error: {0}", ex.Message);
   }
```

The following console application provides us with more information about a particular file or directory; it takes the name of a file or folder as a command-line parameter, and returns some information about this file or folder. This application will use some of the basic and widely-used methods available in the `FileInfo` and the `DirectoryInfo` classes.

The first argument from the command line is taken as the name of the file we wish to examine. Also, it checks to see if our last argument is a "d", which signifies that the name specified is in fact that of a directory. `chosenFile` will be set to `true` if we only wish to examine a file.

```
using System;
using System.IO;

namespace Wrox.FTrackCSharp.BaseClasses.GetFilesInfo
{
   class GetFileInfo
   {
      static void Main(string[] args)
      {
         bool chosenFile = true;
         string fName = "";

         try
         {
            fName = args[0];
            if (args.Length==0)
               throw new Exception("No file specified");
            if (args.Length>1 && args[args.Length - 1]==" d")
            {
               chosenFile = false;
            }
```

The next code segment is the code for examining a file. We check if the file exists with the `Exists` property of the `FileInfo` class after instantiating it, and if `true`, displays the information about the file; if not, a `FileNotFoundException` is thrown. The properties of the file that are of interest to us are highlighted in bold below:

```
if(chosenFile)
{
    FileInfo fileOne = new FileInfo(fName);
    if(fileOne.Exists)
    {
        Console.WriteLine("File exists");
        Console.WriteLine("It was created on: " +
            fileOne.CreationTime.ToString());
        Console.WriteLine("It was last modified on: " +
            fileOne.LastWriteTime.ToLongDateString());
        Console.WriteLine("It was last accessed on: " +
            fileOne.LastAccessTime.ToLongDateString());
        Console.WriteLine("The file length is: " +
            fileOne.Length + " bytes");
    }
    else
        throw new FileNotFoundException();
}
```

Next, we handle the code for examining a directory. Again, we use the `Exists` property (of `DirectoryInfo` this time) to determine if the directory chosen exists. If it does exist, various properties of the directory are displayed, highlighted in bold in the code below, or else a `DirectoryNotFoundException` is thrown.

```
else
{
    DirectoryInfo dirOne = new DirectoryInfo(fName);

    if(dirOne.Exists)
    {
        FileInfo [] listOfFiles = dirOne.GetFiles();
        DirectoryInfo [] subDirs = dirOne.GetDirectories();

        Console.WriteLine("Directory " + dirOne.FullName +
                        " exists with " + subDirs.Length +
                        " subdirectories and " +
                        listOfFiles.Length + " Files.");
    }
    else
        throw new DirectoryNotFoundException();
}
```

Finally, we catch all our exceptions:

```
        catch(FileNotFoundException ex)
        {
            Console.WriteLine("Error : File not found!");
        }
        catch(DirectoryNotFoundException ex)
        {
            Console.WriteLine("Error : Folder not found!");
        }
        catch(Exception ex)
        {
            Console.WriteLine(ex);
        }
    }
  }
}
```

```
Command Prompt                                              _ □ x
C:\FTrack\BaseClasses>GetFilesInfo GetFilesInfo.exe
File exists
It was created on: 3/12/2002 4:43:57 PM
It was last modified on: Tuesday, March 12, 2002
It was last accessed on: Tuesday, March 12, 2002
The file length is: 4608 bytes

C:\FTrack\BaseClasses>
```

It is straightforward to loop through each file in a particular directory, using the `FileInfo` array returned from the `GetFiles()` method of `DirectoryInfo`:

```
DirectoryInfo dirOne = new DirectoryInfo(@"C:\FTrack\BaseClasses");
FileInfo [] listOfFiles = dirOne.GetFiles();

foreach(FileInfo file in listOfFiles)
{
    Console.WriteLine(file.Name);
}
```

Copying, Deleting, and Moving Files and Folders

Files (and directories) can be copied with the `CopyTo()` method of `FileInfo` (and `DirectoryInfo`):

```
FileInfo fileOne = new FileInfo(@"C:\FTrack\BaseClasses\ReadMe.txt");
fileOne.CopyTo(@"C:\FTrack\BaseClasses\Copies\TestCopy.txt", true);
```

This copies the `ReadMe.txt` file in `C:\FTrack\BaseClasses` to another directory, giving the file a new name. The value of `true` for the last parameter in the `CopyTo()` method indicates that the file `C:\FTrack\BaseClasses\Copies\TestCopy.txt` would be overwritten if it existed. The following code has the same effect:

```
File.Copy(@"C:\FTrack\BaseClasses\ReadMe.txt",
          @"C:\FTrack\BaseClasses\Copies\TestCopy.txt", true);
```

You can see how easy copying a file from one location to another was with the help of the `File` class. If your application only needs to perform simple operations on a file and does not need an object to represent it, you can use the `File` class with its static methods. Other methods in the `File` class include creating a new file, opening a file for reading or writing, deleting a file, copying a file, and so on. Similarly, you can use the `Directory` class to do the same with folders in a file system.

For deleting files, the `File` and the `FileInfo` classes both have a `Delete()` method. Here it is:

```
FileInfo fileOne = new FileInfo(
                    @"C:\FTrack\BaseClasses\DeleteMe\TestCopy.txt");
fileOne.Delete();
```

Or:

```
File.Delete(@"C:\FTrack\BaseClasses\DeleteMe\TestCopy.txt ");
```

The `Directory` and `DirectoryInfo` classes also both have a `Delete()` method. However, these `Delete()` methods are different from those of the `File` and `FileInfo` classes. The `Delete()` method of the `Directory` class has two overloads, one that takes in only the path and deletes the directory permanently, throwing an `IOException` if the directory is not empty or read-only, and another overload with two parameters, the first being the path to the directory and the second is a Boolean; a value of `true` indicates recursive deletion, meaning that all subdirectories of the directory will be deleted as well. If a directory has further subdirectories and you call the `Delete()` method with a `false` Boolean parameter, an `IOException` will be raised.

```
DirectoryInfo directoryInfo = new DirectoryInfo(
                    @"C:\FTrack\BaseClasses\DeleteMe");
directoryInfo.Delete();
```

Or, to delete recursively:

```
DirectoryInfo directoryInfo = new DirectoryInfo(
                    @"C:\FTrack\BaseClasses\DeleteMe");
directoryInfo.Delete(true);          // Delete recursively
```

Or simply:

```
// Delete recursively
Directory.Delete(@"C:\FTrack\BaseClasses\DeleteMe", true);
```

And now we look at our final example for this section – moving files and folders. In the code below, we first create a `FileInfo` object and point it to the file `C:\FTrack\BaseClasses\ReadMe.txt`. We then use the `MoveTo()` method to move the file to `C:\FTrack\BaseClasses\Moved` with a new name. The last line of code moves the file back to its original name and location using the static `Move()` method of the `File` class.

```
FileInfo fileOne = new FileInfo(@"C:\FTrack\BaseClasses\ReadMe.txt");
fileOne.MoveTo(@"C:\FTrack\BaseClasses\Moved\Test.txt");
fileOne.Refresh();    // Important that you update the state
```

```
File.Move(@"C:\FTrack\BaseClasses\Moved\Test.txt",
         @"C:\FTrack\BaseClasses\ReadMe.txt");
```

To move directories, we do something similar:

```
DirectoryInfo dirOne = new DirectoryInfo(@"C:\FTrack\BaseClasses\MoveMe");
dirOne.MoveTo(@"C:\FTrack\BaseClasses\NewLocation");
```

Note that if we tried to move the directory to another disk volume or to a directory that already existed, an exception would be raised.

Reading, Writing, and Streams

For reading and writing to files, the generic `Stream` class of the `System.IO` namespace can assist you with all that you need to do; whether it's reading data from a text file, a binary file, another variable or even the Internet. Since the `Stream` class is generic and does not assume any particular data source, it means that you can inherit from it to create a class for dealing with a particular data source.

As far as reading and writing to files is concerned, here are some of the many classes in the `System.IO` namespace at our disposal:

Class	Used For
FileStream	Reading and writing binary data from and to files
StreamReader	Reading text files
StreamWriter	Writing text files

Let us now proceed to discuss each of these classes and their use.

Binary Files

We will use the `FileStream` class to demonstrate how you can go about reading or writing binary data from or to a binary file, or any other file. First let's see how the `FileStream` class works.

The `FileStream` constructor has many overloads, but we are interested only in three of them: the first takes four parameters, the second takes three and the last one takes two. Basically, when creating or writing or reading to a file, we can control three key properties of it, namely:

❑ FileMode – Sets the mode of the file, for example, `Create`, `Append`, `Open`, or `Truncate`

❑ FileAccess – Indicates whether you want to read the file, write to it, or do both

❑ FileShare – Allows other streams to simultaneously access the file or not, and if so, in what mode: `Read`, `ReadWrite` or `Write`

Let us now see an example of the three constructors at work:

```
FileStream fStream = new FileStream(@"C:\FTrack\BaseClasses\ReadMe.txt",
                                    FileMode.Open);
```

Or:

```
FileStream fStream = new FileStream(@"C:\FTrack\BaseClasses\ReadMe.txt",
                                    FileMode.Create, FileAccess.ReadWrite);
```

Or:

```
FileStream fStream = new FileStream(@"C:\FTrack\BaseClasses\ReadMe.txt",
                                    FileMode.Append, FileAccess.Read,
                                    FileShare.Write);
```

Writing to a Binary File

Our first example will be writing to a binary file; we can use the `FileStream` class since it implements methods for writing to files. The following demonstrates writing a set of characters to a file named `Testing.dat`, but uses a fiendishly clever scheme to encrypt the vital, top-secret message:

```
using System;
using System.IO;

namespace Wrox.FTrackCSharp.BaseClasses.BinaryDataWriting
{
    class BinaryDataWriter
    {
        static void Main(string[] args)
        {
            string message="This is a secret message.";

            FileStream fStream = new FileStream(
                                    @"C:\FTrack\BaseClasses\Testing.dat",
                                    FileMode.Create, FileAccess.Write);

            for(int i=0; i < message.Length; i++)
            {
                int c = message[i] + 15;
                if (c > 255) c -= 255;

                fStream.WriteByte((byte)c);
            }
            fStream.Close();
        }
    }
}
```

We begin by defining a string and initializing it with our message "This is a secret message.". Next, we instantiate a `FileStream` object and make it point to a file named `Testing.dat`, and indicate that this file should be created with write access with `FileAccess.Write`. The `for` loop runs through the string, and after "adjusting" each character in the string, we call the `WriteByte()` method of the `FileStream` object and pass it a single byte that we explicitly convert from the single character we have just "adjusted".

Finally, the stream is automatically flushed and then closed with the `Close()` method of `FileStream`.

In Notepad, this is the result of our writing:

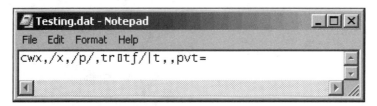

Reading From a Binary File

We can obtain a `FileStream` instance from the `FileInfo` class and use that for our purpose of reading binary data. Here, we shall decode the message that we have just encoded:

```
using System;
using System.IO;
namespace Wrox.FTrackCSharp.BaseClasses.BinaryDataReading
{
    class BinaryDataReader
    {
        static void Main(string[] args)
        {
            FileStream fStream = new FileStream(
                                    @"c:\FTrack\BaseClasses\Testing.dat",
                                    FileMode.Open, FileAccess.Read);
            int iData;
            do
            {
                iData = fStream.ReadByte();
                if(iData != -1)
                {
                    iData -= 15;
                    if (iData<0) iData += 255;
                    Console.Write((char)iData);
                }
            }
            while(iData != -1);
            fStream.Close();
        }
    }
}
```

We first obtained an instance of the `FileStream` class by creating a new `FileInfo` object and calling the `OpenRead()` method that prepares the file to be read. We have two available methods for reading data from the file: the `Read()` method, which reads an array of bytes, and the `ReadByte()` method, which reads one byte at a time. In the code, we check if the `ReadByte()` call returned −1, which indicates end of file, and if it's not −1, we suitably "adjust" the value and then display it on the console. Again, we call the `Close()` method to automatically flush the stream and then close it.

Unsurprisingly, the output of this code is:

```
This is a secret message.
```

Note that there is in fact a `CryptoStream` class in the `System.Security.Cryptography` namespace that is derived from `Stream`, and provides genuine, robust security for `Stream` communication.

Text Files

So far we've been working with binary files and the `FileStream` class. This section (and the next) will introduce you to these two classes:

❏   `StreamReader` for reading text files

❏   `StreamWriter` for writing text files

These classes are specially designed to read and write to text files, and offer a number of methods that you can use in your applications.

Writing to a Text File

The `StreamWriter` class is specifically to assist you in writing text files. This class implements a `Write()` method and a `WriteLine()` method, similar to that of the `Console` class. Both of these methods in the `StreamWriter` class have a number of overloads, and so they can accept anything from an `object` to a string or several other data types. Thus, the flexibility of this class allows us to write almost anything to the text file with ease:

```csharp
using System;
using System.IO;

namespace Wrox.FTrackCSharp.BaseClasses.WritingTextExample
{
    class TextWritingExample
    {
        static void Main(string[] args)
        {
            StreamWriter sWriter = new StreamWriter(
                            @"C:\FTrack\BaseClasses\TextTesting.txt");
            sWriter.WriteLine("StreamWriter turned out to be " +
                                            "such a useful class!");
            sWriter.WriteLine("Let's see if it allows the following to " +
                                            "be written in the file:");
            sWriter.WriteLine(99.5 + @"%");
            sWriter.WriteLine("It's " + true + " that learning C# is " +
                                            "a piece of cake");
            sWriter.Close();
        }
    }
}
```

Our code starts by instantiating the `StreamWriter` class and writing to a file named `TextTesting.txt` in `C:\FTrack\BaseClasses`. We used the `WriteLine()` method of the class and passed strings, `float` values and a Boolean – a mixture of types. This simply shows you how flexible these methods are, and how easy it is to manipulate an object of any type as long as it has a `ToString()` method, since this is implicitly the method called behind the scenes. Consider the following line of code:

```
sWriter.WriteLine("It's " + true + " that learning C# is " +
                                            "a piece of cake");
```

The `true` Boolean type used here calls the `ToString()` method to implicitly return a string that will be concatenated with the rest, effortlessly.

Reading from a Text File

To look at the `StreamReader` class, here is an example that will display the output written to the `TextTesting.txt` file in the previous example:

```
using System;
using System.IO;

namespace Wrox.FTrackCSharp.BaseClasses.ReadingTextExample
{
    class TextReadingExample
    {
        static void Main(string[] args)
        {
            string data;
            StreamReader sStream = new StreamReader(
                            @"C:\FTrack\BaseClasses\TextTesting.txt");
            do
            {
                data = sStream.ReadLine();
                Console.WriteLine(data);
            }
            while(data != null);
            sStream.Close();
        }
    }
}
```

This application instantiates the `StreamReader` class, opens the `TextTesting.txt` file (from our last section), and reads one line at a time until it bumps into a `null` value, since a `null` value signals the end of the file. Finally, we close the stream by calling the `Close()` method. Another way of reading the file could be reading it character by character with the `Read()` method, or reading a block of characters with the `ReadBlock()` method.

The output of our code is:

```
Command Prompt                                                    _ □ ×
C:\FTrack\BaseClasses>TextWriterExample

C:\FTrack\BaseClasses>TextReaderExample
StreamWriter turned out to be such a useful class!
Let's see if it allows the following to be written in the file:
99.5%
It's True that learning C# is a piece of cake

C:\FTrack\BaseClasses>
```

Using XML in C#

XML has been around for quite a while now, and since XML provides such a elegant way to describe information or to store data in a well organized manner that permits easy exchange of this data, the .NET Framework has the System.Xml namespace dedicated to XML.

This section is not going to tell you about XML standards or details of what XML is capable of, instead we will acquaint you with a number of the .NET classes you can use for:

❑   Reading XML documents

❑   Writing XML documents

❑   XML Serialization

Here is a list of some of the classes from the System.Xml and System.Xml.Serialization namespaces that we shall learn about in the following sections:

Classes	Description
XmlTextWriter	Implements the abstract XmlWriter class. Provides a forward-only cursor for writing to a stream.
XmlTextReader	Implements the abstract XmlReader class. Provides a fast, non-cached, forward-only cursor for reading XML data from a stream.
XmlSerializer	In the System.Xml.Serialization namespace; used for serializing objects. Provides methods for both serializing and deserializing data.

In the following sections, we will be using the XmlTextWriter and the XmlTextReader classes for writing and reading to XML documents, respectively. It should be noted that the XmlTextReader class provides a fast, non-cached, forward-only cursor and does not support methods for manipulating documents. For that purpose, there are other classes in the System.Xml namespace that you can explore such as the XmlValidatingReader class, for validation, or the XmlDocument class for further manipulation, storage or retrieval of XML data.

Writing to an XML File

The `XmlTextWriter` class provides you with methods for writing XML to a stream. You can not only write data to a file but also choose how to write it by using its configurable features such as changing indentation, formatting, or even the indent character itself.

Before we show you how to work with an `XmlTextWriter` class, let's assume that we want the following XML produced by our code:

```xml
<?xml version="1.0" encoding="us-ascii"?>
<profile company="Wrox Press">
    <employee>
        <name>Julian Skinner</name>
        <age>21</age>
        <job>
            <title>Commissioning Editor</title>
        </job>
    </employee>
</profile>
```

Now that we have the output before us, let's see how we'd accomplish this with code.

```csharp
using System;
using System.Text;
using System.Xml;

namespace Wrox.FTrackCSharp.BaseClasses.WriteXml
{
    class XmlTextWriting
    {
        static void Main(string[] args)
        {
            //
            // TODO: Add code to start application here
            //
            XmlTextWriter xmlWr = new XmlTextWriter(
                        @"C:\FTrack\BaseClasses\profiles.xml", Encoding.ASCII);

            xmlWr.Formatting = Formatting.Indented;

            xmlWr.WriteStartDocument();
            xmlWr.WriteStartElement("profile");
            xmlWr.WriteAttributeString("company", "Wrox Press");
            xmlWr.WriteStartElement("employee");
            xmlWr.WriteElementString("name", "Julian Skinner");
            xmlWr.WriteElementString("age", "21");
            xmlWr.WriteStartElement("job");
            xmlWr.WriteElementString("title", "Commissioning Editor");
            xmlWr.WriteEndElement();
            xmlWr.WriteEndElement();
            xmlWr.WriteEndElement();
            xmlWr.WriteEndDocument();
```

```
        xmlWr.Flush();
        xmlWr.Close();
    }
  }
}
```

In the code, our first call was to the `XmlTextWriter` constructor with two parameters, the file name and the encoding type, which we set to ASCII through `Encoding.ASCII`. Note the `Encoding` class is in the `System.Text` namespace. Next, we asked the `XmlTextWriter` object to indent the output for us since there is no default indentation and the output will clutter up if you don't explicitly do so. It is the next few lines that attract our attention:

```
xmlWr.WriteStartDocument();
```

This line writes the header, or the start of the XML document, which in our case is:

```
<?xml version="1.0" encoding="us-ascii"?>
```

Then we have:

```
xmlWr.WriteStartElement("profile");
xmlWr.WriteAttributeString("company", "Wrox Press");
```

This produces the second line: a starting tag named `profile` with an attribute named `company`, which further has `Wrox Press` as a value. Note that you can have as many attributes as you want by repeating the `WriteAttributeString()` method with the different parameters. We continue to output the elements with the `WriteElementString()` method:

```
xmlWr.WriteElementString("name", "Julian Skinner");
xmlWr.WriteElementString("age", "21");
```

Next, we start another element named `job`. Note that the `WriteElementString()` method has created another element, inside the first.

```
xmlWr.WriteStartElement("job");
xmlWr.WriteElementString("title", "Commissioning Editor");
```

You end an element tag with the `WriteEndElement()` method, and so we end all our element tags, and the document:

```
xmlWr.WriteEndElement();
xmlWr.WriteEndElement();
xmlWr.WriteEndElement();
xmlWr.WriteEndDocument();
```

Finally, we flush the stream and close it.

```
xmlWr.Flush();
xmlWr.Close();
```

Reading an XML File

Just as there is a class for writing XML to a stream, so there's the XmlTextReader class for reading XML. Since we've already created a file with XML data in it, we'll now see how to read and output this data.

When our application, XmlTextReaderExample, starts, it loads the XML file that we created earlier into an XmlTextReader object, loops through the file and simply outputs the appropriate data.

```
using System;
using System.Xml;

namespace Wrox.FTrackCSharp.BaseClasses.ReadXml
{
    class XmlTextReading
    {
        static void Main(string[] args)
        {
            XmlTextReader xmlRd = new
                        XmlTextReader(@"C:\FTrack\BaseClasses\profiles.xml");

            string nodeText;
            string txt = null
            string output = null;

            while(xmlRd.Read())
            {
                if(xmlRd.NodeType == XmlNodeType.Element)
                {
                    nodeText = xmlRd.Name;
                    txt = null;
                    output = nodeText;
                    switch(nodeText)
                    {
                        case "profile":
                            xmlRd.MoveToAttribute("company");
                            output = xmlRd.Name;
                            txt = xmlRd.Value;
                        break;
                        case "name":
                            txt = xmlRd.ReadString();
                        break;
                        case "age":
                            txt= xmlRd.ReadString();
                        break;
                        case "title":
                            txt = xmlRd.ReadString();
                        break;
```

```
                }
            if (txt!=null) Console.WriteLine(output + " : " + txt);
                }
            }
        }
    }
}
```

The key line is the following:

```
if (xmlRd.NodeType == XmlNodeType.Element)
```

This line checks if the NodeType of what is read from the file is a XmlNodeType.Element, and if so, it allows the code to go further and read the Name property of the node and then read the appropriate information.

For dealing with the company attribute of the profile tag, we use the MoveToAttribute() method. The line:

```
xmlRd.MoveToAttribute("company");
```

moves us to the company attribute of the current element, from where we can access the value of the attribute, Wrox Press, and also the name of the attribute. XmlTextReader also has a GetAttribute() method that simply returns the value of a particular attribute.

To read the string between the other tags, we use the ReadString() method.

Here's the output of our XML reader:

```
Command Prompt
C:\FTrack\BaseClasses>XmlTextReaderExample
company : Wrox Press
name : Julian Skinner
age : 21
title : Commissioning Editor

C:\FTrack\BaseClasses>
```

ADO.NET, the data access technology of the .NET Framework is heavily based on XML, and we will see more about the interplay between ADO.NET and XML in Chapter 10.

XML Serialization

Serialization is a process for saving the state of an object in a form suitable for transporting over a stream, which could be a file or a network. Correspondingly, deserialization is the process of storing or loading an object from a stream.

The XmlSerializer class in the System.Xml.Serialization namespace allows you to serialize public fields, and public properties of an class that support get and set operations, into XML.

Let's look an example to see how XML serialization and deserialization works with C#. We begin with the namespaces:

```
using System;
using System.Xml.Serialization;
using System.IO;
```

Next, we have the object that is to be serialized, a Product class. Note the presence of a private field:

```
public class Product
{
    string strName = "";
    long lPrice = 0;
    private int privateValue = 0;

    public void SetPrivateValue(int value)
    {
        privateValue = value;
    }
    public int GetPrivateValue()
    {
        return privateValue;
    }
    public string Name
    {
        get { return strName; }
        set { strName = value; }
    }

    public long Price
    {
        get{ return lPrice; }
        set{ lPrice = value; }
    }

    public Product()
    {
    }
}
```

Now we move onto the code that will actually serialize and then deserialize a Product object. We begin by creating a Product object named Car, and initializing its values:

```
class XmlSerializing
{
    static void Main(string[] args)
    {
        Product Car = new Product();
        Car.Name = "Mercedez Benz";
        Car.Price = 56400;
        Car.SetPrivateValue(18);
```

We open a stream to write to the file `Serialized.xml`:

```
// Open a stream and write to file
StreamWriter sWriter = new
            StreamWriter(@"C:\FTrack\BaseClasses\Serialized.xml");
```

Next, we create an `XmlSerializer` object and serialize the `Car` object by passing the `StreamWriter` object and the `Car` object to the `Serialize()` method, and then close the stream.

```
XmlSerializer xmlSer = new XmlSerializer(Car.GetType());

xmlSer.Serialize(sWriter, Car);
sWriter.Close();
```

Now we deserialize, creating a new object of type `Product` from the information contained in `Serialized.xml`.

```
Product newCar = new Product();

// Open the file for reading
FileStream fStream = new FileStream(
                @"C:\FTrack\BaseClasses\Serialized.xml",
                FileMode.Open, FileAccess.Read);
// Create a new XmlSerializer of the new object type
XmlSerializer newXmlSer = new XmlSerializer(newCar.GetType());

// Deserialize and display on console
newCar = (Product) newXmlSer.Deserialize(fStream);
Console.WriteLine("Product name: " + newCar.Name);
Console.WriteLine("Product price: " + newCar.Price);
Console.WriteLine("A Private Value: " + newCar.GetPrivateValue());

fStream.Close();
Console.Read();
    }
}
```

Observe that the private value is 0, even though the `Car` object originally had a value of 18, since this field was not serialized:

This application performed the serialization and deserialization of the object that we defined by a class named `Product`. The code performed these steps for XML serialization:

- ❑ Create an object of type `Product`
- ❑ Initialize the `Name` and the `Price` properties of the object
- ❑ Open a stream for the object to be serialized to
- ❑ Create a `XmlSerializer` of the object type
- ❑ Call the `Serialize()` method and pass it the stream along with the object we wanted to serialize
- ❑ Close the `Stream`

Below are the contents of the `Serialized.xml` file that we serialized our object to:

```
<?xml version="1.0" encoding="utf-8"?>
<Product xmlns:xsi="http://www.w3.org/2001/XMLSchema-instance"
         xmlns:xsd="http://www.w3.org/2001/XMLSchema">
  <Name>Mercedez Benz</Name>
  <Price>56400</Price>
</Product>
```

The steps taken for deserialization were:

- ❑ Create a new object of type `Product`
- ❑ Open a stream for reading the file
- ❑ Create a new `XmlSerializer` of the new object type
- ❑ Call the `Deserialize()` method, pass it the stream and explicitly cast the deserialized object to the `Product` type and store it in the object
- ❑ Display the properties on the console

This ends our discussion of XML serialization. Notice how convenient it is to store your information in a serialized form, and then deserialize it anytime you need to reconstruct your object. With this new tool, you can easily extend the power of your applications and even use this technique in writing configuration files or documenting your code.

To serialize a class's private data members, the .NET Framework makes it possible to employ serialization formatter objects from within the
`System.Runtime.Serialization.Formatters.Binary` or
`System.Runtime.Serialization.Formatters.Soap` namespaces for serializing into binary format or SOAP format. We shall see XML serialization again in Chapter 13, in the context of Web Services.

An HTML Content Describer

Now that we've learned quite a bit about string manipulation, file operations, and reading/writing XML documents, it is time we incorporated this knowledge into a more complete application. Our application takes the name of a folder as a command-line parameter, looks through each HTML file in that folder for its `<title>` tag using `StreamReader`, and when found, it extracts the contents of the tag and populates an XML document with this information, using `XmlTextWriter`. Finally, we include a simple XML stylesheet, to view the XML file in a more helpful manner. Let's get to work:

```csharp
using System;
using System.Text;
using System.IO;
using System.Xml;

namespace Wrox.FTrackCSharp.BaseClasses.HtmlContentDescriber
{
    class DescribeHtmlContent
    {
        [STAThread]
        static void Main(string[] args)
        {
            try
            {
                string temp;
                bool htmlFile = false;

                StreamReader sStream;

                XmlTextWriter xmlWr = new XmlTextWriter(
                        @"C:\FTrack\BaseClasses\HtmlContents.xml", Encoding.ASCII);
                xmlWr.Formatting = Formatting.Indented;
                xmlWr.WriteStartDocument();
                xmlWr.WriteRaw(
                    "\n<?xml:stylesheet type=\"text/xsl\" href=\"StyleSheet.xsl\"?>");
                xmlWr.WriteStartElement("describer");

                DirectoryInfo dirOne = new DirectoryInfo(args[0]);

                FileInfo [] listOfFiles = dirOne.GetFiles();

                foreach(FileInfo file in listOfFiles)
                {
                    if(file.Extension.ToLower().Equals(".html") ||
                        file.Extension.ToLower().Equals(".htm"))
                    {
                        htmlFile = true;

                        sStream = new StreamReader(file.FullName);

                        do
                        {
                            temp = sStream.ReadLine();
                            if(temp != null &&
                                temp.ToLower().IndexOf("<title>") != -1)
                            {

                                int a = temp.ToLower().IndexOf("<title>") + 7;
                                int b = temp.ToLower().IndexOf("</title>");
```

```
        temp = temp.Substring(a, b - a);

                        xmlWr.WriteStartElement("file");
                        xmlWr.WriteElementString("name", file.Name);
                        xmlWr.WriteElementString("description", temp);
                        xmlWr.WriteElementString("path", file.DirectoryName);
                        xmlWr.WriteEndElement();
                        xmlWr.Flush();
                    }
                }
                while(temp != null);

                sStream.Close();

                Console.WriteLine("Reading contents from file:
                        {0}", file.FullName);
            }
        }

        if(!htmlFile)
            Console.WriteLine("No HTML file found in the directory!");
        else
        {
            xmlWr.WriteEndElement();
            xmlWr.WriteEndDocument();

            xmlWr.Flush();
            xmlWr.Close();
        }
    }
    catch(Exception ex)
    {
        Console.WriteLine("Error: {0}", ex.Message);
    }
    }
    }
}
```

The first command-line argument the program receives is a valid path to a folder containing HTML files. It should be kept in mind that the comparison between strings with the Equals() method is case-sensitive and so throughout this example, we have used the ToLower() method to be sure we don't miss a file if its extension is .HTML rather than .html, for example.

```
XmlTextWriter xmlWr=new XmlTextWriter(@"C:\FTrack\BaseClasses\HtmlContents.xml",
                        Encoding.ASCII);
xmlWr.Formatting = Formatting.Indented;

xmlWr.WriteStartDocument();
xmlWr.WriteRaw("\n<?xml:stylesheet type=\"text/xsl\" href=\"StyleSheet.xsl\"?>");
```

The code above creates a new XML file named HtmlContents.xml, but note the addition of the WriteRaw() method immediately following the WriteStartDocument() method. This method is used to manually insert raw markup in XML documents, and in this case, we have added a line of our own as a processing instruction to the XML file, indicating that a stylesheet, StyleSheet.xsl, is to be used. This stylesheet will be used later when displaying the data we collect. Note the use of \ in the string as an escape sequence to ignore quotation marks.

Our next task is to create a `StreamReader` object for reading in the HTML files, then loop through the array of `FileInfo` objects returned from the `GetFiles()` method of `DirectoryInfo`. As we loop through, we check the extension of the files to see if they are HTML files, and if so, we begin to extract the title from this document:

```
temp = sStream.ReadLine();
if(temp != null && temp.ToLower().IndexOf("<title>") != -1)
{
    int a = temp.ToLower().IndexOf("<title>") + 7;
    int b = temp.ToLower().IndexOf("</title>");
    temp = temp.Substring(a, b - a);
```

The portion of code shown above searches through the file line by line for a `<title>` tag. When it is found, the position of `<title>` and `</title>` within the string is found using the `IndexOf()` method (once again making use of `ToLower()`), and the text between the two tags is extracted with the `Substring()` method. This string now holds the actual contents of the `<title>` tag and thus can be used as a short description of the file.

Next, we pay a visit to our `XmlTextWriter` object, and start creating nodes in the XML document. The following lines of code do the main work:

```
xmlWr.WriteStartElement("file");
xmlWr.WriteElementString("name", file.Name);
xmlWr.WriteElementString("description", temp);
xmlWr.WriteElementString("path", file.DirectoryName);
xmlWr.WriteEndElement();
xmlWr.Flush(); /* Must call to flush data to file */
```

Here is the XSL template that will be used to format `HtmlContent.xml`. The file is named `StyleSheet.xsl` and should be present in the same folder where the XML file resides, which in this case would be the `C:\FTrack\BaseClasses` folder:

```
<?xml version='1.0'?>
<xsl:stylesheet xmlns:xsl="http://www.w3.org/1999/XSL/Transform" version="1.0">
  <xsl:template match="/">
    <html>
      <body>
        <table border="1" width="100%">
          <tr bgcolor="#C0C0C0">
            <td>Name of File</TD>
            <td>Description</TD>
            <td>Directory Path</TD>
          </tr>
          <xsl:for-each select="describer/file">
            <tr>
              <td><xsl:value-of select="name"/></TD>
              <td><xsl:value-of select="description"/></TD>
              <td><xsl:value-of select="path"/></TD>
            </tr>
```

```
      </xsl:for-each>
    </table>
  </body>
  </html>
  </xsl:template>
</xsl:stylesheet>
```

Since a stylesheet is an XML file itself, it begins with the standard XML declaration along with a `<xsl:stylesheet>` element, indicating that this document is a stylesheet and providing a location for declaring the XSLT namespace. We set the `xsl:template` element's `match` attribute to `"/"` to indicate that this template corresponds to the root (`/`) of the XML source document.

We will not dwell on any of the details of this stylesheet, except to say that the `<xsl:for-each>` element loops through a set of elements in the XML data, and finally, the `<xsl:value-of>` element selects a specific child and then inserts the text content of that child into the template, and the `select` attribute finds the relevant set of elements in the source document.

Now we can view the data in the XML document in a suitable form from a browser. Below is a screenshot of `HtmlContents.xml` displaying the output from one of the subdirectories of `WINNT\Help`:

We will see XSLT again in Chapter 10. Of course, the methods used here to extract the title of the HTML document are rather crude; the `System.Text.RegularExpression` namespace contains classes for using regular expressions that will provide far more powerful string checking.

Summary

In this chapter, we have taken a quick tour of some of the classes in the .NET Framework class library. We looked at these topics, which are concerned with strings:

- ❑ Strings in C# are immutable and interned
- ❑ Methods for manipulating strings in C#
- ❑ The `StringBuilder` class in the `System.Text` namespace

In the `System.IO` namespace, we saw:

- ❑ The `FileSystemInfo`, `FileInfo`, and `DirectoryInfo` classes for handling files and directories
- ❑ The `FileStream` class for reading from and writing to binary files
- ❑ The `StreamReader` and `StreamWriter` classes for reading from and writing to text files

In the `System.Xml` namespace, we saw:

- ❑ The `XmlTextReader` and `XmlTextWriter` classes for reading and writing XML documents

In the `System.Xml.Serialization` namespace, we saw:

- ❑ The `XmlSerializer` class for XML serialization

We finished off our tour by combining elements from the earlier sections to produce an application for describing the content of static HTML files.

Take the

Fast Track

to

C#

8

Building Windows Applications

Despite the increasing importance of browser-based applications able to run on your system without installation there is still an important role for a Windows application to perform. An application installed onto your system can offer more control over your system and exploit more local processing power if needed. The user can also have a much richer environment to work in than the client area of a browser window.

The .NET Framework brings with it the System.Windows.Forms namespace which exposes several classes such as Form, Menu and Application that offer an object-oriented view of some of the basic elements your application may use. Treating your forms in an object-oriented way promotes code that is easier to read and maintain. For example, you can deal with interaction with a form by processing events that the form will raise or overriding methods within your form such as OnPaint(). Both methods are a lot easier to maintain than a lengthy switch statement to process messages as they are received.

You can create Windows Applications with any text editor and the C# command-line compiler, but Visual Studio .NET makes it much easier by allowing you to draw up your forms graphically and generating the code necessary to build your forms. Although your application can use resource files, these are not used to create forms and place controls within those forms as they were with the MFC. Everything about your form is defined within your source code, but it is not hidden from view, as was the case with the Visual Basic Forms Designer.

With Visual Studio.NET we also get a comprehensive installer for our applications so that they can be packaged up into a single installable file for easy installation. Customizable dialogs and easy access to the target file system and registry remove the need for you to create your own installation program or look to other vendors for most deployment options.

In this chapter we will look at:

- ❑ Windows forms
- ❑ Windows controls
- ❑ Event handlers
- ❑ Creating a simple Windows application
- ❑ Deploying an application

Windows Forms

Windows forms give you a simple yet powerful way to create a user interface for your Windows applications. Windows forms share some similarities with both the Windows Foundation Classes used in C++ and the drag and drop methodology of Visual Basic. We can determine the appearance and characteristics of a form by setting properties such as MaximizeBox, MinimizeBox and Size, but we also have the power to override methods and process events to give us control over the functionality of the form.

To create a form you simply have to create a class that is derived from System.Windows.Forms.Form. This base class contains all the functionality you need to create and display a form on the screen. Like all other applications you need a Main() method which is the entry point where execution will start and finish – there is no WinMain() method as may be familiar to Visual C++ developers. So, to display a form we could write the following:

```
using System;
using System.Windows.Forms;

public class BasicForm : Form
{
    public static void Main()
    {
        BasicForm myForm = new BasicForm();
        Application.Run(myForm);
    }
}
```

To compile this code from the commandline, you execute the following; no further reference to the System.Windows.Forms.dll assembly is required:

```
csc BasicForm.cs
```

The code here is mostly self-explanatory; we create a class called BasicForm, derived from Form. The Main() method creates a new instance of our class and calls the static member Run() from the Application class which acts as a message loop for our form. The Windows operating system sends messages to a Windows form within the .NET runtime exactly as it would to a form that is not run within the .NET runtime, notifying it of any interactions with the form. A Windows form under .NET has the functionality to deal with these messages and raise events that we can deal with accordingly. We will take a closer look at dealing with events later when we look at handling events with delegates. In this example, however, the application will sit idle until the form is closed.

The `Application` class is within the `System.Windows.Forms` namespace and contains static methods, properties, and events to deal with managing your application, including dealing with Windows messages and idle processing.

To handle user interaction with your form, you can override methods from the base `Form` class or create an event handler – we will look more at event handlers later in the chapter. In the example below, the code is similar to that above but we now have overridden the `OnClick()` method to provide a response to the user clicking on the form. After we do our processing within the method we have overridden, we need to call the base method so that any other processing required by the form is performed.

```
using System;
using System.Windows.Forms;

public class BasicForm : Form
{
    public static void Main()
    {
        BasicForm myForm = new BasicForm();
        Application.Run(myForm);
    }
    protected override void OnClick(System.EventArgs e)
    {
        MessageBox.Show("You have clicked the form");
        base.OnClick(e);
    }
}
```

The `MessageBox` class is also located within the `System.Windows.Forms` namespace, and the static `Show()` method can be overloaded to provide different button combinations and an icon if needed.

It is also possible to contain several forms within a Multiple Document Interface (MDI) form. You can create an MDI form by setting the `IsMdiContainer` property to `true`, and add child forms by setting their `MdiParent` property to the name of the MDI Parent form. Unfortunately, there is no support for the Document and View architecture which MFC users will be familiar with.

Windows Controls

Windows controls can be placed onto Windows forms to provide functionality to the user and provide a means for the user to input data for your application. They provide methods, properties, and events that can be controlled and monitored by the application.

The .NET Framework provides an extensive set of standard controls for Windows forms. The standard controls are easy to use with a consistent common naming structure; for example the `Text` property is now available on all controls, whereas the Windows controls of the past would vary between a `Caption` property or a `Text` property for representing displayed text.

There are many common controls to help you build your user interface; there are the controls you would expect such as Label, Button, TextBox, CheckBox, RadioButton, PictureBox, ListView, and TreeView. You also get some new controls which are more specialized; the screenshot below lists some of the controls that are available to you:

All controls are derived from System.Windows.Forms.Control, which defines the basic functionality that a control must provide. You can create your own controls by deriving from that base class. The Form class which we use to create our forms was also derived from the Control class.

We will now create a form and place a control on it using Visual Studio .NET, so we can examine what code has been generated to do this. Create a new **Windows Application** project and place a textbox on the form that was created for you. We will call the textbox myTextBox and change the Text property to **Example Text**.

If you view the code behind the form, you will see that Visual Studio .NET has created some code for us to create the form and the textbox. A private variable has been created for our textbox and an InitializeComponent() method has been added to the constructor of our form class. Let's take a look at these two pieces of code:

```
public class Form1 : System.Windows.Forms.Form
{
    private System.Windows.Forms.TextBox myTextBox;

    private void InitializeComponent()
    {
        this.myTextBox = new System.Windows.Forms.TextBox();
        this.SuspendLayout();
        //
        // myTextBox
        //
        this.myTextBox.Location = new System.Drawing.Point(32, 24);
        this.myTextBox.Name = "myTextBox";
        this.myTextBox.Size = new System.Drawing.Size(144, 20);
        this.myTextBox.TabIndex = 0;
        this.myTextBox.Text = "Example Text";
        //
        // Form1
        //
        this.AutoScaleBaseSize = new System.Drawing.Size(5, 13);
        this.ClientSize = new System.Drawing.Size(292, 266);
        this.Controls.AddRange(new System.Windows.Forms.Control[] {
                               this.myTextBox});
        this.Name = "Form1";
        this.Text = "Control Test";
        this.ResumeLayout(false);
    }
```

In the `InitializeComponent()` method, the `TextBox` control is created and its properties set. It is then added to the `Controls` collection of the form. Similar code is generated for all components you add to the form using Visual Studio .NET. The Form Designer does not store any data other than your source code, so if you alter the code here the properties would be reflected in the Form Designer. However, if you enter any invalid code the designer will not allow you to make further changes to the form until the code is corrected.

One of the great new features of these controls is that they have anchoring. In the example above, set the `Anchor` property of the `TextBox` control to "Bottom ,Right". Whenever the form is resized, either at run-time or through Visual Studio .NET, the textbox will maintain the distance between itself and the sides of the form. This can greatly assist with creating forms that resize gracefully.

Event Handling

Events are the primary mechanism used to notify your form that something has happened, usually due to user interaction. This could be anything from moving the mouse over a control, inputting data into a control, or even dragging another window over our form. Earlier in the chapter the `OnClick()` method of our form was overridden to capture mouse clicks and then display a message box. When the user clicks on our form, not only is the code within the `OnClick()` method processed, but the form will also raise a `Click` event. Using a delegate we can specify what method should run as a response to that event. In this section of the chapter we will look at how to deal with events using delegates.

With C#, events are exposed in almost the same fashion as properties and methods. We can assign a delegate to the event, thus setting the method that will deal with that particular event within our application. A delegate in C# holds a reference to a method; if the method is not static, the delegate will hold a reference to an instance of that class and method. We will be looking at the System.EventHandler delegate as that is used to handle events.

All a delegate requires is an object and a method whose arguments and return types match those of the method to be delegated. All event handlers have two arguments and do not return any values, so any method to receive events delegated to it must be created with these arguments. The following function is capable of receiving an event; it will display a message box when it does. Unlike the earlier example where the OnClick() method was overridden to capture the mouse click, with the use of a delegate we do not need to call the base method to ensure any further processing is done.

```
private void myControl_Event(object sender, System.EventArgs e)
{
    MessageBox.Show("Event raised");
}
```

The sender parameter refers to the object that raised the event, such as a button or textbox. The second parameter will contain any additional information regarding the event, if appropriate. To connect the above method to our textbox from the previous example we would add the following line into the InitializeComponent() method:

```
this.myTextBox.TextChanged += new System.EventHandler(
                            this.myControl_Event);
```

Now whenever the text is changed within the textbox, a TextChanged event will be raised and passed onto our myControl_Event() method via the System.EventHandler delegate we assigned. You can list the available events for an object in Visual Studio .NET through the **Properties** dialog by selecting the Events icon, which looks like a bolt of lightning. You can also create an event handler by entering a method name there, or by double-clicking for Visual Studio .NET to generate a method with an appropriate name. You do not have to enter a unique method name for each event handler.

The main benefit of handling events with delegates is that it is an extremely clean and effective way to manage the events your application will receive. You still get the flexibility in choosing what methods events receive, thus allowing you to specify a central event handler method. This gives you the power offered by languages such as C++ or Java, but the delegates can be set up in a straightforward manner that produces code that is easy to read and maintain.

Custom Drawing onto your Form

Although the controls shipped with the .NET Framework are flexible enough to deal with many scenarios, there are situations where you will need to draw onto the form manually to achieve the desired effect. Many applications use custom drawing techniques to provide the desired display to the user, such as Internet Explorer rendering the current web page.

If you need to draw onto your form you will need to use GDI+ to perform your drawing operations. GDI+ contains the .NET base classes that are available for the purpose of carrying out custom drawing on the screen. This functionality can be found within the System.Drawing and System.Drawing.Drawing2D namespaces. The Form class exposes the event Paint, raised whenever the form surface needs redrawing. A Paint event can be raised by the Invalidate() method. We will not go into drawing operations in any detail here but building on our earlier example the following code will write some text onto our form.

To create the Graphics object used to draw the text onto the form we use the PaintEventArgs object that is passed to our method. This contains a graphics object with the clipping parameters for our form so that we can draw or redraw what is necessary.

```
using System;
using System.Drawing;
using System.Windows.Forms;

public class BasicForm : Form
{
    public static void Main()
    {
        BasicForm myForm = new BasicForm();
        Application.Run(myForm);
    }
    protected override void OnPaint(PaintEventArgs e)
    {
        Graphics dc = e.Graphics;
        dc.DrawString ("This is my string!", new Font("Arial", 12),
                    Brushes.Black, 25, 25);
        base.OnPaint(e);
    }
}
```

We have declared that we are using the System.Drawing namespace to allow us to use the Graphics object.

Simple Calculator Application

We are going to build a simple application using Visual Studio .NET to create the user interface. We are going to create a simple calculator using a label for the display and command buttons to enter values and operators. We will also implement a menu for our application.

Our application will need to use sixteen buttons, one for each number, together with four operators (+, –, *, /) a cancel button, and an "equals" button. To implement sixteen different event handlers for each button would make our code heavily fragmented with a different function for each button. However using delegates we can set up event handlers to deal with inputting numbers or performing calculations, which will make our code easier to understand and maintain.

Using Visual Studio .NET, create a new C# Windows Application project named **Calculator**, this gives you a blank form ready for you to start creating your application. Change the following properties of the form:

Property	Setting
Name	frmMain
Text	Calculator
FormBorderStyle	FixedDialog
MaximizeBox	False
Size	250; 300

Create a label on the form and set the following properties:

Property	Setting
Name	lblDisplay
BackColor	White
Location	25; 20
Size	185; 20
TextAlign	MiddleRight
Text	0

Let's now look at the code generated by Visual Studio .NET. Here is the code within the `InitializeComponent()` method which deals with setting the properties of our label and form. The `lblDisplay` variable was declared as part of the class definition.

```
private void InitializeComponent()
{
    this.lblDisplay = new System.Windows.Forms.Label();
    this.SuspendLayout();
    //
    // lblDisplay
    //
    this.lblDisplay.BackColor = System.Drawing.Color.White;
    this.lblDisplay.Location = new System.Drawing.Point(25, 20);
    this.lblDisplay.Name = "lblDisplay";
    this.lblDisplay.Size = new System.Drawing.Size(185, 20);
    this.lblDisplay.TabIndex = 0;
    this.lblDisplay.Text = "0";
    this.lblDisplay.TextAlign = System.Drawing.ContentAlignment.MiddleRight;
    //
    // frmMain
    //
    this.AutoScaleBaseSize = new System.Drawing.Size(5, 13);
    this.ClientSize = new System.Drawing.Size(244, 255);
```

```
    this.Controls.AddRange(new System.Windows.Forms.Control[]
                    {this.lblDisplay});
    this.FormBorderStyle = System.Windows.Forms.FormBorderStyle.FixedDialog;
    this.MaximizeBox = false;
    this.Name = "frmMain";
    this.Text = "Calculator";
    this.ResumeLayout(false);
}
```

The SuspendLayout() *and* ResumeLayout() *methods are called so that the controls are not visibly placed onto the form, and properties altered step by step, but are visually updated in one go. Specifying* true *in the* ResumeLayout() *method will force the update to be executed immediately.*

Our calculator also requires some buttons that the user can press to input data into the application. Rather than adding each button and setting the properties of each one manually, we can create a function to do this and call it with the relevant information.

```
private void AddButton(int Left, int Top, string Key, KeyType Type)
{
    // Create button and add to the Controls collection of our form
    Button newButton = new Button();
    this.Controls.Add(newButton);

    //Set Properties of our new button
    newButton.Top    = Top;
    newButton.Left   = Left;
    newButton.Width  = 35;
    newButton.Height = 35;
    newButton.Text   = Key;

    //Assign an event handler for our new button
    switch(Type)
    {
        case KeyType.Number:
            newButton.Click += new System.EventHandler(NumberClick);
            break;
        case KeyType.Operator:
            newButton.Click += new System.EventHandler(OperatorClick);
            break;
        case KeyType.Equal:
            newButton.Click += new System.EventHandler(EqualsClick);
            break;
        case KeyType.Cancel:
            newButton.Click += new System.EventHandler(CancelClick);
            break;
    }
}
```

The code in this method creates a new `Button` control, adds it to the `Controls` collection of the form and sets the properties as required. We use the `Text` property to display what the button is for, and also to allow us to determine what button was clicked. Additionally, we use the `System.EventHandler` delegate to point the click event to various methods based on what type of button we are creating. The various types are held in the enumeration `KeyType`.

We will create a method to call this function and create the buttons as needed. This method can then be called from within the form constructor.

```
private void CreateButtons()
{
    // Add buttons for digits 1 to 9
    int j;
    for (int i = 0; i < 9; i++)
    {
        j = (int)(i / 3);
        this.AddButton(25 + (i %3 ) * 50, 50 + ((2 - j) * 50),
                       (i + 1).ToString(), KeyType.Number);
    }
    // Add zero, operators, equals and cancel.
    this.AddButton(25, 200, "0", KeyType.Number);
    this.AddButton(75, 200, "C", KeyType.Cancel);
    this.AddButton(125, 200, "=", KeyType.Equal);
    this.AddButton(175, 50, "+", KeyType.Operator);
    this.AddButton(175, 100, "-", KeyType.Operator);
    this.AddButton(175, 150, "*", KeyType.Operator);
    this.AddButton(175, 200, "/", KeyType.Operator);
}
```

After `InitializeComponent()` has been called to set up our form and label, we have added code to create our buttons. The code in the `AddButton()` method gives the buttons a width and a height of 35 pixels, and we space the buttons 50 pixels apart to give us some spacing between buttons. We also add padding of 25 pixels from the left edge and 50 from the top edge of the form to allow for our label.

To create the buttons 1 through to 9 we use two variables, i and j. i is used to calculate the horizontal point and j for the vertical point of our button, and we pass a KeyType of Number and a string representing the number on the key to our AddButton() method. The remaining buttons are created by a series of calls with the relevant parameters. This leaves us with a form which looks like this at run-time:

We can now amend the form constructor to add a call to our CreateButtons() method. The form constructor will already have a call to the InitializeComponent() method that Visual Studio .NET has added for us. The constructor now looks like this:

```
public frmMain()
{
    //
    // Required for Windows Form Designer support
    //
    InitializeComponent();
    CreateButtons();
}
```

Now we need to write the code that deals with the button clicks and provides the correct output via the label control. To do this we need to declare some additional variables in the form constructor:

```
public class frmMain : System.Windows.Forms.Form
{
    private System.Windows.Forms.Label lblDisplay;
    private float Value1 = 0;
    private float Value2 = 0;
    private enum OperatorFlag {None, Plus, Minus, Multiply, Divide};
    private enum KeyType {None, Number, Cancel, Operator, Equal};
    private OperatorFlag OperatorType;
```

We will use Value1 and Value2 for the values that our calculator will use to perform its calculations and the OperatorFlag enumeration will store what the current operation is. When any of our buttons are clicked, the event handler we set up will call the appropriate method, so now we write the code for these methods.

As we discussed earlier in the chapter, a method must accept exactly the same parameters as specified by the delegate; thus, like all other event handlers, our `NumberClick()` method will be of the form:

```
public void NumberClick(Object sender, System.EventArgs e)
```

We then need to determine what button was pressed to raise the event. This can be retrieved from the `sender` object. To access properties of the relevant button, we need to cast the object to a button so that they are exposed. In this scenario, we are only interested in the `Text` property that we set, so we retrieve it with the following line of code:

```
string Key = ((System.Windows.Forms.Button) sender).Text;
```

However, if we needed an object so that we could manipulate more than one property, we could create it like this:

```
Button thisButton = (System.Windows.Forms.Button)sender;
```

That line of code would give us an object called `thisButton`, representing the button that the user clicked on, and allow us to read and write to the properties of that button.

After determining which button has been pressed, we can use that information to increment the value for our calculation and the display accordingly. This is done via the following method:

```
public void NumberClick(Object sender, System.EventArgs e)
{
    string Key = ((System.Windows.Forms.Button)sender).Text;

    Value1= Value1 * 10 + int.Parse(Key);
    lblDisplay.Text = Value1.ToString();
}
```

We also need methods to deal with the cancel button and the operator buttons. These are implemented as follows:

```
public void CancelClick(Object sender, System.EventArgs e)
{
    Value1 = 0;
    Value2 = 0;
    lblDisplay.Text =" 0";
}

public void OperatorClick(Object sender, System.EventArgs e)
{
    string Key = ((System.Windows.Forms.Button)sender).Text;

    switch(Key)
    {
        case "+":
            OperatorType = OperatorFlag.Plus;
            break;
        case "-":
```

```
        OperatorType = OperatorFlag.Minus;
        break;
    case "*":
        OperatorType = OperatorFlag.Multiply;
        break;
    case "/":
        OperatorType = OperatorFlag.Divide;
        break;
    }
    Value2 = Value1;
    Value1 = 0;
}
```

Finally, we implement a method to handle the equals button, which will perform the necessary calculations and display the result using the `lblDisplay` control.

```
public void EqualsClick(Object sender, System.EventArgs e)
{
    switch(OperatorType)
    {
        case OperatorFlag.Plus:
            Value1 = Value2 + Value1;
            break;
        case OperatorFlag.Minus:
            Value1 = Value2 - Value1;
            break;
        case OperatorFlag.Multiply:
            Value1 = Value2 * Value1;
            break;
        case OperatorFlag.Divide:
            Value1 = Value2 / Value1;
            break;
    }
    OperatorType = OperatorFlag.None;
    lblDisplay.Text = Value1.ToString();
    Value2 = 0;
}
```

We now have a functioning calculator that can be used to add, subtract, divide and multiply numbers. Now, we will add a menu to the application which will allow users to change the font or color of the calculator display, or view the "About" box.

Menus

The majority of Windows applications have a menu system, and therefore users will probably expect to see one on your application as well. Fortunately, menus are extremely easy to create using the Form Designer in Visual Studio .NET. You can graphically draw your menu and assign event handlers for the items.

There are two types of menus that can be created and used within your forms. Context-sensitive menus are usually invoked when you right-click over a certain item, such as a textbox, and give items relevant to the control that has been clicked on. To implement this you have the `System.Windows.Forms.ContextMenu` class.

The second type of menu is the main menu of an application, located at the top left of the form. To create a main menu for your application you need to use the `System.Windows.Forms.MainMenu` class. Both classes can be added to your form by dragging the appropriate control onto your form.

Both menu classes are populated by creating instances of the `System.Windows.Forms.MenuItem` class, and adding them to the relevant parent object. A `MenuItem` can either be a clickable item or a separator for the menu.

For our application we will create a main menu by dragging a **MainMenu** control from the ToolBox onto the form. This instance of the **MainMenu** control will be named `mainMenu1` by default. Add the following items as shown in this screenshot:

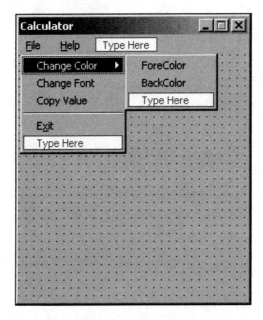

There is also one item under **Help** which is labeled **&About**. By using **&** in the label, the character following the **&** is underlined, and the menu item is made accessible through a keyboard shortcut. If you right-click on a menu item you can switch view to the names of the menu items by selecting **Edit Names**. You can rename the default created names to more meaningful names such as menuFile, menuColor, and so on. For our application, the names of the items are listed below:

Menu Name	Display Text
menuFile	&File
menuColor	Change Color
menuColorFore	ForeColor
menuColorBack	BackColor
menuFont	Change Font
menuCopy	Copy Value
menuItem5	- (displayed as the separator)
MenuExit	E&xit
MenuHelp	&Help
MenuAbout	&About

To exit from the application we need just one line of code. Double-click the **E&xit** item in the **File** menu to create an event handler and add the following line of code so your method looks like this:

```
private void menuExit_Click(object sender, System.EventArgs e)
{
    this.Close();
}
```

Our application also needs an "**About**" box so the users can find out who is responsible for its creation. Create an event handler for menuAbout, and add the following code:

```
private void menuAbout_Click(object sender, System.EventArgs e)
{
    frmAbout AboutForm = new frmAbout();
    AboutForm.ShowDialog();
}
```

Create a new form called `frmAbout` and set the following properties for it:

Property	Setting
Name	frmAbout
FormBorderStyle	FixedDialog
MinimizeBox	False
MaximizeBox	False
ShowInTaskBar	False

Create a button called `cmdExitAbout`, and add some labels to hold text that will create an about box which looks similar to the one shown below.

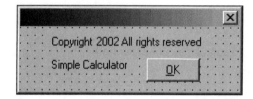

The following code will close this form when the **OK** button is clicked:

```
private void cmdExitAbout_Click(object sender, System.EventArgs e)
{
    this.Close();
}
```

Note that the `Button` class has the property `DialogResult` which can be set to one of the following: `Ok`, `Cancel`, `Abort`, `Retry`, `Cancel`, `Yes`, or `No`. This value will be returned by the `ShowDialog()` method when it is called from the parent form, providing a simple way to check how the dialog box was closed.

The two menu items for color will allow the user to change the display color for the calculator. The code to do this is practically identical for changing either the foreground or background color of the label control, so it makes sense to have a common method for changing color that both menu items will execute. Create an event handler for the `Click` event of both menu items called `menuColor_Click` and enter the following code:

```
private void menuColor_Click(object sender, System.EventArgs e)
{
    bool back;
    if (((System.Windows.Forms.MenuItem)sender).Text == "BackColor")
        back = true;
    else
        back = false;
    ColorDialog aClrDialog = new ColorDialog();
    aClrDialog.AllowFullOpen = false;
    if (back==true)
        aClrDialog.Color = this.lblDisplay.BackColor;
```

```
        else
            aClrDialog.Color = this.lblDisplay.ForeColor;
        if (aClrDialog.ShowDialog() == DialogResult.OK)
        {
            if (back==true)
                this.lblDisplay.BackColor  = aClrDialog.Color;
            else
                this.lblDisplay.ForeColor  = aClrDialog.Color;
        }
        aClrDialog.Dispose();
    }
```

As you can see in the above code, it is very simple to call up the predefined color dialog box, by creating an instance of the ColorDialog class. In this example we check the Text property of the calling MenuItem object and depending on that, we set the selected color of the dialog box before displaying it. If the dialog box is exited via the OK button we then set the color appropriate to the users selection. The standard font dialog box is just as simple to set up as shown in the following piece of code which should be set as the event handler for the menuFont menu item:

```
    private void menuFont_Click(object sender, System.EventArgs e)
    {
        FontDialog aFontDialog = new FontDialog();
        aFontDialog.ShowColor = true;
        aFontDialog.ShowEffects = true;
        aFontDialog.MinSize = 1;
        aFontDialog.MaxSize = 35;
        aFontDialog.Font = this.Font;
        if (aFontDialog.ShowDialog() == DialogResult.OK)
        {
            this.lblDisplay.Font = aFontDialog.Font;
        }

        aFontDialog.Dispose();
    }
```

Finally, we also want to add code so that the user can copy the displayed value from the calculator onto the clipboard. Within the System.Windows.Forms namespace there is the Clipboard class which has static methods we can use to set and get the clipboard contents. Here we check that the display actually contains some text, and if so, we set the clipboard contents to that text.

```
    private void menuCopy_Click(object sender, System.EventArgs e)
    {
        if(lblDisplay.Text != "")
            Clipboard.SetDataObject(lblDisplay.Text);
    }
```

Now our menu is fully built, and functional, we have to instruct our form to display the menu. This is done by setting the `Menu` property to our `mainMenu1` object. This can be done via Visual Studio .NET, which will have the main menu name in a dropdown box for that property ready for us to select. This will add the following line of code to our project within the `InitializeComponent()` method, or we can simply add the code ourselves to the `InitializeComponent()` method:

```
this.Menu = mainMenu1;
```

We now have a fully functional calculator that can be partially customized in appearance and allows data to be copied to the clipboard. In doing so, we have touched on many of the basic classes within the `System.Windows.Forms` namespace that will almost certainly be the foundation of any Windows applications you will develop.

Deploying Applications

Once you have built and tested your application it is ready to be sent to anyone who is going to use it. Unfortunately, this is not a simple task for most applications as you cannot just send the main executable of your application and expect it to work in most scenarios. Although .NET promotes an XCOPY scenario where you can copy your application files onto the destination machine and your application can be executed without any further installation, there are situations where this is not appropriate. For instance, you may need to create a directory for your application to be installed into, or your application may require files other than the main executable installed in either the same folder or a shared location such as the global assembly cache, which we shall visit in the next chapter. You may also want a shortcut to your application placed on the user's desktop or the Start menu.

To perform all these actions you need an application that can copy all the data into the correct locations on the target system, and perform any necessary actions, such as creating Registry keys. Additionally you need to ensure your application can be uninstalled when no longer required by the user. With Visual C++ there was no real support for this within the IDE, and it was generally easier to use a third party product such as InstallShield.

Although not shipped with Visual Studio 6 there was an application called Windows Installer that integrated with the Visual InterDev IDE. Although it did not accept C++ projects, you could add files into the installer projects manually and build an executable that would install your files and proprietary settings. Those of you who did use Windows Installer through InterDev will immediately feel at home with the installer projects found within Visual Studio .NET, as they work in much the same way, although there is a lot more functionality and support for all .NET languages.

Setup and Deployment Projects

There are two **Setup and Deployment** projects that you can create using Visual Studio .NET which will result in an executable ready to install your application. There is also a wizard to help you select the initial settings for your setup and deployment project and two projects that can encapsulate data for multiple Setup projects:

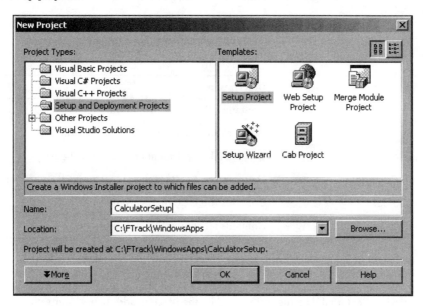

Here is a brief description of what the two Setup projects allow you to do:

❑   **Setup Project**: This is used to create a setup file designed for Windows applications allowing you to manipulate the Registry and file system as needed

❑   **Web Setup Project**: This is used to install web applications, and includes appropriate functionality such as stopping and restarting the web server.

The two other projects allow you to package part of an application:

❑   **Cab Project**: A CAB Project is used to store files that can be called upon from your setup project. Your CAB files can be held remotely and requested over the Internet for deployment. After creating the .CAB file you will notice an additional file within it with an extension of OSD. This file contains information about the other files allowing the CAB to be utilized by the installation application.

❑   **Merge Module**: merge modules can store files, but unlike CAB projects they are held within the main installation package. A merge module holds locations of where the files will be installed to, as well as Registry settings and custom actions. They have nearly all the functionality of a full Setup project. One use for merge modules would be to provide several versions of components, each with different localized resources. The installation application would decide which merge module to use based on the destination locale.

For the purposes of this chapter, we will look at using the standard Setup project for which we will specify the initial settings through the Setup Wizard and use it to package the Calculator application we have built. The Setup Wizard will create a basic setup project for us and add the relevant files from our Windows Application project.

Using Visual Studio .NET, add a new Setup Wizard project to our existing solution, calling the project CalculatorSetup.

The Setup project can take 6 types of files from your existing .NET project(s), as well as files used by your application that are not in your project at all. The types of files are listed below:

File Type	Description
Content	Contains all content files in the project
Debug Symbols	Contains the debugging files for the project
Documentation Files	Contains the documentation files for the project
Localized Resources	Contains the satellite assemblies for each culture's resources
Primary Output	Contains the DLL or EXE built by the project
Source Files	Contains all source files in the project

After the Welcome screen of the wizard, the next screen shows that the default selection with the wizard is for a **Windows Application**. From the next screen, choose the **Primary Output** files from Calculator to be included. We do not need any of the other types as listed above. We will not specify any additional files; if we used any external data files this would be the place to add them to our setup project.

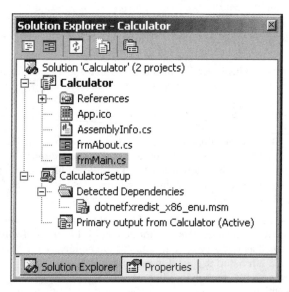

As shown in the above screenshot, the wizard has added both our primary output from the Calculator project, as we specified, and a merge module containing the .NET redistributable files. However this merge module is not the appropriate way to install the .NET Framework. If we wish to distribute the .NET Framework with our application, we need to include the file DotNetfx.exe which can be found on the Component Media that accompanies Visual Studio .NET, or downloaded from the Microsoft web site. This will need to be installed if the .NET Framework is not present on the target machine your application needs to run on. To disable the merge module you can right-click the module in the Solution Explorer and select Exclude. You can also add additional files, merge modules and assemblies as required to the project from the context menu when you right-click on the title of the project.

The project has some properties that affect the appearance of your setup module; the default values are taken from your project name and the details that you registered with your copy of Visual Studio .NET. It is worth reviewing these properties before going onto the individual items within the installation package.

For the Calculator application we set the following properties:

Property	Value
Author	Neil
Description	Simple Calculator
Keywords	Calculator
Manufacturer	Wrox Press LTD
ManufacturerURL	http://www.wrox.com
ProductName	Calculator
Title	Calculator

If you right-click the project name in the Solution Explorer window, as shown in the screenshot below, you can select a number of views to help you configure the destination system for your application:

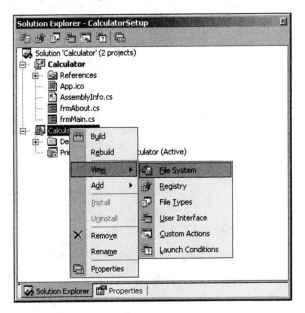

Here is a summary of the views you can use:

View	Description
File System	This allows you to configure what files and shortcuts are created
Registry	This allows you to create Registry keys and values
File Types	You can create custom file types for your application's documents
User Interface	This details what dialogs are shown when the installer is run
Custom Actions	You can specify a script or executable file to run as part of installation
Launch Conditions	You can add install-time checks for conditions that would prevent your application running properly, and prevent installation accordingly

The File System page shows us a view of the destination file system. The Primary Output file has been placed in the Application Folder. Navigate to the User's Desktop and add a shortcut to our Primary Output file. The screenshot below shows a shortcut placed in the User's Programs Menu.

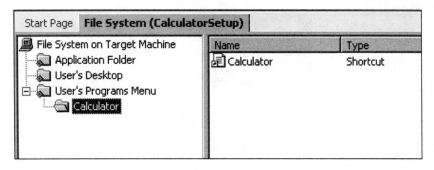

We can add more folders to the view by right-clicking on **File System on Target Machine** and selecting **Add Special Folder**. This presents us with the following menu:

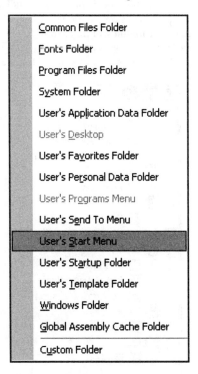

This allows us to add, say, a **User's Start Menu** and create a directory to hold our shortcut in.

In the **Registry** view you can see that two keys have already been created for you. The [Manufacturer] key will take its name from the **Manufacturer** property of your Setup project. You can create additional keys and values as appropriate; if you try to create a value that already exists you will overwrite the current value. The screenshot below shows the default keys that get created for you as part of the default setup project:

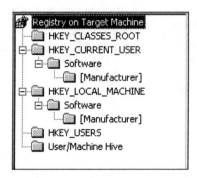

We can also alter the user interface of our installation package. Within the User Interface view, you will see the order in which dialogs for guiding the user through the installation process are displayed. You can add and remove dialogs and set properties on each one, giving you scope to customize their appearance. Generally, the dialogs under Install will be used but an administrator could use the Administrator Install to facilitate installation over a network. To access the Administrator Install you need to call the main setup package file with /a as a command line parameter.

The default settings are adequate for our application, so we can now go ahead and build the setup project. This may take some time due to the size of the .NET Framework merge module we have included. The files produced depend on the Bootstrapper and PackageFiles properties of the Setup project. We used the default properties that packaged all the files within the main setup file and produced a Windows Installer bootstrap. Once finished, you will find five files in your output directory as follows:

Filename	Description
CalculatorSetup.msi	Main package file containing the files for our application and settings we specified in the setup project. Can be executed if Windows Installer is present on the destination system.
InstMsiA.exe	Windows Installer Setup file for Alpha processors
InstMsiW.exe	Standard Windows Installer Setup file
Setup.exe	Executable which will determine whether Windows Installer is present and either install your application or the installer.
Setup.ini	Data file for Setup.exe

If you are confident that the target machine has an up-to-date version of Windows Installer, you can distribute just the main package file by not building the bootstrap files.

If you execute either CalculatorSetup.msi or Setup.exe, you should be greeted with the following dialog, and be able to install your application. The installation package will also take care of removing the application through Add/Remove Programs in the Control Panel if needed.

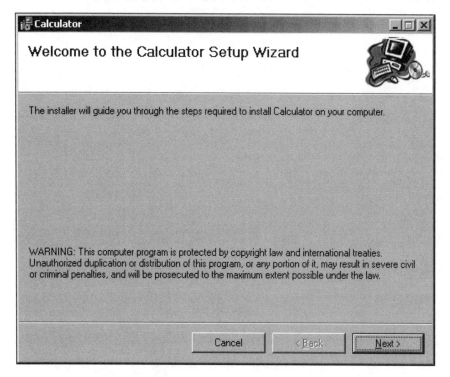

Summary

Although the .NET Framework is very much geared towards the scenario of distributed applications, in this chapter we have seen that it still retains an excellent set of base classes for the more traditional Windows applications. Windows Forms moves handling windows into an object-oriented environment providing an easy to use model without sacrificing any real flexibility in the process.

Visual Studio .NET gives us a quick and simple way to create forms and place controls onto them. In this chapter, we have seen how Visual Studio .NET handles forms and controls so we can manipulate properties and set up event handlers using the IDE. In particular, we looked at:

❑ The controls offered by the .NET Framework for Windows Forms applications

❑ Some of the classes in the System.Windows.Forms namespace that represent controls

❑ Using delegates for event handling to respond to user interaction with our forms

❑ Creating forms and using controls

❑ Using menu items, and standard color, and font dialogs

Finally, we used Visual Studio .NET to package up our application for deployment on other systems.

Take the **Fast Track** to *C#*

9

Assemblies and ILDASM

An **assembly** is a package containing executable code and resources for the .NET runtime, produced each time you build a C# program.

In this chapter, we'll look at the concepts and vocabulary used in C# and .NET when talking about assemblies. We'll show the assembly **manifest** describing the contents of the assembly, and how assemblies are used as a version, deployment, security, type, and reference unit by the .NET runtime.

Assemblies may be one of two types: **private** or **shared**. We'll show how to create each of these types of assembly. Assemblies have a name, version number, and culture, and we'll show how these may be combined with a public/private key into a **strong name** uniquely identifying the assembly.

We'll look at single-file, multi-file, and satellite assemblies. We'll examine assembly attributes, and learn how to view the contents of an assembly with the Ildasm tool. We'll look at the search methods used by the .NET runtime to locate assemblies, how the runtime performs version checking, and how both searching and version checking can be changed by configuration files.

Finally, we'll learn about the **global assembly cache** for shared assemblies, as well as briefly looking at code access security, digital signatures, reflection, dynamic assemblies, and assemblies for interfacing with legacy systems such as COM.

What is an Assembly?

An assembly is a self-describing package of executable code and resources for the .NET environment. It may be a one file or a set of files. The main file in an assembly may be either an executable (.EXE) or dynamic link library (.DLL), and a multi-file assembly may have a mix of file types.

As described in Chapter 1, the executable code contained in the assembly is MSIL (Microsoft Intermediate Language code), which is compiled by the .NET runtime's Just-In-Time (JIT) compiler to machine code for whatever machine the assembly happens to be executing on. Assemblies are directly executable by Windows and use the Windows portable executable (PE) format.

Besides executable code, an assembly also contains a **manifest** describing its contents. The word "manifest" comes from the metaphor of a real-world package – the delivery truck dumps the big box on your doorstep and you pull the manifest out of the envelope taped to the side to find out what has been shipped to you. The manifest of a .NET assembly contains **assembly metadata** describing the assembly's properties and its external references to other assemblies. The manifest also contains **type metadata** describing what classes, methods, and properties are inside the assembly. We'll look at the details of this in just a bit.

Assemblies are **self-describing**. The manifest and metadata enable the assembly to tell the .NET runtime and the operating system what it contains without having to resort to external resources such as the Registry.

Benefits of Assemblies: The End of "DLL Hell"

The self-description is a key benefit of .NET: this makes it much easier to install components and have client programs find them. The difficulties with multiple instances and versions of DLLs and COM components on legacy Windows systems has been called **"DLL Hell"**, because it's so difficult to manage. Components from different software packages may share names, making it very hard to sort out which DLL belongs to which application. Multiple versions of a support library may be needed; for example application A needs utility.dll version 1.1, but application B needs version 2.0. The Registry is used to track elements of applications, but the way the Registry is used is often up to the application. COM provides some means for addressing these issues, with GUIDs (globally unique identifiers), but the system is still far from perfect. .NET addresses these deployment and versioning issues by giving applications a self-contained way to identify themselves.

Benefits of Assemblies: Side-by-Side Execution

Assemblies in .NET support **side-by-side execution**, where two different versions of a component (say, v1.1 and 2.0) can both be installed and execute simultaneously on a system automatically without conflicts.

The benefit of side-by-side execution is that old and new versions of a software product can both be used; for example, if an application is being upgraded in stages from an old version to a new version, the new and old versions can both be used even if they use assemblies with the same names. Also, if two different software products use a common component but require different versions of that component, they can both be installed and execute at the same time without interfering with one another.

We'll look at the details as to how all this is accomplished later in the chapter.

What is in an Assembly?

The assembly is the defining packaging unit for everything contained inside it. This includes almost all aspects of the way the assembly relates to the .NET runtime, operating system, and other external code. In particular it includes:

❑   Version – all code and resources inside the assembly share a single version number.

❑   Security – all code security checking is done at the assembly level. Everything in the assembly has the same security context.

❑   Type Checking – all types (classes, methods, properties, enumerations, events, and so on) are defined to the .NET runtime by the assembly in which they are contained. This means that even if two assemblies both define the same class with the same name, properties and methods, the .NET runtime will still treat them as different classes because they originate from different assemblies.

❑   Deployment – when you install a .NET program or library on a system, the assembly is what is copied to the system and becomes known to the system.

❑   References – When you add a reference within a C# project in Visual Studio .NET, the reference is to an assembly.

.NET System Assemblies and References

All the .NET runtime classes that you are now familiar with in the .NET class library are themselves contained in a collection of assemblies. You can see these assemblies, and where they are located, in the Project | Add Reference dialog of Visual Studio .NET, in the .NET tab:

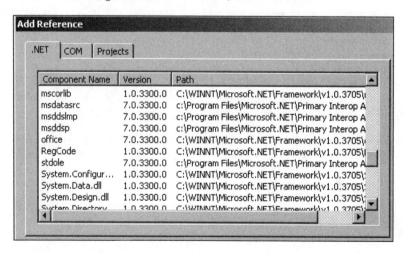

The core assembly of the .NET runtime is mscorlib. A reference to this assembly is included by default in any .NET assembly, so you don't need to explicitly add it. Many of the basic classes in System are defined in this assembly, including part or all of System.Collections, System.IO, System.Math, and others. Many of the other system assemblies are named in a way that relates to the namespace of the classes they define, such as the System.Data.dll and System.Xml.dll assemblies. However, the namespace and the assembly name may be different.

241

Namespaces and Assemblies are Different

Let's elaborate on that last point about namespaces being different from assemblies. The namespace defined in a using directive in C# simply declares that you are going to use a set of names in the declared namespace. Using the namespace within the code does not tell the system what assembly contains the code being referred to. For example, at the beginning of a C# source file:

```
using System.Drawing;
```

does not create an assembly reference to System.Drawing.dll by itself; you still have to add a reference to System.Drawing.dll in your project in order to use those classes.

You can define classes in multiple namespaces in a single assembly, and the same namespace may also be used in other assemblies.

> *For example, the* System.Data.dll *assembly is part of the .NET runtime; almost all of its classes are defined, as you would expect, in the* System.Data *namespace. However, there is one class (XmlDataDocument) contained in* System.Data.dll *that exists in the* System.Xml *namespace, even though the other classes in the* System.Xml *namespace are defined in* System.Xml.dll.

Culture

An assembly can be associated with a particular **culture**, which specifies the national language and set of related locale conventions such as calendars, time and number formats, and so on.

> *The culture is determined by a special abbreviation set by the Internet standard RFC 1766; it consists of a 2-character language code specified by the ISO 639 standard, followed sometimes by an additional abbreviation specifying a country, dialect, or other specific subculture. The ISO 3166 standard specifies the country codes.*

An example culture is "en-US" meaning English language as used in the United States. Other examples include "fr" for French, "fr-CA" for French language within Canada, and so on. If no culture is specified for an assembly, it is assumed to be culture-neutral; that is, to not have any language or national convention dependencies. The culture is one of a number of **assembly attributes** that can be configured within the source code; we'll show how those are set in just a bit.

Support for multiple cultures has several implications in the structure and version checking of assemblies, which will be described in the section ahead on satellite assemblies.

Private and Shared Assemblies

An assembly is categorized either as a **private assembly**, that is, the assembly is deployed as part of a single application, or as a **shared assembly,** used by multiple programs simultaneously. The .NET Framework has special facilities to support shared assemblies.

Private Assemblies

By default, an assembly is private to your project. Private assemblies **must** be in the same directory as the application. When you make a reference to a private assembly in another project, Visual Studio .NET will make a copy of the referenced assembly that is private to the referencing project's directory.

Copying the assembly ensures that the referencing project can execute even if the original assembly is unavailable because of ongoing development. However, making copies on disk of every referenced DLL is not very efficient for widely-used components, so the .NET Framework provides for **shared assemblies**.

Shared Assemblies

Shared assemblies are available for use by all the programs on the system. Because they are available system-wide, the .NET runtime imposes several extra checks on shared assemblies to ensure that they are valid for the program requesting them, such as security and version compatibility. All .NET system assemblies are shared.

Global Assembly Cache (GAC)

A program referencing a shared assembly does not need to know its location because all shared assemblies are stored in a fixed .NET system directory called the **global assembly cache**, often abbreviated as the **GAC**. The GAC is actually more than just a directory; it has a special implementation because of its unique role in supporting the execution of assemblies in the .NET Framework. We talk about that in more detail when we show how to install assemblies into the GAC later in this chapter.

Strong Names

How many programmers in the world are shipping a file called `utility.dll` or `database.dll` with their programs? If my program includes `database.dll` v1.0 and your program includes `database.dll` v2.0, and an end user installs both of our programs on his or her system, how do we avoid a DLL-Hell-style disaster? What happens when I update that end-user with v2.0 of my `database.dll`? .NET protects against problems caused by multiple versions by requiring that shared assemblies be given **strong names**.

A strong name is guaranteed to be globally unique to your assembly. With strong names, my `database.dll` and your `database.dll` are identified as different assemblies by the .NET runtime, and can co-exist in the global assembly cache without colliding. The .NET Framework provides tools that use **public/private key cryptography** to generate a unique identifier within the assembly that only you have access to. References to your assembly in client programs use the assembly's public key to ensure that they are referencing your assembly and not some other assembly with the same file name.

This process of generating a strong name is called **signing** an assembly. We'll describe the process of signing an assembly in detail later in this chapter.

Strong names also include the version number. This ensures, for example, that v2.0 of your `database.dll` is correctly identified as a newer version of your `database.dll` v1.0.

The strong name can include the **culture** of the assembly, also. Therefore, if `database.dll` v1.0.1 has both a French version and an English version, you can ship both with v1.0.1 of your application and both users will automatically get the correct version for their culture loaded onto their respective systems at run time.

Besides protecting against name/version conflicts, the strong name helps ensure that your assembly really came from you and is not an altered version, perhaps changed, for example, by a virus. .NET provides facilities for even stronger digital certification of assemblies as well, which we will describe briefly when we show how to sign assemblies.

Version Numbers

Let's talk in more detail about version numbers. The version number for a .NET assembly has four parts:

MajorVersion.MinorVersion.BuildNumber.Revision

The major and minor numbers are the familiar version numbers we see all the time in software development: version 1.0, version 1.1, version 2.0, and so on.

The build number and revision number assign a much finer level of detail to the version. The build number typically changes every time the assembly is rebuilt. The .NET Framework uses this mechanism; the current one I am using is 1.0.3706, indicating build 3706.

The revision number is designed to be used for a patch or a "hot fix" to an assembly that is exactly the same as a predecessor build except for one patch. So one could have version 1.0.3706.1 to distinguish this fixed version.

Do you have to follow this set of meanings? No, you can assign any set of numeric version numbers you want to an assembly. However, the conventions described here are normally expected in the .NET development environment.

Shared Assembly Version Checking

The important point about assembly version numbers is that for shared assemblies, the version being referenced and the actual version of the assembly must match exactly. This is the **default version policy** of the .NET runtime for shared assemblies.

The manifest of an assembly contains both the version number of the current assembly, as well as the version numbers of referenced external assemblies. When the .NET runtime loads a referenced assembly, it checks the version in that assembly's manifest and compares it to the version stored in the reference to make sure the versions are the same.

If the assemblies have different version numbers they are assumed to be incompatible and the referenced assembly will not load – for example, utility.dll v1.1 is not compatible with a program referencing utility.dll v1.0, 1.0.2, or 2.0. If you have two programs, one referencing utility.dll v1.1 and utility.dll v2.0, the solution is to load both versions onto the system and use side-by-side execution to let them co-exist (they can co-exist in the GAC because their strong names will differ). This is why your install program for v2.0 of your program should not necessarily remove v1.0 if it is installed.

So what happens if you want the assembly that references version 1.0 to use version 1.1? You can change the version policy with **configuration files**, which we'll discuss in more detail at the end of the chapter.

OK, enough concepts for now. Let's look next at how the different pieces of an assembly fit together.

Each of the satellite assemblies has a manifest, so they are true assemblies. However, they all have the same strong name, and as such are regarded by the .NET runtime as the same assembly, except each has a different culture attribute:

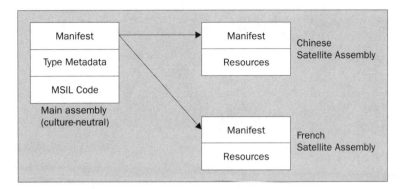

The .NET runtime knows to load the satellite assembly that matches the culture of the machine where the assembly executes. The strong name match on everything except the culture attribute ensures that the satellite is correctly matched with the main assembly, even if two versions of the main assembly are executing side-by-side.

The culture-specific assemblies cannot contain any executable code, so your code needs to be structured to be culture-neutral and use the resources and information the culture-specific resource files contain to implement culture-specific behavior differences.

This structure can be carried down to another level with "sub-satellite" assemblies; for example, there could be a generic German file for resources used with all variations of German, and in addition one or more country-specific resources, for example the Austrian variant of German.

Example Assembly: Shapes Class Library

Let's create an example assembly to examine in detail. I'm going to use a simple class library to start with. This class library is called Shapes, and has classes for doing operations with different kinds of shapes, such as circles and ellipses.

To create this library in Visual Studio .NET, create a C# Class Library project called Shapes. We change the **Default Namespace** of this project to Wrox.FTrackCSharp.Assemblies.Shapes by right-clicking on the project in the Solution Explorer and selecting **Properties**. We rename the Class1.cs file to Shapes.cs, and edit its contents to match the code shown below:

```csharp
using System;
using System.Drawing;

namespace Wrox.FTrackCSharp.Assemblies.Shapes
{
    public class Circle
    {
```

```
    float x;        // x coordinate of center
    float y;        // y coordinate of center
    float radius;   // radius of circle

    // construct circle with only radius given
    public Circle(float inputRadius)
    {
       this.x = this.y = 100; // default location
       this.radius = inputRadius;
    }
    // construct circle with given location and radius
    public Circle(float inputX, float inputY, float inputRadius)
    {
       this.x = inputX;
       this.y = inputY;
       this.radius = inputRadius;
    }

    public double Area()
    {
       // area = pi r squared
       return System.Math.PI * (radius * radius);
    }

    public void Draw(Graphics g)
    {
       Pen p = new Pen(Color.Red);        // define a pen
       // draw circle using radius for both width and height
       g.DrawEllipse(p, x, y, radius, radius);
    }
}

public class Ellipse
{
    float x;         // x coordinate of center
    float y;         // y coordinate of center
    float width;     // width of Ellipse
    float height;    // height of Ellipse

    // construct Ellipse with given height, width
    public Ellipse(float inputWidth, float inputHeight)
    {
       this.x = this.y = 100; // default location
       this.width = inputWidth;
       this.height = inputHeight;
    }

    // construct Ellipse with given location, width, height
    public Ellipse(float inputX, float inputY,
               float inputWidth, float inputHeight)
    {
       this.x = inputX;
       this.y = inputY;
```

```
        this.width = inputWidth;
        this.height = inputHeight;
    }

    public double Area()
    {
        // area = pi * height * width
        return System.Math.PI * height * width;
    }
    public void Draw(Graphics g)
    {
        Pen p = new Pen(Color.Black);       // define a pen
                // draw ellipse using object's instance variables
        g.DrawEllipse(p, x, y, width, height);
    }


    }
}
```

The one slight bit of complexity in this code is that the `Circle` and `Ellipse` classes each have two constructors, one that takes just the size parameters and another that takes parameters to initialize the location (x, y) as well as the size. We take notice of this because we will see it when we examine the assembly.

To build this library in Visual Studio .NET, you'll need to add a reference to the `System.Drawing.dll` assembly in the Project | Add Reference | .NET tab because we use some graphics calls in the `Draw()` method.

After creating the code and references as shown, build the `Shapes` library. The binary result assembly `Shapes.dll` will be in the `bin\debug` directory beneath the `Shapes` project directory. Before we take a direct look at that assembly, let's see how to set the attributes of the assembly from within C#.

Assembly Attributes

Visual Studio .NET automatically creates a second C# source file as part of a C# project. This file, `AssemblyInfo.cs`, is used to set attributes of the assembly such as the assembly version number, name, and so on:

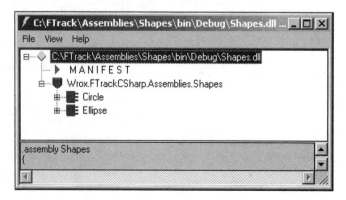

249

Let's look at the contents of `AssemblyInfo.cs`. At the start you see code that looks like this:

```
using System.Reflection;
using System.Runtime.CompilerServices;

//
// General Information about an assembly is controlled through the following
// set of attributes. Change these attribute values to modify the information
// associated with an assembly.
//
[assembly: AssemblyTitle("")]
[assembly: AssemblyDescription("")]
[assembly: AssemblyConfiguration("")]
[assembly: AssemblyCompany("")]
[assembly: AssemblyProduct("")]
[assembly: AssemblyCopyright("")]
[assembly: AssemblyTrademark("")]
```

Each of the `[assembly: AssemblyXxxxx]` statements is an *attribute*, as described in the first chapter. The word `assembly:` at the beginning of each attribute tells the compiler that the attribute directive following is targeted at the assembly itself, not a class, method, or other part of the program. These attributes are defined in the `System.Reflection` and `System.Runtime.CompilerServices` namespaces referenced at the start of this code.

Visual Studio .NET supplies this file as a template for you to fill in with the properties you want your assembly to have. You could use these attributes in any of your source files, for example directly in `shapes.cs`, but the `AssemblyInfo.cs` file is a convenience that keeps the assembly attributes separate from the program logic.

Let's go through the meaning of each of these attributes in the order that they appear in the Visual Studio .NET-generated `AssemblyInfo.cs` file.

Informational Assembly Attributes

The attributes at the beginning such as title, company, etc. are purely informational and can be filled in with any descriptive value you want associated with your assembly component, such as:

```
[assembly: AssemblyTitle("Shapes Class Library")]
[assembly: AssemblyDescription("Circles and Ellipses")]
[assembly: AssemblyConfiguration("Professional Version")]
[assembly: AssemblyCompany("AnyCompany, Inc.")]
[assembly: AssemblyProduct("Shapes")]
[assembly: AssemblyCopyright("Copyright 2002, AnyCompany, Inc.")]
[assembly: AssemblyTrademark("Shapes is a trademark of AnyCompany, Inc.")]
```

Just for fun change some of these attributes in the `AssemblyInfo.cs` file as shown above; we'll see how these show up in the assembly itself when we learn how to examine assemblies with `Ildasm`, just ahead.

Culture Attribute

The next attribute appearing in `AssemblyInfo.cs` is the `AssemblyCulture` attribute, which is to specify the culture, as described in the earlier part of this chapter.

The default value for this attribute is an empty string (`""`), indicating the assembly is culture-neutral:

```
[assembly: AssemblyCulture("")]
```

This is the default value and should almost always be left empty.

> The culture cannot be set for an executable, so setting this attribute for an executable produces this compile error: **Executables cannot be localized, Culture should always be empty.**
>
> DLLs that contain executable code should not specify a culture, so this attribute needs to be left empty for most DLLs as well.

A DLL can be localized by specifying a culture, but this should only be done if you are creating a culture-specific satellite assembly that does **not** contain executable code. The culture becomes part of the assembly's version, so if your assembly contains executable code, applications seeking to use the DLL may not find the correct entry points for the methods and properties exposed by the DLL unless they specify a matching culture reference.

You can set the culture for a satellite assembly with the `AssemblyCulture` attribute as in the following example:

```
[assembly: AssemblyCulture("en-US")]   // English, USA culture
```

While the definitive list of language and country codes is specified by the ISO 639 and 3166 standards as described before, a comprehensive list of .NET-supported codes is listed in the .NET Framework documentation – search for "CultureInfo Class" with a titles-only search, then scroll down to the bottom of the `CultureInfo` class description.

For more information, also see the `System.Globalization` namespace, as well as globalization, localization and culture in the Visual Studio .NET and .NET Framework online documentation. Visual Studio .NET provides tools to assist with generating applications to support multiple cultures.

Version Attribute

Next within the `AssemblyInfo.cs` file comes the `AssemblyVersion` attribute. In a new project, the default setting of this attribute looks like this:

```
[assembly: AssemblyVersion("1.0.*")]
```

You can replace this version number with any set of numbers separated by periods; any parts you don't specify default to zero. For example, you could replace the version number with "1" (equivalent to 1.0.0.0), "1.1" (equivalent to 1.1.0.0), "1.2.1" (same as 1.2.1.0), or a full 4-part version number:

```
[assembly: AssemblyVersion("1.0.3706.1")]
```

Do you have to change this every time you build a new version? No, you don't. The asterisk (*) in the default version specifies that you want Visual Studio .NET to generate automatic version numbers; let's see how that works.

Automatic Version Numbers

Let's go back to that default version number setting for a new project; the version number looks like this:

```
[assembly: AssemblyVersion("1.0.*")]
```

The `AssemblyVersion` attribute allows an asterisk (*) to be specified for the last two parts of the version number. This directs Visual Studio .NET to set the build and revision numbers automatically. You can also specify the asterisk just for the revision number:

```
[assembly: AssemblyVersion("1.0.1.*")]
```

You cannot have an automatic version for the major and minor version numbers (1.* is not allowed).

If you look at the actual generated version number (we'll show you how to do that just ahead) you'll see that if you specify, say, `AssemblyVersion("1.0.*")`, then the version number Visual Studio .NET generates will be something like this:

1:0:757:24332

If we touch some code to make the compiler rebuild the assembly, we'll see the number change automatically to something like:

1:0:757:25005

The build number did not change but the revision number leaped ahead! With automatic version numbers, the build number will change once a day (it is defined as the number of days since January 1, 2000) and the revision number changes every few seconds (it is the number of seconds since midnight, divided by 2). Unless you rebuild more than once every 2 seconds you can be assured you'll get different version numbers for every build with this mechanism.

The nice thing about this is that you don't have to do anything to generate those numbers, but you can check them to verify that two assemblies are truly different or the same. This is handy for verifying, say, that an end-user's version of an assembly matches yours.

Strong Name Attributes

The default `AssemblyInfo.cs` file ends with lines for the `AssemblyKeyName` attribute, `AssemblyKeyFile` attribute, and `AssemblyDelaySign` attribute, as shown here:

```
[assembly: AssemblyDelaySign(false)]
[assembly: AssemblyKeyFile("")]
[assembly: AssemblyKeyName("")]
```

These attributes enable you to sign the assembly, generating a strong name for a shared assembly. This subject is described in more detail towards the end of this chapter where we talk about shared assemblies. We'll describe these attributes briefly here but don't change any of them; we'll do that in the shared assembly section.

The `AssemblyDelaySign` attribute reserves space in the assembly for a signature to be added later; this might be used in a larger corporate environment where a group other than the developer's is responsible for signing and verifying the company's products.

> *Note that there is more detail on delay signing available in the .NET online documentation, under the heading "Delay Signing an Assembly".*

The `AssemblyKeyFile` attribute specifies a file containing the keys for the strong name; this is the typical method for signing an assembly. We'll go through the steps for creating such a file later in this chapter.

The `AssemblyKeyName` attribute specifies a key for the strong name; instead of a file containing the key, this is the name of a key registered with the Crypto Service Provider (CSP) on this machine. If you're familiar with the CSP and have keys registered in it, you may want to use this instead of a file. However, if you're not familiar with CSPs already, just use the key file, it is much easier to deal with.

Go ahead and build the `Shapes` assembly, if you have not done so already, and we'll look at it with the `Ildasm` tool.

Viewing the Contents of an Assembly: ILDASM

The .NET Framework SDK and Visual Studio .NET come with a useful tool for looking at the contents of an assembly. The tool is called `Ildasm`, the Intermediate Language Disassembler. The .NET Framework Documentation calls it the MSIL Disassembler. The name of the executable is `Ildasm.exe`.

This tool lets us look directly at the contents of an assembly in its executable, binary form without having to have the source code accessible. It is helpful for understanding how assemblies are put together and how references and metadata appear within the assembly; it is sometimes useful as a debugging tool but in our case it is mainly a tool to let us directly look at assemblies and help us understand how they work.

Ildasm is located with the other .NET Framework tools in this directory path:

```
C:\Program Files\Microsoft Visual Studio .NET\FrameworkSDK\Bin
```

You can add this to your system's PATH environment variable so it is searched automatically.

I find the easiest way to access Ildasm.exe is to choose the **Visual Studio .NET Command Prompt** from Start | Programs | Microsoft Visual Studio .NET | Visual Studio .NET Tools, which automatically starts a command prompt with the path set for Ildasm and all other VS.NET command line tools. You can also add it as an external tool to Visual Studio .NET by browsing to its directory.

So, assuming you've located Ildasm and executed it, you'll see a graphical screen with a standard File menu on the left. Use File | Open to browse to the directory where Shapes.dll is located on your system (probably in the bin\debug subdirectory of your project), and open it.

> *Note: you can also specify the assembly name on the command line, for example:*
> *Ildasm c:\path\file.dll.*

Once you have specified an assembly and opened it, you'll see a display something like this:

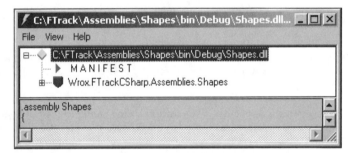

Ildasm provides a tree-based hierarchical view of the assembly contents. What we are seeing in the top level of the display are the files in the assembly, in this case only one, Shapes.dll. The contents of Shapes, as shown in our previous diagram, are first the manifest, and then the type metadata, which begins with the namespace Wrox.FTrackCSharp.Assemblies.Shapes declared in the first line of our class library. If you click on the plus sign by the namespace Shapes shield icon, you will see it expanded as follows:

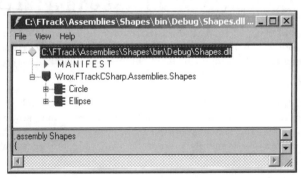

We can see the Circle and Ellipse classes that we defined. Expand the view again on each of these:

We now see our classes Circle and Ellipse, with the instance variables as well as the Area() and Draw() methods for each class. We also see some things we don't immediately understand, like that funny .ctor repeated twice in each class?

The .ctor is the MSIL notation for a constructor method; recall we defined two constructors for each class in Shapes, one with just the radius as a parameter and one with center x,y coordinate location, and radius parameters? There is a .ctor defined for each of these constructors.

The various float64 declarations are the .NET Framework/MSIL notation for the double data type in C#. double compiles to a 64-bit floating point number.

If you double-click on the Area() method you will see the actual MSIL code for that method. Ildasm follows the reference from the type metadata into the MSIL code storage section of the assembly to show this. However, as I said at the beginning we're not going to cover the details of MSIL code in this chapter, we're here to talk about assemblies.

By the way, we're going to see some MSIL (Microsoft Intermediate Language) code in this part of the chapter. We're not going to try to teach you MSIL, but we'll cover just enough to understand the contents of an assembly. MSIL looks a lot like a very simple assembler language, so if you've seen assembly language before it will be easy to pick up. It is also a lot like the Java byte codes that a Java VM executes, so familiarity with that will be helpful. If you haven't seen either of these, no problem; we'll explain the important parts as we encounter them and you can safely ignore the rest; just program in C# and let the compiler and runtime worry about the MSIL code.

If you're really voraciously curious about the details of MSIL, see the CLI (Common Language Infrastructure) documents in the Tool Developers Guide directory of the .NET Framework SDK. This is located in

```
C:\Program Files\Microsoft Visual Studio .NET\FrameworkSDK\Tool
Developers Guide\docs
```

on my system, but may differ in another version of Visual Studio .NET and the .NET Framework.

Just to be confusing, these documents call the language CIL for Common Intermediate Language. This is because CIL (nee MSIL) has been submitted to the ECMA standards body.

Viewing Contents of the Manifest

Double-clicking on the MANIFEST section at the start of the ILDASM display brings up the MANIFEST display, which looks like the following screenshot:

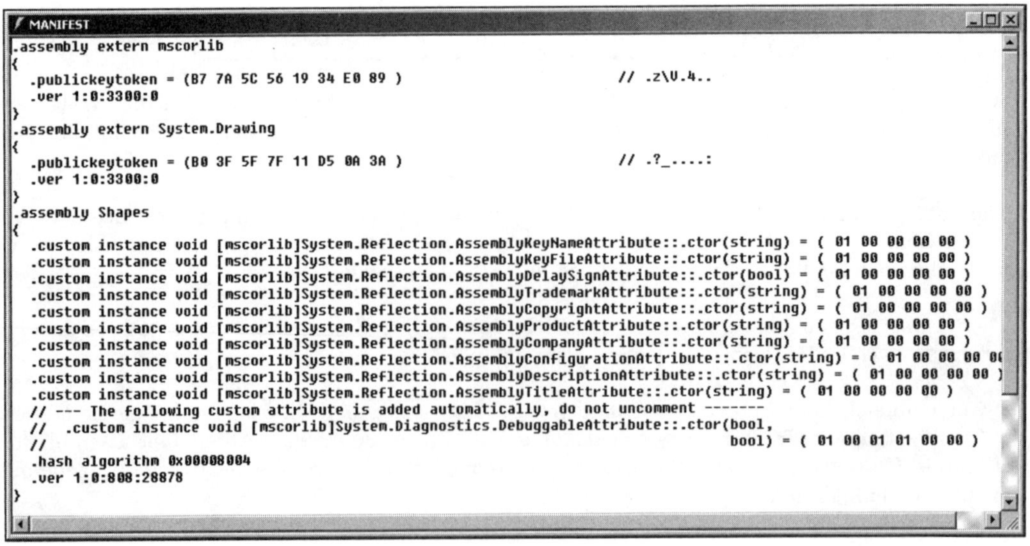

There's a lot of stuff here; however you will see it's all pretty straightforward if you look at it piece by piece.

The first section is an external assembly declaration:

```
.assembly extern mscorlib
{
  .publickeytoken = (B7 7A 5C 56 19 34 E0 89 )          // .z\V.4..
  .ver 1:0:3300:0
}
```

This is the reference to the .NET runtime core assembly mscorlib.dll, where the root of all the classes defined in the System namespace reside. The System.Math.PI constant that we use comes from here, for example. The mscorlib reference is generated by default, so it will always be there.

The .publickeytoken directive inside the mscorlib declaration refers to the public/private key encryption that establishes the strong name identity of mscorlib.dll.

The .ver directive is the version number; this tells the system what version of mscorlib the Shapes.dll binary was bound to and is compatible with. Note the four-part version number.

The next section is an external reference to the System.Drawing.dll assembly, needed for the Draw() methods. It also has a version number, as well as a public key token similar to the previous reference to mscorlib.

The final section describes the Shapes assembly itself:

```
.assembly Shapes
{
```

within the Shapes section are the many **assembly attribute** lines that look similar to these:

```
.custom instance void
    [mscorlib]System.Reflection.AssemblyKeyNameAttribute::
        .ctor(string) = ( 01 00 00 00 00 )
.custom instance void
    [mscorlib]System.Reflection.AssemblyKeyFileAttribute::
        .ctor(string) = ( 01 00 00 00 00 )
```

The attributes are constructed and initialized when the assembly is loaded, which is why you see a .ctor beside them. Notice that the attributes are the same as we saw in the AssemblyInfo.cs file, just in reverse order. The numbers beginning with 01 00 00 00 are the actual hexadecimal value of the initialized attribute; since we left this particular one empty we see the 01 00 00 00 indicating an empty value.

If you initialized some of the informational attributes you will see initialized values for those; for example, if you set the `AssemblyTitleAttribute` to "Shapes" you would see this in the Ildasm display, showing the hex value of the initialized string and a comment with the actual characters:

```
.custom instance void
[mscorlib]System.Reflection.AssemblyTitleAttribute::.ctor(string)
   = ( 01 00 06 53 68 61 70 65 73 00 00 )              // ...Shapes..
```

Finally, the `Shapes` assembly section ends with its version number declaration:

```
  .ver 1:0:808:28878
}
```

Now we see what version number Visual Studio .NET came up with when we specified the automatic version number generation using the asterisk (*) for the build and revision numbers. You can try making a small change to the source code and rebuilding; you'll see the same build number but a different revision.

Finally, after the assembly, there is a module declaration for the main (and only) module in this assembly.

```
  .module Shapes.dll
```

There are some details following the module statement but they're pretty obscure so we're going to skip those.

If you press *Ctrl-M* while looking at the **Area** method, another window pops up detailing all the metadata for the assembly displayed as text. If you scroll to the end of this display you will see the assembly metadata listed. This is just another way of looking at the data displayed graphically, without having to guess what all the icons are.

Viewing Contents of a Method

Just for fun, while we're in ILDASM let's click on a method, say the `Area()` method for `Circle`:

```
Circle::Area : float64()
.method public hidebysig instance float64
        Area() cil managed
{
  // Code size       29 (0x1d)
  .maxstack  3
  .locals init ([0] float64 CS$00000003$00000000)
  IL_0000:  ldc.r8     3.1415926535897931
  IL_0009:  ldarg.0
  IL_000a:  ldfld      float32 Wrox.FTrackCSharp.Assemblies.Shapes.Circle::radius
  IL_000f:  ldarg.0
  IL_0010:  ldfld      float32 Wrox.FTrackCSharp.Assemblies.Shapes.Circle::radius
  IL_0015:  mul
  IL_0016:  conv.r8
  IL_0017:  mul
  IL_0018:  stloc.0
  IL_0019:  br.s       IL_001b
  IL_001b:  ldloc.0
  IL_001c:  ret
} // end of method Circle::Area
```

Here is the actual IL code for the `Circle` method. You can see it loads the constant 3.1415926... (obtained from `System.Math.PI` in our code but compiled inline for efficiency), then loads the `radius` field twice, finally calling the multiply instruction (`mul`) to get the answer.

Well, that was fun but not too practical, perhaps. Most of the time you will not need to look at assembly contents this way; however, if there is ever a question as to which version of an assembly is actually installed or what version of the source made it into the last build, `Ildasm` is one way to answer these questions directly from the binary assembly. You can also explore the Microsoft .NET system assemblies or any other .NET assembly to see undocumented methods and other interesting trivia.

Outputting the Contents of an Assembly as IL

With the command line option `/out`, you can have Ildasm write the contents of an assembly to a file instead of the screen. For example,

```
>Ildasm Shapes.dll /out=Shapes.il
```

produces the file `Shapes.il` that contains the IL of our `Shapes` assembly. We have seen some of the contents of this file already when we viewed the assembly from Ildasm, but using a text editor the IL of the assembly can be edited directly. We can use the MSIL assembler `Ilasm.exe` to produce an executable file from `Shapes.il`:

```
Command Prompt                                                    _ □ ×
C:\FTrack\Assemblies\Shapes>ilasm Shapes.il /DLL

Microsoft (R) .NET Framework IL Assembler.  Version 1.0.3512.0
Copyright (C) Microsoft Corporation 1998-2001. All rights reserved.
Assembling 'Shapes.il' , no listing file, to DLL --> 'Shapes.DLL'
Source file is ANSI

Assembled method Circle::.ctor
Assembled method Circle::.ctor
Assembled method Circle::Area
Assembled method Circle::Draw
Assembled method Ellipse::.ctor
Assembled method Ellipse::.ctor
Assembled method Ellipse::Area
Assembled method Ellipse::Draw
Creating PE file

Emitting members:
Global
Class 1 Fields: 3;       Methods: 4;
Class 2 Fields: 4;       Methods: 4;
Resolving member refs: 26 -> 26 defs, 0 refs
Writing PE file
Operation completed successfully
```

Private Assemblies

Now let's look at what happens when our `Shapes` assembly is referenced by a program. We'll start by using it as a private assembly, which is the default and simplest case.

Simple Client Program

We'll make a simple client for Shapes named AreaCircle:

```
using System;
using Wrox.FTrackCSharp.Assemblies.Shapes;

namespace Wrox.FTrackCSharp.Assemblies.AreaCircle
{
    public class CircleArea
    {
        public static void Main()
        {
            Circle c = new Circle(1.0F);
            Console.WriteLine("Area of Circle(1.0) is {0}", c.Area());
        }
    }
}
```

Build this program as a console application. Add the reference to the Shapes class library with **Solution Explorer | References | Add Reference**, browsing to the location of Shapes.dll in the Shapes bin\Debug directory. We are using Shapes as a private assembly at this point.

Now build AreaCircle and run it. We will see the following:

Note that if you browse to the AreaCircle\bin\Debug directory, you will see that Visual Studio .NET has made a local copy of Shapes.dll:

```
Directory of C:\FTrack\Assemblies\AreaCircle\bin\Debug

02/03/2002  01:05p            4,608 Shapes.dll
02/03/2002  01:12p            5,632 AreaCircle.exe
```

Visual Studio .NET makes a local copy because, you will recall, private assemblies must be in the same directory as the application that uses them. However, the compile-time reference information in the Visual Studio.NET project for AreaCircle (viewable in **Solution Explorer | References | Shapes | Properties**) shows where the Shapes reference came from, and the local copy is updated automatically if Shapes.dll has been updated when AreaCircle is rebuilt.

At run-time, however, the local copy is the only one referenced in the private AreaCircle assembly. If you just run AreaCircle.exe outside of Visual Studio .NET, the local copy of Shapes.dll will be what the .NET runtime loads, even if the Shapes project has been rebuilt and there are changes to Shapes.dll. Only when AreaCircle is rebuilt will the local copy be renewed.

We can use `Ildasm` to look at the manifest of `AreaCircle.exe` to see the external reference to `Shapes.dll`:

```
MANIFEST                                                    _ □ ✗
.assembly extern mscorlib
{
  .publickeytoken = (B7 7A 5C 56 19 34 E0 89 )
  .ver 1:0:3300:0
}
.assembly extern Shapes
{
  .ver 1:0:808:28878
}
.assembly AreaCircle
```

Note that there is no path name, just the assembly name and version number. In order to find the assembly the .NET runtime has to apply its rules for searching for assemblies in order to satisfy the reference.

Private Assembly Binding and Searching

So what happens if you remove the private copy of `Shapes.dll` from the `bin\Debug` directory of `AreaCircle`? Let's see what happens (I'm going to use the command prompt since we built it as a console application):

```
>C:\FTrack\Assemblies\AreaCircle\bin\Debug>del Shapes.dll
>C:\FTrack\Assemblies\AreaCircle\bin\Debug>AreaCircle

Unhandled Exception: System.IO.FileNotFoundException: File or assembly name
Shapes, or one of its dependencies, was not found.
File name: "Shapes"
   at Wrox.FTrackCSharp.Assemblies.AreaCircle.CircleArea.Main()

Fusion log follows:
=== Pre-bind state information ===
LOG: DisplayName = Shapes, Version=1.0.808.28878, Culture=neutral,
PublicKeyToken=null
 (Fully-specified)
LOG: Appbase = C:\FTrack\Assemblies\AreaCircle\bin\Debug\
LOG: Initial PrivatePath = NULL
Calling assembly : AreaCircle, Version=1.0.808.29243, Culture=neutral, PublicKey
Token=null.
===

LOG: Application configuration file does not exist.
LOG: Policy not being applied to reference at this time (private, custom,
partial, or location-based assembly bind).
LOG: Post-policy reference: Shapes, Version=1.0.808.28878, Culture=neutral,
PublicKeyToken=null
LOG: Attempting download of new URL
```

```
file:///C:/FTrack/Assemblies/AreaCircle/bin/Debug/Shapes.DLL.
LOG: Attempting download of new URL
file:///C:/FTrack/Assemblies/AreaCircle/bin/Debug/Shapes/Shapes.DLL.
LOG: Attempting download of new URL
file:///C:/FTrack/Assemblies/AreaCircle/bin/Debug/Shapes.EXE.
LOG: Attempting download of new URL
file:///C:/FTrack/Assemblies/AreaCircle/bin/Debug/Shapes/Shapes.EXE.
```

That's quite a screenful of error messages! Why does it not find it when we just said Visual Studio .NET keeps track of the reference and updates the copy automatically? And why is it looking for `Shapes.exe` when we had a reference to `Shapes.dll`?

The answer to the first question, about Visual Studio .NET's reference, is that here we are not using Visual Studio .NET; we are just executing the assembly directly from the command line. Therefore, we are relying on the .NET runtime's **binding rules** to locate assemblies at execution time.

The .NET runtime follows a predefined set of rules in order to locate an external assembly at execution time.

❑   For private assemblies, the local directory is searched first, and then the system looks for a subdirectory with the same name as the assembly. The runtime also looks for either a DLL or EXE file having the same name as the requested assembly.

❑   For a shared assembly, the local directory is searched first, then the global assembly cache.

Version checking is performed for a shared assembly. We'll discuss search rules for shared assemblies after we show how to build them.

Note that the version checking was not performed since `Shapes.dll` is a private assembly, as can be seen from the message:

```
LOG: Policy not being applied to reference at this time (private, custom,
partial, or location-based assembly bind).
```

The private assembly **search rules** for our `Shapes` class the combination of these results in the following set of searches:

```
/Shapes.DLL
/Shapes/Shapes.DLL
/Shapes.EXE
/Shapes/Shapes.EXE
```

It is not a good idea to have EXEs and DLLs having the same name within your application, because of this binding behavior, in addition to avoiding confusion with names. If you want to structure your application directory differently, you can use an application configuration file to specify where the parts of your application are located within the application directory.

Application Configuration Files

Additional search paths may be specified with an **application configuration file**. A configuration file is a small text file in XML format specifying additional properties for the application. It is located in the same directory as the application main assembly binary, in our case in bin\Debug where AreaCircle.exe resides.

To try this, make a simple text file using Notepad or Visual Studio .NET, with these contents:

```
<configuration>
    <runtime>
        <assemblyBinding xmlns="urn:schemas-microsoft-com:asm.v1">
            <probing privatePath="I\never\thought\to\look\here"/>
        </assemblyBinding>
    </runtime>
</configuration>
```

Configuration files have the same name as the application they apply to, with a .config extension added to the name. Save the file as AreaCircle.exe.config in the same bin\debug directory as AreaCircle.exe.

Now make a new set of subdirectories under \bin\Debug: like I\never\thought\to\look\here. Copy Shapes.dll to the new directory, and try to run AreaCircle again. You'll see it runs correctly now that the runtime knows where to look. Why not just give it a reference to ..\..\Shapes\bin\Debug directly, you might ask? If that worked, it would be great for our example, but configuration files can redirect only within an application's private directory. This prevents a program from poking around in other directories on a system that it shouldn't.

Shared Assemblies

Next, we will make a shared version of Shapes.dll, and see how this affects the assembly binding and the assembly itself.

Building a Shared Assembly

In order to create a shared assembly with a strong name, you must generate a public/private key pair that is used to sign the assembly. Public/private key cryptographic systems use a private key known only to the sender of an encoded message, and a public key available to anyone.

In the .NET Framework, the public key of an assembly is used when another assembly references a strongly named (shared) external assembly. When the external assembly is loaded, the .NET runtime compares its strong name private key with the public key to be sure they match; if they do not, the referenced assembly will not load.

Using the sn Tool to Sign the Assembly

The .NET Framework provides a tool for generating the strong name called sn.exe (named for Strong Name). Let's create a strong name for our Shapes assembly. From the command-line, change directory to your project directory. Use the following command to generate a key, also giving a file name you will reference from your assembly (which usually has the .snk extension):

```
>sn -k shapes.snk
```

This creates the key file shapes.snk in the current directory; you'll see output like:

```
Microsoft (R) .NET Framework Strong Name Utility  Version 1.0.3705.0
Copyright (C) Microsoft Corporation 1998-2001. All rights reserved.

Key pair written to shapes.snk
```

To now sign the assembly with this key file, modify the AssemblyKeyFile attribute in the last part of the AssemblyInfo.cs file for your project:

```
[assembly: AssemblyKeyFile(@"..\..\shapes.snk")]
```

This path specifies the root directory of our project. If you don't specify the path, Visual Studio .NET will look in the obj\debug or obj\release directory for the key file.

Rebuild the Shapes.dll assembly. The assembly is now signed. If we now examine the manifest of the Shapes.dll assembly with Ildasm, we see that a public key has been generated and embedded within:

That big block of hexadecimal code shows the encrypted public key that other assemblies can reference.

Note that if we try to execute a client program that uses Shapes now without recompiling it, we get the following error because the Shapes.dll assembly no longer matches (the external reference is to a private assembly, but Shapes is now a shared assembly):

```
Unhandled Exception: System.IO.FileLoadException: The located assembly's manifest
definition with name 'Shapes' does not match the assembly reference.
```

We need to recompile the client program to update its external assembly reference to use the signed version of Shapes.dll.

Installing a Shared Assembly Into the Global Assembly Cache

The final step in deploying the shared assembly is to copy the now strongly-named assembly into the global assembly cache (GAC) ,where all applications can find it without having to search paths and/or have private copies of the assembly.

Note that administrator privileges on a Windows machine are required in order to place assemblies into the GAC.

Using Windows Installer

To work with the GAC during development, it's easier to use Gacutil or the assembly Windows shell extension, both described in the next section. However, these utilities should not be used for production applications, as the Windows Installer is the preferred way to deliver a production application to end-users.

Windows Installer version 2.0 and greater supports installation of .NET shared assemblies and can load these assemblies into the GAC.

Windows Installer can keep track of how many client applications have references to an assembly (that is, when client applications are installed with Windows Installer), and can remove unused versions when client applications are no longer referring to them. The installer can repair, patch, or remove assemblies in the GAC or even in private locations. It uses a transaction-based approach to rollback an unsuccessful, partial installation. It can also support install-on-demand, installing only when an application actually runs and needs to load the assembly.

Each shared assembly must be in its own Windows Installer component to support all the assembly functionality. Windows Installer is a table-driven tool; assembly information is loaded into the MsiAssembly and MsiAssemblyName tables. In the last table, the usual components of identifying a strongly-named assembly are specified (name, version, language (culture), and public key).

The background of how to use Windows Installer itself is beyond the scope of a C# book. See the documentation on Windows Installer in the Platform SDK, under Windows Installer, for more information.

Using the Gacutil Utility

One common way of installing an assembly into the global assembly cache during development is to use a .NET command line tool called Gacutil (Global Assembly Cache Utility). To install Shapes.dll into the GAC, use Gacutil with the /i flag at the Visual Studio .NET command-line tools prompt:

```
>Gacutil /i Shapes.dll
```

The message "Assembly successfully added to the cache" will indicate successful installation of the assembly.

To prove that Shapes.dll is in the GAC, do this:

❑ Rebuild AreaCircle (updating the reference to the now shared assembly version of Shapes.dll).

❑ Delete the copy of Shapes.dll from deep within the bin\Debug directory of AreaCircle.

❑ Now run AreaCircle.exe :

```
C:\FTrack\Assemblies\AreaCircle\bin\Debug >AreaCircle
Area of Circle(1.0) is 3.141596
```

It still runs even with Shapes.dll absent because it is loading the assembly from the GAC. Next, use Gacutil to uninstall Shapes:

```
>Gacutil /u shapes
```

Note that the .dll extension is omitted for the uninstall option.

Now try to run AreaCircle:

```
C:\FTrack\Assemblies\AreaCircle\bin\debug>AreaCircle
Unhandled Exception: System.IO.FileNotFoundException: File or assembly name
shapes, or one of its dependencies, was not found.
```

This shows that Shapes.dll was previously being loaded from the GAC. You can look at the GAC directly with the global assembly cache shell extension. Microsoft recommends that only users with Administrator privileges be allowed to uninstall assemblies from the global assembly cache. For more information on this, see the "Global Assembly Cache" entry in the .NET documentation.

Using the GAC Shell Extension (shfusion.dll)

The GAC is located in the Assembly subdirectory of the Windows directory of your system (C:\WINNT\Assembly on my machine). If you browse to this directory with Windows Explorer, you'll see that the files are uniquely displayed:

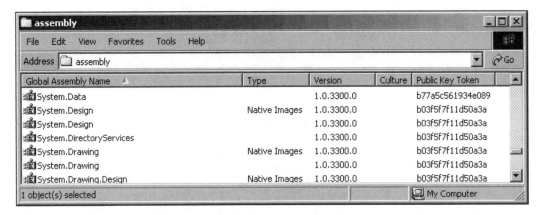

We see global (shared) assembly names, version, culture, and public keys – it's those parts of a strong name again. We are using a Windows Shell extension designed specifically for displaying the contents of the GAC; it is called `shfusion.dll` and is installed by the .NET Framework.

> *The Type column shows if the assembly is a special variation of the standard assembly, like the System assembly at the bottom of the screenshot above with a Native Images type. These are already compiled, high-performance machine-language versions of that `System` assembly.*

You can use this tool to view the assemblies in the GAC; it also supports drag-and-drop! You can install `Shapes.dll` into the GAC by using Windows Explorer to copy `Shapes.dll` from its development `bin\debug` folder and drop it into this view of `C:\WINNT\Assembly`. This requires that the assembly be signed just as with other methods of installing into the GAC. When we paste into the window, we see:

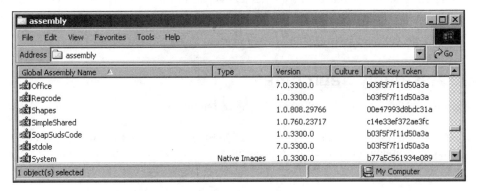

You can right-click on an assembly to delete it from the GAC, or to get its Properties in detail.

Side-by-Side Installation of Different Versions in the GAC

We can install different versions of Shapes.dll side-by-side in the GAC. To see this, place the current version of Shapes.dll into the GAC using one of the above methods. Then, change the AssemblyVersionAttribute of Shapes.dll to 2.0.0.0 and rebuild it. Place the rebuilt version into the GAC.

Notice that both versions of Shapes.dll appear in the list. Each has the same public key (since they are signed with the same shapes.snk file) but a different version number. These versions will coexist in the GAC; the AreaCircle application will continue to use the 1.0.x version until the AreaCircle assembly is rebuilt with a reference to the 2.0 version of Shapes.dll.

Note that if a newer 1.0.x version of Shapes.dll (say, version 1.0.999) were to be placed in the GAC, the 1.0.999 would also coexist with the first two. Try this; change the 2.0.0 version number back to 1.0.999, and then install Shapes.dll into the GAC again. You will see a display like this:

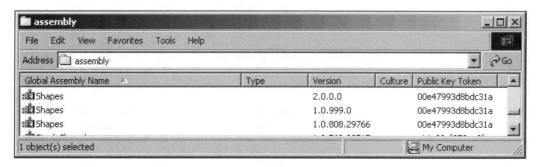

All three versions coexist. AreaCircle still has a reference to 1.0.808.29766, and will use that version until AreaCircle is rebuilt. AreaCircle will not use either of the newer versions of Shapes, unless a configuration file directs it to the newer version. However, another client program with a reference to, say, Shapes.dll version 2.0.0.0, would use that version.

Shared Assembly Searching

When a program references a shared assembly, the search follows this order:

1. The .NET runtime checks to see if the assembly has been loaded already, perhaps by a reference in another assembly in the same application. In this case, the previously loaded version in memory is used; there is no sense going through the search process twice.

2. The runtime checks the global assembly cache. It checks to make sure the name, version, culture, and public key of the requested assembly match the assembly found in the GAC. If a match is found in the GAC, then the assembly is loaded from the GAC and the binding request is satisfied.

3. The runtime searches in the path of the original reference, if such a path exists (references directly to assemblies in the GAC do not have a path to follow). The shared assembly configuration files may prevent this from happening.

4. If a path is found in the configuration files, it searches that location.

5. It searches the paths we described earlier for a private assembly.

6. Finally, if none of the above matches, it requests Windows Installer to provide the assembly, as an install-on-demand feature. The requested assembly must have been marked as install-on-demand at the time the application containing the assembly was installed with Windows Installer, or else the install-on-demand request will not be issued.

Shared Assembly Configuration Files

The configuration files that can affect the binding and version matching for an assembly are the following:

❏ The application configuration file, described earlier. It is located in the application's directory and has the same name as the application's main assembly with a `.config` suffix; for example, `AreaCircle.exe.config`.

❏ The publisher policy file. This is similar to the application configuration file but is associated not with the application but with the assembly being referenced (`Shapes` in our example). It is implemented in a way designed for shared assemblies installed in the GAC. You build an assembly containing the publisher policy and install that assembly in the GAC. The publisher policy is designed to implement policies from the assembly publisher (you, the software developer or vendor) for patches and updates to shared components. This process is described later in this section.

❏ The machine configuration file, which implements system-wide policies. It is called `machine.config` and is located in the .NET Framework's `Config` subdirectory; on my machine currently this is

`C:\WINNT\Microsoft.NET\Framework\v1.0.3705\config\machine.config`

The machine configuration file is the highest authority, overruling policies from other sources. This gives the System Administrator for a machine the ultimate say over how these policies are enforced.

Contents of Configuration Files

Each of the configuration files starts as a text file in XML format and supports the same XML schema, so the syntax shown here applies to all of these.

Version Redirection

Here is an example configuration file with an entry directing applications using the `Shapes` assembly to a new "hot fix" version:

```
<configuration>
  <runtime>
    <assemblyBinding xmlns="urn:schemas-microsoft-com:asm.v1">
    <dependentAssembly>
      <assemblyIdentity name="Shapes"
                        publicKeyToken="00e47993d8bdc31a"/>
```

```
        <!-- Assembly versions can be redirected in application,
               publisher policy, or machine configuration files. -->
          <bindingRedirect oldVersion="1.0.0.0"
                           newVersion="1.0.0.1"/>
        </dependentAssembly>
        <dependentAssembly>
        </dependentAssembly>
      </assemblyBinding>
    </runtime>
</configuration>
```

The <assemblyIdentity> XML element indicates that this configuration applies to the Shapes.dll assembly; note that the name and the public key are both specified so we know that it is our Shapes.dll we are redirecting and not someone else's assembly of the same name.

The <bindingRedirect> element directs the .NET runtime to load Shapes.dll v1.0.0.1 instead of 1.0.0.0.

Download Assembly from URL

Here is another example, showing how to download an assembly from a web location:

```
<configuration>
  <runtime>
    <assemblyBinding xmlns="urn:schemas-microsoft-com:asm.v1">
      <dependentAssembly>
        <assemblyIdentity name="Shapes"
                          publicKeyToken="00e47993d8bdc31a"/>
        <codeBase version="1.0.0.1"
                  href="http://localhost/Shapes.dll"/>
      </dependentAssembly>
    </assemblyBinding>
  </runtime>
</configuration>
```

The <assemblyIdentity> element is the same as in the previous example.

The <codeBase> element directs the .NET runtime to load Shapes.dll from a web address, in this case the root directory of the web server on the local machine (http://localhost). Note that this assumes Shapes.dll is in the web server root directory (c:\inetpub\wwwroot for Microsoft IIS).

There are several other XML elements controlling various aspects of assembly loading. For a complete description, see the .NET Framework online documentation under the heading "Configuration File Schema".

Creating Configuration Files

For the application configuration file, you would place the XML text shown above in the application configuration file (for example, AreaCircle.exe.config) just as described earlier for private assemblies.

For the machine configuration file, the System Administrator can place the above text within that file. Don't do this lightly, however – the `machine.config` file is quite complex. If I were a System Administrator I would create an application `.config` file or publisher policy file myself rather than mess with the machine configuration file.

As we said before, the publisher policy implements policies from the assembly publisher, that is, the company that created the assembly. If you have shipped shared assemblies and need to specify a version policy for an update or patch for all your customers, the publisher policy lets you do this in a way that works for shared assemblies.

For the publisher policy configuration file, you create an XML source text file with the contents as shown above for the application configuration file. The name and location of the XML source text can be anything; as an example we'll call it `shapes.pub.config`. Then you use `al.exe` (the assembly linker, available under the Visual Studio .NET Command Line Tools) to create an assembly based on this XML source text file. The assembly created must be named in this format:

```
policy.majorVersion.minorVersion.mainAssemblyName.dll
```

The policy assembly is linked with the same strong name public/private key file used to name the main assembly. For example, to create a publisher policy assembly for `Shapes.dll`, we would use a command like:

```
>al /link:shapes.pub.config /out:policy.1.0.Shapes.dll /keyfile:shapes.snk
```

The policy assembly is then placed in the GAC using one of the methods mentioned before for placing assemblies in the GAC. Any application referencing that assembly will then be redirected by the publisher policy.

> *There is one exception to this – the application configuration file or machine configuration file can use the* `publisherPolicy` *configuration tag to tell the runtime to ignore the publisher policy, by placing the tag* `<publisherPolicy apply="no"/>` *in the configuration file.*

Digital Signatures and SignCode

The strong-name mechanism described earlier in this chapter provides only a minimal level of trust for an assembly. In particular:

❑ The strong name protects against assembly name/version confusion, accidental or deliberate

❑ If you already trust a strong-named assembly, a new version using the same public key provides strong evidence that the new assembly contains code from the same trusted source.

However, when you run a program from a particular vendor for the first time, you do not yet trust the source.

Also, you may trust program A from a certain source, but encounter program B that claims to be from the same source, but has a different key – you don't know that program B's key really has anything to do with the source of program A.

To provide a greater level of security the .NET Framework provides a way to put an additional **digital signature** on an assembly in addition to the strong name public/private key.

> A digital signature indicates that an independent trusted authority (called a Certificate Authority or CA) verifies that your code really comes from you or your company and that your code hasn't been altered or corrupted since it was created and signed. Certificate authorities are independent of Microsoft; they are third-party companies such as VeriSign Corporation (http://www.verisign.com) or Thawte (http://www.thawte.com), which sell their certification services to software vendors. You or your company have to pay for this certification if you want your customers to have this independent verification of your assembly's identity; it adds an additional layer of trust to the strong name.

Digital signatures in .NET use a Microsoft technology called Authenticode which was introduced for verification of downloads with Microsoft Internet Explorer; third-party certificate authorities such as VeriSign and Thawte support the Authenticode specification. The Authenticode-compatible digital signature is contained in a **Software Publisher Certificate (SPC)**. VeriSign, Thawte, and other certification authorities can provide these certificates or utilities to create them. The certificates are files created using the X.500 and X.509 standard formats.

The decision as to whether to use a digital signature with your assembly is a business decision for you, your company, and your customers. Microsoft provides the tools to add the signature, but you must make arrangements to get the certificate from a valid certification authority. It is purely an optional step on your part.

Adding a Digital Signature to an Assembly with SignCode

If you decide to use a digital signature, you add it to the assembly using a command-line utility called signcode.exe, found in the same location as sn.exe and Ildasm.

signcode.exe signs the assembly in much the same way that sn.exe signs the assembly, except that it puts the digital signature in a different location within the assembly (there is a specific field in the Portable Executable (PE) file format for this purpose).

To use signcode, you must have a Software Publisher Certificate to sign with. For testing purposes only, the .NET Framework has two tools, makecert and cert2spc, that make a test SPC so you can try out the process of adding a digital signature. We'll go through this process now – bear in mind that for a commercially-valid digital signature, you will need to get an SPC from a recognized commercial supplier of digital signatures such as VeriSign or Thawte as described previously.

Here is an example of creating a test SPC using makecert and cert2spc, for Shapes.dll. Go to the directory containing Shapes.dll and type the following from the command line:

```
>makecert -sk ShapesKey -n "CN=ShapesKey" shapes.cer
```

This creates a certification file referencing (and creating) a private key container in the registry called `ShapesKey`. `"CN=ShapesKey"` gives the certificate a standard X.500 name. Now to transform the certificate into the SPC format, use the `cert2spc` tool:

```
>cert2spc shapes.cer shapes.spc
```

Now that you have a test SPC file, you can sign the assembly, referencing the `ShapesKey` private key container created with `makecert`:

```
>signcode /spc shapes.spc /k ShapesKey Shapes.dll
```

`Shapes.dll` is now signed with a digital signature in addition to its strong name signature. An assembly can have a digital signature without a strong name, but you would want both to get the security benefits.

Code Access Security

Traditional security in computer systems depends on assigning permissions to a particular user, who logs in with a password. Any program run by that user requires the permissions assigned to that user.

This worked well enough when computers were isolated from one another, but in the modern environment where users download and run programs from the Internet, a user may run a program and not realize what that program is doing to their system using their permissions. Code may have bugs that a hacker can exploit, or a user may inadvertently execute code from an untrustworthy source.

To protect against this the .NET Framework provides **code access security** in addition to the traditional login-based security. Code security is enforced at the assembly level, which is why we discuss it in this chapter. Code access security provides these protections:

- ❑ It can require that code prove its origin from a trusted source by providing a digital signature.
- ❑ It assigns different levels of trust to code, and lets code request permissions or require that all callers have certain permissions.
- ❑ It allows permission levels to be defined that are required for access to system resources.
- ❑ It enables system administrators to define and control code access security groups and access levels.

Evidence and Security Policy

A digital signature and strong names are both examples of **evidence** of an assembly's trustworthiness. An administrator will assign code access permissions based on the level of trustworthiness desired. Another example of evidence is the origin of code; for example, code downloaded from the Internet executing in the context of a web browser is in a different context from code resident on the machine that is part of the operating system or .NET Framework.

The runtime's decision to load an assembly or allow a certain operation to execute is based on the evidence for a particular assembly.

For example, an administrator may set a policy of not granting permission to access the file system or execute unmanaged code on an assembly downloaded from the Internet, but will allow an exception for assemblies signed with a digital signature from a certain trusted vendor.

The `ZoneIdentityPermission` class allows downloaded code to be categorized by its originating URL, into zones of lesser and greater trust. The zones identified are, in order of least trust to greatest trust, the restricted sites zones (URLs known to have caused trouble in the past), the general Internet zone, the trusted sites zone, the local intranet zone, and the local machine zone.

Code Permissions

The `System.Security.Permissions` namespace defines a variety of permissions that may be given or denied to an assembly based on the evidence associated with that assembly. For example, a typical security policy may not allow downloaded code to have the `FileIOPermission` for general file access, but would allow such code the `IsolatedStoragePermission` for access to anonymous storage, isolated from the general file system of the host computer.

Permissions are granted based on the evidence of all the assemblies in the stack of callers, as shown here:

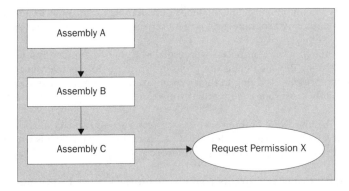

For example, in this diagram assembly A binds to assembly B which then binds to assembly C. Code in assembly C attempts to do something that requires permissions such as file manipulation. When assembly C requests this permission or attempts to do the operation, the entire chain of caller evidence from C back to B back to A is examined for evidence. This can have an performance effect if activity at a lower level generates many permission checks; it is more efficient for assembly A to explicitly request all the permissions needed at one time if assembly A "knows" what permissions will be needed.

For example if assembly A "knew" that all the permissions granted local intranet applications were needed, it could request that set of permissions at assembly load time by adding an assembly `PermissionSet` attribute directive in its `AssemblyInfo.cs` file; this would be processed at the time assembly A is loaded:

```
[assembly:PermissionSetAttribute(SecurityAction.RequestMinimum,
                        Name = "LocalIntranet")]
```

For more information see the topic "Requesting Permissions" in the .NET online documentation.

Advanced Assembly Topics

Now we'll look at some advanced topics that go beyond understanding the basic use of assemblies. The topics show some of the unique features of the .NET runtime and how those features are made available within assemblies.

Reflection and the Assembly Class

The .NET Framework provides classes in the System.Reflection namespace to allow you to get information about classes and types in assemblies without having access to the source code. This allows construction of very generic applications. The System.Reflection namespace provides the Assembly class to get information about, and do operations with, the assembly itself. For example, we can use reflection to find out what version of an assembly we are using, as in the next example, GetAreaCircleVersion:

```
using System;
using System.Reflection;

using Wrox.FTrackCSharp.Assemblies.Shapes;

namespace Wrox.FTrackCSharp.Assemblies.GetShapesVersion
{

   public class ShapesVersion
   {
      public static void Main()
      {
         Circle c = new Circle(1.0F);
         Console.WriteLine("Area of Circle(1.0) is {0}", c.Area());
         // display the assembly we are binding to

         Assembly shapesAssembly;
         // get the assembly object that implements the circle object
         shapesAssembly = Assembly.GetAssembly(c.GetType());
         // Tells us the full name, version, culture, and public key (if any)
         // of the assembly

         Console.WriteLine("Shapes version is :" + shapesAssembly.FullName);
      }
   }
}
```

This example declares an Assembly object, and then calls the GetAssembly() method to get information about the assembly that defines the Circle object – it calls the GetType() method of Circle to get its class information, and then passes this to GetAssembly.

We then use the FullName property of the Assembly class to get the name, version number, culture, and public key (if present) of the containing assembly:

```
C:\FTrack\Assemblies\GetShapesVersion\bin\Debug>GetShapesVersion
Area of Circle(1.0) is 3.14159265358979
Shapes version is :Shapes, Version=1.0.808.29766, Culture=neutral, PublicKeyToken
=00e47993d8bdc31a
```

Explicit and Implicit Loading

All the examples of assembly binding we have looked at so far are **implicit**, that is, the loading of the assembly is performed by the runtime when it encounters the reference in the assembly manifest. You can also load **explicitly**, without a reference, using the Load() or LoadWithPartialName() methods of the System.Reflection.Assembly class. Here is an example called LoadExample.cs:

```
using System;
using System.Reflection;

namespace Wrox.FTrackCSharp.Assemblies.LoadExample
{
    public class LoadExample
    {
        public static void Main()
        {
            Assembly shapesAssembly; // declare assembly object
            // load specifying only assembly name
            shapesAssembly = Assembly.LoadWithPartialName("Shapes");
            if (shapesAssembly != null) {
                Console.WriteLine("Shapes version is :"
                + shapesAssembly.FullName);
            }
        }
    }
}
```

Note that LoadWithPartialName() will load any version of Shapes, and as such is to be used with caution to ensure the correct version is loaded. The Assembly.Load() method takes an AssemblyName object, which has properties representing each component of a strongly-named assembly, including the name, version, culture, and public key. By specifying all these parts, you can ensure the same version-checking as with an implicit assembly load. Explicit loads are useful if you have a program that works with a variety of interfaces to other programs that load different assemblies depending on some logic your program controls, such as interfacing to different network protocols with code specific to each protocol in its own assembly.

Dynamic Assemblies

One of the most interesting "gee-whiz" capabilities of the reflection classes is contained in the System.Reflection.Emit namespace. You can use this class to generate an entire assembly programmatically including the metadata, classes and the MSIL code they contain. These generated assemblies can be created on-the-fly and executed dynamically without having to go through a separate link and execute step. Saving the assembly to an executable file is optional. This capability obviously is of interest to writers of compilers or scripting languages; it could be used, for example, to dynamically generate a customized, object-oriented class interface to some complex external object without having to know the object's structure ahead of time.

Cross-Language Support

Another "gee-whiz" capability of .NET assemblies is their object-oriented **cross-language** capability. I can write a class library in C#, generate an assembly, and use the assembly from a Visual Basic .NET program with all the same data types, classes, properties, methods, inheritance, and other object-oriented features used by C#.

This is a significant advance over the cross-language capabilities of DLLs and COM, which enabled cross-language use at an API or interface level but did not really support cross-language inheritance or a common type subsystem.

There were many cross-language data type issues between VB, C++, and other languages; these are now solved with the common type system (CTS) of .NET. The CLS (Common Language Specification) describes how to write classes that are fully cross-language capable.

Another related topic is the CodeDOM facility that enables source code for multiple languages to be generated from one source. This is great if you deliver a CLS compliant application such as a class library intended to be used by C#, VB.NET or any other .NET language – you can generate samples in both VB.NET and C# from one source.

COM Interop Assemblies

The .NET framework also allows components or libraries written using classic COM and other legacy technologies to be used with C# and other .NET languages.

This mechanism also works via self-describing assemblies; what happens is that a **wrapper** assembly is created for the legacy code that allows it to describe itself to the .NET runtime, convert the COM data types to .NET data types, and allow calls back and forth from the .NET languages to the legacy code, and vice versa. Visual Studio .NET automatically creates a wrapper assembly when you add a reference to a COM component (using the COM tab in the Add Reference dialog).

This diagram shows such a wrapper (also called a runtime callable wrapper) in use; calls made by the .NET client assembly go through the wrapper to get to the COM component. From the .NET assembly's point of view the wrapper **is** the component.

Note that the COM component is still COM; the wrapper does not protect against conflicting versions, registration failures, and other problems from the COM legacy environment.

We will look at COM interoperability in more detail in Chapter 11.

Summary

In this chapter, we have learned the concepts and vocabulary associated with assemblies, and taken an in-depth look at these topics:

- ❑ The assembly is a self-describing package of executable code and resources for the .NET environment.

- ❑ Each assembly has a manifest describing the contents of the assembly and any references to other assemblies.

- ❑ An assembly is a version, deployment, security, type, and reference unit treated by the .NET runtime as a single entity.

- ❑ Assemblies may be private or shared.

- ❑ Each assembly has a name, version number, and culture.

- ❑ Shared assemblies may be signed with a public/private key and/or a digital signature.

Strong names for shared assemblies combine the assembly name, version, culture, and key; the strong name is nearly impossible to confuse with another assembly's identity. Assembly references and the assemblies they reference must match exactly for the .NET runtime to load them (unless a configuration file redirects the runtime to load a different version).

- ❑ Assemblies come in single-file and multiple-file forms. A special kind of assembly used to support multiple national language applications is the satellite assembly.

- ❑ Assemblies have attributes such as the trademark, product name, version number, strong name key information, and culture.

- ❑ You can view the contents of an assembly with the ILDASM tool. The .NET runtime uses specific search strategies to find both private and shared assemblies when satisfying references.

- ❑ For shared assemblies the runtime performs version checking. Both searching and version checking can be changed by configuration files.

- ❑ We learned how to sign an assembly so that it can be given a strong name.

- ❑ We learned various ways to place signed assemblies in the global assembly cache (GAC), thus making the assembly accessible to any application.

- ❑ Finally, we learned about code access security, digital signatures, reflection, dynamic assemblies, and COM interop assemblies.

Take the **Fast Track** to **C#**

10

Data Access with ADO.NET

ADO.NET is the part of the .NET framework that enables access to data in relational databases and other data sources. Microsoft calls this part of the .NET framework ADO.NET because it is the .NET successor to ADO (ActiveX Data Objects), the most common Microsoft API for accessing data before .NET. ADO.NET data providers serve a similar role to JDBC in Java, providing a standard set of classes for basic database access. ADO.NET goes further by providing many new data handling facilities not found in classic ADO or JDBC, for example, the DataSet object with its awareness of relationships between tables, and the XML support integrated directly into ADO.NET.

In this chapter, we will look at:

- ❑ An overview of ADO.NET
- ❑ .NET data providers
- ❑ The ADO.NET class structure – the data consumer classes and the .NET provider classes
- ❑ Using a data reader with the SQL, OLE DB and ODBC .NET providers
- ❑ Stored procedures and transactions within ADO.NET
- ❑ Using the DataSet and navigating relationships within tables
- ❑ Displaying data with the Windows DataGrid control
- ❑ XML in ADO.NET

ADO.NET

ADO.NET provides simple access to relational and non-relational data. As with classic ADO, ADO.NET provides a high-level set of classes that allow us to manipulate data without worrying too much about the low-level implementation.

We can use ADO.NET to access many different types of data source. .NET data providers are specific to particular kinds of databases and data sources. The SQL Server provider gives us direct access to SQL Server 2000 databases, while the OLE DB and ODBC providers give us access to any data source that OLE DB or ODBC support. It's generally faster to use a native provider, because it cuts out the middle tier. As .NET gains popularity, more native providers will appear.

ADO.NET supports disconnected data processing. This means that we can continue to manipulate data when we do not have a connection to the database, and then reopen the connection to update the source with our changes. This makes it much easier to write multi-tier applications, because we can pass data efficiently between tiers without passing a database connection – we can even pass data objects to client applications, then receive them back and update the data source with changes.

XML is central in the design of ADO.NET, and as you will see the multi-tier and XML capabilities goals build on one another as ADO.NET uses XML internally to communicate between tiers as well as externally. The XML classes in ADO.NET unify the hierarchical XML view of data with the table-oriented view of relational systems.

Finally, ADO.NET is extensible (you can write your own .NET data provider and you can inherit from ADO.NET classes to construct higher-level objects).

The `System.Data.dll` assembly contains the ADO.NET classes, many of which are in the `System.Data` namespace and its children.

.NET Data Providers

In ADO.NET, each particular type of data source can have a .NET data provider. These deal with the messier lower-level business, either interfacing with the data source's own API, or a bridge technology such as OLE DB.

The .NET Framework comes with two bundled .NET data providers, one dedicated to SQL Server and the other for the more generic OLE DB interface that works with multiple data formats. Currently, Microsoft offers the ODBC provider as a separate download.

More providers will appear over time, from Microsoft and other vendors. Of course, if a provider avoids additional layers then performance will improve. It is possible to access SQL Server 2000 via OLE DB, but it's far slower than using the native SQL Server provider. The same will be true of new database-specific drivers – they will improve performance, and can also provide extra database-specific features.

SQL Server .NET Provider

This is the Microsoft SQL Server .NET Data Provider. Its classes have names beginning with `Sql`, as in `SqlConnection`. These classes are in the `System.Data.SqlClient` namespace.

OLE DB .NET Provider

The other provider that comes bundled with the framework is the OLE DB provider, for access to Microsoft Access, Oracle, and other data sources that support the Microsoft OLE DB data component interface. The OLE DB provider classes begin with an `OleDb` prefix, as in `OleDbConnection`. These classes are in the `System.Data.OleDb` namespace.

ODBC .NET Provider

This is one example of a .NET data provider supplied separately from the .NET Framework. The ODBC .NET Data Provider is available for download from http://www.microsoft.com/data. Its classes have names beginning with `Odbc`, as in `OdbcConnection`. Its namespace, `Microsoft.Data.Odbc`, follows the *vendor*`.Data.`*xxx* convention recommended for vendor-supplied data providers.

By default, it installs as a separate DLL in the location:

```
C:\Program Files\Microsoft.NET\Odbc.Net\Microsoft.Data.Odbc.dll
```

You must add a reference to this file in any projects that use ODBC.

ODBC is the oldest and most established Windows database API with wide support from hundreds of vendors. Almost every database and data format has an ODBC driver somewhere that supports it. ODBC is very portable but generally not as fast as a native driver, and also does not support all the database features and behavior that a native driver does.

ADO.NET Class Structure

We can divide the ADO.NET-related classes into three groups:

❑ Data Consumer Classes – we use these classes for manipulating data. They are independent of the data source, and we can manipulate data using these classes without an open connection to the database.

❑ .NET Data Provider Classes – these classes interface with the database, and provide some features for manipulating the retrieved data. Each data provider will have a different set of classes – for example, the SQL provider has `SqlCommand`, `SqlConnection`, and so on. We can easily pass data between these classes and the consumer classes.

❑ Other .NET Framework Classes – these classes are related to data handling, but are not part of the `System.Data` namespace. For example, there are data-bound controls that are part of the `System.Windows.Forms` namespace. We can easily pass data between these classes and the data consumer classes.

Let's look at each of these categories in turn.

Data Consumer Classes

High-level data processing in ADO.NET revolves around the ADO.NET data consumer classes – the `DataSet` class and its related classes `DataTable`, `DataRow`, `DataColumn` and `DataRelation`. These classes are in the `System.Data` namespace. As you might guess, these classes represent data in the familiar relational database form of tables, rows, columns, and relationships between tables.

> *The relational database concepts of constraints and views are also represented, in the* `Constraints` *and* `DefaultView` *properties of the* `DataTable` *class. For more information, see the* "`Constraint` *Class" and* "`DataView` *Class" topics within the .NET Framework online documentation.*

This diagram shows the structure of a `DataSet`:

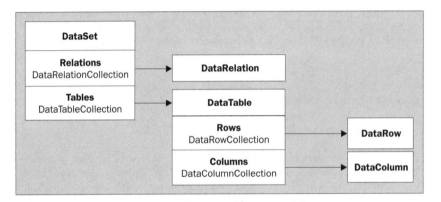

The consumer classes are connected to the actual database or data source via the .NET Data Provider classes, which define the connection, send commands to and from the database, and read data from and write data into the database.

The DataSet

The `DataSet` object can contain data from a set of related tables, stored in memory in an application. For example `Customers`, `Orders`, and `Products` might all be tables in one `DataSet`.

The `DataSet` lets us examine and change this data while disconnected from the server, then update the server with the changes in one efficient operation. The contents of the `DataSet` can be converted to XML, and then saved or sent over a network where the XML can be turned back into a `DataSet`.

The `DataSet` has properties for accessing individual tables and relationships via the objects that represent them. The main objects are:

The DataRelation

The `DataRelation` object represents the relationship between two tables via a shared column. For example, the `Orders` table might have a `CustomerID` column identifying the customer who placed the order. A `DataRelation` object might be created representing the relationship between `Customers` and `Orders` via the shared column `CustomerID`.

> *The shared columns may have different names, but must have the same data type. Also, the two related tables may be be based on views as well as tables in the database, since the `DataTable` may be filled using any SQL query; we'll look at this later in the chapter.*

The `Relations` property of a `DataSet` enables access to the `DataRelation` objects. The `Relations` property is a `DataRelationCollection` – we can access each `DataRelation` contained within it with a `foreach` loop in C#.

> *Data relations enable you to easily navigate between related tables in the `DataSet`. This is a totally new capability in ADO.NET that was not present in predecessors such as ADO, which had very limited support for multiple results or tables within the same `Recordset` object.*

The DataTable

The `DataTable` object represents one of the tables in the `DataSet`. The `Tables` property of a `DataSet` provides access to the `DataTable` object for each table in the `DataSet`. The `Tables` property is a `DataTableCollection`.

The DataRow

The `DataRow` object represents a single row in a table. The `Rows` property of a `DataTable`, a `DataRowCollection`, provides access to the `DataRow` object for each row in the table.

The DataColumn

The `DataColumn` object represents one column in the table, for example `OrderID` or `CustomerName`. The `Columns` property of a `DataTable`, a `DataColumnCollection`, enables access to the `DataColumn` object for each column in the table.

We've seen the data consumer objects, and how they relate to each other, catering for our data manipulation needs. Now let's look at how to interface with the data source – the .NET Provider Classes.

.NET Provider Classes

There is a different .NET Data Provider for each particular target database or data source, and the class names vary according to which provider the class is for.

The provider classes for the SQL Server .NET Provider, from the `System.Data.SqlClient` namespace, all begin with `Sql`. The classes for the OLE DB provider begin with `OleDb`, and the ODBC provider classes begin with `Odbc`. As non-Microsoft vendors implement their own .NET providers, their classes will also have a prefix specific to that vendor. Let's look at each of the major .NET provider classes:

xxxConnection Class

The `Connection` objects are the first objects that we use and are required before using any of the other ADO.NET provider objects. They provide the basic connection to your data source. If you are using a database that requires a user ID and password, or one on a remote network server, the connection object takes care of the details of establishing the connection and logging in. The connection class for the providers discussed above are `SqlConnection`, `OleDbConnection`, and `OdbcConnection`.

> *`Connection` and other objects that serve a similar function in ADO.NET and classic ADO have similar names in both versions.*

xxxCommand Class

We use the `Command` objects to issue commands, such as SQL queries, to a data source. The provider-specific names include `SqlCommand` for SQL Server, `OleDbCommand` for OLE DB, and `OdbcCommand` for ODBC.

xxxCommandBuilder Class

This `CommandBuilder` objects build SQL commands for data modification. For example, we can use it to construct commands for deleting rows from a given table – we don't need to know the SQL. We'll look at this object in more detail when we study how to update data. The provider-specific names include `SqlCommandBuilder` for SQL Server, `OleDbCommandBuilder` for OLE DB, and `OdbcCommandBuilder` for ODBC.

xxxDataReader Class

`DataReader` objects provide fast, forward-only, read-only access to data. To use them, we must have an open connection to the database. It gives maximum performance for reading data by using a "fire hose" cursor to stream data out of the source as fast as possible. The provider-specific names include `SqlDataReader` for SQL Server, `OleDbDataReader` for OLE DB, and `OdbcDataReader` for ODBC.

xxxDataAdapter Object

The `DataAdapter` classes provide the main link between the provider classes and the consumer classes. We use them for writing `DataSet` changes back to the source, filling `DataSet` objects, and several other operations that we'll see in the following examples. The provider-specific names include `SqlDataAdapter` for SQL Server, `OleDbDataAdapter` for OLE DB, and `OdbcDataAdapter` for ODBC.

xxxException Object

This object represents exceptions from errors generated by accessing or manipulating the data source. The provider-specific names include `SqlException` for SQL Server, `OleDbException` for OLE DB, and `OdbcException` for ODBC.

SQL Data Type Support

The SQL data type classes in the `System.Data.SqlTypes` namespace provide SQL-compatible implementations of integer, decimal, floating, string, date, time, and other basic data types that are completely compatible with the SQL-92 and SQL Server definitions of these data types. These classes provide a way to manipulate values obtained from SQL queries without data type conversion issues. Use of these types helps bridge differences between native C# and .NET types, and the SQL data types. The `System.Data.SqlDbType` enumeration provides a set of constants to specify a particular SQL data type when passing data to SQL support methods.

There are good reasons for new .NET Data Providers to supply special data type support in this way. As new providers appear, they are likely to support native data types.

Other .NET Framework Classes

The .NET Framework contains some classes that bridge between ADO.NET and other areas of the Framework. Examples include the XML and Forms classes.

XML .NET Framework classes

Because the `DataSet` is based on XML, the .NET Framework's XML classes are relevant. For example, the `XmlDataDocument` class connects ADO.NET data to all of the built-in XML support classes in the .NET Framework. It inherits from the .NET XML DOM implementation class, `XmlDocument`, while adding a property that is a `DataSet` from ADO.NET, allowing relational or other data contained in a `DataSet` to be read, written, and navigated as an XML document. We'll go through this in more detail later in the chapter.

.NET Windows and Web Forms Classes

Many of the Windows and Web Forms classes can bind to data from consumer classes. For example, the `DataGrid` class displays `DataSet` or `DataTable` data on Windows or Web forms. We'll examine `DataGrid` later in the chapter. The `DataGrid` is one of the most useful and flexible data bound controls, but many of the other controls work in a similar way.

Using ADO.NET

Now that we've seen how ADO.NET fits together, let's start to get our hands dirty with some examples. First we need to get a sample database up and running.

Example Database: MSDE and Northwind

In this chapter, we will base our examples on the Microsoft Northwind sample database. If you want to try out the examples, you will need to set up the Northwind database in SQL Server 2000 or the Microsoft Data Engine.

> **Visual Studio.NET includes the desktop version of SQL Server, called the Microsoft Data Engine (MSDE). The examples will use MSDE, but they will also work with SQL Server 2000 Standard or Enterprise Edition. MSDE is compatible with SQL Server 2000, but has limits on database size and the number of simultaneous users it supports.**

MSDE is installed with Visual Studio .NET, but must be set up separately. By default, Visual Studio .NET places setup instructions in the following folder:

```
C:\Program Files\Microsoft Visual Studio .NET\FrameworkSDK\
                                        Samples\StartSamples.htm
```

Be sure to perform both "Step 1: Install the .NET Framework Samples Database" and "Step 2: Set up the Quick Starts" in order to install the MSDE server and the Northwind sample database.

When the .NET Framework MSDE is installed as described above, it creates a default SQL Server instance name as follows:

```
(local)\NetSDK
```

We will specify NetSDK as the SQL Server to connect to in all the following samples. If you are using a different SQL Server instance (for example, (local)\VSdotNET or just (local) for the default SQL Server 2000 instance) you can substitute that server instance name. If the server instance does not have the Northwind database, use the instnwnd.sql script in the .NET Framework Samples Setup directory to load the Northwind sample data.

The Server Explorer in Visual Studio .NET shows the SQL Servers available to the development environment. If the server and database are visible in Server Explorer, the installation was successful.

Microsoft Access Northwind Sample for OLE DB

The Northwind sample database also comes with Microsoft Access, and we can access it through the ADO.NET OLE DB or ODBC provider. We can use the Microsoft Access database sample Northwind.mdb that comes with Microsoft Office. My copy is located at:

```
C:\Program Files\Microsoft Office\Office\Samples\Northwind.mdb.
```

If you don't have this file, no problem, most of the examples in this chapter use SQL Server; there is one example that shows how to use OLE DB as well as SQL.

.NET Data Provider Examples

Now let's look at how to use the ADO.NET classes. We'll start with the lower-level operations in the various .NET Data Providers. The best way to demonstrate the lowest-level ADO.NET operations is the output data with a data reader. Doing this will show how to use connection and command objects too.

Data Reader for SQL Server

For our first example we'll write a simple console-based application that reads data from a single table stored in SQL Server. This example shows how to connect to an SQL Server data source, open the database, issue a query, and read the results using the `SqlDataReader` class.

This example uses only the `SqlClient` .NET Data Provider classes. For simply reading a stream of data there is no need to use a `DataSet` or any in-memory representation of data. We'll show the code sample in its entirety first, and then explain it piece by piece:

```
using System;
using System.Data.SqlClient;

namespace Wrox.FTrackCSharp.DataAccess.DataReader_Sql
{
    public class DataReader_Sql
    {
        public static void Main()
        {
            try
            { // specify SQL Server-specific connection string
                SqlConnection thisConnection = new SqlConnection(
                    @"Data Source=(local)\NetSDK;" +
                    "Integrated Security=true;" +
                    "Initial Catalog=Northwind;" +
                    "Connect Timeout=5");

                thisConnection.Open();
                SqlCommand thisCommand = thisConnection.CreateCommand();
                // specify SQL query for this command
                thisCommand.CommandText =
                    "SELECT CustomerID, CompanyName from Customers";
                SqlDataReader thisReader = thisCommand.ExecuteReader();
                while (thisReader.Read())
                {
                    Console.WriteLine("\t{0}\t{1}",
                        thisReader["CustomerID"], thisReader["CompanyName"]);
                }
                thisReader.Close();

                thisConnection.Close();
            }
            catch (SqlException e)
            {
                Console.WriteLine(e.Message);
            }
        }
    }
}
```

The last part of the output should look like this:

```
      . . .
      WHITC    White Clover Markets
      WILMK    Wilman Kala
      WOLZA    Wolski Zajazd
Press any key to continue
```

If it looks like:

```
SQL Exception thrown!
SQL Server does not exist or access denied.
Press any key to continue
```

then SQL Server or MSDE may not be installed and/or the SQL Server service may not be running (or you may have a different SQL Server instance name, (local) or (local)\VSdotNET).
If you see this message:

```
SQL Exception thrown!
Cannot open database requested in login 'northwind'. Login fails.
Login failed for user 'YOURCOMPUTERNAME\yourusername'.
Press any key to continue
```

then the connection to SQL Server was made but the Northwind sample database is not installed.

SQL Data Reader Example Code Review

The first step in this code is to create a SqlConnection object:

```
SqlConnection thisConnection = new SqlConnection(
    @"Data Source=(local)\NetSDK;" +
    "Integrated Security=true;" +
    "Initial Catalog=Northwind;" +
    "Connect Timeout=5");
```

SqlConnection takes a connection string as a parameter, which specifies the server, the kind of user/password information needed to log in to SQL Server, and what database to start with (Northwind in our case).

Recall from Chapter 7 that the '@' preceding the string indicates a string literal in C# so that escape prefixes for the backslash characters are not needed.

If you've used ADO before, the Connection object and connection string in ADO.NET are almost exactly the same as what you're used to. If you've used JDBC, the connection string serves a similar function to a JDBC connection. But for the SQL Server .NET provider, the connection string does not specify the driver since the .NET data provider is driver-specific. We do need to specify a driver for OLE DB and ODBC connections, as we will see later.

The connection string is specified in a series of clauses separated by semicolons. The SQL Server name is specified in the `Data Source`. In our example, we use `(local)\NetSDK`, where `(local)` refers to the machine where this program is executing:

```
Data Source=(local)\NetSDK;
```

The next clause tells SQL Server to use the Windows login and password as its security authorization, rather than a separate SQL Server-specific password:

```
Integrated Security=true;
```

You will also see SSPI in the .NET Framework examples, which means the same thing as `true`. SSPI stands for Security Support Provider Interface, which is the component that links SQL Server security with Windows security.

The next clause tells SQL which database within the `(local)\NetSDK` instance to connect to:

```
Initial Catalog=Northwind
```

Finally, the connect timeout is specified so we don't spend the default 30 seconds waiting for the program to tell us it failed to connect because we forgot to start SQL Server.

The next call is to the `Open()` method of `SqlConnection`:

```
thisConnection.Open();
```

The connection isn't activated until `Open()` is called, so connect exceptions are not thrown until this line executes. The next line creates an `SqlCommand` object.

```
SqlCommand thisCommand = thisConnection.CreateCommand();
thisCommand.CommandText =
    "SELECT CustomerID, CompanyName from Customers";
```

`SqlCommand` contains a command for the database server written in the SQL language. The SQL command is stored in the `CommandText` property. `SqlCommand` has methods for executing an SQL command and obtaining the results, one of which is `ExecuteReader()`:

```
SqlDataReader thisReader = thisCommand.ExecuteReader();
```

The `ExecuteReader()` call sends the command to the server for execution. The results are returned to the program in the `SqlDataReader` object. We continue to call this object to get the results from the query:

```
while (thisReader.Read())
```

Read() gets the first and following rows from the query result; it returns `true` if there are results in this row and `false` when we've finished. Note that it will return `false` on the initial call if there are no rows in the result set, so our loop is set up to test the result on the initial Read call. Inside the `while` loop, we display the content of the reader:

```
{
    // output ID and name columns
    Console.WriteLine("\t{0}\t{1}",
        thisReader["CustomerID"], thisReader["CompanyName"]);
}
```

Here is an interesting use of the C# indexer construct, which is the expression inside `[]` like an array index. The column name is an indexer for the data readers, so we can use `thisReader[column name]` to get the data in that particular column with a simple elegant expression. This is used extensively in ADO.NET, as we will see when we get to the `DataSet`. We could also use numeric indexes, as in `thisReader[0]`, `thisReader[1]`. However, references by name are easier to remember and understand when reading code. They also make the code easier to maintain, since often the order of database columns change (which would mess up numerical referencing), but the column names do not. If you know for sure that the column order will not change, using enumerations offer an even better solution – they are faster than referencing by name, and spelling is checked at compile time.

Finally, we close the both the reader and the connection:

```
        thisReader.Close();
        thisConnection.Close();
    }
```

Note that the `Close()` call for the connection is especially important because connections are expensive objects in terms of memory and system resources.

Finally, if an error is encountered within the .NET data provider, it throws one of its exceptions, which we catch:

```
    catch (SqlException e)
    {
        Console.WriteLine(e.Message);
    }
```

The error message for the .NET data provider is specific to its particular database or data source. Additional information may be available within the properties of the exception; for example `SqlException` has a `Server` property to get the name of the server that was being accessed when the error occurred, an `Errors` collection to provide detailed information if an operation results in more than one error, as well as `Class` and `State` properties to get detailed information on the SQL Server status codes associated with an exception.

Data Reader with OLE DB .NET Data Provider

Let's look at the same example but with a different .NET data provider. This time we'll get the data from a Microsoft Access database and use the OLE DB provider to access it. The parts that have changed from the SQL Server example are highlighted:

```
using System;
using System.Data;
using System.Data.OleDb;

namespace Wrox.FTrackCSharp.DataAccess.DataReader_OleDb
{
   public class DataReaderExample
   {
      public static void Main()      // everything is in the Main function
      {
         try
         {
            OleDbConnection thisConnection = new OleDbConnection(
               @"Provider=Microsoft.Jet.OLEDB.4.0;Data Source=" +
               @"C:\Program Files\Microsoft Office\Office\" +
               @"Samples\Northwind.mdb");
            thisConnection.Open();
            // create SQL command object on this connection
            OleDbCommand thisCommand = thisConnection.CreateCommand();
            thisCommand.CommandText =
               "SELECT CustomerID, CompanyName FROM Customers";
            OleDbDataReader thisReader = thisCommand.ExecuteReader();

            while (thisReader.Read())
            {
               Console.WriteLine("\t{0}\t{1}",
                  thisReader["CustomerID"], thisReader["CompanyName"]);
            }
            thisReader.Close();
            thisConnection.Close();
         }
         catch (OleDbException e)
         {
            Console.WriteLine(e.Message);
         }
      }
   }
}
```

The code is very similar to the SqlClient example except for the namespace, class names, and connection string.

> *.NET data providers implement a set of common interfaces that standardize the properties and methods within most of the classes; the data reader classes, for example, implement the IDataReader interface.*

For details on OLE DB connection string clauses and other OLE DB information, see the Visual Studio .NET online documentation under the topic "OleDbConnection.ConnectionString Property".

In our connection string we specify the `Provider` clause to specify the Microsoft Jet Engine for Microsoft Access driver, and the `Data Source` to specify the location of the Microsoft Access `Northwind.mdb` file. Other parts of the program function in the same way as the previous example, except for using the `OleDb` class names.

Data Reader with ODBC .NET Data Provider

Let's finish looking at data readers with an example using the ODBC .NET Data Provider. This gets data from the same Microsoft Access database as the OLE DB example, but uses ODBC instead, which works with hundreds of different databases and data formats.

> To use the ODBC provider you must download and install it as described in the *.NET Data Providers* section earlier in this chapter, then add a reference in your project to **Microsoft.Data.Odbc.dll** in the directory **\Program Files\Microsoft.NET\Odbc.Net**.

Once again the code is very similar. Differences from the SQL Server example are highlighted:

```
using System;
using System.Data;
using Microsoft.Data.Odbc;

namespace Wrox.FTrackCSharp.DataAccess.DataReader_Odbc
{
    public class DataReaderExample
    {
        public static void Main()
        {
            try
            {
                OdbcConnection thisConnection = new OdbcConnection(
                    @"Driver={Microsoft Access Driver (*.mdb)};"+
                    @"DBQ=C:\Program Files\Microsoft Office\" +
                    @"Office\Samples\Northwind.mdb");
                thisConnection.Open();
                OdbcCommand thisCommand = thisConnection.CreateCommand();
                thisCommand.CommandText =
                    "SELECT CustomerID, CompanyName FROM Customers";
                OdbcDataReader thisReader = thisCommand.ExecuteReader();

                while (thisReader.Read())
                {
                    Console.WriteLine("\t{0}\t{1}",
                    thisReader["CustomerID"], thisReader["CompanyName"]);
                }
                thisReader.Close();
                thisConnection.Close();
            }
            catch (OdbcException e)
            {
                Console.WriteLine(e.Message);
            }
        }
    }
}
```

See the ODBC .NET Data Provider documentation, installed in its own program group when you download and install ODBC .NET, for details on connection strings and other information specific to this driver.

In our example we use the `Driver` clause to specify the Microsoft Access driver, and the `DBQ` (database qualifier) to specify the location of the Microsoft Access `Northwind.mdb` file. Other parts of the program function in the same way as the previous example, except for using the `Odbc` class names.

For our other examples, we will only look at the code for the SQL Server version – we have seen how trivial the differences are.

Stored Procedures

Stored procedures are a feature of most SQL database servers. They allow us to define a program consisting of SQL commands and execute it as one command at the server. Stored procedures are highly recommended for performance – the SQL is pre-compiled in SQL Server, whereas with SQL code in your application it is passed to the compiler at run-time every time it needs to be executed. They provide a better way of encapsulating SQL operations that are invoked by a C# program, because you can call them like a function, passing parameters and getting defined results that match the structure of your program. Also for security it is better to have the SQL operations encapsulated in a stored procedure; some database administrators insist on all access through stored procedures for this reason, and also to ensure referential integrity is maintained as well. Stored procedures are the best way to interact with the database in ADO.NET, if the back-end database supports them.

The `Northwind` sample database comes with several predefined stored procedures. The example below calls the predefined `CustOrderHist` stored procedure showing the products ordered by a given customer; you can see its code by viewing the stored procedure within the Server Explorer in Visual Studio .NET:

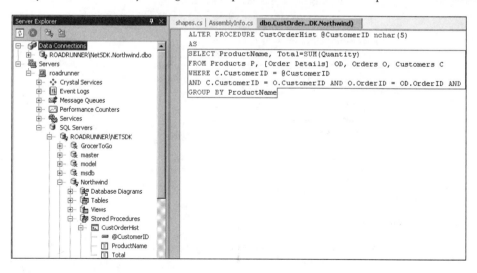

When the `CustOrderHist` stored procedure is called, an `SqlDataReader` returns the results, as in the previous examples:

```
using System;
using System.Data;
using System.Data.SqlClient;
namespace Wrox.FTrackCSharp.DataAccess.DataReader_SP

{
    public class DataReader_SP
    {
        public static void Main()
        {
            try
            {
                SqlConnection thisConnection = new SqlConnection(
                    @"Data Source=(local)\NetSDK;" +
                    "Integrated Security=true;" +
                    "Initial Catalog=Northwind;" +
                    "Connect Timeout=5");
                thisConnection.Open();
                SqlCommand thisCommand = thisConnection.CreateCommand();
                thisCommand.CommandText =
                    "CustOrderHist";
                thisCommand.CommandType = CommandType.StoredProcedure;

                // Set stored procedure parameters
                SqlParameter thisParameter =
                thisCommand.Parameters.Add("@CustomerID",
                                           SqlDbType.NVarChar,
                                           5);
                thisParameter.Value = "WILMK";

                // execute DataReader for specified command
                SqlDataReader thisReader = thisCommand.ExecuteReader();
                while (thisReader.Read())
                {   // output ID and name columns
                    Console.WriteLine("\t{0}\t{1}",
                    thisReader[0], thisReader[1]);
                }
                // close reader
                thisReader.Close();
                // close connection
                thisConnection.Close();
            }
            catch (SqlException e)
            {
                Console.WriteLine("SQL Exception thrown!");
                Console.WriteLine(e.Message);
            }
        }
    }
}
```

This example works in the same way as the previous data reader examples, except for setting the `CommandType` property of the `SqlCommand` object to `StoredProcedure`. This allows you to set the name of the procedure in the `CommandText` property. The other element we haven't seen earlier in this chapter is setting a parameter – we'll take a look at that now.

Command Parameters and Stored Procedures

Command parameters let you pass a variable into a SQL command. They are specified within the SQL Server statement text with a name preceded by an @ sign (in this case, the @ sign must be *inside* the string), as in `@CustomerID`:

```
// Set stored procedure parameters
SqlParameter thisParameter =
    thisCommand.Parameters.Add("@CustomerID",
                               SqlDbType.NVarChar,
                               5);
thisParameter.Value = "WILMK";
```

You can pass parameters to any SQL Server command, but they are most often used with stored procedures. The parameter name is defined in the definition of the stored procedure. You can see the stored procedures defined within a database and their parameters and return types in the Server Explorer within Visual Studio .NET.

SQL Execute Methods in .NET Data Providers

Besides reading data, you can use the .NET data provider classes in a standalone fashion to interact with database servers via the SQL language. Let's look at a few examples of this before moving on to the `DataSet` and high-level ADO.NET usage.

The `SqlCommand` object provides a way for you to specify any SQL command, including SQL DDL (data definition language), DML (data manipulation language) and DCL (data control language) commands, and `SqlCommand` provides a number of ways of executing SQL commands. If you are familiar with SQL Query Analyzer or a similar SQL command tool, think of `SqlCommand` as an object that encapsulates the actions you would take while using such a command tool. The core property of `SqlCommand` is the `CommandText` property which contains the `SELECT`, `UPDATE`, `INSERT`, `DELETE` or other SQL command you wish to execute. `SqlCommand` provides a variety of ways to execute the command and handle the expected results, whether the results are a single or multiple query result or count of affected rows; we saw how to handle multiple results when we looked at the data reader – we'll look at the others now.

ExecuteScalar Method of SqlCommand

As a first example, let's consider a program that gets a count of the rows in a table using the standard SQL `COUNT` function. This function is similar to the `DataReader` example but uses the `ExecuteScalar()` method of `SqlCommand` to execute the query. This method is used to execute SQL commands that return only a scalar (single value), as opposed to returning multiple rows and columns, as with `ExecuteReader()`:

```
using System;
using System.Data;
using System.Data.SqlClient;
```

```
namespace Wrox.FTrackCSharp.DataAccess.ExecuteScalarExample
{
    public class ExecuteScalarExample
    {
        public static void Main()
        {
            SqlConnection thisConnection = new
            SqlConnection(@"Data Source=(local)\NetSDK;" +
                        "Integrated Security=true;Initial Catalog=northwind");
            thisConnection.Open();

            SqlCommand thisCommand = thisConnection.CreateCommand();
            thisCommand.CommandText = "SELECT COUNT(*) FROM Customers";
            object countResult = thisCommand.ExecuteScalar();
            Console.WriteLine("Count of Customers = {0}", countResult);
            thisConnection.Close();
        }
    }
}
```

If multiple rows and/or multiple columns are returned, ExecuteScalar() will return the first value (first row/first column). Note that the return type is object; ExecuteScalar() returns a single value, which may be any data type. For the COUNT query shown above the object returned happens to be an integer.

ExecuteNonQuery Method of SqlCommand

You can use the ExecuteNonQuery method of SqlCommand to execute a SQL command that does not return any data at all. Data modification operations such as INSERT, UPDATE, and DELETE do not return data but instead return the number of rows affected. The program below shows how to use the ExecuteNonQuery method to execute a SQL UPDATE command to increase all the prices by five percent for products supplied by that supplier:

```
using System;
using System.Data;
using System.Data.SqlClient;
namespace Wrox.FTrackCSharp.DataAccess.ExecuteSqlNonQueryExample
{
    public class ExecuteNonQueryExample
    {
        public static void Main()
        {
            SqlConnection thisConnection = new
            SqlConnection(@"Data Source=(local)\NetSDK;" +
                        "Integrated Security=true;Initial Catalog=northwind");
            thisConnection.Open();

            SqlCommand thisCommand = thisConnection.CreateCommand();
            thisCommand.CommandText = "UPDATE Products SET " +
                        "UnitPrice=UnitPrice*1.05 WHERE SupplierId=12";
            int rowsAffected = thisCommand.ExecuteNonQuery();
            Console.WriteLine("Rows Updated = {0}", rowsAffected);
            thisConnection.Close();
        }
    }
}
```

Transactions

We can encapsulate changes to the database as in the previous example in transactions. Transactions give us the ability to back out of a set of related changes if not all of them are successful. They also give higher performance in many cases by allowing the database system to defer I/O operations until the entire set of related changes is committed.

We begin by getting a transaction object from the connection `BeginTransaction()` method, then calling the `Commit()` or `Rollback()` methods of the transaction object as needed, to control the transaction:

```
using System;
using System.Data;
using System.Data.SqlClient;
namespace Wrox.FTrackCSharp.DataAccess.DataSqlTransactionExample
{
   public class DataSqlTransactionExample
   {
      public static void Main()
      {
         SqlConnection thisConnection = new
         SqlConnection(@"Data Source=(local)\NetSDK;" +
            "Integrated Security=true;Initial Catalog=northwind");

         try
         {
            thisConnection.Open();
            SqlCommand thisCommand = thisConnection.CreateCommand();
            SqlTransaction thisTransaction =
                  thisConnection.BeginTransaction();
            thisCommand.Transaction = thisTransaction;
            try
            {
               // first command in the transaction
               thisCommand.CommandText = "UPDATE Products SET " +
                     "UnitPrice=UnitPrice*1.05 WHERE ProductId=12";
               int ProdRowsAffected = thisCommand.ExecuteNonQuery();

               // second command in the transaction
               thisCommand.CommandText = "UPDATE [Order Details] SET " +
                     "UnitPrice=UnitPrice*1.05 WHERE ProductId=12";
               int DetailRowsAffected = thisCommand.ExecuteNonQuery();

               thisTransaction.Commit();  // commit both changes
               Console.WriteLine("Product Rows Updated = {0}",
                     ProdRowsAffected);
               Console.WriteLine("Detail Rows Updated = {0}",
                     DetailRowsAffected);
            }
            catch ( SqlException e)
            {
               Console.WriteLine(e.Message);
               thisTransaction.Rollback();  // undo all changes
```

```
                    Console.WriteLine("No Rows Updated! Transaction " +
                        "rolled back.");
                }
            }
            catch ( SqlException e )
            {
                Console.WriteLine(e.Message);
                Console.WriteLine("Error happened before starting the " +
                    "transaction!");
            }
            finally
            {
                thisConnection.Close();
            }
        }
    }
}
```

In the above example, the five percent price increase is to be applied to the records in both tables where ProductID 12 is referenced. The transaction ensures that no partial changes are made.

The exception handling in this example is a bit more complex than what we have shown before now; there are two nested try blocks, one to handle an error before beginning the transaction, and another within the transaction itself to handle an error during the transaction.

The reason for this kind of exception handling is that you cannot abort a transaction if the transaction has not yet begun. For example, if there were an error when opening the database, that would occur before the transaction had started, and it would not be logical to abort a non-existent transaction. The finally block ensures that the connection is always closed at the end of the program whether an error occurred or not. This is a superior way of handling errors where errors might come from multiple sources.

Note also that the examples in this chapter illustrate how to use the ADO.NET classes, but omit extra error handling and other contingency code to make the examples simpler and easier to understand. This particular example uses a hard-coded UPDATE statement making a specific change for a particular product. In a real-world application your logic would be much more complex, with some kind of input for the product and the required price change.

DataSet Examples

Now that we've looked at the data provider classes in ADO.NET, we can move on to the data consumers – the DataSet class and its supporting objects. The DataSet provides an in-memory data structure for working with data. Since we've been talking about the data providers, first we'll describe the connection between the data provider classes and the DataSet, then move on to its structure and examples of working with it.

Data Adapter Class

The **data adapter** objects connect the data consumer classes such as the DataSet with the data access of the .NET data provider. It enables us to update the database and read data from it. Each .NET data provider implements its own data adapter.

The data adapter class in the SQL Server provider is called SqlDataAdapter. Like all data adapters, it has four SqlCommand objects as properties, corresponding to the 4 basic SQL commands SELECT, INSERT, UPDATE, and DELETE. These properties are the SelectCommand, InsertCommand, UpdateCommand, and DeleteCommand. When data is read into the DataSet, the SelectCommand is called to fill in the data. When changes made in memory to the DataSet are written back to the database, the InsertCommand, UpdateCommand, or DeleteCommand is executed to perform the operation.

Usually the INSERT, UPDATE, and DELETE commands associated with a data adapter deal with the same set of columns and tables that the SELECT command does. The data adapter's CommandBuilder object can be invoked to build the corresponding INSERT, UPDATE, and DELETE commands for a given SELECT command. This works only for single tables, but you can deal with more complicated table structures by writing the SQL commands explicitly, or by using multiple data adapters. Let's look at the structure of the DataSet now.

DataSet Structure for Tables, Rows, and Columns

The DataSet holds data in memory, with structures that let you work with the individual tables, rows, and columns that make up the DataSet. The simplified structure looks like the following diagram:

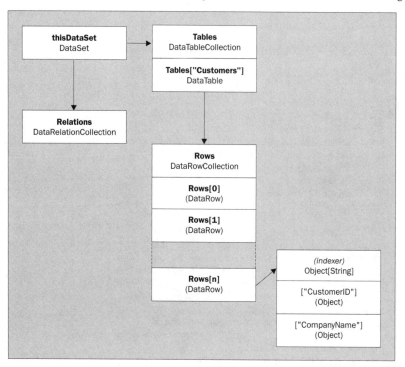

The variable names in this diagram match the source example we are going to look at next. We will declare a DataSet called `thisDataSet`. `thisDataSet` has `Tables` and `Relations` properties. `Tables` is a `DataTableCollection` and the individual members of this collection are of type `DataTable`, accessed by table name.

`DataTable` has a property `Rows` of type `DataRowCollection` – the members of this collection are of type `DataRow` and are accessed by row number. We will use `foreach` to move through all of the rows.

Each row has an indexer that lets you access the columns within that row by column name or index position. This allows long references such as in this line of code:

```
string companyName = thisDataSet.Tables["Customers"].Rows[2]["CompanyName"];
```

This reference gets the `CompanyName` field from the third row (remember that indexers are zero-based) of the `Customers` table in `thisDataSet`.

The `Relations` collection contains information on the relationships between the tables in the data set. Let's look at how this is used in a code example.

Navigating Relationships and Tables using a DataSet

We'll discuss this in some detail following this listing:

```csharp
using System;
using System.Data;
using System.Data.SqlClient;

namespace Wrox.FTrackCSharp.DataAccess.DataRelationExample
{
    class DataRelationExample
    {
        public static void Main()
        {
            // connect to SQL
            SqlConnection thisConnection = new SqlConnection(
                @"Data Source=(local)\NetSDK;" +
                "Integrated Security=true;" +
                "Initial Catalog=northwind;" +
                "Connect Timeout=5");
            thisConnection.Open();

            DataSet thisDataSet = new DataSet();
            // set up DataAdapter objects for each table and fill
            SqlDataAdapter custAdapter = new SqlDataAdapter(
                "SELECT * FROM Customers", thisConnection);
            SqlDataAdapter orderAdapter = new SqlDataAdapter(
                "SELECT * FROM Orders", thisConnection);
            custAdapter.Fill(thisDataSet, "Customers");
            orderAdapter.Fill(thisDataSet, "Orders");
            // set up DataRelation between customers and orders
            DataRelation custOrderRel =
                thisDataSet.Relations.Add("CustOrders",
```

```
                     thisDataSet.Tables["Customers"].Columns["CustomerID"],
                     thisDataSet.Tables["Orders"].Columns["CustomerID"]);

            // print out nested customers and their order ids
            foreach (DataRow custRow in
                               thisDataSet.Tables["Customers"].Rows)
            {
                Console.WriteLine("Customer ID: " +
                                       custRow["CustomerID"] +
                             " Name: " + custRow["CompanyName"]);
                foreach (DataRow orderRow in
                           custRow.GetChildRows(custOrderRel))
                {
                    Console.WriteLine("  Order ID: " +
                                           orderRow["OrderID"]);
                }
            }
            thisConnection.Close();
        }
    }
}
```

Within the code, we create two data adapters, one for each table we are reading. We call the `Fill()` method for each adapter to load the rows into `thisDataSet`. We set up a `DataRelation` object and `Add()` it to the `thisDataSet.Relations` collection. The nested `foreach` loop walks through the data structure we just created, printing out the information for each customer and that customer's orders. The `GetChildRows()` method of the `DataRow` takes a `DataRelation` as a parameter, and finds the related order rows for each customer.

The last part of the output from this example is shown here:

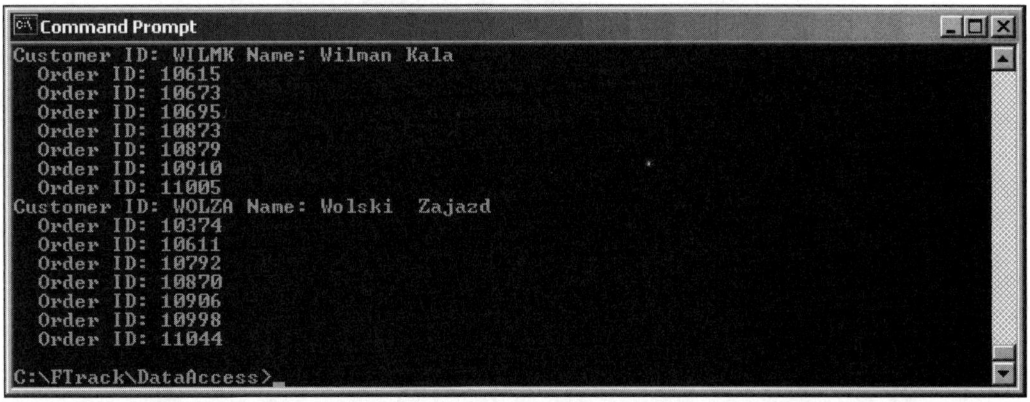

We see the **Customer** IDs and child **Order** IDs indented underneath them. Customers with no orders have no indented child Order IDs.

Updating Data

Changing a row's data values is basically a matter of updating the in-memory values in the `DataSet` structure, then calling the `Update()` method to change the data. We also have to set up the `INSERT`, `UPDATE`, and `DELETE` commands in the `SqlDataAdapter` object.

Let's imagine that the Northwind company has just made new shipping arrangements, so that all shipments to Madrid now go by the Speedy Express company. We'll update the orders destined for Madrid with this new information.

The program is similar to the one just shown, with some additions to the center section:

```
// set up DataAdapter objects for each table and fill
SqlDataAdapter custAdapter = new SqlDataAdapter(
    "SELECT * FROM Customers", thisConnection);
    // create command builder to fill in insert/update/delete commands
SqlCommandBuilder custBuilder = new SqlCommandBuilder(custAdapter);
SqlDataAdapter orderAdapter = new SqlDataAdapter(
                    "SELECT * FROM Orders", thisConnection);
SqlCommandBuilder orderBuilder = new SqlCommandBuilder(orderAdapter);
custAdapter.Fill(thisDataSet, "Customers");
orderAdapter.Fill(thisDataSet, "Orders");

// set up DataRelation between customers and orders
DataRelation custOrderRel = thisDataSet.Relations.Add("CustOrders",
        thisDataSet.Tables["Customers"].Columns["CustomerID"],
        thisDataSet.Tables["Orders"].Columns["CustomerID"]);

// print out nested customers and their order ids
foreach (DataRow custRow in thisDataSet.Tables["Customers"].Rows)
{
    // if city is Madrid, change shipping instructions
    if (custRow["City"].ToString() == "Madrid") {
        Console.WriteLine("Customer ID: " + custRow["CustomerID"] +
            " Name: " + custRow["CompanyName"]);
        foreach (DataRow orderRow in custRow.GetChildRows(custOrderRel))
        {
            Console.WriteLine("changed Ship Via for Order ID: " +
                orderRow["OrderID"]);
            orderRow["ShipVia"] = 1; // Speedy Express
        }
    }
}
orderAdapter.Update(thisDataSet, "Orders");
```

The additions are as follows:

❑   We call `SqlCommandBuilder` to create `INSERT`, `UPDATE`, and `DELETE` commands for our two data adapters (we can do this since they are both based on single-table queries).

❑   We check in our loop for the city of Madrid, and change the `ShipVia` column in `orderRow` if there is a match.

❑   When we have changed all the values in the `DataSet` in memory, we call the `Update()` method of the `SqlDataAdapter` to issue the appropriate `INSERT`, `UPDATE`, or `DELETE` commands to the SQL Server.

The Update() method checks the RowState property of each row in the Rows collection. RowState tracks whether a DataRow has been marked as modified. For all modified rows, the appropriate SQL UPDATE command is issued to update the database.

Finding and Adding Rows

Now, let's look at the methods for adding rows to a DataTable with the Add() method of the DataRowCollection class. We want to check of course to make sure that a row we add isn't already present. The DataRowCollection class provides a method called Find(), which is very useful for this purpose. Here's the modified Main() method, with the new section highlighted:

```csharp
public static void Main()
{
    // connect to SQL
    SqlConnection thisConnection = new SqlConnection(
            @"Data Source=(local)\NetSDK;" +
            "Integrated Security=true;" +
            "Initial Catalog=northwind;" +
            "Connect Timeout=5");
    thisConnection.Open();
    // create DataAdapter object for update and other operations
    SqlDataAdapter thisAdapter = new SqlDataAdapter(
        "SELECT CustomerID, CompanyName FROM Customers", thisConnection);
    // create CommandBuilder object to build SQL commands
    SqlCommandBuilder thisBuilder = new SqlCommandBuilder(thisAdapter);
    // create DataSet to contain related data tables, rows, and columns
    DataSet thisDataSet = new DataSet();
    // get primary key information from database
    thisAdapter.MissingSchemaAction = MissingSchemaAction.AddWithKey;
    // fill DataSet using query defined previously for DataAdapter
    thisAdapter.Fill(thisDataSet, "Customers");

    Console.WriteLine("# rows before change: {0}",
            thisDataSet.Tables["Customers"].Rows.Count);

    DataRow findRow = thisDataSet.Tables["Customers"].Rows.Find("AARON");

    if (findRow == null)
    {
        Console.WriteLine("AARON not found, will add to Customers table");

        DataRow thisRow = thisDataSet.Tables["Customers"].NewRow();
        thisRow["CustomerID"] = "AARON";
        thisRow["CompanyName"] = "Arnold Arons Ltd.";
        thisDataSet.Tables["Customers"].Rows.Add(thisRow);

        Console.WriteLine("AARON successfully added to Customers table");

    }
    else
    {
        Console.WriteLine("AARON already present in database");
    }
```

```
        thisAdapter.Update(thisDataSet, "Customers");

        Console.WriteLine("# rows after change: {0}",
        thisDataSet.Tables["Customers"].Rows.Count);
        thisConnection.Close();
    }
```

The beginning of the program up to the `Fill()` call is the same as previous examples. We use the `Count` property to output the number of rows that currently exist, then use `Find()` to check that the row we want to add is already present.

We need a primary key before we can use `Find()`. The primary key information is stored in the `PrimaryKey` property of the `DataTable`. ADO.NET will set the primary key based on the primary key defined in the database itself, but only if we tell it to do so by setting the `MissingSchemaAction` property to add data with a key to the `DataSet` when calling the `Fill()` method.

> *The schema that the `MissingSchemaAction` name refers to is the definition of the columns in `Columns` collection of the `DataTable`; these are set automatically when the `Fill()` method is called (we could set them explicitly by creating `DataColumn` objects for the `Columns` collection of the `DataTable`, but it is easier to just let them be set using the definitions from the database). The values that the `MissingSchemaAction` property can take are described in the .NET Framework online documentation.*

The primary key uniquely identifies this particular row in the table, so that when we search by the key we will find one and only one row. The `Customers` table in the Northwind database uses the `CustomerID` column as its primary key:

With the primary key set we can now find the row:

```
DataRow findRow = thisDataSet.Tables["Customers"].Rows.Find("AARON");
```

`Find()` returns a `DataRow`, so we set up a `DataRow` object named `findRow` to get the result. `Find()` takes a parameter which is the value to look up; this can be an array of objects for a multi-value key, but in our case with just one value we can simply pass a string containing the value `AARON` which is the `CustomerID` we want to look up.

If `Find()` does not find a match, it returns a `null` reference, which we check for:

```
if (findRow == null)
{
    Console.WriteLine("AARON not found, will add to Customers table");
```

We have already constructed the new `DataRow`, we now call the `Add()` method to add it to the table:

```
    thisDataSet.Tables["Customers"].Rows.Add(thisRow);
```

To demonstrate that the add was successful, we do a `Find()` again immediately after the `Add()` operation.

Deleting Data using a DataSet with SQL Server

The DataRow object has a Delete() method that deletes the current row. Our new code changes the sense of the if statement on findRow so that we test for findRow **not** equal to null (so that it's true if the row we were searching for was found). Then we remove the row by calling Delete on findRow:

```csharp
using System;
using System.Data;
using System.Data.SqlClient;

namespace Wrox.FTrackCSharp.DataAccess.DataDeleteExample
{
    class DataDeleteExample
    {
        public static void Main()
        {
            // connect to SQL
            SqlConnection thisConnection = new SqlConnection(
                @"Data Source=(local)\NetSDK;" +
                "Integrated Security=true;" +
                "Initial Catalog=northwind;" +
                "Connect Timeout=5");
             // open connection
            thisConnection.Open();
            // create DataAdapter object for update and other operations
            SqlDataAdapter thisAdapter = new SqlDataAdapter(
                "SELECT CustomerID, CompanyName FROM Customers",
                thisConnection);
            // create CommandBuilder object to build SQL commands
            SqlCommandBuilder thisBuilder = new SqlCommandBuilder(thisAdapter);

            DataSet thisDataSet = new DataSet();
            // get primary key information from database
            thisAdapter.MissingSchemaAction = MissingSchemaAction.AddWithKey;
            // fill DataSet using query defined previously for DataAdapter
            thisAdapter.Fill(thisDataSet, "Customers");

            Console.WriteLine("# rows before change: {0}",
            thisDataSet.Tables["Customers"].Rows.Count);

            DataRow findRow =
                        thisDataSet.Tables["Customers"].Rows.Find("AARON");

            if (findRow != null)
            {
                Console.WriteLine("AARON already in Customers table");
                Console.WriteLine("Removing AARON . . .");
                findRow.Delete();
                thisAdapter.Update(thisDataSet, "Customers");
            }
            Console.WriteLine("# rows after change: {0}",
            thisDataSet.Tables["Customers"].Rows.Count);
            thisConnection.Close();
        }
    }
}
```

Note that when `Delete()` is called it doesn't remove the row in the database until `Update()` is called to commit the change.

> *The `Delete()` method doesn't actually delete, it just marks the row for deletion. Each `DataRow` object in the `Rows` collection has a property, `RowState`, that tracks whether this row is deleted, added, modified, or is unchanged. The `Delete()` method sets the `RowState` of the row to `Deleted`, and then `Update()` deletes any rows it finds in the `Rows` collection marked for deletion.*

> *The Visual Studio .NET online documentation advises you to call the `AcceptChanges()` method of the `DataSet` after `Delete()`. However, this removes the row from the `DataSet` but has no effect on the row in the database – except that when you next call `Update()`, only changes made **since** `AcceptChanges()` will have any effect.*

> *Do not call `AcceptChanges()` before `Update()` if you want to delete the row in the database itself.*

Displaying Data with a DataGrid

We'll now look at the data-related interface classes – particularly, we'll see examples of using the Windows `DataGrid`. Other databound controls work in a similar way – this will show the principles.

Because we're working with Windows interfaces, we'll take the opportunity to look at using ADO.NET in Visual Studio .NET (or Visual C# .NET). We've spent most of our time looking at using ADO.NET from code, but it's sometimes easier to let Visual Studio .NET handle some of the code for us. In this example we will use Visual Studio .NET to build an application that displays a `DataSet` in a `DataGrid`.

Let's create a new C# Windows Application project in Visual Studio .NET called `DataGrid1`. This will bring up the standard Windows Forms application with **Form1** in design view. In the toolbox on the left, click on the **Data** tab and then select the **SqlDataAdapter** object:

As we drop these objects onto our form, they appear at the bottom of the screen. Visual Studio .NET generates code to create an ADO.NET object of the correct type.

In order to connect to a data source in ADO.NET, we have to use an appropriate .NET Data Provider object; let's pick the `SqlDataAdapter` for a SQL Server database. Click on the object and drop it onto Form1. Note how it drops to the bottom of the form window; `SqlDataAdapter` is one of those objects that has no visible control associated with it, so Visual Studio .NET displays it below the form window (in the "components tray").

When you drop the `SqlDataAdapter`, the DataAdapter Configuration Wizard appears. Click Next to get to the Choose Your Data Connection screen. Enter (local)\NetSDK as the server, check Windows NT authentication, and specify Northwind as the database. This connects your application to the SQL Server MSDE version that comes with Visual Studio .NET. Click Next.

The Choose a Query Type dialog comes up, asking you to choose between Use SQL Statements, the default, Create New Stored Procedures, or Use Existing Stored Procedures. Click on the Create New Stored Procedures choice. Next is the Generate the Stored Procedures wizard, which takes a SELECT statement and generates stored procedures for INSERT, UPDATE, and DELETE statements to go with it. Just type:

```
SELECT CustomerID, CompanyName, Address, City, Country FROM Customers
```

or choose Query Builder to build the same query. Now click on Next.

Following this you are asked to name the stored procedures; just click on Next to use the default names. The View Wizard Results dialog appears, indicating the wizard generated the stored procedures for SELECT, INSERT, UPDATE, and DELETE, as well as table mappings. Press Finish.

Notice that `SqlDataAdapter1` and `SqlConnection1` appear at the bottom of your form. These represent the `SqlDataAdapter` and `SqlConnection` objects that have been generated in the Windows Form code.

Now we need to generate a `DataSet` object to hold the data we get from the `SqlDataAdapter`. Right-click on the **sqlDataAdapter1**, and choose Generate DataSet. It presents a dialog where you can choose the name of the `DataSet`, defaulting to DataSet1. Click OK, and **dataSet11** appears at the bottom of the form (note that the object's name becomes **dataSet11**, although the `DataSetName` property is set to **DataSet1**; we'll explain this when we look at the generated code, below.

Now let's place a `DataGrid` on the form in order to see some data. Choose `DataGrid` from the Windows Forms tab of the ToolBox, and drop it on your form.

Make the form and the `DataGrid` pretty big, so that everything is visible when you run the program. Fill the form with the `DataGrid`. Now connect the `DataGrid` to **dataSet11** by specifying `dataSet11.Customers` as the DataSource:

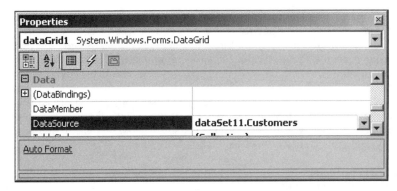

Next we add a couple of buttons: one to fill the `DataSet` (call it Fill), and another to update it (call it Update). Now double-click the Fill button, and add the following code to the event handler that Visual Studio .NET generates:

```
public void fill_Click(object sender, System.EventArgs e)
{
    this.sqlDataAdapter1.Fill(this.dataSet11, "Customers");
}
```

Now return to the form designer and double-click the Update button, and add the following to the event handler:

```
public void update_Click(object sender, System.EventArgs e)
{
    this.sqlDataAdapter1.Update(this.dataSet11, "Customers");
}
```

That's all there is to it. Build and run the application and press Fill to see the `DataGrid` filled with data from the Northwind `Customers` table. Change a cell value and press Update to update the database:

Here we can see the data flow from the SQL database through the .NET data provider objects into the consumer objects in the middle, finally going to the Windows Forms for display at the client. This corresponds to the classic 3-tier architecture for which ADO.NET is designed. The database itself is the data tier, ADO.NET sits in the middle tier, and the client display logic is on the client tier.

Code for DataGrid Example

Now let's take a look at the C# code generated for this example. We'll only pull out some highlights, but of course if you've followed the steps above you'll be able to look at all of the code. We will look at where the ADO.NET objects are in the generated code and how they relate to one another.

The variables for the `DataSet`, `SqlDataAdapter`, the `SqlCommand` objects for SELECT, INSERT, UPDATE, and DELETE, and the other ADO.NET objects are declared at the top of `Form1.cs`. They are initialized within `InitializeComponent()`:

```
private void InitializeComponent()
{
    this.sqlDataAdapter1 = new System.Data.SqlClient. SqlDataAdapter();
    this.sqlSelectCommand1 = new System.Data.SqlClient.SqlCommand();
    this.sqlInsertCommand1 = new System.Data.SqlClient.SqlCommand();
        . . .
    this.dataGrid1 = new System.Windows.Forms.DataGrid();
```

Preceding the UPDATE command there is code to set up a `DataTableMapping`:

```
this.sqlDataAdapter1.TableMappings.AddRange(new
System.Data.Common.DataTableMapping[]
{
    new System.Data.Common.DataTableMapping("Table", "Customers",
    new System.Data.Common.DataColumnMapping[] {
    new System.Data.Common.DataColumnMapping("CustomerID", "CustomerID"),
    new System.Data.Common.DataColumnMapping("CompanyName", "CompanyName"),
    new System.Data.Common.DataColumnMapping("Address", "Address"),
    new System.Data.Common.DataColumnMapping("City", "City"),
    new System.Data.Common.DataColumnMapping("Country", "Country")
})});
```

The `DataTableMapping` lets you use different column names in the `DataTable` from the database column names. We're not doing that, but the code is there for us if we want to rename a column. The first parameter refers to the source column name in the database table, and the second parameter indicates what the name of that column will be in the `DataTable`.

Further down in the file are the definitions of the stored procedures we created:

```
//
// sqlUpdateCommand1
//
this.sqlUpdateCommand1.CommandText = "[NewUpdateCommand]";
this.sqlUpdateCommand1.CommandType=System.Data.CommandType.StoredProcedure;
this.sqlUpdateCommand1.Connection = this.sqlConnection1;
this.sqlUpdateCommand1.Parameters.Add(new
```

```
            System.Data.SqlClient.SqlParameter("@RETURN_VALUE", . . .
    this.sqlUpdateCommand1.Parameters.Add(new
            System.Data.SqlClient.SqlParameter("@CustomerID", . . .
    this.sqlUpdateCommand1.Parameters.Add(new
            System.Data.SqlClient.SqlParameter("@CompanyName", . . .
    this.sqlUpdateCommand1.Parameters.Add(new
            System.Data.SqlClient.SqlParameter("@Original_CustomerID", . . .
    this.sqlUpdateCommand1.Parameters.Add(new
            System.Data.SqlClient.SqlParameter("@Original_Address", . . .
```

Here we see the name of the Visual Studio .NET-generated stored procedure and the parameters passed from the form to it. Note that the stored procedures for performing an UPDATE and DELETE take additional parameters specifying the original values so that they can correctly identify the row to update or delete.

Strongly Typed DataSets

Although we never used the term, this example uses a strongly typed DataSet. Below the parameter setup in the auto-generated forms code you'll come across the initialization of the DataGrid and the DataSet. Skipping over the obvious stuff, you'll see a couple of lines that may intrigue you:

```
//
// dataGrid1
. . .
this.dataGrid1.DataSource = this.dataSet11.Customers;
```

First off, isn't it supposed to be dataSet11.Tables["Customers"] or something like that? And why are there two 1 digits anyway? How did we get something that looks a real object attribute for Customers?

The answer is revealed by looking near the beginning of the Form1 class, where you can see the declaration of dataSet11:

```
public class Form1 : System.Windows.Forms.Form
    {
        private System.Data.SqlClient.SqlDataAdapter sqlDataAdapter1;
        . . .
        private dataGrid1.DataSet1 dataSet11;
```

The extra 1 in the name of dataSet11 is there to distinguish the instance variable dataSet11 from the type DataSet1. So why, you might, ask, is DataSet1 a type?

What we did was generate a **strongly typed dataset**. A strongly typed dataset is generated from a table so that you can use the column names as actual names in your code, without having to rely on the odd-looking use of indexers to get fields by number.

Where is the definition of this `DataSet1 DataSet`? You might expect to see some C# code in `Form1.cs` or some other file. It is nowhere to be found, except that in the Solution Explorer you find a new file called `DataSet1.xsd`. This is an XSD (XML Schema Definition) file that defines a data structure such as a `DataSet`, and indeed is used internally for `DataSet` implementation. If you view the XML source of `DataSet1.xsd`, you see at its core the five columns selected from the `Customers` table:

```
<xs:element name="CustomerID" type="xs:string" />
<xs:element name="CompanyName" type="xs:string" />
<xs:element name="Address" type="xs:string" minOccurs="0" />
<xs:element name="City" type="xs:string" minOccurs="0" />
<xs:element name="Country" type="xs:string" minOccurs="0" />
```

The .NET Framework has a tool called `xsd.exe` that takes an XSD source file and generates C# code from the XSD source. Visual Studio .NET hides this process, generating the XML schema for you and directly integrating the processing with `xsd.exe` into your project without your having to do this extra step. If you look in your project directory for `DataGrid1` (or click on the Show All Files icon in the Solution Explorer) you'll see a `DataSet1.cs` file that was generated by `xsd.exe`. It has definitions for the columns that correspond to the database columns, such as:

```
internal DataColumn CityColumn
{
    get
    {
        return this.columnCity;
    }
}
```

The `Customers DataSet` has fields named `CityColumn`, `CountryColumn`, and so on, that you can reference directly in C# code. The advantage of this is cleaner C# code and a better opportunity for the compiler to optimize column access. The XML Schema designer tool within Visual Studio .NET can be used to customize a strongly typed `DataSet`.

Using XML in ADO.NET

Speaking of XML, we'll wrap up by describing the support for XML integrated into the ADO.NET interfaces. You can generate XML data for consumption by other tools, or read in XML schemas and data directly into an ADO.NET `DataSet`. We already had a quick look at reading and writing simple XML documents in Chapter 7.

ReadXml() and WriteXml()

The `DataSet` has a `ReadXml()` method to read the contents of an XML file into a `DataSet`. You can also write XML out to a text file with `WriteXml()`. Here is a program that constructs a `DataSet` and writes its contents out. This is similar to the program that we used to demonstrate the `DataRelation` earlier in the chapter, but with the complex nested `foreach` loops replaced by the single call to `WriteXml()` as shown here:

```
using System;
using System.Data;
```

```
using System.Data.SqlClient;

namespace Wrox.FTrackCSharp.DataAccess.DataWriteXmlExample
{
    public class DataWriteXmlExample
    {
        public static void Main()
        {
            SqlConnection thisConnection = new SqlConnection(
                    @"Data Source=(local)\NetSDK;" +
                    "Integrated Security=true;" +
                    "Initial Catalog=northwind;" +
                    "Connect Timeout=5");

            thisConnection.Open();
            DataSet thisDataSet = new DataSet();

            SqlDataAdapter custAdapter = new SqlDataAdapter(
                    "SELECT CustomerID, CompanyName, ContactName, Phone " +
                    "FROM Customers", thisConnection);
            custAdapter.Fill(thisDataSet, "Customers");

            SqlDataAdapter orderAdapter = new SqlDataAdapter(
                    "SELECT OrderID, CustomerID FROM Orders", thisConnection);
            orderAdapter.Fill(thisDataSet, "Orders");

            DataRelation custOrderRel = thisDataSet.Relations.Add("CustOrders",
                    thisDataSet.Tables["Customers"].Columns["CustomerID"],
                    thisDataSet.Tables["Orders"].Columns["CustomerID"]);
            custOrderRel.Nested = true;

            string outfile = @"nwinddata_sql.xml";
            thisDataSet.WriteXml(outfile);
            Console.WriteLine(
                    @"Successfully wrote XML output to file {0}\n", outfile);

            thisConnection.Close();
        }
    }
}
```

This example outputs two levels of nested XML, one for Customers, and another for Orders. The beginning of the output file nwinddata_sql.xml looks like the following:

```xml
<?xml version="1.0" standalone="yes"?>
<NewDataSet>
  <Customers>
    <CustomerID>ALFKI</CustomerID>
    <CompanyName>Alfreds Futterkiste</CompanyName>
    <ContactName>Maria Anders</ContactName>
    <Phone>030-0074321</Phone>
    <Orders>
```

```
    <OrderID>10643</OrderID>
    <CustomerID>ALFKI</CustomerID>
  </Orders>
  <Orders>
    <OrderID>10692</OrderID>
    <CustomerID>ALFKI</CustomerID>

  </Orders>...
```

This is the raw XML output, showing the customer information and each related order underneath; the formatting into XML is done automatically for us (we set the `Nested` property of the `DataSet` to `true` to make each customer's orders immediately follow the customer.) This raw XML text can easily be read by any program that understands the XML format. In the next section we'll show a way to transform the XML into HTML for a web browser.

XmlDataDocument

The XML specification defines standard language or object structure for viewing an XML document in memory called the DOM (Document Object Model). The .NET Framework supplies a set of XML manipulation classes that conform to the DOM standard in the `System.Xml` namespace.

The highest-level object in the DOM model is the `XmlDocument` which describes an entire XML document from its beginning to end. ADO.NET supplies a bridge object called `XmlDataDocument` that unifies the `XmlDocument` object and the `DataSet`. `XmlDataDocument` is a subclass of `XmlDocument` with an addition of a `DataSet` property. With `XmlDataDocument` you can view that relational data easily in XML and use XML-standard APIs to work with the contents of the XML document.

Here is an example showing how to transform the XML data into HTML output for a web browser. It uses an input XML document written in XSLT, which is an XML-standard way to transform an XML document into another format.

Here is the XSLT document itself; to try it, enter the following contents into a file called `customer_orders.xsl` and copy the file into the web root directory (`c:\inetpub\wwwroot\`) of the Microsoft web server (IIS or Personal Web Server):

```
<xsl:stylesheet xmlns:xsl="http://www.w3.org/1999/XSL/Transform"
      version="1.0">
  <xsl:template match="CustomerOrders">
    <html>
      <body>
        <xsl:apply-templates select="Customers"/>
      </body>
    </html>
  </xsl:template>
  <xsl:template match="Customers">
    <table border="2">
      <tr>
        <th>Customer</th>
        <th>Name</th>
        <th>Contact</th>
        <th>Phone</th>
```

```
                </tr>
                <tr>
                    <td><xsl:value-of select="CustomerID"/></td>
                    <td><xsl:value-of select="CompanyName"/></td>
                    <td><xsl:value-of select="ContactName"/></td>
                    <td><xsl:value-of select="Phone"/></td>
                </tr>
            </table>
            <xsl:apply-templates select="Orders"/>
    </xsl:template>
    <xsl:template match="Orders">
        <table border="1">
            <tr>
                <td>Order:</td>
                <td><xsl:value-of select="OrderID"/></td>
            </tr>
        </table>
    </xsl:template>
</xsl:stylesheet>
```

Here is the C# code that uses the XSLT file as its input. The first part of this code that creates and fills the data set is exactly the same as the previous example:

```csharp
using System;
using System.Data;
using System.Data.SqlClient;
using System.Xml;
using System.Xml.Xsl;

namespace Wrox.FTrackCSharp.DataAccess.DataXSLTexample
{
    public class DataXSLTexample
    {
        public static void Main()
        {
            SqlConnection thisConnection = new SqlConnection(
                @"Data Source=(local)\NetSDK;" +
                "Integrated Security=true;" +
                "Initial Catalog=northwind;" +
                "Connect Timeout=5");

            thisConnection.Open();
            DataSet thisDataSet = new DataSet();

            SqlDataAdapter custAdapter = new SqlDataAdapter(
                "SELECT CustomerID, CompanyName, ContactName, Phone " +
                "FROM Customers", thisConnection);
            custAdapter.Fill(thisDataSet, "Customers");

            SqlDataAdapter orderAdapter = new SqlDataAdapter(
                "SELECT OrderID, CustomerID FROM Orders", thisConnection);
            orderAdapter.Fill(thisDataSet, "Orders");
            DataRelation custOrderRel = thisDataSet.Relations.Add("CustOrders",
                    thisDataSet.Tables["Customers"].Columns["CustomerID"],
                    thisDataSet.Tables["Orders"].Columns["CustomerID"]);
            custOrderRel.Nested = true;

            thisConnection.Close();

            XmlDataDocument thisXmlDataDoc = new XmlDataDocument(thisDataSet);
```

```
        XslTransform thisXslTran = new XslTransform();
        thisXslTran.Load(@"c:\inetpub\wwwroot\customer_orders.xsl");

        XmlTextWriter thisXmlWriter = new
            XmlTextWriter(@"c:\inetpub\wwwroot\customer_orders.html",
            System.Text.Encoding.UTF8);

        thisXslTran.Transform(thisXmlDataDoc, null, thisXmlWriter);
        thisXmlWriter.Close();
        Console.WriteLine(
          @"Output available at http://localhost/customer_orders.html");
    }
  }
}
```

In this example a `DataSet` is created holding Northwind data, filled just like the `DataSet` examples we worked with earlier in this chapter. An `XmlDataDocument` is constructed using the Northwind `DataSet` as an input parameter to the `XmlDataDocument` constructor. The `XmlDataDocument` is an in-memory image of the XML document; if we were to output it to a text file that file would contain the same raw XML text as shown in the previous example. However, the `XmlDataDocument` saves us the step of writing it to a text file; we can manipulate the context of the XML document in memory. We create an `XslTransform` object and load it with the XSLT document shown above. Then we transform the XML contained within the `XmlDataDocument` into HTML; we can then look at this with a web browser, as shown here:

This is a bit prettier than the raw XML output, isn't it? We could work on the XSLT template to improve the look of the generated HTML even further, but this is enough to illustrate the idea.

There are many classes and methods within the .NET Framework XML namespace for manipulating XML documents in memory like this; you can select a subset of the XML elements for processing, search for contents, and direct XML to streams for output to other programs or services located on other machines.

For more details on these and other capabilities, see the topic "Employing XML in the .NET Framework" in the .NET Framework Developer's Guide within the Visual Studio.NET online documentation.

Summary

We've covered quite a lot of ground in this chapter:

❑   We learned how to use the ADO.NET standard framework for accessing relational and other data in .NET.

❑   We saw that ADO.NET is designed to deliver simple data access with support for SQL and XML, supporting disconnected processing in the DataSet object and low-level database access within the .NET data providers.

❑   We explored the two built-in .NET data providers for SQL Server and OLE DB, and also briefly looked at the separately downloadable ODBC .NET Data Provider.

❑   We learned about the different classes within .NET data providers and the higher-level ADO.NET data consumer classes.

❑   We generated ADO.NET objects and support code within Visual Studio .NET and learned how that code can be used in programs.

❑   We looked at the XML support within ADO.NET and used some simple examples of writing out XML from a DataSet and transforming data from a DataSet contained within an XML document into HTML for display in a web browser.

Even with covering this much, we've only begun to introduce you to the many capabilities and features of ADO.NET. There are a number of very good books dedicated to ADO.NET and data access in .NET, among them *Professional ADO.NET*, *ADO.NET Programmer's Reference*, and *Data-Centric .NET Programming with C#* from Wrox Press.

Take the

Fast Track

to

C#

COM and COM+ Interoperability

Tremendous resources have been devoted to building solutions based on the technologies preceding .NET. There is plenty of business logic and system software packaged in COM components and dynamic link libraries, and you can expect these technologies to remain entrenched in the software around us for years to come. Fortunately, the .NET framework enables us to work with legacy software by allowing us to call COM components and exported functions from DLLs. This interoperability (called interop for short in .NET) also works in reverse. You can expose your .NET objects as COM components for the world of unmanaged code to use. The flexibility offered by interoperability allows more options when planning the migration of existing software to .NET technologies.

In this chapter we will discuss how to move between the managed environment of .NET and unmanaged code. Specifically, we will cover the following topics:

- ❑ Consuming COM components from C#
- ❑ Packaging C# code as a COM component
- ❑ Taking advantage of COM+ services from a C# class
- ❑ Invoking DLL functions from C#

Along the way, we will present examples of putting interop to work in .NET applications.

COM Interop

If you already have an extensive investment in COM components, you are probably thrilled by the fact that you can continue using your existing code from within .NET. Although there are many advantages to porting your code to C#, porting is not always an option when schedules are tight and you already have a foundation of tested software to build upon. You may also be using software packaged in COM components from a third party with no .NET version forthcoming.

To move between C# and COM code is to move between **managed** and **unmanaged** code. C# code targets the managed environment of the common language runtime and uses services provided by the runtime, including garbage collection and code access security. COM components, in contrast, run in the unmanaged environment where data types, exception handling, and memory management strategies can drastically differ.

The .NET Framework will make transition between the two environments look seamless. The first step is describing the COM component to .NET by translating the component's type library into .NET metadata. The tool we will use to do the translation is known as the Type Library Importer. Using this imported information, the .NET runtime will provide us with objects to sit between the managed and unmanaged code to facilitate the transition. These wrapper objects will help manage the lifetime of the COM component, as well as translate data and error codes between .NET and COM.

To demonstrate COM interop, we will first build a small COM component using the C++ ATL Project Wizard in Visual Studio .NET. This component will contain two methods. The first method gives us the amount of free disk space in megabytes for a given disk. The second method tells us the volume name and serial number for a given root path. Under the covers these methods call `GetDiskFreeSpaceEx()` and `GetVolumeInformation()` in the Win32 API. We are not going to look at the detailed implementation, but you can download the full source code from www.wrox.com. The name of the project is `atlwrox.sln`, which produces a COM DLL with the name of `atlwrox.dll`.

Since we do want to know what the methods look like, the interface definition language for the component is shown below.

```
// IDriveInfo
[
    object,
    uuid ("7CD3F32A-7D8B-44BD-9544-8BFC93314B68"),
    dual,   helpstring("IDriveInfo Interface"),
    pointer_default(unique)
]

interface IDriveInfo : IDispatch
{
    [id(1)] HRESULT GetFreeDiskSpace([in] BSTR sDirectoryName,

                            [out,retval] LONG* plTotalFreeMBytes);

    [id(2)] HRESULT GetVolumeNameAndSerial([in]BSTR sRootPath,
                            [out] ULONG* plVolumeSerial,
                            [out,retval] BSTR* psVolumeName);
};
```

Once the C++ project compiles and is registered, we are ready to create a new C# console application, named `TestAtlWrox`, for our first test of calling unmanaged code from .NET.

Generating Metadata

The first step in using our component from C# is generating .NET metadata for the COM component. Information about a COM component is often stored inside of a type library. You can usually find a type library embedded in the DLL or OCX with the component's code, but you may also find type libraries as standalone files with a `.TLB` or `.OLB` extension. In our example project above, the type library is embedded into the DLL itself. The Visual Studio .NET IDE can automatically import a type library for you using the **Add Reference** menu item on the **Project** menu. On the resulting dialog, we select the **COM** tab and browse to the DLL with our component, as shown below:

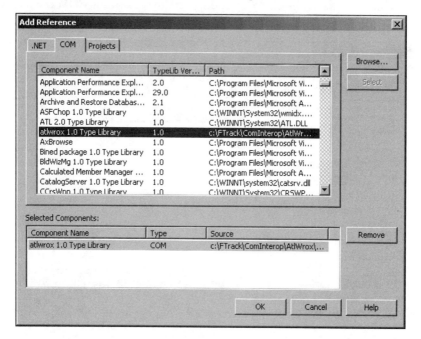

Visual Studio .NET will then create an interop assembly for you in the project's output directory. In this example, the name is `Interop.atlwrox.dll`. The interop assembly will provide all of the type definitions needed for the runtime to make COM components appear as native .NET types. There are also three other options available for generating interop assemblies. If you want more control over interop assembly generation you can use the Type Library Importer command line tool (`Tlbimp.exe`). `Tlbimp` allows you to control additional parameters, such as the filename and namespace of the generated interop assembly. For example, we could produce the same interop assembly from the debug directory of `TestAtlWrox` using the following command line (assuming `Tlbimp` is in the path):

```
>Tlbimp ..\..\..\atlwrox\debug\atlwrox.dll /out:Interop.atlwrox.dll
```

Once a reference is added to the project, we can switch to the IDE's object browser (select **Other Windows** from the **View** menu and click **Object Browser**), to see how the COM component looks in managed code.

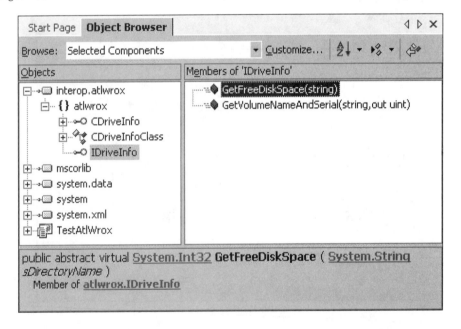

We can see in the object viewer how `Tlbimp` has produced one managed class, and two managed interfaces. The class (`CDriveInfoClass`) represents the COM class factory for the component (the coclass). `Tlbimp` always appends `Class` to the name when generating a managed class for a COM coclass. Creating a new instance of this managed class is similar to calling `CoCreateInstance()` in C++. `Tlbimp` also generates an interface with the same name as the coclass (`CDriveInfo`) as a placeholder for class identifier (CLSID) and interface identifier (IID) of the default interface of the component. Finally, `Tlbimp` generates an interface for `IDriveInfo` with methods corresponding to each of the COM interface methods.

You can also use `Tlbimp` to produce a **primary** interop assembly. The **publisher** of a software component typically produces the primary interop assemblies for their components. A primary interop assembly contains a strong name and a digital signature to uniquely identify and guarantee the integrity of the assembly. Microsoft provides primary interop assemblies for several of their COM libraries, including ADO and MSHTML. It is recommended you use a primary interop assembly for a component, when one exists.

If you need to programmatically create interop assemblies you can use the `TypeLibConverter` class from the `System.Runtime.InteropServices` namespace. This class contains methods to convert type libraries into assemblies and vice versa. Finally, it is possible to create custom wrappers by hand. You would typically resort to this option in the rare case you need to correct or optimize the metadata generated by one of the methods listed above. The situation might also arise when the type library has incomplete information about a component. Type libraries contain only automation-compatible information, which restricts the data types to the types friendly to late binding clients like VBScript. If you come across, for example, a COM method parameter attributed with `size_is`, you'll need to do some hand tweaking. In the majority of cases the tools listed will provide everything you need to easily use a COM component, as we will demonstrate in the next section.

Creating and Invoking

With the interop assembly referenced by our project, we can use the code below to call the methods on our component in `atlwrox.dll`.

```
using System;

namespace Wrox.FTrackCSharp.ComInterop.TestAtlWrox
{
    class Class1
    {
        [STAThread]
        static void Main(string[] args)
        {
            atlwrox.IDriveInfo driveInfo;
            driveInfo = new atlwrox.CDriveInfoClass ();

            string path = @"C:\";
            long megabytes = driveInfo.GetFreeDiskSpace(path);

            uint serialNumber;
            string name = driveInfo.GetVolumeNameAndSerial(path,
                                                    out serialNumber);

            string output;
            output = String.Format("There are {0}MB free on {1}",
                                megabytes, path);
            Console.WriteLine(output);

            output = String.Format("Volume on {0}, name={1} and SN={2}",
                                path, name, serialNumber);
            Console.WriteLine(output);
            Console.ReadLine();
        }
    }
}
```

The Runtime Callable Wrapper

You'll notice in the previous sample how the COM component is as easy to use as any native object from the .NET framework. C++ programmers will notice how there is no need to call CoCreateInstance() or manage reference counting through AddRef() and Release(). This is all done through the magic of the **Runtime Callable Wrapper (RCW)**.

When the COM object is created, the .NET runtime will generate an instance of an RCW from the metadata imported from the type library. This RCW will sit between your code and the COM component as a proxy. The RCW takes responsibility for creating the COM object and managing the reference counts. The RCW also marshals parameters between .NET and COM to provide you, for example, a System.String reference where the COM component uses a BSTR. In short, the RCW will hide all of the details needed to move between managed and unmanaged code. There is exactly one RCW for each instantiated COM object.

Error Handling

It is also the responsibility of the RCW to convert failed HRESULTs into exception objects. COM methods typically return an HRESULT to indicate success or failure. The interop layer will try to match a failed HRESULT code with a corresponding .NET exception, for example, the COM HRESULT E_OUTOFMEMORY maps to a System.OutOfMemoryException. Unknown HRESULTs produce an instance of the System.Runtime.InteropServices.COMException class. If the component you are calling implements the ISupportErrorInfo interface (achieved through a simple check box in most ATL COM class wizards), the runtime will try to retrieve additional error information. For example, the implementation for GetFreeDiskSpace() in our C++ code is shown below.

```
STDMETHODIMP CDriveInfo::GetFreeDiskSpace(BSTR sDirectoryName,
                                          LONG* plTotalFreeMBytes)
{
    unsigned __int64 i64FreeBytesAvailable,
                     i64TotalNumberOfBytes,
                     i64TotalNumberOfFreeBytes;
    BOOL result;
    result = ::GetDiskFreeSpaceEx(CW2A(sDirectoryName),
                    (PULARGE_INTEGER)&i64FreeBytesAvailable,
                    (PULARGE_INTEGER)&i64TotalNumberOfBytes,
                    (PULARGE_INTEGER)&i64TotalNumberOfFreeBytes);
    if(!result)
    {
        Error("GetDiskFreeSpaceEx returned failure");
        return E_FAIL;
    }

                                              // 2^20
    *plTotalFreeMBytes = (long)(i64TotalNumberOfFreeBytes / 1048576);

    return S_OK;
}
```

To force an exception, we just need to pass an invalid drive letter into the method. This results in GetDiskFreeSpaceEx() returning false. The C++ code inspects the return value and in the case of failure will set a textual error message and return an HRESULT indicating a generic error. The resulting exception, if not caught, will pop open the following dialog box from the client.

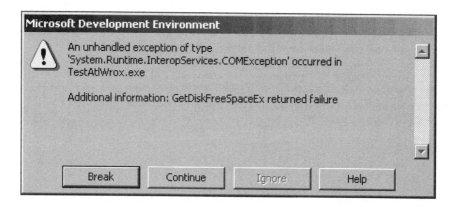

Threading Models

Experienced COM programmers might be interested in knowing how the runtime interacts with COM apartments. As a brief overview, there are two COM apartment models. Components built to run in a **single threaded apartment (STA)** require that all method calls happen on the same thread that created the object. The STA is easier to develop for, since all instance data is protected from multithreaded access by COM. The **multithreaded apartment model (MTA)** has no such restrictions, and the component developer must use locks and synchronization primitives to ensure concurrent threads do not corrupt instance data.

Any thread using a COM component needs to enter one of these two apartment types. This implies that .NET runtime threads will also need to enter one of these apartment types before interop takes place. By default, the CLR will join the MTA. If the COM component you are using is designed to run in an STA, COM will build an additional proxy and stub pair to marshal calls between the different apartments. This extra layer of code might result in a small performance hit. The good news is you can override the default behavior of an application via the STAThreadAttribute and MTAThreadAttribute classes. Applying the STAThread attribute, as we have done in our example, overrides the default setting and ensures that all of our application's interop threads join an STA. If you want to control the threading model for a specific thread, you can set the ApartmentState property of the System.Threading.Thread class before the thread begins running. No COM apartments are used unless your application is performing COM interop.

Using Reflection

You may find situations where a late binding approach to interop is advantageous. Although early binding offers performance benefits, strong type checking, and IntelliSense features, late binding allows a program to use a component without an interop assembly, so the program does not need to know anything about the component until runtime.

The late binding approach uses classes from the System.Reflection namespace to create a COM component and invoke methods. Using the static Type.GetTypeFromProgID() method, we can generate a System.Type reference from a COM programmatic identifier. The static CreateInstance() method of the System.Activator class will use this reference to create a new instance of the component for us. The next step is to setup the call to InvokeMember() by building an array of objects with the parameters for a given method. This technique is demonstrated in the following example where we use our DriveInfo component again, but this time the project contains no reference to an interop assembly.

```csharp
using System;
using System.Reflection;

namespace Wrox.FTrackCSharp.ComInterop.ReflectAtl
{

    class Class1
    {

        [STAThread]
        static void Main(string[] args)
        {
            Type type;
            type = Type.GetTypeFromProgID("ATLWrox.DriveInfo");

            object driveSpace;
            driveSpace = System.Activator.CreateInstance(type);

            string path = @"C:\";
            object [] iArgs = new object [] { path };

            object result = type.InvokeMember("GetFreeDiskSpace",
                                        BindingFlags.InvokeMethod,
                                        null,
                                        driveSpace,
                                        iArgs);

            string output;
            output = String.Format("There are {0}MB free on {1}",
                                result, path);
            Console.WriteLine(output);
            Console.ReadLine();


        }
    }
}
```

Interop with ActiveX Controls

ActiveX controls have a slightly different flavor from the example component we have used so far. ActiveX controls require the designer and consumer to implement a number of specific COM interfaces. ActiveX implies a control you want to host inside of a form, with some user interface features and plenty of properties to set and events to handle. Once again, .NET will allow the ActiveX control to look and feel just like a native .NET forms control. The easiest approach to importing an ActiveX control for use in .NET is to right-click on the .NET Toolbox window and select **Customize Toolbox**. After selecting the item you need, the control will appear in your toolbox, ready to drag and drop onto a form.

You can also use a command line tool, the Windows Forms ActiveX Control Importer (AXIMP.EXE). AXIMP is different from TLBIMP (the tool we used earlier in this chapter) because AXIMP must generate wrapper classes derived from System.Windows.Forms.AxHost for ActiveX controls. AXIMP generates two files. The first file is the same type of interop assembly we saw before, with the programmatic identifier (PROGID) of the control used as the filename (for instance, progid.dll). The second file contains the additional wrapper classes derived from AxHost, and uses the same filename with an Ax prefix (for instance, Axprogid.dll). These wrapper classes allow .NET forms to host the control. In design mode you can use the **Properties** window to set properties and manage event handlers. If you need to perform the import programmatically, use the AxImporter class from the System.Windows.Forms.Design namespace.

So far in this chapter we have investigated how to use unmanaged code packaged in COM components from our C# applications. But what about the reverse scenario of using our C# components from unmanaged code? This is the topic for the next section.

Interop with COM Clients

Packaging your C# components as COM components for COM clients to invoke might sound a little awkward at first, but it offers even more options when developing .NET migration strategies or continuing software development for existing customers who are not ready to move to the new platform. In this section we will create a new version of the DriveInfo component, this time written in C#, to see how to use the component from a couple different types of COM clients.

There are a few rules to keep in mind when designing a C# class to use from a COM client:

❑   Only public types in an assembly are visible to COM clients

❑   Only public methods, properties, and events on a type are visible to COM clients

❑   COM clients can only create types that have a default (empty) constructor

With these rules in mind, let's take a look at the C# version of the DriveInfo class. This class was added to the ConsumeFromCOM project, which was generated by the C# Class Library wizard. In this listing, we will skip all of the implementation details and cover them later in the chapter.

```
using System;

namespace Wrox.FTrackCSharp.ComInterop.ConsumeFromCOM
{
```

```
public class DriveInfo
{
    public DriveInfo()
    {
    }

    public int GetFreeDiskSpace(string directoryName)
    {
    // implementation detail
    }

    public string GetVolumeNameAndSerial(string rootPath,
                    ref uint serialNumber)
    {
    // implementation detail
    }
}
}
```

Our class appears as a simple C# class, with no special attributes or namespaces. We will continue to add to this class as we work through the section, but for now we can see just how easy it is to get a simple COM server up and running from C#.

Registration

The next step we need to take is to register our class with COM. We do this from the command line with the Assembly Registration Tool (Regasm.EXE). If you remember anything about COM, you probably remember the Registry entries needed by the COM runtime to locate and load your components. Regasm performs this job for .NET components by creating the required registry entries, similar to the regsvr32 tool in COM development. The name of the assembly produced by our project is ConsumeFromCOM.dll. If you are in the directory with the DLL and the PATH includes the framework's bin directory, all you need to type is:

```
>Regasm ConsumeFromCOM.dll
```

The resulting output will look like the following.

```
Microsoft (R) .NET Framework Assembly Registration Utility 1.0.3705.0
Copyright (C) Microsoft Corporation 1998-2001. All rights reserved.

Types registered successfully
```

For the purposes of a quick demonstration, we are going to try to use our C# class as a COM component from VBScript. Before we do this, however, it is important to understand how to deploy our assembly.

Private Deployment

There are two types of deployment. We will cover shared assembly deployment later in this section, but right now we are going to use the assembly as a private assembly. Now typically, when you register a COM server, there is an entry under the CLSID for InProcServer32 with the complete path to the component's DLL. This allows COM to find and load the DLL into a process. However, if we use REGEDIT to view the registry entries for DriveInfo, we find the following information under InProcServer32.

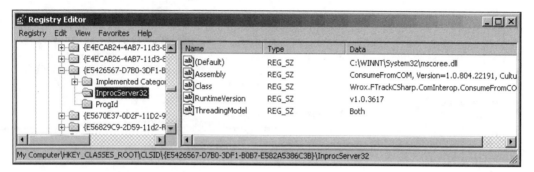

Notice that the default entry does not point to ConsumeFromCOM.dll, but to mscoree.dll. This DLL contains the Common Language Runtime. Allowing COM to load this DLL into the client's process gives the CLR a chance to set up the managed environment required for our object to run. After loading, the .NET runtime will go to the Registry and use the **Assembly** and **Class** entries to locate our assembly and class. You will notice, however, that there is not a complete path to our assembly. With private deployment the assembly must reside in the application's directory or a subdirectory.

Since we are going to use CSCRIPT.EXE from the %SYSTEMROOT%\system32 directory to execute VBScript, we will make a subdirectory named ConsumeFromCom under system32 and copy ConsumeFromCOM.dll into the subdirectory. This gives any application in the system root or system32 directory access to our assembly, which may present problems. A typical private deployment is for a single application only, and later in this section we will examine how to do a shared deployment for multiple applications in a more robust manner.

Also notice the **ThreadingModel** entry in the Registry for the component. By specifying a threading model of **Both**, the component will load into either an STA or the MTA and avoid cross-apartment marshalling. This is the default behavior for a .NET class registered as a COM component.

With the Registry entries and assembly in place we can try the following VBScript in Test.vbs.

```
option explicit

dim sPath
sPath = "C:\"

dim oDriveInfo
set oDriveInfo =
CreateObject("Wrox.FTrackCSharp.ComInterop.ConsumeFromCOM.DriveInfo")

dim lMBFree
```

```
lMBFree = oDriveInfo.GetFreeDiskSpace(sPath)

dim lSerial
dim sName

sName = oDriveInfo.GetVolumeNameAndSerial(sPath, lSerial)

Wscript.Echo "There are " + CStr(lMBFree) + "MB free on " + sPath
Wscript.Echo "The volume on " + sPath + " has a name of " + sName
```

Once again, the .NET runtime will provide some magic to make our C# object look and feel just like a COM component. This magic is in the form of a wrapper object known as a **COM Callable Wrapper (CCW)**. Much like the RCW, the CCW sits between the managed and unmanaged environments as a proxy, marshaling method calls and data between the two sides. There is one CCW for each .NET component created via COM. The CCW provides reference counting by implementing IUnknown, and allows late binding clients to work (such as VBScript) by implementing IDispatch. Managed exceptions are translated into COM HRESULTs by the CCW, which also offers the ISupportErrorInfo interface for extended error reporting.

A C++ Client

Now that our C# class has undergone a simple test from VBScript we want to try to use the component from C++. First, we are going to take a few steps to make the component easier to use from C++. We add the following code to our DriveInfo class.

```
using System;
using System.Text;
using System.Runtime.InteropServices;

namespace Wrox.FTrackCSharp.ComInterop.ConsumeFromCOM
{
    [ClassInterface(ClassInterfaceType.AutoDual)]
    public class DriveInfo
    {
    ...
    }
}
```

Type Library and Interface Generation

This ClassInterface attribute we applied to our class controls the generation of the class interface. In the previous example, with no attribute applied, the default setting is equivalent to using ClassInterfaceType.AutoDispatch. This setting only allows late binding through the IDispatch interface. By only allowing late binding COM clients you can update your component without too many versioning headaches. However, writing late binding code from C++ has always been a bit more work, so in this example we will use the AutoDual option to support both late binding clients through IDispatch, and early binding clients through a class interface generated from the public types of our class.

In order to see the effects of the `ClassInterfaceAttribute` directly, we can take a look at the type library we must generate for early binding to our component. You can generate a type library and have the library registered using the `Regasm` tool as shown below.

```
>Regasm.exe /TLB ConsumeFromCOM.dll
```

This generates a `ConsumeFromCOM.tlb` file we can view with the View TypeLib option on the File menu of OLEVIEW. You should be able to find this tool in the C:\Program Files\Microsoft Visual Studio .NET\Common7\Tools directory of your Visual Studio installation. Browsing to the `.tlb` file of our class with **no** `ClassInterfaceAttribute` set reveals the following.

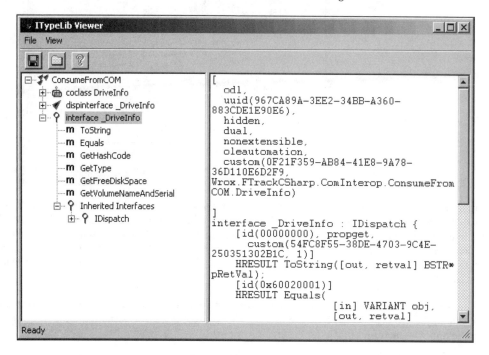

As you can see, the `_DriveInfo` interface contains no information for early binding clients. The only way to use the class's methods is via the `IDispatch` interface, which is how our VBScript worked. Next, we will regenerate the type library using the `ClassInterfaceAttribute` with `ClassInterface.AutoDual` specified, compiling, and running `Regasm /TLB` again. Viewing this type library reveals the following interface.

Our interface still derives from IDispatch, but now defines all of our public methods for early binding clients. Notice also how we picked up the public methods of our base class, System.Object. We can now use early binding from C++ or VB to invoke these methods (and we get IntelliSense features too). The drawbacks to this approach are mainly apparent when you make changes to your C# class that affect the layout of the interface. These changes force early binding clients to recompile in order to work properly.

With our early binding type library in place we are ready to create a simple C++ program, which we will create in the project cppclient. We use the **Win32 Project** type in Visual Studio .NET to generate a console application, and replace the generated code with the following.

```
#include "stdafx.h"
#import "mscorlib.tlb" rename("ReportEvent", "mscorlibReportEvent")
#import "C:\FTrack\ComInterop\ConsumeFromCOM\bin\Debug\ConsumeFromCOM.tlb"

using namespace ConsumeFromCOM;

int _tmain(int argc, _TCHAR* argv[])
{
    HRESULT hr = ::CoInitialize(NULL);
    if(FAILED(hr))
    {
        return -1;
    }
```

```
_DriveInfoPtr spDriveInfo(__uuidof(DriveInfo));

_bstr_t sPath = "C:\\";
long lMBytes = spDriveInfo->GetFreeDiskSpace(sPath);

_bstr_t sName;
long lSerialNumber;
sName = spDriveInfo->GetVolumeNameAndSerial(sPath,
                                        &lSerialNumber);

printf("Drive %S (%S) has %ldMB free",
        sPath.GetBSTR(),
        sName.GetBSTR(),
        lMBytes);

::CoUninitialize();

return 0;
}
```

The `#import` feature of Visual Studio lets us generate smart pointer wrapper classes from the component's type library. We will also need to import `mscorlib.tlb`. Remember, since we are still privately deploying our assembly we need to copy `ConsumeFromCOM.dll` into the directory or subdirectory where our C++ client executable resides before executing the program. A second option, as we mentioned earlier, is to look at doing a shared deployment of our component.

Shared Deployment

As we detailed in Chapter 9, shared deployment allows multiple applications to use an assembly. The first step in deploying our C# component in a shared assembly is generating a strong name with the Strong Name Tool.

>**sn -k ConsumeFromCOM.snk**

You can now have the assembly signed for you during a build using the `AssemblyKeyFileAttribute` in the `AssemblyInfo.cs` file, as shown below.

```
[assembly: AssemblyKeyFile(@"..\..\ConsumeFromCOM.snk")]
```

The final step is to install the freshly built assembly into the global assembly cache (GAC) with the global assembly cache tool.

>**gacutil /i ConsumeFromCOM.dll**

The component is now available to all the COM clients on the machine. Don't confuse this step with using `Regasm`, you'll still need `Regasm` to make the appropriate Registry entries for COM to bootstrap `mscoree.dll` into the client process, but now the runtime will locate the assembly in the GAC.

Taking Advantage of COM+ Services

COM programming has changed dramatically since the release of Microsoft Transaction Server (MTS) in the NT 4.0 Option Pack. This release was the beginning of Enterprise Services, such as distributed transactions, making their way into COM. Windows 2000 introduced COM+, and Windows XP extends these services even further. The .NET framework allows you to take advantage of this built-in infrastructure. The following list is representative of the COM+ Services available:

❑ Automatic, distributed transactions

❑ Object pooling

❑ Just-In-Time activation

❑ Queued components

❑ Loosely coupled events

❑ Synchronization

A .NET component taking advantage of a COM+ feature is known as a **serviced component**. A serviced component is derived from the ServicedComponent class in System.EnterpriseServices. The COM+ runtime will host the serviced component and make the serviced component available to COM clients and .NET client alike. The serviced component will live inside a specific COM+ **context**, as do all COM+ components. Each context has some associated properties, for example a context may have a property set requiring a database transaction. Components with similar property requirements can live inside the same context.

The System.EnterpriseServices namespace is chock full of attributes allowing you to declaratively configure the services you need for your objects. Unlike COM+ programming, where most of the configuration information resided in the COM+ catalog, .NET uses the metadata inside an assembly to configure the services for you. This allows a developer to specify at compile time the exact settings required for his or her components. The following table outlines a subset of the attributes available for use. You'll find most of these attributes correspond to configuration items inside in the Component Services Manager MMC. There are application-level, component-level, interface-level, and method-level attributes, and we will revisit these attributes shortly.

Attribute Class	Description
ApplicationAccessControlAttribute	Enables security at the application level. Also sets the access check, authentication, and impersonation levels.
ApplicationActivationAttribute	Configures the assembly to run as a library (in process) or server (out of process) application
ApplicationNameAttribute	Configures the name of the application
ApplicationQueueingAttribute	Configures queued component support for the application

Attribute Class	Description
AutoCompleteAttribute	Configures a method for auto-complete. Transactions are automatically committed or aborted depending on the outcome of the method call.
DescriptionAttribute	Sets the description of an application, component, method, or interface
ExceptionClassAttribute	Sets the name of the queuing exception class to instantiate before a queued component message is routed to the dead letter queue.
InterfaceQueuingAttribute	Enables queuing on an interface
ObjectPoolingAttribute	Enables object pooling. Sets the minimum and maximum pool size and creating timeout length
SynchronizationAttribute	Sets the synchronization requirements for a component
TransactionAttribute	Configures the transaction support required by the component

Building a Serviced Component

To see how the classes and attributes from the `System.EnterpriseServices` namespace work, we will begin to walk through an example project. Ultimately, we want to build a queued component with transactional support, but it is an interesting demonstration to start with something very simple and work up. We create a C# Class Library project named `QueuedComponent` and add a reference to the `System.EnterpriseServices.dll` assembly. We also need to generate a strong name for the assembly, so we create a key pair using the Strong Name Tool and reference the key file in `AssemblyInfo.cs`. The code for our starting experiment is listed below:

```
using System.Data.SqlClient;
using System.Runtime.InteropServices;

namespace Wrox.FTrackCSharp.ComInterop.QueuedComponent
{
    public interface IQAuthor
    {
        void UpdateContract(string authorId, bool contract);
    }

    [ClassInterface(ClassInterfaceType.AutoDual)]
    public class Author : ServicedComponent, IQAuthor
    {
        public Author()
        {
        }
```

```
public void UpdateContract(string authorId, bool contract)
{
    SqlConnection connection = new SqlConnection();
    connection.ConnectionString = "data source=localhost;" +
                                "initial catalog=pubs;user id=sa";
    connection.Open();

    SqlCommand command = new SqlCommand();
    command.Connection = connection;

    string sql = String.Format("UPDATE authors SET contract = {0} " +
                               "WHERE au_id = '{1}'",
                               contract ? "1" : "0",authorId);
    command.CommandText = sql;
    command.ExecuteNonQuery();

    if(authorId == "172-32-1176")
    {
        throw new ApplicationException("Invalid author id for update");
    }
}
}
}
}
```

Our example will connect to the pubs database on the local SQL Server and attempt to update the contract field for the given author. We plan on throwing an exception if the author's identifier is equal to 172-32-1176. This will help us test transactional support when we add it later. Notice we have also provided a separate interface containing the most interesting method to call. Defining a separate interface is generally a good design, as the interface is separated from the implementation class and this gives you more control over the types exposed to clients.

Now, the last step is to register the ServicedComponent, and here we will use Regsvcs.exe. This installs the component, but not as a COM component. We will look at how we can dynamically install this component as a COM component below, but for now, simply register it as follows:

>Regsvcs QueuedComponent.dll

There are several options for regsvcs.exe, but the major ones are:

❑   /tlb<tlbfile>
    Filename for the exported type library

❑   /u
    Uninstall target application

A C# Client

After building the project, we create a new C# console application. Again we add a project reference to System.EnterpriseServices.dll, and also the new QueuedComponent.dll we created above. The code for the console application follows:

```
using System;
using System.Runtime.InteropServices;
using Wrox.FTrackCSharp.ComInterop.QueuedComponent;

namespace Wrox.FTrackCSharp.ComInterop.QueuedCSharpClient
{
    class Class1
    {
        [STAThread]
        static void Main(string[] args)
        {
            IQAuthor author = new Author();
            author.UpdateContract("172-32-1176", false);
        }
    }
}
```

Without performing any additional registration steps we build and launch the console application. Since we are passing the special "exception" value for the author ID, the component generates an exception. However, if we examine our database we can see that the method did actually update the record because we do not yet have a transaction in effect. Also, at the beginning of this section we mentioned how a serviced component is hosted in a COM+ environment. We can see the most amazing side effect of running our client application by looking in the Component Services manager.

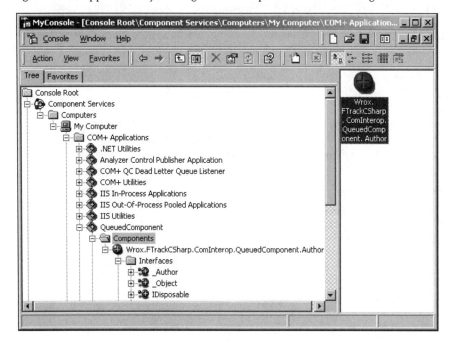

Without performing any explicit registration steps ourselves, the C# component has appeared as a configured COM+ component in the COM+ catalog. Serviced components have a special capability called **dynamic registration**. The first time a managed client tries to create an instance of a serviced component, the CLR will dynamically register the assembly, register the type library, and configure the component in the COM+ catalog (if it is not already present). Note, however, that dynamic registration does not place our assembly in the GAC. The COM+ catalog entry still points to mscoree.dll as the server to load for the component, so the CLR still has the job of trying to locate our assembly. In the previous section we moved the assembly under the running application's directory, but in this example we did not. If we take a look at the Registry entry for our component, we can see how this trick works.

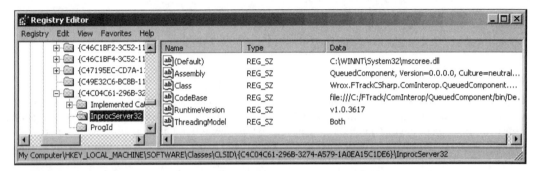

There is a new value under InProcServer32 named CodeBase pointing to the path of our assembly. The CLR will follow this link to our code. We could have used this technique in the previous section with ConsumeFromCOM.dll by passing the /codebase argument to Regasm.exe. You need to have a signed (strong named) assembly in order for this technique to work.

Configuration Attributes

Since we have not used any attributes to explicitly configure our component, all of the COM+ settings have default values. The following table outlines default values for a subset of the available attributes. The attribute column gives the name of the class to apply when you need to modify the default value. Scope indicates where you will find the setting in the COM+ property pages, and also where to apply the attribute in your C# code (package is equivalent to an assembly level attribute).

Attribute	Scope	Default Value
ApplicationAccessControl	Package	False
ApplicationActivation	Package	Library
ApplicationName	Package	Name of the assembly
ApplicationQueuing	Package	None
AutoComplete	Method	False

Attribute	Scope	Default Value
Description	Package	None
	Component	
	Interface	
	Method	
ExceptionClass	Component	False
InterfaceQueuing	Component	False
	Interface	
ObjectPooling	Component	False
PrivateComponent	Component	None
Synchronization	Component	False
Transaction	Component	False

Our next step is to put these attributes to work in order to take advantage of the COM+ services we need, primarily transaction support and queuing.

Configuring Transaction Support

Transactions allow you to perform a series of tasks as a single logical unit of work. If one task fails, you can abort the transaction and rollback any changes made by the other tasks inside the same transaction. Transactions are most popular in database applications when multiple components are writing to the database and you need to ensure the changes are committed or aborted as a single task.

Underneath the covers, the **Microsoft Distributed Transaction Coordinator (MSDTC)** manages these transactions. MSDTC can span transactions across multiple machines, and across multiple resources. For example, a single distributed transaction could control the changes to a SQL Server database, an Oracle database, and a Microsoft Message Queue.

Automatic transactions are configured by applying `TransactionAttribute` at the class level. You can set the transaction option to one of the following enumerated values: `Disabled`, `NotSupported`, `Required`, `RequiresNew`, or `Supported`.

These following transaction options are available to specify the type of context required by the component.

Transaction Option	Description
Disabled	Allows a component to load into any context by ignoring the transactional property
NotSupported	The default setting: forces a component into a new context if the context attempting to load the component is transactional
Required	Forces a component into a transactional context by creating a new context with a transaction if needed. This is the default setting if you apply a TransactionAttribute but do not explicitly set the transaction option.
RequiresNew	Guarantees that the component is placed into a context with a newly created transaction
Supported	Signifies that the component will participate in a transaction if one exists in the current context, but a transaction is not created if one does not exist

With these rules in mind, let's take a look at the updated code for our transactional component.

```
[Transaction(TransactionOption.Required)]
[ClassInterface(ClassInterfaceType.AutoDual)]
public class Author : ServicedComponent, IQAuthor
{
    public Author()
    {
    }

    [AutoComplete]
    public void UpdateContract(string authorId, bool contract)
    {
        // same implementation
    }
}
```

In addition to adding a transaction attribute to the class, we add an AutoComplete attribute to our method. Any time a transaction is in effect we need to let the runtime know if we want the transaction to commit or abort. AutoComplete will tell the transaction to commit if the method returns normally, but if an exception is thrown, the runtime is told to abort the transaction. All of the parties involved in a transaction must vote for success if the transaction is to commit – it only takes one dissenter to abort the entire transaction.

An alternative to using the AutoComplete attribute is to vote for success or failure explicitly. Voting is done using the static SetComplete() and SetAbort() methods of the System.EnterpriseServices.ContextUtil class. If we decided to go down this route, our UpdateContract() method would look like the following

```
public void UpdateContract(string authorId, bool contract)
```

```
{
    // SQL connection and update command …

    if(authorId == "172-32-1176")
    {
      ContextUtil.SetAbort();
        throw new ApplicationException("Invalid author id for update");
    }

    ContextUtil.SetComplete();
}
```

Configuring Queuing

While the asynchronous capabilities of .NET are feature-rich and robust, queued components offer a slightly different twist on the same feature, and provide a good deal more infrastructure. When a client requests a queued component, the COM+ runtime synthesizes a recorder component with the same interfaces. The recorder takes all the method calls and parameters and packages them into a Microsoft Message Queue (MSMQ) message. The client will return to processing while MSMQ will move messages, if needed, across machines in a reliable fashion. There is a built-in retry mechanism in case of a network, software, or hardware failure. When the message comes out of the queue, the COM+ listener instantiates a player component to play back the method calls into the queued component.

To configure our component as a COM+ queued component, we add the following attribute to our interface:

```
[InterfaceQueuing]
public interface IQAuthor
{
    void UpdateContract(string authorId, bool contract);
}
```

The InterfaceQueuing attribute indicates that the method calls on this interface may be queued. Queued interfaces have a few more stringent rules than regular interfaces for COM components. Since the client is detached, all of the parameters must be in parameters – there are no out parameters or return values allowed. Reference parameters are only allowed when the parameter marshals by value.

The rest of our attributes are placed in the AssemblyInfo.cs file.

```
using System.Reflection;
using System.EnterpriseServices;

[assembly: AssemblyKeyFile(
      @"C:\FTrack\ComInterop\QueuedComponent\bin\Debug\QueuedComponent.snk")]

[assembly: ApplicationName("WroxQC")]
[assembly: ApplicationActivation(ActivationOption.Server)]
[assembly: ApplicationQueuing(Enabled=true, QueueListenerEnabled=true)]
[assembly: ApplicationAccessControl(Value=false,
                        Authentication=AuthenticationOption.None)]
```

Let's look at a few of these attributes in more depth. The activation option (Server) tells COM+ to run this application out of process. A queued component needs to run in an out of process surrogate since the client process may have stopped long before the method call reaches the component. Unlike other COM+ applications, a queued application does not automatically start when a client requests a new queued component. Instead, you will need to start the application manually or programmatically. This is actually a useful feature, since you can use queuing to batch together operations. For example, you could write a queued component to process resource-intensive database imports and schedule the package to run in the middle of the night. Requests for a non-queued component from this package will still launch the package immediately.

You can also control whether or not the package will pull messages from MSMQ with the QueueListenerEnabled value. We set this value to true to ensure that the package will listen to the queues and process our method calls. If the COM+ package is launched without this attribute enabled, no messages are processed from the queue.

One last attribute is required if you have MSMQ installed in workgroup mode. MSMQ configures itself in workgroup mode if an Active Directory service is unavailable during the time of installation. In this scenario we need to set the authentication option to none. Typically, MSMQ will use certificates stored in an Active Directory service to verify the origin and integrity of the messages arriving in the queues. Without an Active Directory service, we need to turn off all authentication for a queued component to work correctly. Obviously, you need to avoid this scenario in secure production applications. Workgroup mode also lacks some of the high availability features available with Active Directory.

Manual Registration

With our attributes in place we can rebuild the application, delete the COM+ package created when we used dynamic registration, and now take a look at the Framework Services Installation Tool (Regsvcs.exe). This tool is specifically designed for registering Serviced Components with the COM+ catalog. Using this tool manually is a more robust approach to registration, since the tool can catch and report any errors. For example, COM+ registration requires system administrator privileges, so you probably do not want just any user with a client application to initiate a dynamic registration. Providing an installation script using Regsvcs.exe offers a professional installation.

A successful install for the author component should look like the following.

```
>Regsvcs QueuedComponent.dll
Microsoft (R) .NET Framework Services Installation Utility Version 1.0.3617.0
Copyright (C) Microsoft Corporation 1998-2001. All rights reserved.

Installed Assembly:
        Assembly:
C:\FTrack\ComInterop\QueuedComponent\bin\Debug\QueuedComponent.dll
        Application: WroxQC
        TypeLib:
c:\ftrack\cominterop\queuedcomponent\bin\debug\QueuedComponent.tlb
```

If you check the Component Services MMC plugin, you'll notice that the WroxQC package has been added. In addition, COM+ has created queues for us to support the queued application. You can also view these in the MMC as shown below.

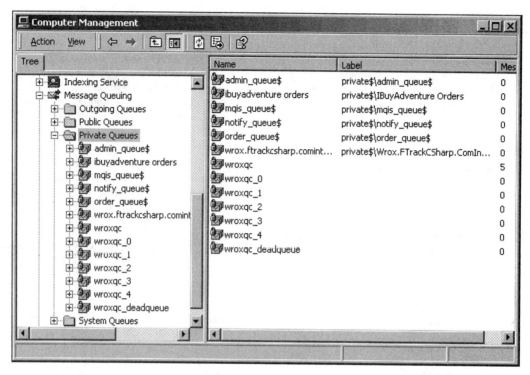

Since we are using MSMQ in workgroup mode, the queues for our package are all private queues. There is one primary queue created (wroxqc), five retry queues (wroxqc_0 through wroxqc_4), and one dead message queue (wroxqc_deadqueue). The retry and dead queues are always private queues. With Active Directory, COM+ would create one public queue: the primary queue.

Retry Queues

One of the interesting features in the queued component infrastructure is the built-in retry mechanism. When the COM+ queue listener picks a message out of the queue for a component, it does so under a transaction. If the component throws an exception, the transaction is aborted and the message is placed back in the queue. However, COM+ does not allow a poison message to indefinitely keep coming off the queue and generating exceptions. Instead, the message is allowed three chances at success. After three failures, the message is moved into the next queue down, so a message failing three times in the primary queue (wroxqc) is sent to the first retry queue (wroxqc_0).

COM+ also waits for a specific amount of time before replaying a message after it arrives in a retry queue. One minute for the first retry queue, two minutes for the second, four minutes for the third, eight minutes for the fourth, and 16 minutes for the final retry queue. If the message still generates an exception, the message is placed in the dead queue and no more work is performed. This retry behavior can help you to solve a number of problems in distributed systems, particularly when trying to send or receive information across external networks of unknown reliability.

Back to the C# Client

With transaction support and queuing in place we can now return to the client application. If you execute the application we demonstrated earlier, you might be surprised to see an exception generated. Why wasn't our program disconnected from the Author component? The answer is that even though the Author component is configured for queuing, it is the client who decides if the calls are made synchronously or asynchronously. To use the Author component as a queued component we need to create the object using a moniker.

Using Monikers

Typical COM programs create a COM component from a CLSID or a PROGID. However, you can also use a moniker to create a component. A moniker is useful when locating and creating a component requires more information than the usual PROGID. In our case, queued components require a queue moniker. This allows COM+ to give us a reference to a recorder object as a proxy for the real Author object. Remember the recorder object is the object responsible for packaging method calls and parameters into MSMQ messages. The Marshal class from the System.Runtime.InteropServices namespace allows us to use monikers. The updated C# client looks like the following:

```
using System;
using System.Runtime.InteropServices;

namespace Wrox.FTrackCSharp.ComInterop.QueuedCSharpClient
{
    class Class1
    {
        [STAThread]
        static void Main(string[] args)
        {
            IQAuthor author;
            string moniker =
             "queue:/new:Wrox.FTrackCSharp.ComInterop.QueuedComponent.Author ";

            author = (IQAuthor)Marshal.BindToMoniker(moniker);
            author.UpdateContract("172-32-1176", true);
            Marshal.ReleaseComObject(author);
        }
    }
}
```

Looking at all members of the Marshal class will reveal quite a mix of methods to help with writing interop code. We only use two of these methods here, but we will cover some more of the class later in the chapter. BindToMoniker() gives us back an object reference to a recorder, and this time the method call we make happens asynchronously. ReleaseComObject() allows you to explicitly manage the lifetime of an object. Remember that the RCW manages the lifetime of a COM object for you, but there may be times when you want to explicitly control the order of multiple releases or release a component at a specific time.

If we make sure the WroxQC COM+ package is stopped, we can run the client program and then check the MSMQ queues for a message. As we can see below, running our program has produced a single message in the primary queue.

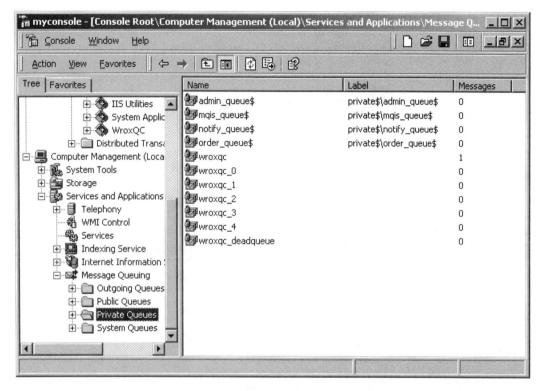

Since the `authorId` parameter we pass into the component dooms the call to failure, we can watch as the message works its way down the retry queues once the application has started. You can manually start and stop COM+ applications by right-clicking on the package in the Component Services.

Platform Invocation Services

Before COM came along it was fashionable to package code into a dynamic link library of exported functions. DLLs allowed applications to share common code and offered binary interoperability between the different C and C++ compilers on the market. Even today, the vast array of functionality offered by the Win32 API comes from code inside of non-COM DLLs. Although the .NET Framework has tremendous coverage of the Win32 APIs, even extending and improving upon it, the framework does not cover 100% of the available methods. **Platform Invocation Services (PInvoke**, for short) allow .NET programmers to execute the C-style functions exported by these DLLs.

Identifying DLL Functions

Every DLL function you use from C# needs to be identified with the name (or ordinal number) of the function, and the name of the DLL where the function lives. Uncovering the DLL name for Win32 API methods is as easy as finding the function documentation in MSDN. Most of the Win32 APIs are from the "big three": `GDI32.dll`, `kernel32.dll`, or `user32.dll`. For third party libraries you may need to perform some additional research if the information is not in the associated documentation.

One useful tool deployed with Visual Studio .NET for this purpose is dumpbin.exe. You can see all of the exported functions in a DLL using dumpbin with the /exports switch. For example, if we dump the file we created with C++ at the beginning of the chapter (atlwrox.dll) we can see the five functions implemented in almost every COM DLL:

```
C:\FTrack\ComInterop\AtlWrox\Debug>dumpbin /exports atlwrox.dll
Microsoft (R) COFF/PE Dumper Version 7.00.9447
Copyright (C) Microsoft Corporation. All rights reserved.


Dump of file atlwrox.dll

File Type: DLL

  Section contains the following exports for atlwrox.dll

    00000000 characteristics
    3C91E4BF time date stamp Fri Mar 15 12:10:39 2002
        0.00 version
           1 ordinal base
           5 number of functions
           5 number of names

    ordinal hint RVA      name

          1    0 000117D5 DllCanUnloadNow
          2    1 00011EC9 DllGetClassObject
          3    2 00011302 DllMain
          4    3 00011E92 DllRegisterServer
          5    4 00011032 DllUnregisterServer

  Summary

        4000 .data
        2000 .idata
        7000 .rdata
        2000 .reloc
        2000 .rsrc
       25000 .text
       10000 .textbss
```

If you remember our C# COM component from this chapter, you might recall we hid the implementation from the earlier code listing. This component exposed methods to retrieve the free drive space, as well as the volume name and serial number. Taking a look at the implementation listed below, we can see the component used two Win32 API functions from Kernel32.

```
public int GetFreeDiskSpace(string directoryName)
{
    ulong freeBytesAvailable = 0;
    ulong totalNumberOfBytes = 0;
    ulong totalNumberOfFreeBytes = 0;

    bool result = GetDiskFreeSpaceEx(directoryName,
                           ref freeBytesAvailable,
```

```
                                    ref totalNumberOfBytes,
                                    ref totalNumberOfFreeBytes);
        if(!result)
        {
            throw new ApplicationException("GetDiskFreeSpaceEx ailure");
        }
                                        // 2^20
        return (int)(totalNumberOfFreeBytes / 1048756);

    }

    public string GetVolumeNameAndSerial(string rootPath,
                                ref int serialNumber)
    {
        StringBuilder volumeName = new StringBuilder(255);
        uint uSerial = 0;
        uint comLength = 0;
        uint fsFlags = 0;

        bool result = GetVolumeInformation(rootPath,
                                    volumeName,
                                    (uint)volumeName.Capacity,
                                    ref uSerial,
                                    ref comLength,
                                    ref fsFlags,
                                    null, 0);
        if(!result)
        {
            throw new ApplicationException("GetVolumeInformation failure");
        }

        serialNumber = (int)uSerial;
        return volumeName.ToString();
    }


    [DllImport("kernel32")]
    static extern bool GetDiskFreeSpaceEx(
                                    string Path,
                                    ref ulong freeBytesAvailable,
                                    ref ulong totalNumberOfBytes,
                                    ref ulong totalNumberOfFreeBytes);


    [DllImport("kernel32")]
    static extern bool GetVolumeInformation(
                                string rootPath,
                                StringBuilder volumeNameBuffer,
                                uint volumeNameSize,
                                ref uint volumeSerialNumber,
                                ref uint maximumComponentLength,
                                ref uint fileSystemFlags,
                                StringBuilder fileSystemNameBuffer,
                                uint fileSystemNameSize);
    }
}
```

349

Using the DllImportAttribute

Most of the work needed to interop with managed DLL code centers around writing the correct function prototype. The work begins by decorating the unmanaged function prototype with a DllImportAttribute. As a minimum, the DllImportAttribute constructor requires just the name of the DLL where the unmanaged function resides.

The extern keyword applied on these two methods above indicates they are implemented externally. Because of this, no implementation is provided and the declaration ends with a semicolon.

PInvoke Marshalling

When writing the function prototype itself, special care is required to ensure that the data transfer from managed code to unmanaged code and back is successful. There are many options available to accomplish what you need to call any Win32 API function, so we are only able to cover a subset of the information here.

Many managed data types have a direct mapping to an unmanaged data type. For example, you can use a System.Byte for C functions expecting an unsigned char, because both are 8 bits and no data conversion needs to take place. Other data types require some amount of translation. As an example, let's take a look at the C prototype for the GetVolumeInformation() function we used in this example.

```
BOOL GetVolumeInformation(LPCTSTR lpRootPathName,
                          LPTSTR lpVolumeNameBuffer,
                          DWORD nVolumeNameSize,
                          LPDWORD lpVolumeSerialNumber,
                          LPDWORD lpMaximumComponentLength,
                          LPDWORD lpFileSystemFlags,
                          LPTSTR lpFileSystemNameBuffer,
                          DWORD nFileSystemNameSize);
```

If you compare the C prototype to our C# declaration, you'll notice that many of the parameters are passed as basic string or ref int data types. One exception is the lpVolumeNameBuffer parameter where the Win32 function expects a writeable, fixed length string buffer. Since the System.String class implements an immutable string, we instead instantiate a StringBuilder object from the System.Text namespace. If you are simply passing strings "by value" (like the first parameter), you can pass System.String objects.

Many DLL functions require structures, or pointers to structures, as parameters. In these situations you can declare a matching structure in C# and use the StructLayoutAttribute to wrest control of the structure's memory layout away from the runtime. The LayoutKind enumeration allows you to specify the structure layout as Auto, Explicit, or Sequential. Auto layout allows the runtime to choose the memory layout of a structure. Explicit gives you unambiguous control over the layout, down to the memory offset for each field. Selecting a Sequential layout forces the runtime to lay out the type's members in the order they appear. As an example, look at the SYSTEMTIME structure as defined by the Win32 API.

```
typedef struct _SYSTEMTIME
{
    WORD wYear;
    WORD wMonth;
    WORD wDayOfWeek;
    WORD wDay;
    WORD wHour;
    WORD wMinute;
    WORD wSecond;
    WORD wMilliseconds;
} SYSTEMTIME, *PSYSTEMTIME;
```

This structure is used by several API functions, including the GetSystemTime() function from Kernel32.dll. The API takes a pointer to the structure, as shown here.

```
void GetSystemTime(LPSYSTEMTIME lpSystemTime);
```

To use the function from C#, we simply declare ourselves a managed version of the structure using a sequential layout. The following console mode application would give us the current system time by calling the GetSystemTime() API function directly.

```csharp
using System;
using System.Runtime.InteropServices;

namespace Wrox.FTrackCSharp.ComInterop.PInvokeGetTime
{
    class Class1
    {
        [StructLayoutAttribute(LayoutKind.Sequential)]
        private struct SYSTEMTIME
        {
            public short year;
            public short month;
            public short dayOfWeek;
            public short day;
            public short hour;
            public short minute;
            public short second;
            public short milliseconds;
        }

        [DllImport("kernel32.dll")]
        static extern bool GetSystemTime(ref SYSTEMTIME time);


        [STAThread]
        static void Main(string[] args)
        {
            SYSTEMTIME systemTime= new SYSTEMTIME();

            GetSystemTime(ref systemTime);
```

```
            Console.WriteLine("System time is {0}/{1}/{2} {3}:{4}:{5}",
                        systemTime.month, systemTime.day,
                        systemTime.year, systemTime.hour,
                        systemTime.minute, systemTime.second);
            Console.ReadLine();
        }
    }
}
```

Summary

This chapter has covered the various interoperability technologies available in .NET. We have seen how to use classic COM components in our .NET programs, including how to manually import type libraries using TLBIMP.EXE. We also wrote a .NET component to use from a COM client, and a .NET component to use COM+ services. Finally, we have seen how to use functions from legacy DLLs from out .NET components. As .NET continues to penetrate the market we may find less of a need for interop capabilities, but for the time being it is nice to know the tools support legacy technology so well.

12

ASP.NET

ASP.NET refers to parts of the .NET Framework that provide tools and infrastructure for web applications. We will look at two types of application built with ASP.NET. The first type, the **web forms** application, is the topic for this chapter. In the next chapter we will discuss **web services**. Both of these application types rely on technologies provided by ASP.NET. ASP.NET provides built-in state management, caching algorithms, tracing support, flexible authentication schemes, and many other features that enable us to build solid and scalable web applications.

In this chapter we will:

- ❑ Build a simple e-mail application to demonstrate how to create **web forms**, use validation controls, and create our own user controls

- ❑ Work with the ASP.NET `DataGrid` control, and see how to use ADO.NET in web applications

- ❑ Look at how to configure our ASP.NET applications and take advantage of built-in authentication and authorization

- ❑ See how to use diagnostic tools to debug our ASP.NET applications

Along the way, we will learn about the implementation and structure of ASP.NET applications. But before we start, let's look at how ASP.NET came to be.

ASP.NET – Why is it Here?

The name implies that ASP.NET is a new version of ASP. In fact, the differences are radical. ASP was a stand alone scripting language. ASP.NET is really just a web interface for our .NET applications – we have full access to the .NET Framework and our own classes, we just happen to be creating web pages instead of a Windows forms or console output.

We can still use ASP.NET the old way – mixing server-side instructions in with our HTML. But it is now far easier to separate the HTML from the server-side logic, for two reasons:

1. We can call our own compiled classes, without needing a Registry entry or any special component installation

2. ASP.NET supports code-behind files, which separate the HTML from most of the page's server-side code – we will see more of these in our example application

Classic ASP used scripting languages like VBScript, but ASP.NET uses full C# (or any other .NET language) to get strong typing, decent exception handling, inheritance. The code compiles instead of being interpreted, which gives performance a good boost.

ASP.NET enables us to write web forms in an event-driven way. We can respond to click events, manipulate the properties of objects, and so on, without needing to understand the underlying HTTP requests, or changing the attributes of HTML tags. If you want to work that way, you still can, but you don't have to.

If we create our ASP.NET applications in Visual Studio .NET, we don't even need to code our own HTML. Visual Studio .NET enables us to create interfaces by dragging controls onto a form, as we would when creating a Windows application. We can create our own controls, making it easy to create common interface elements for our site such as menu bars, headers, and footers.

Now we've heard some of the reasons why ASP.NET is great, let's see it in action. We will use Visual Studio .NET for the examples, although everything will work the same in Visual C# Standard. Many of the principles we cover will be the same when using a text editor and C# compiler, although you will need to code the HTML manually.

When Microsoft released Active Server Pages, the technology quickly became a favorite instrument for developing web applications. The mixed environment of scripting language and HTML markup was easy to learn and simple to use. The amount of time and expertise required to bring a web application to market decreased considerably.

As time progressed, the web matured and web applications became more complex. The very features that endeared us to ASP became a source of pain. The loose typing allowed data mismatch errors to slip into production environments, and the lack of structured error handling made these errors harder to handle. As user interfaces became more intricate, the mix of HTML markup, client-side script, and server-side script inside of the same source file began to feel cumbersome. Although encapsulation techniques existed to reduce the burden, such as VBScript classes and include files, for example, developing a user interface for the Web was a completely different experience to developing an interface with Visual Basic or Visual C++.

Using C# or VB.NET to develop an ASP.NET application gives you a strongly typed, compiled language environment with structured exception handling, performance gains over ASP, and access to a rich class library. In contrast to ASP, ASP.NET is a drastically different setting. As web applications continue to grow in complexity and scale, the advantages gained by using a robust, object-oriented language will only grow in importance.

However, the biggest improvement in ASP.NET is arguably the interface construction. Building a web forms application is now incredibly similar to building a forms-based application for Windows using C# or Visual Basic .NET. Of course, web forms offer unique properties for web applications, as we will start to see in the next section.

Creating a Web Forms Project

In Visual Studio .NET, the ASP.NET Web Application project icon is listed in the New Project dialog box alongside the familiar Windows project types. When we create an ASP.NET Web Application, we specify a location for it on a web server – not our local hard drive. The location we specify must be a machine running IIS 5.0 or above. A new virtual directory is created if none exists. Our first example project is called WebEmail:

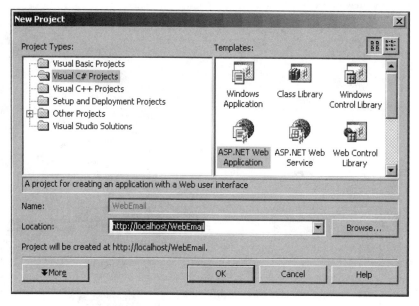

Once the project is created, the next screen contains a blank web form for us to work with. If not, double click on the WebForm1.aspx file in the Solution Explorer window.

Without Visual Studio .NET, we can create an ASP.NET application by creating a virtual directory in IIS, and creating our ASPX files in a text editor.

If you are downloading the accompanying source code for the book, in Windows Explorer you can navigate to the AspNet folder, which contains the ASP.NET projects for this chapter, and right-click. Select the Properties option and click on the Web Sharing tab, then select the Share This Folder option. These steps will create a virtual directory in IIS pointing to the sample code and allow you to execute it.

Adding Controls

If we open the Toolbox window we should see two sets of controls to drag and drop onto the form. The first set is under the HTML tab of the Toolbox window, while the second set is under the Web Forms tab. There are other tabs available, but we will concentrate on these two for most of the chapter. Some of the controls seem to overlap, for instance, there is an entry for a Label control in both the Web Forms and HTML tabs. But don't worry – the difference will soon become clear!

The first control we will drag onto the form is an Image control from the HTML tab. Right-click this control to bring up a property dialog, and set the ImageSource to the GIF file with the Wrox logo (or whatever image you want, of course).

Next, drag a Button control from the Web Forms tab onto the ASPX page. With two controls placed so far, our designer view looks like the following screen:

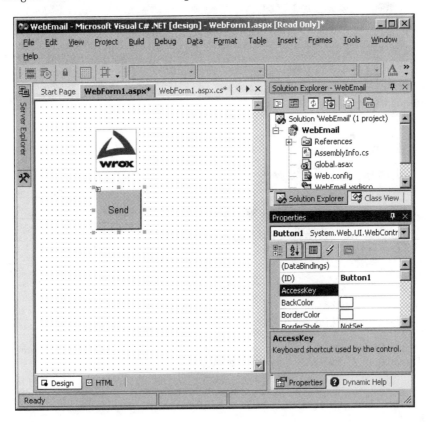

To clearly see the effects of dragging these two controls onto the form we can switch to the HTML view using the flat button on the bottom of the designer's window. The HTML looks like this, although a few tags and attributes have been removed here to save space:

```
<%@ Page language="c#" Codebehind="WebForm1.aspx.cs" AutoEventWireup="false"
    Inherits="WebEmail.WebForm1" %>
<html>
   <head>
      <title>WebForm1</title>
   </head>
   <body MS_POSITIONING="GridLayout">
      <form id="Form1" method="post" runat="server">
         <img src="images\newwroxlogo.gif">
         <asp:Button id="Button1"runat="server" Text="Button"></asp:Button>
      </form>
   </body>
</html>
```

There are several key points to make about the example above. We can see the HTML Image control has placed an HTML element into the ASPX page. HTML controls are great for relatively static content, such as this image, where all the properties are set at design time and are rendered into HTML immediately.

Other controls are more dynamic and are useful when we do not know all of their properties at design time, or wish them to change during execution. The button we placed on the form is an interactive control, and the user will expect something to happen after clicking the button. One of the incredible features of ASP.NET is that we can raise a Click event on the server when a user clicks the button. This truly brings the same event-driven model from Windows applications to web applications. So how does this happen?

You probably already noticed that the button control looks different from the image control in the ASPX source. The Button control is inside of markup that includes a **tag prefix** (asp) and a **tag name** (Button). The controls under the **Web Forms** tab are server-side controls, meaning that the ASP.NET runtime instantiates an object on the server to represent the control. These server-side controls have properties to set (such as the Text property), and render themselves as HTML at run time. The class used for this control is the Button class from the System.Web.UI.WebControls namespace. Server-side controls must always contain a runat="server" attribute inside of the tag to work properly.

In Visual Studio .NET we are discouraged from manipulating this object in the ASPX file itself – instead, each ASPX file has a 'code-behind', which is where we put our real C# code.

Code-Behind Files

The top line of our ASPX file is the Page **directive**. The directive applies attributes to the page for the parser and compiler to use. We will look at the Codebehind attribute, which points to a C# source code file:

```
<%@ Page language="c#" Codebehind="WebForm1.aspx.cs"
    AutoEventWireup="false" Inherits="WebEmail.WebForm1" %>
```

If we switch back to the design view we can right-click on the button and select **Properties** from the context menu. Just like Windows form development, there is a **Properties** window to set the events and properties for any object in the designer. We want to change the ID of our button to `SendButton` and then switch to the **Events** tab of the **Properties** window (click on the lightning bolt). If we double-click in the cell next to the **Click** event, the IDE adds an event handler to our code and opens the **code-behind** file `WebForm1.aspx.cs`. Here is the source:

```csharp
using System;
using System.Collections;
using System.ComponentModel;
using System.Data;
using System.Drawing;
using System.Web;
using System.Web.SessionState;
using System.Web.UI;
using System.Web.UI.WebControls;
using System.Web.UI.HtmlControls;
using System.Web.Mail;

namespace WebEmail
{
    /// <summary>
    /// Summary description for WebForm1.
    /// </summary>
    public class WebForm1 : System.Web.UI.Page
    {
        protected System.Web.UI.WebControls.Button SendButton;

        private void Page_Load(object sender, System.EventArgs e)
        {
            // Put user code to initialize the page here
        }

        #region Web Form Designer generated code
        override protected void OnInit(EventArgs e)
        {
            //
            // CODEGEN: This call is required by the ASP.NET Web
            // Form Designer.
            //
            InitializeComponent();
            base.OnInit(e);
        }

        /// <summary>
        /// Required method for Designer support - do not modify
        /// the contents of this method with the code editor.
        /// </summary>
        private void InitializeComponent()
        {
            this.SendButton.Click += new
                System.EventHandler(this.SendButton_Click);
            this.Load += new System.EventHandler(this.Page_Load);
        }
        #endregion

        private void SendButton_Click(object sender, System.EventArgs e)
        {
        }
    }
}
```

The above code defines a single class derived from `System.Web.UI.Page`. The class includes a `protected` member variable representing our button, as well as a method to handle the button's `Click` event. There is no information here about the position of the button or any other page layout – as we've seen, that's all in the ASPX.

This separation of page layout from page logic is an important part of ASP.NET. The ASP.NET environment uses the ASPX file to generate a class that inherits from the class defined in the `Inherits` attribute of the `Page` directive. This is why the button is declared as `protected` – the ASPX class inherits from the code-behind class, and needs to access the button.

Visual Studio .NET sets all this up for us. When using a text editor to program ASP.NET, we can choose to do this or to combine our layout and logic in the ASPX file. If you choose to separate, there are two ways you can do it:

❑ Create your code-behind class, compile it to an accessible assembly, and then manually set the `Inherits` attribute of the `Page` directive. You do not need a `Codebehind` attribute – this is only used by Visual Studio .NET.

❑ Create your code-behind class, do not compile it, set the `Inherits` attribute to the class name, and the `src` attribute to point to the code-behind source. ASP.NET will compile the code-behind automatically when it is needed. If the source file changes, ASP.NET will automatically recompile.

Separating layout from logic makes site maintenance far easier in all but the smallest ASP.NET applications. Of course, in some circumstances there are advantages in having everything in a single file, classic ASP style. ASP.NET lets you choose.

> **If you want to mix C# code into the HTML, use `<%` to open a C# section, and `%>` to close it.**

Anyway, back to our application. Press *Ctrl+F5* (or select **Start Without Debugging** from the **Debug** menu) to run the form. Visual Studio .NET will launch the browser and navigate to the project's main ASPX on the web server. You could even set a breakpoint on the `SendButton_Click` event and run with the debugger to watch the breakpoint hit when you click the button in the browser. So far our form doesn't do anything, so we need to add some additional features.

Sending e-Mail from a Web Form

For our first working example we want to build a form from which a user can send email. First, we drop an HTML `GridLayoutPanel` onto the form, and drag our `SendButton` control into the panel.

> **The panel controls are containers for other controls and allow us to manipulate a group of controls as a single unit.**

Next, we will drop three `TextBox` controls from the **Web Form** tab of the **Toolbox** into the panel and name them `toText`, `subjectText`, and `messageText`. We set the `TextMode` property of the `messageText` control to `MultiLine`, and drop a server-side `Label` control into the panel and name it `lblStatus`. After adding some HTML label controls, changing the controls' position, and playing with some of the visual properties, our form looks like this:

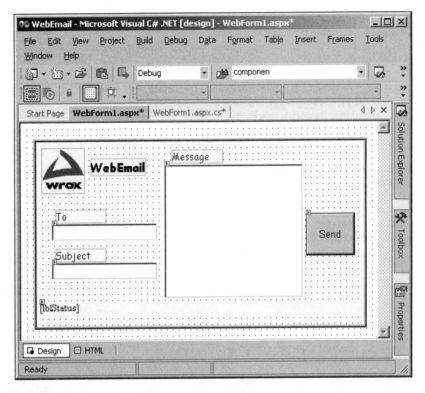

This form is going to send an e-mail for us using the `SmtpMail` class from the `System.Web.Mail` namespace, so we need to add the following to the top of our code-behind:

```
using System.Web.Mail;
```

As we added each Web Form control, the designer added a member variable to the code-behind class to represent the control. The variable name matches the `id` attribute of the control in the ASPX page. We can now get and set properties for these controls in our C# code.

The members of `SmtpMail` that we will be using are static, so we do not need to instantiate an object – we just call the property and method on the class itself. We need to add the following code to the button's event handler:

```
private void SendButton_Click(object sender, System.EventArgs e)
{
    try
    {
        SmtpMail.SmtpServer = "my.smtpserver.net";

        SmtpMail.Send("TestWroxWebEmail@wrox.com",  // from address
            toText.Text, subjectText.Text, messageText.Text);
```

```
        toText.Text = "";
        subjectText.Text = "";
        messageText.Text = "";

        lblStatus.Text = "Your message has been sent!";
    }
    catch(Exception exception)
    {
        lblStatus.Text = "Error: " + exception.Message;
    }
}
```

Change the static `SmtpMail.SmtpServer` property to point to a valid SMTP server machine (if you do not have your own, use your ISP's). The form will send the e-mail or report an error. For instance, if the user leaves the To field blank, the `SmtpMail.Send()` generates an exception. In the next section we will take steps to prevent this exception by validating user input.

Validation Controls

The `SmtpMail` class provides some **server-side validation** for us. We have seen how it will raise an exception if there is no valid e-mail address in the To box. However, forgetting to enter a valid email address is a very common problem. If every time a user leaves the box blank we rely on the server to detect the problem, we slow down the application and place added stress on the server. For this reason, we also employ client-side validation.

Client-side validation involves writing scripts into the web page that cause the browser to validate fields itself, and to provide immediate feedback. Client-side validation will speed the application up for most users, but we cannot trust it – some users turn off JavaScript, and others might have malicious schemes for submitting invalid data. Client-side scripting can take a load off the server, but we always *need* to validate on the server too. Good web applications will do both.

Coding two versions of the validation, and making sure they both do the same thing gives developers many headaches. ASP.NET uses validation controls to do the job for you – automatically creating client- and server-side validators that do the same thing. There are even five types of validation controls included in ASP.NET:

- ❑   `RequiredFieldValidator` – Ensures the user populates a field with some value.

- ❑   `CompareValidator` – Compares input against a constant value or against the value in another control.

- ❑   `RangeValidator` – Compares the input to an upper and lower boundary. The boundaries are numbers, alphabetic characters, or dates.

- ❑   `RegularExpressionValidator` – Compares the entry against a pattern defined by a regular expression.

- ❑   `CustomValidator` – Enables developers to add custom validation code on the client and server.

Our first step is to require the user to populate the Subject field by dropping a `RequiredFieldValidator` onto the form where you want the error message to appear (in this case, immediately below the Subject text box. Set the `ControlToValidate` property to `subjectText`.

The `ErrorMessage` property specifies what to display when the validation condition is not met. Validation occurs when the user clicks on a server-side button control. We can select whether a `Button`, `ImageButton`, or `LinkButton` will invoke the validator with the `CausesValidation` property. For instance, if we had a button allowing the user to start over by blanking out all of the form fields, we would want to avoid validation by setting `CausesValidation` to `false`.

We also need to ensure that the user has entered a valid e-mail address. This is more complicated, but Visual Studio .NET makes it easy with the `RegularExpressionValidator`. We can drag this control underneath the To textbox and point the `ControlToValidate` at `toText`. Visual Studio .NET provides a number of built-in regular expressions you can use from the `ValidationExpression` property dialog:

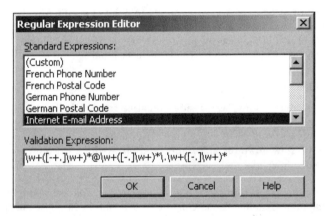

A `RegularExpressionValidator` only runs the input through the regular expression if there is text available in the input control. If the input control is empty then the `RegularExpressionControl` always accepts it. Since we are going to require an email address, we will need an additional `RequiredFieldValidator` also pointing to `toText` as the `ControlToValidate`. This ensures that the field is not left blank.

Our ASPX file now includes the additional three control tags.

```
<asp:RequiredFieldValidator id="RequiredFieldValidator1"
      style="Z-INDEX: 111; LEFT: 25px; POSITION: absolute; TOP: 182px"
      runat="server" Font-Size="X-Small"
      ErrorMessage="Subject field is required"
      ControlToValidate="subjectText">
</asp:RequiredFieldValidator>

<asp:RegularExpressionValidator id="RegularExpressionValidator1"
      style="Z-INDEX: 113; LEFT: 25px; POSITION: absolute; TOP: 120px"
      runat="server" Width="139px" Font-Size="X-Small"
      ErrorMessage="Valid email is required"
      ControlToValidate="toText"
      ValidationExpression="\w+([-+.]\w+)*@\w+([-.]\w+)*\.\w+([-.]\w+)*">
</asp:RegularExpressionValidator>

<asp:RequiredFieldValidator id="RequiredFieldValidator2"
```

```
        style="Z-INDEX: 113; LEFT: 25px; POSITION: absolute; TOP: 120px"
        runat="server" Font-Size="X-Small"
        ErrorMessage="Email is required"
        ControlToValidate="toText">
</asp:RequiredFieldValidator>
```

> **If you are using a text editor, simply type the code as shown above. The regular expressions look horrible, but they are really quite simple. Most of the regular expressions you will ever need are available from http://regxlib.com.**

If the user presses the Send button without entering any text in the required fields, the client-side validation script produces the following error messages under the text boxes:

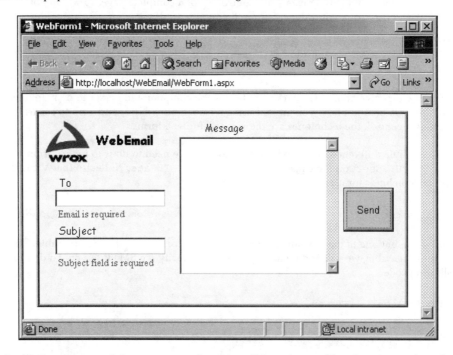

If we disable JavaScript and then try again, the page will be submitted but the server-side code will catch the error and produce the same error message.

User Controls

When we were discussing ASP.NET's features, we mentioned the ability to create our own controls. In this section we will create a control that we can drop onto any web page, and that does the same thing as the page we developed above. To do this we will create a **user control**. Most of what we do will be very similar to the technique we used to create the page. In fact, you can view user controls as mini pages.

Start a new ASP.NET solution in Visual Studio.NET called EmailControl. Once the project is loaded select Add New Item from the Project menu and select the Web User Control icon. We give the file a name of WebEmail.ascx.

To create the user control, add the form elements to the control in exactly the same way as we did for the web form. There are two key differences between the control's ASCX file and the page's ASPX file:

❏ The directive – in the case of a control we have a Control directive, instead of Page:

```
<%@ Control Language="c#" AutoEventWireup="false"
        Codebehind="WebEmail.ascx.cs" Inherits="UserControl.WebEmail"
        TargetSchema="http://schemas.microsoft.com/intellisense/ie5"%>
```

❏ The opening and closing tags – the control is not a complete page, so we do not open with the <html> tags, we are just declaring a self-contained <div>:

```
<div ms_positioning="GridLayout">
   <!-- Same HTML as for WebEmail page -->
</div>
```

The Control directive applies similar attributes for the compiler and parser to pick up, including the name of the code-behind file. If you are not using Visual Studio .NET, and wish to separate layout from logic in a user control, the techniques are the same as for web forms.

There is very little difference in the code-behind too. All we need to do is to inherit from System.Web.UI.UserControl instead of System.Web.UI.Page. Note also that Visual Studio .NET declares code-behinds for user controls as abstract:

```
public abstract class WebEmail : System.Web.UI.UserControl
```

This will work, but one of the key advantages of User Controls is that they are reusable. To make our control more reusable, we will add a public property to specify the SMTP server. To do this, just add the following code:

```
public string SmtpServer
{
   get { return SmtpMail.SmtpServer; }
   set { SmtpMail.SmtpServer = value; }
}
```

and remove the line from SendButton_Click that specifies the SMTP server, so that it now looks like this:

```
private void SendButton_Click(object sender, System.EventArgs e)
{
    // Smtp server assignment removed
    try
    {
        SmtpMail.Send("TestWroxWebEmail@wrox.com",
                    toText.Text,
```

```
                      subjectText.Text,
                      messageText.Text);

      toText.Text = "";
      subjectText.Text = "";
      messageText.Text = "";

      StatusLabel.Text = "Your message has been sent!";
   }
   catch(Exception exception)
   {
      StatusLabel.Text = "Error: " + exception.Message;
   }
}
```

We can now drop the control onto any web form we like, and instantly have a page for sending email.

Adding a User Control to a Web Form

Including the WebEmail user control in a web form requires only a few extra lines in an ASPX file. Firstly, we need a Register directive. The Register directive enables a developer to create a new tag prefix and tag name for a user control. The directive is also used to tie the control to the ASCX file where the control resides. Here is the code for an ASPX file that uses our control:

```
<%@ Register TagPrefix="Wrox" TagName="WebEmail" Src="WebEmail.ascx" %>
<%@ Page language="c#" Codebehind="WebForm1.aspx.cs"
    AutoEventWireup="false" Inherits="EmailControl.WebForm1" %>

<html>
   <head>
      <title>WebForm1</title>
   </head>
   <body ms_positioning="GridLayout">
      <form id="Form1" method="post" runat="server">
         <div align="center" ms_positioning="FlowLayout">
            User Control Demo Application
         </div>
         <hr width="100%" size="1">
         <div ms_positioning="GridLayout">
            <Wrox:WebEmail id="WebEmail1" runat="Server"
                  SmtpServer="smtp.myserver.net" />
         </div>
      </form>
   </body>
</html>
```

We add the control to the form by writing code using the server control syntax with the new tag prefix and name. Inside the tag we can even declaratively set the control's SmtpServer property. Unfortunately, unlike the server controls we cannot manipulate this user control from the code-behind. Let's see a (slightly hacky) way to do this.

Accessing a User Control from the Code-Behind

If we need to manipulate a user control from a web form's code-behind, we need to declare it in the code-behind instead of the ASPX. Here's what we do:

Add a `PlaceHolder` control to the web form (either by dragging it from the **Web Forms** tab on the toolbox, or typing the following HTML:

```
<asp:PlaceHolder id="PlaceHolder1" runat="server"></asp:PlaceHolder>
```

Instantiate the user control in the `Page_Load` event in the web form's code-behind, and `Add()` it to the `PlaceHolder`:

```
private void Page_Load(object sender, System.EventArgs e)
{
    WebEmail myWebEmail = (WebEmail)LoadControl("WebEmail.ascx");
    myWebEmail.SmtpServer = "smtp.myserver.net";

    PlaceHolder1.Controls.Add(myWebEmail);
}
```

Here we declare an object of the correct type, and use the `LoadControl` method to instantiate it – casting it back to the declared type. We then add the control to the `PlaceHolder.Controls` collection, causing it to be displayed.

Additional Server Controls

So far the server-side controls we have used have been very simple. They typically match up with a single HTML element, such as a textbox or button. ASP.NET also offers some more advanced controls, which use a combination of HTML and client-side script to offer a sophisticated interface such as a calendar. Before we demonstrate some of the more powerful controls, let's take a look at all of the Web form controls ASP.NET provides. The following table lists all of the server-side controls except for the validation controls we detailed earlier:

Class	Description
AdRotator	Displays a random advertisement banner based on information in an XML configuration file. We can also manipulate it from code.
Button	Displays a push button. In addition to a `Click` event, we can use a `Command` event to handle multiple buttons on a form. Set the `CommandName` and `CommandArgument` properties to provide additional information to the `Command` event handler.
Calendar	Displays a monthly calendar in a highly flexible control. The calendar control allows users to move to dates in any year, and has the ability to display specific information for a given date.
CheckBox	Displays a checkbox. The `Checked` property indicates if the box is checked or not.

Class	Description
CheckBoxList	Contains multiple checkboxes in a single control. This control is easier to use when more than one checkbox is needed. It is not as flexible when it comes to layout and positioning of individual checkboxes.
DataGrid	Displays information from a data source in a table, and also allows editing, sorting, and paging.
DataList	Displays a list of data using templates and styles. This is similar to a DataGrid, but the DataList allows for the highest control over layout and style.
DropDownList	Displays a dropdown list. Use the SelectedIndex property to retrieve the position of the selected item.
HyperLink	Displays a link as text or as an image. The NavigateUrl property controls the location to link to.
Image	Displays an image. The ImageUrl property controls the image to display.
ImageButton	Displays an image, but like a Button, has a click event.
Label	Displays text. Useful as a placeholder for status messages. If you include HTML code in the Text property, it will be encoded so that the HTML code itself displays.
LinkButton	Looks like a hyperlink, but fires a click event.
ListBox	Displays a list of items for the user to select from. The Selected property indicates the selected item. If multi-selections are possible, loop through the Items collection and test the Selected property.
Literal	Renders text directly into a web page. Use a literal control to add text, even HTML markup, programmatically to a page.
Panel	A container for other controls. Use the Visible property to hide and show a group of controls at once. Like the PlaceHolder control, you can use a Panel to programmatically add controls to a page. A BackImageUrl displays a background image in the panel.
PlaceHolder	Used to programmatically add controls to a page. The placeholder produces no output on its own.
RadioButton	Displays a radio button. The Checked property indicates whether the control is selected.
RadioButtonList	Displays a group of radio buttons. Use the SelectedIndex property to find the checked button. The RadioButton list eases the management of a group of radio buttons, but layout is less flexible.

Table continued on following page

Class	Description
Repeater	A container control for lists of data. The data is displayed using templates, allowing for the highest level of customization in the presentation.
Table	Displays a table. Since this is a server-side control you can programmatically add rows and cells.
TextBox	Displays a single line, multi-line, or password textbox. The type of text box to display is controlled with the TextMode property.
Xml	Displays an XML document in a web page. The XML may be transformed using XSL processing instructions.

We will now look at one of the most interesting and powerful of these controls: the DataGrid.

Data Binding with Web Controls

A common task in web applications is displaying data from a data source on a web page. The data source may be an array, a set of database records, or any object implementing the IEnumerable interface. All of the server controls above allow some form of data binding, which means that displaying data is amazingly easy. Some controls, for example Button and Textbox, provide single value bindings. Other controls, such as the DataGrid, can display whole tables of data. We're going to create a new application that uses two of the list controls (DataGrid and Repeater) to display information from the SQL Server sample pubs database.

The DataGrid

We saw the Windows DataGrid when we looked at ADO.NET in Chapter 10. The ASP.NET DataGrid control is also powerful yet simple to use. When the DataGrid binds to an ADO.NET DataSet or a data reader, the DataGrid uses the field names as column headers in an HTML table. Each record in the data object becomes a row in the table. The DataGrid can add a footer row to the table, and also supports sorting and paging of the data.

First, drag and drop a DataGrid into a web form. We can set properties to change almost any aspect of the control's behavior and display. In this application, we want the grid to display data generated from a query on the publishers table. We also want an additional column the user can click to display child records on the same form. These child records list the employee contacts for the selected publisher. By the time we've finished, the page will look like this (with Binnet & Hardley selected):

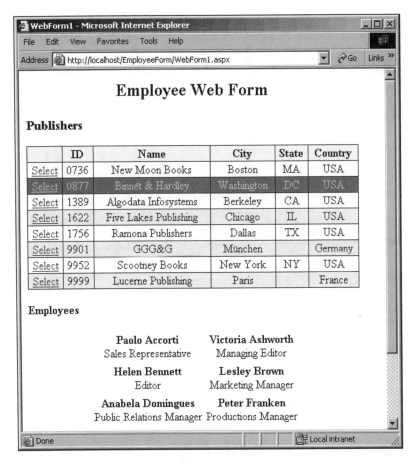

To add additional columns, click the ellipsis in the Columns cell of the grid's Properties window to display the following dialog. We leave the Create columns automatically at run time checkbox selected, allowing the grid to dynamically build columns from the data source. In addition, we move a Select column (found under the Button Column branch) from the Available Columns into the list of Selected Columns:

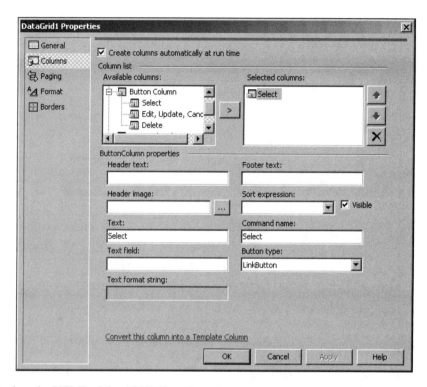

Take a look at the HTML of the ASPX file, where the DataGrid properties are expressed as XML elements. The designer understands how to read and modify the properties, but you can also code the XML by hand. The ASPX source for the DataGrid in this application is shown below:

```
<asp:datagrid id="DataGrid1" runat="server"
      BorderColor="#400040" BorderStyle="Solid">
   <SelectedItemStyle ForeColor="Lime" BackColor="IndianRed"/>
   <AlternatingItemStyle BackColor="#C0FFFF"/>
   <ItemStyle BackColor="White"/>
   <HeaderStyle Font-Bold="True" HorizontalAlign="Center"
                BackColor="#FFFF80">
   </HeaderStyle>
   <Columns>
      <asp:ButtonColumn Text="Select" CommandName="Select"/>
   </Columns>
</asp:datagrid>
```

The only step left is to populate the `DataGrid` from the data source. Let's just review what we want the page to do:

❑ The user navigates to our page. We want to populate the page's `DataGrid` with data from the database, which we will do in the `Page_Load()` method.

❑ The user selects one of the rows. This will reload the page with some new parameters, and will call `Page_Load()` again.

We only need to populate the `DataGrid` in the first of these cases. Subsequent page loads can reuse the data we already obtained the first time. After the first page load, the `DataGrid` will persist the values it displays in a property named `ViewState`. `ViewState` is encoded into a hidden variable on the client's browser.

Although this technique increases the amount of data sent to the client's browser, it saves us from re-querying the database when the user posts the page back to the server. The grid will simply recreate the data it needs to display from `ViewState` instead.

We can check whether the page is loading for the first time with the `IsPostBack` property of the page. We add the following code to the web form's `Page_Load` event. It checks the `IsPostBack` property and binds a `SqlDataReader` to the `DataGrid`:

```
private void Page_Load(object sender, System.EventArgs e)
{
    if(!IsPostBack)
    {
        string connectString =
                "initial catalog=pubs;user id=sa;server=localhost";
        SqlConnection sqlConnection = new SqlConnection(connectString);
        sqlConnection.Open();
        SqlCommand sqlCommand = new SqlCommand();

        sqlCommand.CommandText =
                "SELECT pub_id AS ID, pub_name AS Name, " +
                "city AS City, state AS State, " +
                "country AS Country " +
                "FROM publishers";

        sqlCommand.Connection = sqlConnection;
        SqlDataReader reader = sqlCommand.ExecuteReader();

        DataGrid1.DataSource = reader;
        DataGrid1.DataBind();
    }
}
```

`ViewState` will only work when the `EnableViewState` property is `true`, which is the default. If you want to repopulate from the data source every time, set `EnableViewState` to `false`, and make the binding unconditional.

Now that the `DataGrid` displays correctly, we can turn our attention to displaying the child records. Each record will display inside a single table cell. We will have two cells to a row. This may not look great, but it gives us a good excuse to get to grips with the `Repeater` control.

The Repeater

The `Repeater` control provides an easy way for repeating HTML snippets a specified number of times. To use the `Repeater` we really need to work with the HTML view of the ASPX file.

But first, we need to provide some data for our `Repeater`. We need an event handler when the user clicks on a **Select** link in the publisher grid. To generate the event handler, switch to design view and double-click on any **Select** link in the grid. Inside the event handler we extract the ID of the selected publisher to use in the new query. The event handler for the form is shown below. Notice that we will be placing the `Repeater` control in an invisible panel to hide the detail display until the user selects a publisher:

```
private void DataGrid1_SelectedIndexChanged(object sender,
                                          System.EventArgs e)
{
    string connectString =
        "initial catalog=pubs;user id=sa;server=localhost";
    SqlConnection sqlConnection = new SqlConnection(connectString);
    sqlConnection.Open();
    SqlCommand sqlCommand = new SqlCommand();

    string pubid = DataGrid1.SelectedItem.Cells[1].Text;

    sqlCommand.CommandText =
        "SELECT employee.emp_id AS ID, employee.fname AS 'First Name', " +
        "employee.lname AS 'Last Name', jobs.job_desc AS Description " +
        "FROM employee INNER JOIN " +
        "jobs ON employee.job_id = jobs.job_id " +
        "WHERE (employee.pub_id = '" + pubid +"')";

    sqlCommand.Connection = sqlConnection;
    SqlDataReader reader = sqlCommand.ExecuteReader();

    Repeater1.DataSource = reader;
    Repeater1.DataBind();

    Panel1.Visible = true;
}
```

To use the `Repeater`, we place display templates with markup and expressions inside of the `<asp:Repeater>` tag. The template types and rendering rules are detailed in the following list:

❑ `HeaderTemplate` – this element is rendered once, before any rows from the data source are rendered

❑ `FooterTemplate` – this element is rendered once, after all data rows in the data source have been processed

❑   `ItemTemplate` – this element is rendered once for each row in the data source

❑   `AlternatingItemTemplate` – when this element is present, alternate rows are rendered using this template instead of the `ItemTemplate`

❑   `SeparatorTemplate` – this element is rendered between each row

The following excerpt from the employee ASPX page demonstrates how the templates are used in our web form:

```
<asp:Repeater id="Repeater1" runat="server">
   <HeaderTemplate>
      <h4>Employees</h4>
      <table cellpadding="2" align="center">
   </HeaderTemplate>

   <ItemTemplate>
      <tr align="center">
      <td>
         <b>
            <%# DataBinder.Eval(Container.DataItem, "First Name")%>
            <%# DataBinder.Eval(Container.DataItem, "Last Name")%>
         </b>
         <br/>
         <%# DataBinder.Eval(Container.DataItem, "Description")%>
      </td>
   </ItemTemplate>

   <AlternatingItemTemplate>
      <td>
         <b>
            <%# DataBinder.Eval(Container.DataItem, "First Name")%>
            <%# DataBinder.Eval(Container.DataItem, "Last Name")%>
         </b>
         <br/>
            <%# DataBinder.Eval(Container.DataItem, "Description")%>
         </td>
      </tr>
   </AlternatingItemTemplate>

   <FooterTemplate>
      </table>
   </FooterTemplate>
</asp:Repeater>
```

You can see the `Repeater` allows very precise control over the layout and styles. Although we only used HTML markup inside of our templates, you can also place controls inside. To extract fields from the data bound source, place a data binding expression between <%# and %> tags. The data binding expression uses the `Eval()` method of the `DataBinder` class to extract an object from the container, given the field name.

Web server controls bring all the advantages of forms-based programming to the web: event handling, data binding, and a robust object model to program against. While web forms provide the user interface for your application, some work is still required on the server to set up the proper environment for your application to use. As you might expect, .NET has made great improvements in the ability to configure an application, as we shall see in the next section.

ASP.NET Configuration

ASP.NET makes it easy to configure web applications. We no longer need to worry about IIS settings. We just include XML configuration files in our application directory that are readable by both machines and developers.

ASP.NET uses configuration files called web.config. Applications can contain multiple web.config files, applying different settings to different folders. These files control the settings for authentication, authorization, diagnostics, and more. The files are also extensible, meaning we can specify new configuration parameters to read from web.config. The schema for the ASP.NET configuration files is rather large, but well documented in the .NET online help. We will briefly highlight a few of the sections that are useful when building a new web forms application.

> When you create a new Web Application in Visual Studio .NET, a simple
> web.config file is created automatically. If you are not using Visual Studio .NET
> then you only need a web.config file if you want to change from the default settings.

Using web.config

This next example builds on the employee application created in the last section. There are two changes to make to the application:

❑   First, we need to restrict the web form to users who have a valid username and password combination

❑   Secondly, we want to move the hard-coded database connection string from our code-behind file to the configuration file

Both of these changes affect the web.config file for the application. The source code for this example can be found in the Authenicate directory. The web.config file for the new application is shown below, with changes from the Visual Studio .NET default settings highlighted:

```
<?xml version="1.0" encoding="utf-8" ?>
<configuration>
   <system.web>
      <compilation defaultLanguage="c#" debug="true"/>
      <customErrors mode="RemoteOnly" />
      <authentication mode="Forms">
         <forms name=".WroxSample" loginUrl="login.aspx"
                timeout="20"
         />
      </authentication>
```

```
        <authorization>
          <deny users="?" />
        </authorization>
        <trace enabled="false" requestLimit="10" pageOutput="false"
              traceMode="SortByTime" localOnly="true"
        />
        <sessionState mode="InProc"
              stateConnectionString="tcpip=127.0.0.1:42424"
              sqlConnectionString="data source=127.0.0.1;user id=sa;password="
              cookieless="false"
              timeout="20"
        />
        <globalization requestEncoding="utf-8" responseEncoding="utf-8" />
      </system.web>
    <appSettings>
      <add key="connectionString"
            value="initial catalog=pubs;user id=sa;server=localhost"
      />
    </appSettings>
  </configuration>
```

For now, we intend to concentrate on the `authentication`, `authorization`, and `appSettings` sections. Later in this chapter we will discuss the `trace` configuration. We will discuss `sessionState` configuration in the next chapter while we're looking at web services.

Authentication

Applications requiring authentication generally fall into one of two categories. The first category is a secure application. The second category is the personalized application, where content changes dynamically based on the user's identity. Obviously, a single application may fall into both categories. In either case, there are three built-in options provided by ASP.NET for authentication:

❑ **Windows Authentication** – relies on IIS to perform authentication using basic, digest, or integrated Windows authentication. The exact type of authentication used depends on the **Directory Security** settings in the IIS directory properties dialog. The user credentials are checked against the server machine or in the server's domain.

❑ **Passport Authentication** – integrates with Microsoft's .NET Passport service. Passport coordinates the authentication steps between your servers, the remote Passport login servers, and the client's web browser. Offering Passport authentication allows over 150 million (and rising) Passport account holders to use your application without completing a tedious registration step.

❑ **Forms Authentication** – uses the ASP.NET runtime to enforce authentication. ASP.NET redirects unauthenticated requests for a protected resource to a login page. A cookie is issued to authenticated users for access to protected areas.

The `web.config` file listed above configures the application for forms authentication. You can find the exact details of the configuration inside of the `forms` subelement. This includes the `name` of the cookie to send to the browser, a `loginUrl` containing the location of the login form, and a `timeout` that specifies in minutes the time before rejecting an authentication cookie after a period of inactivity (effectively logging-out the user).

To implement forms based authentication, we'll need to provide a login page. The login form might be as simple as the form shown below, with two `TextBox` server controls and one `Button` server control. An additional label control is present to provide feedback or instructions when a login attempt fails:

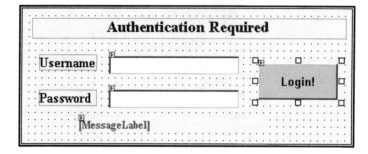

By assigning an event handler to the button's click event, you can examine the incoming credentials and decide if the user has supplied the correct username and password. A common technique is to compare the incoming credentials against credentials stored in a database. If the credentials match, you can use the `FormsAuthentication` class from the `System.Web.Security` namespace. The `RedirectFromLoginPage()` method will issue a cookie to the browser to indicate a successful authentication, and then redirect the browser back to the page originally requested. In the code below, we simply check the incoming username and password against a pair of hard-coded strings:

```
private void LoginButton_Click(object sender, System.EventArgs e)
{
    if(UsernameText.Text == "scott" && PasswordText.Text == "password")
    {
        FormsAuthentication.RedirectFromLoginPage(UsernameText.Text, false);
    }
    else
    {
        MessageLabel.Text = "Invalid login";
    }
}
```

The first parameter in the `RedirectFromLoginPage` method is the name of the user: we will understand more about this parameter when we cover authorization in the next section. The second parameter is a flag for creating persistent cookies. If the parameter is true, .NET creates a persistent cookie for the browser to store on the client's hard drive. A persistent cookie remains alive between browser sessions. If you want to ensure the user is required to log into the application each time a new session starts, pass `false` for this flag.

Authorization

Authentication is being sure of *whom* a user is. Authorization is identifying *what* we allow a specific user to do. The `authorization` element in a `web.config` file consists of `allow` and `deny` elements. You can place a `user` attribute inside one of the sub-tags to grant or revoke authorizations by name. A question mark represents all anonymous users, while an asterisk represents all users. The `web.config` file for our application denies access to all anonymous users with `<deny users="?" />`. These settings apply to all ASP.NET content in the current directory and all subdirectories, unless another `web.config` file in a subdirectory is present and overrides the configuration.

Application Configuration

The `web.config` file can also contain application-specific configuration information. The easiest approach is to use the `appSettings` element in the `web.config` file to add name /value pairs, as we have done with the database connection strings in the configuration file for the current example. You can retrieve these values using the `ConfigurationSettings` class from the `System.Configuration` namespace. We can change the database connection code for our form to the following:

```
string connectString =
  System.Configuration.ConfigurationSettings.AppSettings["connectionString"];

SqlConnection sqlConnection = new SqlConnection(connectString);
```

Both developers and administrators should find the `web.config` files easier to modify and manage than configuring through IIS. This makes ASP.NET applications easier to deploy and keep running.

Another section in the `web.config` file, the `tracing` element, is a part of ASP.NET's diagnostics. We will cover this capability in the next section.

Diagnostics in ASP.NET – Tracing

Once your application is in the final stages of development, you might need to track down performance bottlenecks or identify other problems. Even after the application is released, it is nice to monitor the health of a running system. Fortunately, ASP.NET provides a number of monitoring and tracing options.

Tracing in ASP generally required strategic placement of `Response.Write` commands throughout the code to see exactly what statements were executing. Unfortunately, you had to go back and remove all these statements before releasing the application into production. There was no easy way to implement a switch and turn tracing on and off. With .NET, you do have a switch. There are two levels of trace information in ASP.NET: page-level and application-level.

Page-Level Tracing

The 'switch' for page-level tracing is found in the `Page` directive of each ASPX file. Tracing is disabled by default. Turning tracing on displays the following at the bottom of the page:

- ❑   Request details (time, type, status code)
- ❑   Size in bytes needed to render the page and each control
- ❑   Timing information for critical points of the page's lifecycle
- ❑   Cookie information sent to the server
- ❑   Client HTTP headers
- ❑   Form data

- ❑ Session and application state associated with the request
- ❑ Query strings sent with the request
- ❑ All server variables (REMOTE_HOST, SERVER_NAME, and so on)

The figure below shows the beginning of the trace information when tracing is enabled for the publisher report page we built earlier in this chapter:

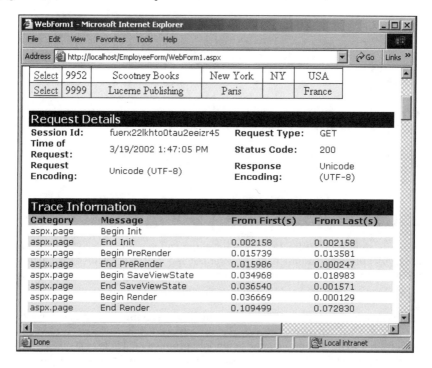

To produce these tracing results, adjust the Page directive for the form to this:

```
<%@
    Page language="c#"
    Codebehind="WebForm1.aspx.cs" AutoEventWireup="false"
    Inherits="EmployeeForm.WebForm1"
    Trace="true"
    TraceMode = "SortByTime"
%>
```

TraceMode is an optional attribute. The SortByTime value instructs the runtime to sort trace messages based on the time they arrived, while SortByCategory sorts the messages by the category name. ASP.NET provides default trace messages with a category of aspx.page.

You can instrument your own code using the Trace property of the Page object. The Trace property is an instance of the TraceContext class. The methods Write() and Warn() place time-stamped custom trace information into the trace log. Using Warn will cause the entry to appear in red instead of black. Also, if you want to avoid expensive calculations in producing trace messages when tracing is not in effect, check the IsEnabled property on the TraceContext object. In our employee report web form, we could add the following statements to the Page_Load method:

```
private void Page_Load(object sender, System.EventArgs e)
{
    if(!IsPostBack)
    {
        Trace.Write("SQL", "Starting SQL code");
        SqlConnection sqlConnection = new SqlConnection(connectString);
        sqlConnection.Open();
        SqlCommand sqlCommand = new SqlCommand();

        sqlCommand.CommandText =
                "SELECT pub_id AS ID, pub_name AS Name, " +
                "city AS City, state AS State, " +
                "country AS Country " +
                "FROM publishers";

        sqlCommand.Connection = sqlConnection;
        SqlDataReader reader = sqlCommand.ExecuteReader();
        Trace.Write("SQL", "Ending SQL code");

        try
        {
            throw new ApplicationException("This exception is intentional");
        }
        catch(Exception ex)
        {
            Trace.Warn("Exception!", "Caught exception :", ex);
        }

        Trace.Write("Begin data binding");
        DataGrid1.DataSource = reader;
        DataGrid1.DataBind();
        Trace.Write("End data binding");
    }
}
```

Each trace method offers three overloaded versions. The simplest call passes just a trace message as an argument, while the most detailed call allows you to pass a category string, a message, and an exception to dump into the trace log. The most common usage is to pass just a category name and a message. The above code produces the following output:

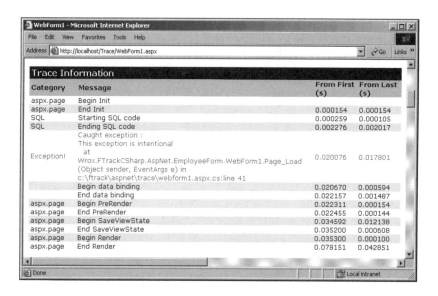

Application-Level Tracing

To enable tracing for an entire application we need to modify the `trace` element of the `web.config` file. This allows the runtime to log trace messages from every page in the application, unless the page has explicitly disabled tracing in the `Page` directive. A special trace viewer (`trace.axd`) is also enabled in the application's root directory. The trace viewer output for our example application is shown below:

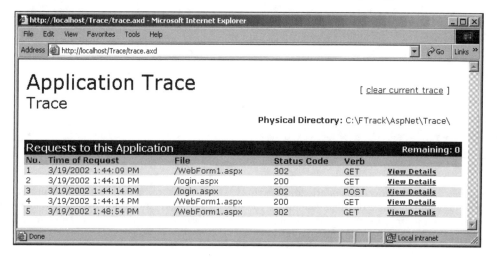

From the `trace.axd` view you can drill down into the individual trace logs for each request. The number of trace logs kept for viewing, and other parameters, are controlled by the attributes in the `web.config` file. The `trace` section for this application is shown below:

```
<trace
      enabled="true"
      requestLimit="5"
      pageOutput="false"
      traceMode="SortByTime"
      localOnly="true"
/>
```

The `enabled` attribute turns tracing on and off, while `requestLimit` controls the maximum number of trace requests to store on the server. Once the number of traces reaches this limit, no new traces are stored. We can clear the current traces by clicking on the **clear current trace** hyperlink in the upper right of `trace.axd`, allowing the server to store new traces.

When the `pageOutput` attribute is `true`, the trace messages are also appended to the end of the page output as we saw earlier. Setting `pageOutput` to `false` allows us to see the trace messages only from `trace.axd`; the messages are not appended to the output of the pages. However, the `Page` directive can override this behavior by explicitly enabling tracing for a page.

The `traceMode` attribute has the same values and behavior as we saw in the page-level example. Finally, the `localOnly` attribute restricts viewing of the `trace.axd` output to the local machine, a good security measure.

Summary

ASP.NET offers tremendous improvements over previous web development tools and runtimes. In this chapter we covered:

- ❑ Event-driven forms
- ❑ User controls
- ❑ Server controls
- ❑ Authentication
- ❑ Diagnostics

To continue to learn more about ASP.NET, try *Professional ASP.NET 1.0*. In the next chapter, we will see a new type of application built on the ASP.NET infrastructure: the web service.

Take the
Fast Track

to
C#

13

Web Services

The primary goal of a web form application is to format information for humans to use. In contrast, the goal of a web service application is to format information for software components to use. In both cases, the consumer is located on a remote machine, sometimes on a local network, but often across the Internet. Trying to place a more specific description of a web service into one line is a difficult task, not because web services themselves are difficult – in fact, the technologies and protocols underlying web services are familiar and simple. The difficulty arises because web services are so flexible and extensible you can use them to solve a number of distinct problems in distributed software development. In this chapter we discuss three primary topics, and see examples of how to put web services to work.

- ❑   Writing, testing, and debugging a web service.
- ❑   Writing a web service client
- ❑   The ASP.NET infrastructure support for web services.

Web Service Problem Domains

Before we begin to jump into web service coding, let's discuss two problem domains where you can use web services, in order to gain a better understanding of what web services can offer.

Platform Interoperability

Looking at the software world from a high level reveals a heterogeneous mix of operating systems, languages, and environments. Trying to have two of these different platforms communicating with each is often time-consuming, expensive, or both. Attempting to invoke a method on a Java object from a C++ object never works until some type of software magic exists in between.

Today, we have XML. One of the reasons HTML became so popular was because the platform-independent markup allowed web browsers and web servers to communicate easily without needing to know who was on the other end of the wire. XML is serving the same role in software-to-software communication. XML has matured quickly to offer robust tools and standards, such as XML Schema, allowing us to not only encode the data moving between platforms in a neutral way, but giving us a metadata format to describe the structure of the data to both parties.

Web services leverage the capabilities of XML to offer interoperability to a wide range of languages. Converting your software components to web services gives you a much larger customer base.

Distributed Computing

There are a number of established technologies available to make remote procedure calls (RPC) across a network. This includes Microsoft's Distributed COM (DCOM), Sun's Remote Method Invocation (RMI), and the OMG's Common Object Request Broker Architecture (CORBA). Each of these technologies works very well in homogeneous environments with well-managed networks. For example, if you need two COM components on different servers to talk, and both servers are behind your corporate firewall, DCOM is a safe choice.

The problem today is that many of these remote calls need to travel across the Internet into unknown networks beyond our control. Each of these proprietary protocols looks unfriendly when they arrive at proxy servers (security on outgoing traffic) or firewalls (security on incoming traffic), and are generally dropped before reaching the destination.

However, there are several open and standard protocols that move across the Internet pretty easily, even through firewalls and proxy servers. The most notable of these protocols is HTTP. If we could simply change our remote procedure calls to use HTTP as a transport, we can offer our components to anyone across the Internet.

Web services use XML for data encoding and HTTP as a transport to produce a platform-neutral protocol for RPC. For example, you can write a C# class with a method to return the current temperature in your area. You place the code on a web server with a connection to the Internet. An associate located on the other side of the continent might write a Java application to call your code and retrieve the current temperature from across the Internet. The same code could support both a browser-based interface and a web service interface. The .NET Framework provides plenty of tools and support to both write and consume web services. Let's begin to take a look at these tools in the next section.

Writing a Web Service

The Visual Studio .NET IDE can easily create a new web service project for you from the New Project dialog box, as shown below. Similar to the web application project, a web service project requires a machine with IIS 5.0 or above installed.

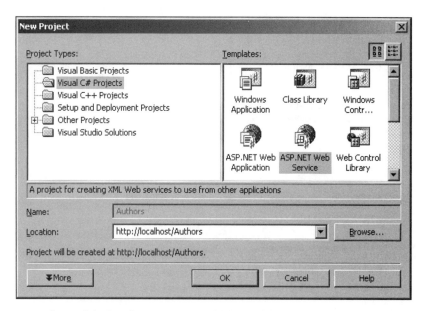

The new project (named **Authors**) contains several files, including `Service1.asmx`. This file is the base URL for a web service call (just like an ASPX page is the base URL for a web form request). Web services also use code-behind files, where the processing logic resides in a separate C# file, in this case `Service1.asmx.cs`. This file does not initially display in the Solution Explorer until you click on **Show All Files** in the Solution Explorer toolbar window. For now, we want to jump into the code-behind file by right-clicking on the ASMX file in design view and selecting **View Code** from the context menu.

Inside, we find a class derived from the `WebService` class of the `System.Web.Services` namespace. Although you do not need to derive your classes from the `WebService` class, the class does offer properties, methods, and events to support web services, and we will examine some of these members later in this chapter. What actually makes your code part of a web service is a `WebMethod` attribute. You should apply this attribute to a public method to allow web service clients to invoke the method. In this example, we add a web service method to return the name of an author from the pubs database in SQL Server.

```csharp
using System;
using System.Collections;
using System.ComponentModel;
using System.Data;
using System.Diagnostics;
using System.Web;
using System.Web.Services;
using System.Data.SqlClient;

namespace Wrox.FTrackCSharp.WebService.Authors
{
    [WebService(Namespace="http://www.wrox.com/FastTrack/Authors",
                Name="Author Web Service")]
    public class Service1 : System.Web.Services.WebService
```

```
    {
       public Service1()
       {
          InitializeComponent();
        }

       #region Component Designer generated code
       //Required by the Web Services Designer
       private IContainer components = null;
       private void InitializeComponent()
       {
       }

       protected override void Dispose( bool disposing )
       {
          if(disposing && components != null)
          {
             components.Dispose();
          }
          base.Dispose(disposing);
       }
       #endregion

       protected readonly string connectionString =
                      "initial catalog=pubs;user id=sa;server=localhost";


       [WebMethod]
       public string GetAuthorName(string id)
       {
          SqlConnection sqlConnection = new SqlConnection(connectionString);

          sqlConnection.Open();
          SqlCommand sqlCommand = new SqlCommand();

          string command = String.Format("SELECT au_fname, au_lname " +
                                         "FROM authors " +
                                         "WHERE au_id = '{0}'" , id);

          sqlCommand.CommandText = command;
          sqlCommand.Connection = sqlConnection;

          SqlDataReader reader = sqlCommand.ExecuteReader();

          string name = "";
          if(reader.Read())
          {
             name = String.Format("{0} {1}", reader["au_fname"],
                                             reader["au_lname"]);
          }
          return name;
       }
    }
}
```

WebService and WebMethod Attributes

The above example is a fairly typical code snippet, and by using just two attributes we configure this class as a web service. The first attribute applied to the class, the WebService attribute, is actually optional. This attribute allows you to set the following descriptive properties for the web service.

- ❏ Description – a string to describe the web service.

- ❏ Name – a string to name the web service.

- ❏ Namespace – a string to specify the default XML namespace for this Web Service.

The most important property to set on the WebService attribute is the Namespace. The runtime uses the namespace to qualify the XML elements and attributes associated with this web service. If a web service does not specify a namespace, the runtime provides a default value of http://tempuri.org. Since namespaces are required to be globally unique, it is always a good idea to apply the attribute and set the property to a URI in your domain.

The WebMethod attribute marks a public method as executable for web service clients. This attribute contains the following properties (all optional).

- ❏ BufferResponse – when true (the default), the runtime attempts to buffer the entire response in memory before starting the response back to the client. This is a performance benefit unless you return large amounts of data.

- ❏ CacheDuration – indicates the number of seconds to hold a response in a memory cache. The default value is 0. This property is described in more detail later in this chapter.

- ❏ Description – a string used to describe the method.

- ❏ EnableSession – indicates if session state is enabled for this method, the default value is false. This property is used later in the chapter.

- ❏ MessageName – a string to uniquely name the web method. Often used to distinguish methods when using overloaded methods.

- ❏ TransactionOption – indicates if the web method should participate as a root object in a distributed transaction coordinated by MSDTC. The default value is disabled, and this property is described in more detail later in the chapter.

Testing and Debugging a Web Service

We will test the web service by viewing the ASMX file with a web browser. This test is going to use the HTTP GET request to invoke the web service. When we are ready to invoke the method, the method name and parameters are passed in the query string to the ASMX page as part of an HTTP GET request. All of the names are **case sensitive**. The ASMX page will extract these parameters, invoke the web service method, and place the return value into a simple XML document to send as the response, as we will demonstrate below.

Press *Ctrl+F5* to build and run the project. A successful build will produce the file `Authors.DLL`, and then the runtime will launch a browser and navigate to the URL of the `Service1.asmx` page. The runtime will generate an interface from metadata in the web service. The first screen we come to is shown below:

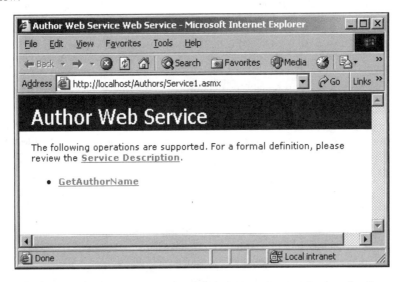

The first link leads to the service description. We will revisit this topic later in the chapter. For now, we want to click on the GetAuthorName link to get to the following page:

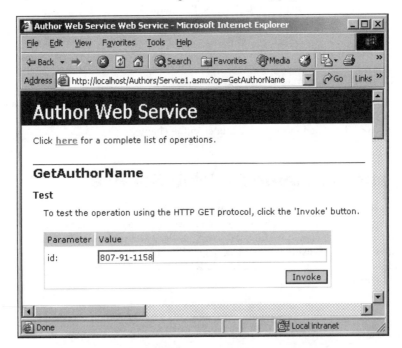

This screen presents us with a form. Any input parameters for the web method will appear with a text entry box, allowing us to specify the values for a web service call. Having an auto-generated web interface for the service is invaluable in quickly getting a web service tested and debugged. Entering an ID from the `authors` table of the `pubs` database gives us the following result:

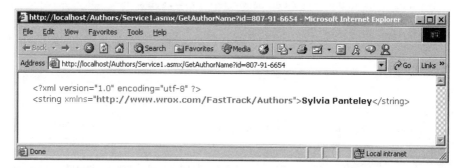

The web method has given us an XML result containing the name of the author. Later in the chapter we will build a Windows client for this web service to demonstrate how seamlessly web services are consumed by .NET; for now we can examine the other protocols supported by ASP.NET web services.

Using HTTP POST

HTTP POST is very similar to the HTTP GET request shown above, except instead of passing parameters in the query string, the parameters are passed in the HTTP payload as name-value pairs, in the same fashion as form values are posted in from a web form. The method name to invoke is still in the query string. The choice between GET and POST is entirely up to the client; both are functionally equivalent. If we actually look at the request coming into the web server with a packet-sniffing utility, we would see the following:

```
POST /Authors/Service1.asmx/GetAuthorName HTTP/1.1
Host: localhost
Content-Type: application/x-www-form-urlencoded
Content-Length: length

id=807-91-6654
```

As before, ASP.NET will extract the parameters and invoke the web service method. The result is placed in an XML document and looks the same as the response for the HTTP GET request above. Both GET and POST have a few limitations; for example, you cannot use out or ref parameters with GET or POST. For more functionality, SOAP is the protocol of choice.

Using SOAP

The Simple Object Access Protocol (SOAP) is an XML-based protocol for exchanging platform-neutral messages between two software applications. SOAP does not specify a specific transport protocol, although HTTP is most commonly used.

A SOAP message is composed of up to three pieces. The SOAP **Envelope** is the top element of a SOAP message. The Envelope may contain namespace declarations and other attributes. The SOAP **Header** is an optional section, provided as an extensibility mechanism. Using the Header you can layer new features on top of a web service, and we will demonstrate this capability later in the chapter. Finally, the SOAP **Body** contains the method name and parameters for the web service call. A SOAP request for the GetAuthorName method looks like the following:

```
POST /Authors/Service1.asmx HTTP/1.1
Host: localhost
Content-Type: text/xml; charset=utf-8
Content-Length: 346
SOAPAction: "http://www.wrox.com/FastTrack/Authors/GetAuthorName"

<?xml version="1.0" encoding="utf-8"?>
<soap:Envelope xmlns:xsi="http://www.w3.org/2001/XMLSchema-instance"
               xmlns:xsd="http://www.w3.org/2001/XMLSchema"
               xmlns:soap="http://schemas.xmlsoap.org/soap/envelope/">
  <soap:Body>
    <GetAuthorName xmlns="http://www.wrox.com/FastTrack/Authors">
      <id>807-91-6654</id>
    </GetAuthorName>
  </soap:Body>
</soap:Envelope>
```

In the above request we see the Envelope and the Body, the Header section is optional (we will use a SOAP header later in the chapter) and not needed for this example. The server will parse the SOAP message for the method and parameters to generate a SOAP response, shown next.

```
HTTP/1.1 200 OK
Content-Type: text/xml; charset=utf-8
Content-Length: 392

<?xml version="1.0" encoding="utf-8"?>
<soap:Envelope xmlns:xsi="http://www.w3.org/2001/XMLSchema-instance"
               xmlns:xsd="http://www.w3.org/2001/XMLSchema"
               xmlns:soap="http://schemas.xmlsoap.org/soap/envelope/">
  <soap:Body>
    <GetAuthorNameResponse xmlns="http://www.wrox.com/FastTrack/Authors">
      <GetAuthorNameResult>Sylvia Panteley</GetAuthorNameResult>
    </GetAuthorNameResponse>
  </soap:Body>
</soap:Envelope>
```

Any language capable of parsing XML can participate in a SOAP message. There are SOAP tools available for many popular languages (including C++, VB, Java, Perl, and Python), and a wide variety of platforms.

Web Services Description Language

Before we write the first real client application for our web service, we need to examine one more significant artifact of our project. Going back to the original view of our web service in the browser (http://localhost/Authors/Service1.asmx) we saw a link to a Service Description. The service description is also an XML document written in Web Services Description Language (WSDL). WSDL defines messages (descriptions of the parameters) and operations (methods). The operations are grouped into a portType, and then a binding couples the portType with a specific network protocol and address. If you have ever written COM interfaces in IDL, you can think of WSDL as the IDL for web services. Many of the same elements are here with different names. WSDL describes parameters, methods, and interfaces, and then where to find them.

WSDL is verbose, and designed to support a variety of message formats and network protocols, which makes WSDL slightly difficult to read. With the tools provided by .NET, however, it will be a rare case when you need to manually read or write WSDL for a web service. A stripped-down version of the WSDL for our web service is shown below:

```xml
<?xml version="1.0" encoding="utf-8" ?>
<definitions xmlns:soap="http://schemas.xmlsoap.org/wsdl/soap/"
             xmlns:s="http://www.w3.org/2001/XMLSchema"
             xmlns:s0="http://www.wrox.com/FastTrack/Authors"
             targetNamespace="http://www.wrox.com/FastTrack/Authors"
             xmlns="http://schemas.xmlsoap.org/wsdl/">
  <types>
    <s:schema elementFormDefault="qualified"
              targetNamespace="http://www.wrox.com/FastTrack/Authors">
      <s:element name="GetAuthorName">
        <s:complexType>
          <s:sequence>
            <s:element minOccurs="0" maxOccurs="1"
                       name="id" type="s:string" />
          </s:sequence>
        </s:complexType>
      </s:element>
      <s:element name="GetAuthorNameResponse">
        <s:complexType>
          <s:sequence>
            <s:element minOccurs="0" maxOccurs="1"
                       name="GetAuthorNameResult" type="s:string" />
          </s:sequence>
        </s:complexType>
      </s:element>
    </s:schema>
  </types>
  <message name="GetAuthorNameSoapIn">
    <part name="parameters" element="s0:GetAuthorName" />
  </message>
  <message name="GetAuthorNameSoapOut">
    <part name="parameters" element="s0:GetAuthorNameResponse" />
  </message>
  <portType name="Author_Web_ServiceSoap">
    <operation name="GetAuthorName">
      <input message="s0:GetAuthorNameSoapIn" />
```

393

```
              <output message="s0:GetAuthorNameSoapOut" />
          </operation>
     </portType>
     <binding name="Author_Web_ServiceSoap" type="s0:Author_Web_ServiceSoap">
       <soap:binding transport=http://schemas.xmlsoap.org/soap/http
                   style="document" />
       <operation name="GetAuthorName">
         <soap:operation
                 soapAction=http://www.wrox.com/FastTrack/Authors/GetAuthorName
                 style="document" />
         <input>
           <soap:body use="literal" />
         </input>
         <output>
           <soap:body use="literal" />
         </output>
       </operation>
     </binding>
     <service name="Author_Web_Service">
       <port name="Author_Web_ServiceSoap"
             binding="s0:Author_Web_ServiceSoap">
         <soap:address location="http://localhost/Authors/Service1.asmx" />
       </port>
     </service>
</definitions>
```

WSDL forms a contract between the web service and client. You don't have to use WSDL to take advantage of web services, but there are advantages to doing so. A software tool can parse the XML in a WSDL file and extract the parameters, methods, and locations for a web service. Using this meta-information, a tool could generate a C#, C++, or Java class, whichever language you target. The class could completely encapsulate the underlying details of making a web service call. In the simplest case, you could make a web service call without seeing any XML encoding, or seeing any HTTP networking. The web service call would appear as a native, local method call to an object in your language of choice. Of course, the .NET Framework provides just such a tool, and we will use the tool in the next section.

Creating a Web Service Client

Any type of application can consume a web service: Windows forms, Web forms, Windows Services, even other web services can act as a client. For our first client we will use a simple C# console application.

The first step is using a tool to generate a web service proxy class. A proxy class is the software we alluded to earlier as the object sitting between our code and the web service to make the calls look seamless. There are two techniques available to generate the proxy. The first technique uses the Web Services Description Language Tool (WSDL.EXE). WSDL is a very flexible tool; you can pass /? as a parameter to see all of the options available. To generate the proxy for our application we use the following command-line command:

```
>wsdl http://localhost/Authors/Service1.asmx?WSDL /namespace:AuthorsClient1
```

```
/out:Authors.cs
```

The only required parameter to WSDL is the URL of a WSDL document, which our ASMX file can produce when given the query string ?WSDL as shown above. We also specify the namespace to place the proxy class in, and the filename for the source code. A successful WSDL run should produce the following output:

```
Microsoft (R) Web Services Description Language Utility
[Microsoft (R) .NET Framework, Version 1.0.3705.0]
Copyright (C) Microsoft Corporation 1998-2001. All rights reserved.

Writing file 'Authors.cs'.
```

We will need to add the Authors.cs file to our console mode project, and also add a reference to the System.Web.Services.dll. Taking a peek into the generated Authors.cs file will reveal the name of the proxy class (AuthorWebService). With all our references in place, the following code is all we need to invoke the web service from a Windows application:

```
using System;

namespace Wrox.FTrackCSharp.WebServices.AuthorsClient1
{
    class Class1
    {
        [STAThread]]
        static void Main(string[] args)
        {
            AuthorWebService authorWebService = new AuthorWebService();
            string name = authorWebService.GetAuthorName("807-91-6654");
            System.Console.WriteLine(name);
        }
    }
}
```

The web service proxy is derived from the SoapHttpClientProtocol class from the System.Web.Services.Protocols namespace. This class uses SOAP to invoke the web service method, but hides these details from our application and makes the call appear the same as a normal method call. There are additional features of the proxy class which we will examine later in this chapter.

The following diagram shows the flow of control of the web service call. We begin with a simple method call to the proxy class. The proxy class formats a SOAP message into the body of an HTTP request and forwards the request to the web server. When the Service1.ASMX page receives the SOAP request on the server it extracts the method name and parameters, and then invokes the call to retrieve an author's name. Our component queries the database and returns a string, which the runtime places into a SOAP message and sends back as a response. The proxy object extracts the result and returns a string to the client application.

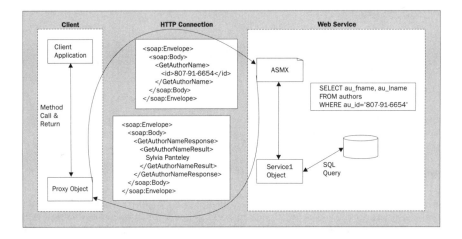

Adding a Web Reference Using Visual Studio .NET

A second technique for generating a web service proxy is to use the Add Web Reference menu item from the Tools menu of the IDE. This approach uses default namespaces and filenames, so is not as flexible as the command-line WSDL tool. However, if you are exploring a new web service, the user interface presented allows you to view the methods available, as well as the WSDL for the service. Entering the URL for the Authors web service (http://localhost/Authors/Service1.asmx) into the address space should reveal the following dialog, and clicking on the Add Reference button in the lower right will generate and add a proxy class to the solution:

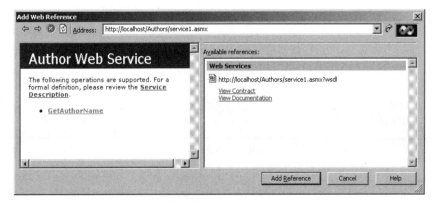

XML Serialization

So far our web service only passes simple strings back and forth, but web services are also capable of moving complex data structures. This includes arrays, collections, and classes. These objects are serialized (translated) into XML when sent or received from a web service. Some classes in the .NET framework are designed with XML serialization in mind, for example, the DataSet, and certainly the XmlDocument. As an example, we will add the following method to our web service to return a DataSet with all of the records in the authors table of the pubs database:

```
[WebMethod]
public DataSet GetAllAuthors()
{

    SqlConnection sqlConnection = new SqlConnection(connectionString);
    sqlConnection.Open();

    string sql = "SELECT au_id AS Id, au_fname AS 'First Name', " +
                 "au_lname As 'Last Name', " +
                 "city AS City, " +
                 "state AS State " +
                 "FROM authors";

    SqlDataAdapter sqlAdapter = new SqlDataAdapter(sql, sqlConnection);

    DataSet dataSet = new DataSet();
    sqlAdapter.Fill(dataSet);
    sqlConnection.Close();

    return dataSet;
}
```

In this method the `DataSet` is implicitly serialized to XML for return from the web service. On the client side, the proxy class is able to recreate a `DataSet` object from the XML in the SOAP message.

You can also define public classes and have the runtime serialize the public fields and properties for you. For example, suppose we wanted to return a single author from the web service with the following classes:

```
public class Author
{
    public string firstName;
    public string lastName;
    public string phone;
    public Address address;
}

public class Address
{
    public string street;
    public string city;
    public string state;
}
```

The following new method uses these new classes. Given an author ID, the method reads a record from the database and moves selected data fields into the public fields of the classes:

```
[WebMethod]
public Author GetAuthor(string id)
{
    SqlConnection sqlConnection = new SqlConnection(connectionString);
    sqlConnection.Open();
    SqlCommand sqlCommand = new SqlCommand();
```

```
        string command = String.Format("SELECT au_fname, au_lname, " +
                                        "city, state, phone, address " +
                                        "FROM authors " +
                                        "WHERE au_id = '{0}'" , id);

        sqlCommand.CommandText = command;
        sqlCommand.Connection = sqlConnection;

        SqlDataReader reader = sqlCommand.ExecuteReader();

        Author author = null;
        if(reader.Read())
        {
            author = new Author();
            author.firstName = reader["au_fname"].ToString();
            author.lastName = reader["au_lname"].ToString();
            author.phone = reader["phone"].ToString();
            author.address = new Address();
            author.address.street = reader["address"].ToString();
            author.address.city = reader["city"].ToString();
            author.address.state = reader["state"].ToString();
        }
        sqlConnection.Close();
        return author;
    }
```

XML serialization will transform the Author class into XML using reflection to find the public fields and properties. This Author class contains only public fields. We could achieve better encapsulation by changing each field into a protected or private field and exposing the field as a public property. Note, however, that a property requires both a get and a set method in order for serialization to take place. If we test the above web service method with a web browser (using the built-in data entry form provided by the ASMX page), we can see the following result:

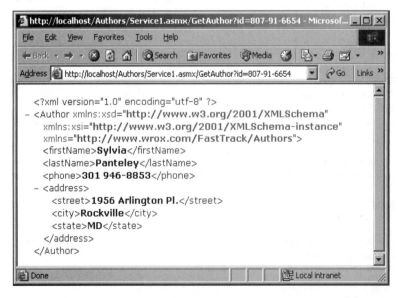

Customizing XML Serialization

The default serialization behavior places the string values inside elements, using the variable names as the names of the elements. You can override this default behavior by decorating a class with attributes imported from the `System.Xml.Serialization` namespace. For example, we could change the serialization of the Author class with the following attributes:

```
public class Author
{
    [XmlElement(ElementName="FirstName")]
    public string firstName;

    [XmlElement(ElementName="LastName")]
    public string lastName;

    [XmlElement(ElementName="PhoneNumber")]
    public string phone;

    [XmlElement(ElementName="Address")]
    public Address address;
}

public class Address
{
    [XmlAttribute(AttributeName="Street")]
    public string street;

    [XmlAttribute(AttributeName="City")]
    public string city;

    [XmlAttribute(AttributeName="State")]
    public string state;
}
```

These attributes explicitly declare the element names for the `Author` class, and change the `Address` class from using XML elements to XML attributes. There are additional attributes you can find in the `System.Xml.Serialization` namespace to ignore fields (`XmlIgnoreAttribute`), set the root element (`XmlRootAttribute`), and more.

These attributes are useful to decouple your code from the corresponding XML representation, allowing you to change your variable names and implementation details without changing the XML produced by the web service, which might force your clients to change their code. These attributes also allow you to tweak your XML output to match a schema defined by an outside party and meet the exact format expected by a third party. The XML produced by the web service call now looks like the following:

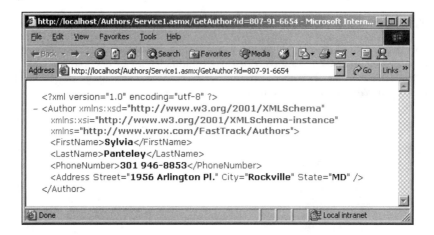

XML Schemas

XML schemas define the structure and data types in an XML document, similar to the way a database schema defines structure and data types in a relational database. XML schemas and web services can work hand in hand. We can define an XML schema for the `Authors` class and publish the schema for anyone working with the raw XML of the `Author` class. This allows, for example, the other party to validate the XML and ensure that the XML is in the expected format. There is, in fact, a schema for the `Authors` class already embedded in the WSDL. If you want to extract the schema for an author, use the XML Schema Definition Tool (`XSD.EXE`). `XSD.EXE` has many capabilities, including the ability to generate the XML schema for a class using the metadata in the class's assembly. To generate an `Author` schema, use the following command line from the `bin\Debug` directory of the web service:

```
>xsd Authors.dll /type:Author
```

This tells the `XSD.EXE` tool to look into the file `Authors.dll` and build a schema for the type `Author`. A successful run of the tool produces the following output.

```
Microsoft (R) Xml Schemas/DataTypes support utility
[Microsoft (R) .NET Framework, Version 1.0.3705.0]
Copyright (C) Microsoft Corporation 1998-2001. All rights reserved.

Writing file 'C:\FTrack\AspNet\Authors\bin\Debug\schema0.xsd'.
```

The following listing shows the generated XML schema:

```
<?xml version="1.0" encoding="utf-8"?>
<xs:schema elementFormDefault="qualified"
           xmlns:xs="http://www.w3.org/2001/XMLSchema">
  <xs:element name="Author" nillable="true" type="Author" />
    <xs:complexType name="Author">
      <xs:sequence>
```

```
            <xs:element minOccurs="0" maxOccurs="1" name="FirstName"
                        type="xs:string" />
            <xs:element minOccurs="0" maxOccurs="1" name="LastName"
                        type="xs:string" />
            <xs:element minOccurs="0" maxOccurs="1" name="PhoneNumber"
                        type="xs:string" />
            <xs:element minOccurs="0" maxOccurs="1" name="Address"
                        type="Address" />
        </xs:sequence>
      </xs:complexType>
    <xs:complexType name="Address">
      <xs:attribute name="Street" type="xs:string" />
      <xs:attribute name="City" type="xs:string" />
      <xs:attribute name="State" type="xs:string" />
    </xs:complexType>
  </xs:schema>
```

The XSD.EXE tool is also extremely useful when working in the opposite direction. If another party gives you an XML schema to use, you can generate a class for the schema with the following command line.

```
>xsd schema0.xsd /classes
```

The above command generates one or more classes from the schema0.xsd file. These classes provide you with a type safe and intuitive interface to generating XML in the required format. We will see how to use the Author XML returned from the web service in the next section.

A Windows Form Client

The next example client is a Windows form application. We are going to use this example to demonstrate how to use the DataGrid and Authors class from the client side, as well as making an asynchronous web service call. The form has one Button control (getAuthorsButton), and one DataGrid control (authorsDataGrid). There are two interesting events to handle for the form. The first, shown below, is the click event for the button. This event loads the DataGrid control with the DataSet returned by the GetAllAuthors web service method. For this project we generated the AuthorWebService proxy class using WSDL.EXE as before. The project also requires a reference to the System.Web.Services assembly.

```
private void getAuthorsButton_Click(object sender, System.EventArgs e)
{
    AuthorWebService authorsWebService = new AuthorWebService();
    DataSet dataSet = authorsWebService.GetAllAuthors();
    authorsDataGrid.DataSource = dataSet.Tables[0];
}
```

The web service proxy is able to recreate a DataSet object from the SOAP message, giving us the following display:

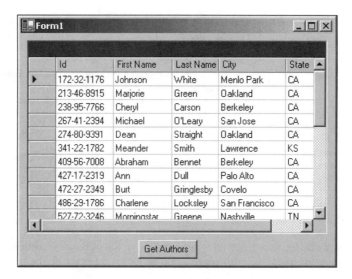

The second interesting event happens when the user double-clicks on the selection column of the DataGrid. When this event occurs, we want to invoke the GetAuthor method of the web service and display more detailed information about the selected author. We will need to handle the XML generated when the web service serializes the Author object. Fortunately, when we generated the web service proxy class with the WSDL.EXE tool, WSDL.EXE also generated local Author and Address classes alongside the proxy. We can see how to use these classes in the event handler method shown below:

```
private void authorsDataGrid_DoubleClick(object sender, System.EventArgs e)
{
    int index = authorsDataGrid.CurrentRowIndex;
    string id =
      ((DataTable)(authorsDataGrid.DataSource)).Rows[index]["Id"].ToString();

    AuthorWebService authorsWebService = new AuthorWebService();
    Author author = authorsWebService.GetAuthor(id);

    object [] formatArgs = {
                            author.FirstName,
                            author.LastName,
                            author.PhoneNumber,
                            author.Address.Street,
                            author.Address.City,
                            author.Address.State
                    };

    string message = String.Format("Name: {0} {1} \n\r" +
                            "Phone: {2} \n\r" +
                            "Address: \n\r" +
                            "{3} \n {4},{5}", formatArgs);

    MessageBox.Show(message, "Author Detail");
}
```

Notice how the client's version of the Author class uses upper case versions for the field names of FirstName, LastName, and PhoneNumber, yet in the web service the Author class used lower case versions (firstName, lastName, phoneNumber). This is because the client-side version of the Author class is generated using WSDL.EXE, and WSDL.EXE parses the XML schema representation of the Author class from the web service's WSDL. Remember, we gave the Author class special XML serialization attributes in the web service to precisely specify the element names as uppercase, and this is the specification used to generate the client-side class to handle the XML. The above method will produce a dialog box similar to the following:

You may or may not notice one small problem with this application. When the user clicks the **Get Authors** button, there is a delay while the proxy class completes the web service call. During this time, the form is unresponsive to the user. We could cover this flaw with a busy mouse cursor and let the user know the program is still processing, but how long will it be until we have a response?

Unlike previous remote procedure call technologies, web services can travel the Internet. Since we cannot predict the behavior of networks beyond our control, we need to realize that there is always the possibility of high latency and long transmission times. Although the delay is hardly noticeable when using a web service on the local host, our applications need to provide a robust user interface in the face of network turmoil. Fortunately, there are additional features in the web service proxy class to help us: asynchronous methods.

Asynchronous Web Service Calls

Asynchronous calls are useful when you need to invoke a method without blocking the calling thread. In the application above, the user interface thread remains blocked while waiting for a response from the web service method. If we could execute the method on a different thread, the user interface thread would remain free to process user events and the application would remain responsive. Managing extra threads is sometimes a tricky task in other environments, but in .NET there is support and encapsulation for asynchronous processing in the form of asynchronous methods.

For each method in our web service the proxy class contains three methods. The first method is the synchronous method. These are the methods we have been using so far in this chapter, for example, GetAllAuthors. The second and third methods are asynchronous methods, and these methods are always prefaced with Begin and End. The proxy class contains methods named BeginGetAllAuthors and EndGetAllAuthors. As you might suspect, these methods respectively begin and end an asynchronous call. To understand how these methods function, the following listing shows the method signature for the asynchronous associates of GetAuthor.

403

```
public System.IAsyncResult BeginGetAuthor(string id,
                                    System.AsyncCallback callback,
                                    object asyncState)

public Author EndGetAuthor(System.IAsyncResult asyncResult)
```

The begin methods will always contain the same input and by-reference parameters as the synchronous methods, plus two additional parameters we will discuss in more detail later. Notice that the return type has also changed since the begin method will return to the caller before the web service call is ever invoked. Instead of returning an Author, then, this method returns an object implementing the IAsyncResult interface. This interface encapsulates the state of an asynchronous call.

IAsyncResult is also a parameter to the EndGetAuthor() method, in addition to any out and ref parameters (in our example method there are none). Notice EndGetAuthor() now returns the Author object we expect as a result. Before we start a more in-depth discussion of the new interfaces and classes presented here, let's take a look at some source code to see just how easy an asynchronous web call can be.

Using Callback Delegates

Once again we will use the Windows form application with a DataGrid and a Button control to display all of the authors in the pubs database. The name of the new project is **AuthorsClient3**. The following source code shows a new version of the event handler for the button click event. This time we invoke the GetAllAuthors web service method asynchronously:

```
private void getAuthorsButton_Click(object sender, System.EventArgs e)
{
    AuthorWebService authorsWebService = new AuthorWebService();
    authorsWebService.BeginGetAllAuthors(new
            AsyncCallback(GetAuthorsCallback), authorsWebService);
}

private void GetAuthorsCallback(IAsyncResult ar)
{
    AuthorWebService authorsWebService = (AuthorWebService)ar.AsyncState;

    DataSet authorsDataSet = authorsWebService.EndGetAllAuthors(ar);
    UpdateDataGrid(authorsDataSet);
}

private delegate void UpdateDataGridDelegate(DataSet ds);

private void UpdateDataGrid(DataSet authorsDataSet)
{
    if(this.InvokeRequired)
    {
        Delegate updateDelegate = new UpdateDataGridDelegate(UpdateDataGrid);

        object [] delegateArgs = { authorsDataSet };

        this.Invoke(updateDelegate, delegateArgs);
    }
    else
```

```
    {
       authorsDataGrid.DataSource = authorsDataSet.Tables[0];
    }
}
```

The first parameter to `BeginGetAllAuthors()` is an `AsyncCallback` delegate. When we invoke `BeginGetAllAuthors()`, the method does not wait for the web service call to finish, instead, the method returns immediately. When the web service call is complete, the runtime will invoke this delegate to let our program know the call is finished. The delegate sends the flow of execution to the `GetAuthorsCallback()` method where we can retrieve the result.

The second parameter is a generic object reference you can use to pass additional context information to the callback method. The runtime will preserve this reference and pass it along to the callback method via the `IAsyncResult` interface. You can retrieve this object reference using the `AsyncState` property of `IAsyncResult`. In this example we pass a reference to the `AuthorWebService` object so the class does not need to be re-instantiated.

When the execution reaches the `GetAuthorCallback()` method, we simply need to retrieve the result of the web service call using the `EndGetAllAuthors()` method and bind the result to the grid. If you try the new version you'll notice the form still responds to events while the web service call is processing.

You might notice that we have encapsulated the code to bind the `DataSet` to the `DataGrid` inside another method. There is some additional logic inside this method to ensure the correct thread updates the `DataGrid`. Underneath the .NET machinery, a Windows form control uses a window handle to make calls into the Windows API. These handles have a thread affinity, meaning they are bound to a specific thread and any calls utilizing the handle must happen on the same thread. Consequently, .NET controls are also bound to a specific thread, and there are only a handful of methods safe to use from a different thread.

We want to make sure the data binding happens on the user interface thread that created the `DataGrid` *control.*

The callback does not happen on the user interface thread owning the controls. When we invoke `BeginGetAllAuthors()`, a worker thread from the runtime pool picks up the request to execute. The worker thread is the same thread invoking the callback method. Because of this, we need to switch back to the interface thread and then update the `DataGrid`. The following code shows how to achieve this.

```
private delegate void UpdateDataGridDelegate(DataSet ds);

private void UpdateDataGrid(DataSet dsAuthors)
{
   if(this.InvokeRequired)
   {
      Delegate updateDelegate = new UpdateDataGridDelegate(UpdateDataGrid);

      object [] delegateArgs = { dsAuthors };

      this.Invoke(updateDelegate, delegateArgs);
   }
   else
   {
```

```
            dgAuthors.DataSource = dsAuthors.Tables[0];
    }
}
```

The `InvokeRequired` property of the form will return `true` if we are not on the same thread as the thread owning the control's window handle. If we are not, we need to use the `Invoke()` method of the form. This method is inherited from the `Control` class and executes the given delegate on the correct thread. The delegate we pass to `Invoke()` points to the same method we are in, and `Invoke()` requires us to pass any parameters to the delegate target in an array of object references.

Additional Asynchronous Techniques

Using a callback delegate is only one technique to finishing an asynchronous web service call. You can pass a `null` reference to the begin method for the `AsyncCallback` delegate and manage the asynchronous call with the returned `IAsyncResult` interface. For instance, you can use the `IsCompleted` property of `IAsyncResult` to poll for completion of the web service call, or block a thread until the operation is completed using the `WaitOne()` method of `WaitHandle` object returned by the `AsyncWaitHandle` property. It is also possible to call the end method before the web service call is complete. The end method will simply block until the response returns. In between the begin and end methods, you can still perform other calculations.

Notice we did not need any additional code on the server for asynchronous web services. The decision is up to the client to decide if the call is made synchronously or asynchronously. There are, however, some additional features we have not covered for the server side of web service programming. These topics are discussed in the next section.

WebMethod Properties in Detail

Earlier in the chapter we outlined all of the properties available to use with the `WebMethod` attribute. Some of these properties enable powerful features for web services and warrant further attention.

Web Service Transactions

You can enable transactions with the `TransactionOption` of the `WebMethod` attribute. These transactions are managed by the Microsoft Distributed Transaction Coordinator (MSDTC) allowing you to span transactions across components (even COM components, as we saw in Chapter 11) and across databases. There are five enumeration values available for the transaction option: `Disabled`, `NotSupported`, `Supported`, `Required`, and `RequiresNew`. Of these five values, only two are applicable to a web method: `Required` and `RequiresNew`. A web method must be the root of any transaction because there is currently no way to flow an existing transaction into a web service. The other three values have no effect on the behavior of a web method. We will need to add a reference to the `System.EnterpriseServices.dll` assembly and import the `System.EnterpriseServices` namespace to use the transaction options. To demonstrate the `TransactionOption`, we will update the `Authors` web service with a new method to modify the telephone number for a given author. The source code for the method is shown below:

```
[WebMethod(TransactionOption=TransactionOption.Required)]
public void UpdateAuthorPhone(string id, string phone)
{
   SqlConnection sqlConnection = new SqlConnection(connectionString);
   sqlConnection.Open();
   SqlCommand sqlCommand = new SqlCommand();

   string command = String.Format("UPDATE authors " +
                                  "SET phone = '{0}' " +
                                  "WHERE au_id = '{1}'", phone, id);

   sqlCommand.CommandText = command;
   sqlCommand.Connection = sqlConnection;

   sqlCommand.ExecuteNonQuery();

   if(phone.Length < 12)
   {
      string message = "Oops, wrong format!";
      throw new ApplicationException(message);
   }
}
```

If the web service returns normally, the runtime will automatically commit the transaction and save any changes. If, however, the method throws an exception, the runtime will automatically abort the transaction and rollback all changes. In this example, we will throw an exception if the phone number string has less than 12 characters, but notice that the method throws the exception after executing the SQL query. If we invoke the web service twice, once with a phone number, and once with a bad phone number, we can view the MSDTC statistics in the Component Services MMC snap-in and see one transaction committed and one aborted, as shown below:

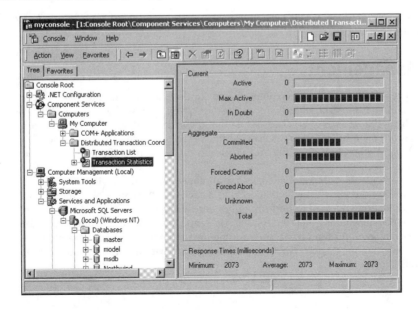

Web Service Caching

One of the great features in ASP.NET is the built-in caching support. Caching holds the results of a web service method call in memory to serve additional, similar requests. Caching is essential to building a high-performance ASP.NET application or web service. By default, caching is disabled for web service methods. You can change this behavior with the CacheDuration property. The CacheDuration property specifies the number of seconds for the runtime to hold a response in memory. For example, we could hold the result of the GetAuthor() method call in memory for 60 seconds with the following code:

```
[WebMethod(CacheDuration=60)]
public Author GetAuthor(string id)
{
    //
    // ... same implementation
    //
}
```

The caching algorithms will place a response into the cache for each unique combination of input parameters arriving in the request. In this example, if a request comes with an ID for an author we already have saved in the cache, there is no need to execute the body of the method, and the runtime fulfills the request with the cached version of the data. This saves time and resources for additional requests.

It might take some time and experimentation with tools like Performance Monitor to find the best cache settings for a specific web service application. You do not want to waste memory trying to cache the response of a web method when the incoming request parameters always vary. Also, trying to cache a web method returning a large amount of information may take away resources needed in other areas of the application.

However, any time spent enabling and tuning the cache settings is worth the effort; the performance gains are often substantial.

State Management

ASP.NET provides two state management objects for both web forms and web services: the Application and Session objects. In web services, you can use these two objects when you derive your class from the WebService class. While the Application object is always available in a web service method, the runtime disables access to the Session by default. You can enable the Session object on a per method basis with the EnableSession property of the WebMethod attribute.

The Application object is a global container of name-value pairs available to all web methods. One of the best uses of the Application object is as a cache for infrequently changing data. For example, if there is a calculation you need to perform only once during the life of a web service application, you can perform the calculation when the service starts, and store the results in the Application object to use later. When an application starts, the runtime fires the Application_Start event. You can modify this event in the Global.asax.cs file associated with the web service project, as we will demonstrate shortly.

The `Session` object is also a container of name-value pairs, but unlike the `Application` object, the `Session` object is specific to a client's session. If you have used `Session` objects in ASP applications, you'll be pleasantly surprised to learn how ASP.NET now allows `Session` contents to be shared across a server web farm, and even persisted in a database. When a new session starts, the runtime fires the `Session_Start` event. The next example tracks the number of active client sessions, the number of method hits for each session, and the total method hits for the entire service. To initialize the counters, we modify the following events in the `Global.asax.cs` file:

```
protected void Application_Start(Object sender, EventArgs e)
{
   Application["TotalSessions"] = 0;
   Application["TotalHits"] = 0;
}

protected void Session_Start(Object sender, EventArgs e)
{
   Application["TotalSessions"] = (int)Application["TotalSessions"] + 1;
   Session["TotalSessionHits"] = 0;
}

protected void Session_End(Object sender, EventArgs e)
{
   Application["TotalSessions"] = (int)Application["TotalSessions"] - 1;
}
```

Notice that there is also a `Session_End` event fired when a session expires after a period of inactivity. The timeout period is a configurable value in the `sessionState` element of the `web.config` file we saw in the last chapter. The default value is 20 minutes. The runtime fires a corresponding `Application_End` event when an application shuts down. With the initialization in place, we can define the following new web method in the web service:

```
[WebMethod(EnableSession=true)]
public Statistics GetServiceStatistics()
{
   Session["TotalSessionHits"] = (int)Session["TotalSessionHits"] + 1;
   Application["TotalHits"] = (int)Application["TotalHits"] + 1;


   Statistics statistics = new Statistics();
   statistics.TotalHits = (int)Application["TotalHits"];
   statistics.TotalSessions = (int)Application["TotalSessions"];
   statistics.TotalSessionHits = (int)Session["TotalSessionHits"];

   return statistics;
}
```

The `Statistics` object we return is a simple class. We define the class inside the web service code-behind file, and we allow the default XML serialization to convert the class into XML:

```
public class Statistics
{
   public int TotalHits;
   public int TotalSessions;
```

```
    public int TotalSessionHits;
}
```

We can test the method by launching two web browsers and invoking `GetServiceStatistics()` repeatedly. If each web browser invokes the service three times, we should reach the following display:

State Management Drawbacks

Be careful not to abuse the state management features provided by ASP.NET. Anything kept in the `Application` object, for example, takes away memory the system could use for processing. Keeping a large amount of infrequently used data in the container could hinder rather than help performance. Also, since the `Application` object services multiple threads in the application, locks are required to avoid corruption from concurrent thread access. This locking can reduce the performance of the web service.

The `Session` object has limited use in a web service. The runtime tracks unique sessions by issuing a cookie to the client. Most web service clients ignore HTTP cookies, which is why the above demonstration required a web browser. If you need to implement a comparable feature to cookies in a web service, you might want to look at using SOAP headers.

SOAP Headers

SOAP headers are an extensibility mechanism to support additional infrastructure in a SOAP message. For example, we might use SOAP headers to implement authentication, or we might require a digital signature in a SOAP header to verify the integrity of the message body. These types of features are completely different from the primary feature set of the web service, so we don't really want to define them in terms of the service interface. This is exactly the type of problem the designers had in mind when writing SOAP headers into the standards document.

As an example, suppose we wanted to bill clients of the web service based on the number of method calls they make. We could assign each client a globally unique identifier (GUID), and use the GUID and a database table to track the number of calls each client makes. There are at least two ways of getting the client's GUID. First, we could add a GUID parameter to every billable method in the web service. Unfortunately, this interferes with the interface design and is completely unrelated to the behavior of the method. The second approach is to place the GUID into a SOAP header, where it does not clutter up the method signatures, yet is still a part of the SOAP message.

The first step is defining a new class in the web service derived from the `SoapHeader` class in the `System.Web.Services.Protocols` namespace. This class is placed in the `Service1.asmx.cs` file of the web service project:

```
public class TicketHeader : SoapHeader
{
    public System.Guid ticket;
}
```

Next, we add a public member variable to the web service class of type `TicketHeader`. The runtime will automatically populate this variable when a request arrives for a method using the header. A method is marked as using a specific header with the `SoapHeader` attribute passing the name of the member variable as a parameter. The following code updates the `GetAuthorName()` method of the web service to use the header:

```
public TicketHeader ticketHeader;

[WebMethod]
[SoapHeader("ticketHeader")]
public string GetAuthorName(string id)
{
    string guid = ticketHeader.ticket.ToString();
    if(guid != null && guid.Length > 0)
    {
        // .. process ticket
    }
    //
    // rest of the implementation...
    //
}
```

The method simply pulls the ticket value out of the `ticketHeader` member variable to use for processing. If the ticket does not exist, we are free to throw an exception and stop processing. SOAP headers are not available when using the HTTP GET or HTTP POST requests, so to test the new feature we require a client application.

Using SOAP Headers from the Client

To test the ticket header we build a new console application. Once again we include a reference to the `System.Web.Services.dll` assembly and use WSDL to generate a proxy class, as we have seen before. We use the following code to invoke the web service method:

```
using System;

namespace Wrox.FTrackCSharp.WebServices.AuthorsClient4
{
    class Class1
    {
        [STAThread]
        static void Main(string[] args)
        {
            TicketHeader ticketHeader = new TicketHeader();
            // this is the guid assigned to this client
            ticketHeader.ticket =
                    new Guid("00BA4A55-B6E3-4D3F-836A-C622528CACAD");

            AuthorWebService wsAuthor = new AuthorWebService();
            wsAuthor.TicketHeaderValue = ticketHeader;

            string result = wsAuthor.GetAuthorName("172-32-1176");
            Console.WriteLine(result);
        }
    }
}
```

As you can see, WSDL is intelligent enough to give us a client-side class for manipulating the SOAP header we need. This class becomes a public member variable of the proxy class. The SOAP request sent from the client to the server looks like the following:

```
POST /Authors/Service1.asmx HTTP/1.1
Content-Type: text/xml; charset=utf-8
SOAPAction: "http://www.wrox.com/FastTrack/Authors/GetAuthorName"
Content-Length: 498
Host: localhost

<?xml version="1.0" encoding="utf-8"?>
<soap:Envelope xmlns:soap="http://schemas.xmlsoap.org/soap/envelope/"
               xmlns:xsi="http://www.w3.org/2001/XMLSchema-instance"
               xmlns:xsd="http://www.w3.org/2001/XMLSchema">
    <soap:Header>
        <TicketHeader xmlns="http://www.wrox.com/FastTrack/Authors">
            <ticket>00ba4a55-b6e3-4d3f-836a-c622528cacad</ticket>
        </TicketHeader>
    </soap:Header>
    <soap:Body>
        <GetAuthorName xmlns="http://www.wrox.com/FastTrack/Authors">
            <id>172-32-1176</id>
        </GetAuthorName>
    </soap:Body>
</soap:Envelope>
```

In order to see the trace as shown above, you can use one of many TCP trace utilities. There is one such utility included in the Microsoft SOAP Toolkit 2.0, available from http://msdn.microsoft.com. The Trace Utility tool (MSSOAPT.EXE) provides a listening port where the program captures incoming traffic and displays the traffic before forwarding the packets to the final destination. You can start a new formatted trace by pressing *Ctrl+F* and entering the listening port and destination as shown below.

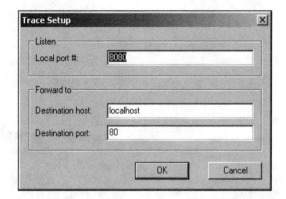

With the trace in place, you need to point the Url property of the client-side proxy to point to the local listening port by adding the following line of code after the AuthorWebService is instantiated in AuthorsClient4:

```
wsAuthor.Url = "http://localhost:8080/Authors/Service1.asmx";
```

You can also define headers to send back to the client from the server. The client is able to access these headers using the same technique as above, but obviously only after the web service method call completes.

Summary

Web services are a flexible technology to use in a variety of situations, from keeping a single user's PDA updated with their latest contact information, to facilitating an enterprise level integration between two businesses. Using open and standardized protocols such as XML and HTTP allows you to integrate with other platforms and other languages.

The .NET Framework provides a variety of tools and classes to build web services, making them easy to build, debug, deploy, and consume. We have demonstrated in this chapter just how flexible the technology is. We can use web services synchronously or asynchronously, and extend the underlying protocol to support our own requirements. The .NET Framework is touted as the first development platform built from the ground up for web services, and is certainly a wonderfully productive tool in this arena.

In this chapter, we have seen:

- How to write a web service
- How to test and debug a web service
- Creating a web service client
- Using XML serialization to return more complex objects from our web service
- Using asynchronous web service calls to allow applications to continue in the face of network turmoil
- State management and SOAP Headers

Take the
Fast Track

to
C#

Index

Symbols

A

E

F

ASP Today

p2p.wrox.com
The programmer's resource centre

A unique free service from Wrox Press
With the aim of helping programmers to help each othe

Wrox Press aims to provide timely and practical information to today's programmer. P2P is a list server offering a host of targeted mailing lists where you can share knowledge with four fellow programmers and find solutions to your problems. Whatever the level of your programming knowledge, and whatever technology you use P2P can provide you with the information you need.

ASP — Support for beginners and professionals, including a resource page with hundreds of links, and a popular ASP.NET mailing list.

DATABASES — For database programmers, offering support on SQL Server, mySQL, and Oracle.

MOBILE — Software development for the mobile market is growing rapidly. We provide lists for the several current standards, including WAP, Windows CE, and Symbian.

JAVA — A complete set of Java lists, covering beginners, professionals, and server-side programmers (including JSP, servlets and EJBs)

.NET — Microsoft's new OS platform, covering topics such as ASP.NET, C#, and general .NET discussion.

VISUAL BASIC — Covers all aspects of VB programming, from programming Office macros to creating components for the .NET platform.

WEB DESIGN — As web page requirements become more complex, programmer's are taking a more important role in creating web sites. For these programmers, we offer lists covering technologies such as Flash, Coldfusion, and JavaScript.

XML — Covering all aspects of XML, including XSLT and schemas.

OPEN SOURCE — Many Open Source topics covered including PHP, Apache, Perl, Linux, Python and more.

FOREIGN LANGUAGE — Several lists dedicated to Spanish and German speaking programmers, categories include. NET, Java, XML, PHP and XML

How to subscribe:
Simply visit the P2P site, at http://p2p.wrox.com/

Got more Wrox books than you can carry around?

Wroxbase is the new online service from Wrox Press. Dedicated to providing online access to books published by Wrox Press, helping you and your team find solutions and guidance for all your programming needs.

The key features of this service will be:

- Different libraries based on technologies that you use everyday (ASP 3.0, XML, SQL 2000, etc.). The initial set of libraries will be focused on Microsoft-related technologies.
- You can subscribe to as few or as many libraries as you require, and access all books within those libraries as and when you need to.
- You can add notes (either just for yourself or for anyone to view) and your own bookmarks that will all be stored within your account online, and so will be accessible from any computer.
- You can download the code of any book in your library directly from Wroxbase

Visit the site at: www.wroxbase.com

Programmer to Programmer™

Registration Code: 711603340X7VK101

Wrox writes books for you. Any suggestions, or ideas about how you want information given in your ideal book will be studied by our team.
Your comments are always valued at Wrox.

Free phone in USA 800-USE-WROX
Fax (312) 893 8001

UK Tel.: (0121) 687 4100   Fax: (0121) 687 4101

Fast Track C# – Registration Card

Name _____

Address _____

_____

_____

City _____ State/Region _____

Country _____ Postcode/Zip _____

E-Mail _____

Occupation _____

How did you hear about this book?

☐ Book review (name) _____

☐ Advertisement (name) _____

☐ Recommendation _____

☐ Catalog _____

☐ Other _____

Where did you buy this book?

☐ Bookstore (name) _____ City _____

☐ Computer store (name) _____

☐ Mail order _____

☐ Other _____

What influenced you in the purchase of this book?

☐ Cover Design ☐ Contents ☐ Other (please specify):

How did you rate the overall content of this book?

☐ Excellent ☐ Good ☐ Average ☐ Poor

What did you find most useful about this book? _____

_____

What did you find least useful about this book? _____

_____

Please add any additional comments. _____

_____

What other subjects will you buy a computer book on soon?

_____

What is the best computer book you have used this year?

_____

Check here if you DO NOT want to receive support for this book ☐

wrox

Programmer to Programmer™

Note: If you post the bounce back card below in the UK, please send it to:

Wrox Press Limited, Arden House, 1102 Warwick Road,
Acocks Green, Birmingham B27 6HB. UK.

Computer Book Publishers